THE CAMBRIDGE ANCIENT HISTORY

PLATES TO VOLUMES VII PART 2 AND VIII

THE CAMBRIDGE ANCIENT HISTORY

PLATES TO VOLUMES VII PART 2 AND VIII

The Rise of Rome to 133 BC

NEW EDITION

Edited by

CHRISTOPHER SMITH

Professor of Ancient History, University of St Andrews and Director of the British School at Rome

CAMBRIDGE UNIVERSITY PRESS
Cambridge, New York, Melbourne, Madrid, Cape Town,
Singapore, São Paulo, Delhi, Mexico City

Cambridge University Press
The Edinburgh Building, Cambridge CB2 8RU, UK

Published in the United States of America by Cambridge University Press, New York

www.cambridge.org
Information on this title: www.cambridge.org/9780521252553

First published 2013

Printed and bound in the United Kingdom by the MPG Books Group

A Catalogue record for this publication is available from the British Library

ISBN 978-0-521-25255-3 Hardback

Dedication

This book is dedicated to the memory of John Lloyd, who was originally commissioned to write the chapter on the Samnites and whose work on the survey of the Biferno valley is a contribution of unrivalled importance to our knowledge of the Samnites. His premature death at a time when he was directing an important study of settlement in the Sangro valley was a grievous blow to Samnite studies. Additionally he was to all the contributors a friend and guide, and is sadly missed.

CONTENTS

ACKNOWLEDGEMENTS

Many of the contributors have incurred debts of one sort or another in the lengthy period of time during which this project has been developing. Many chapters were written first some time ago. Where possible, we have taken account of recent scholarship. The editor is particularly grateful to all the contributors, and to Michael Sharp of Cambridge University Press, for their patience; to Dr Jeremy Armstrong for editorial assistance; and to Chris Jackson for the huge task of copy-editing a complex volume.

For providing, or assisting with acquiring, photographs we would like to thank Maria Pia Malvezzi, Graeme Barker, Jon Coulston, Roger Wilson, Michel Bats, Brigitte Lescure, Anne Roth-Congès and Jonathon Williams.

Thanks are also due from Alastair Small to Michael Crawford and Keith Rutter for comments on the coins; Carola Small for much help in editing digital images; and from Greg Woolf to the librarians of the Bibliothèque Gernet-Glotz and of the École Normale Supérieure (rue d'Ulm).

ABBREVIATIONS

AE	*L'Annee Épigraphique*
AEA	*Archivo Español de Arqueología*
AJA	*American Journal of Archaeology*
Arch. Cl.	*Archeologia Classica*
Arch. Laz.	*Archeologia Laziale*
ARV[2]	J. D. Beazley, *Attic Red-Figure Vase-Painters* (2nd edn, Oxford, 1963)
BAC	*Bulletin Archéologique du Comité des Travaux*
B.Com.	*Bollettino della Commissione Archeologica Comunale di Roma*
BMC Italy	R. S. Poole (ed.), *A Catalogue of the Greek Coins in the British Museum: Italy* (London, *c.* 1873)
BMC Sicily	R. S. Poole (ed.), *A Catalogue of the Greek Coins in the British Museum: Sicily* (London, 1876)
BMCRR	H. A. Grueber, *Coins of the Roman Republic in the British Museum* (London, 1910)
CIE	*Corpus Inscriptionum Etruscarum*
CIL	*Corpus Inscriptionum Latinarum*
CLP	*Civiltà del Lazio Primitivo* (Rome, 1976)
CRAI	*Comptes Rendus de l'Académie des Inscriptions*
FUR	*Forma Urbis Romae*
GRT	*La Grande Roma dei Tarquini* (Rome, 1990)
HN[2]	N. K. Rutter, A. M. Burnett, M. H. Crawford, A. E. M. Johnston and M. Jessop Price, *Historia Numorum, Italy* (2nd edn, London, 2001).
IG	*Inscriptiones Graecae*
ILLRP	*Inscriptiones Latinae Liberae Rei Publicae*
JDAI	*Jahrbuch Des Deutschen Archäologischen Instituts*
JRA	*Journal of Roman Archaeology*
LIMC	*Lexicon Iconographicum Mythologiae Classicae* (Zurich and Munich, 1981–99)
LTUR	*Lexikon Topographicum Urbis Romae*
MAAR	*Memoirs of the American Academy in Rome*
MDAIR	*Mitteilungen des Deutschen Archäologischen Instituts, Römische Abteilung*
MEFRA	*Mélanges de l'École française de Rome, Antichité*
MemPontAcc	*Memorie della Pontificia Accademia di Archeologia*
Mon.Ant.	*Monumenti Antichi* (Reale Accademia dei Lincei)
Monuments Piot	*Fondation Eugène Piot. Monuments et Mémoires*
NSc	*Notizie degli Scavi di Antichità*
OJA	*Oxford Journal of Archaeology*
PBSR	*Papers of the British School at Rome*
PdP	*Parola del Passato*
RA	*Revue Archéologique*
RAN	*Revue Archéologique de Narbonnaise*
RE	Pauly-Wissowa, *Real-Encyclopädie der klassischen Altertumswissenschaft*
REL	*Revue des Études Latines*
RendAccLinc	*Rendiconti della Classe di Scienze Morali, Storiche e Filologiche, Accademia Nazionale dei Lincei*

RendPontAcc	*Atti della Pontificia Accademia Romana di Archeologia: Rendiconti*
RFAp I	A. D. Trendall and A. Cambitoglou, *The Red-Figured Vases of Apulia* I*: Early and Middle Apulian* (Oxford, 1978)
RMR	*Roma Medio-Repubblicana: Aspetti culturali di Roma e del Lazio nei secoli* IV *e* III *a. C.* (Rome, 1973)
RRC	M. H. Crawford, *Roman Republican Coinage* (Cambridge, 1974)
Sc.Ant.	*Scienze dell' Antichità*
SE	*Studi Etruschi*
SEG	*Supplementum Epigraphicum Graecum*
Thes CRA	*Thesaurus Cultus et Ritum Antiquorum*
ZPE	*Zeitschrift für Papyrologie and Epigraphik*

INTRODUCTION

CHRISTOPHER SMITH

The volumes of the *Cambridge Ancient History* to which this volume of Plates is related were published in 1989. This volume is concerned with Italy and the western Mediterranean; in Italy the span is somewhat wide, from the Iron Age on, reflecting the interest in *CAH* VII.II in the beginnings of Rome. Other chapters focus more intensely on the fourth to second centuries, reflecting the interest of both volumes in the expansion of the Roman Empire and the processes of conquest, imperialism and transformation which much of the western Mediterranean experienced through the Punic Wars, as Rome wrested control of the sea coast after the defeat of Carthage. Twenty years on, what can we say now about the state of the subject, and what new light does this volume shed?

Archaeology has changed our view of some areas radically; early Rome is the best example because of the wealth of information provided by more recent excavations. More generally, our capacity to use the variety of mechanisms which archaeology now has to develop richer regional pictures is clearer from this volume than its textual counterparts; aerial photography, survey, excavation and archival work are all represented in most of the chapters, and we made the deliberate decision to allow for more extensive introductions to clarify the interplay of archaeology and history. In this way we hope that this volume escapes the accusation of presenting archaeology merely as a support for the more significant work of the historian by grounding the material culture in a fuller contextual discussion.

This leads us to consider the specific ways in which material culture has become important in the re-evaluation of the period. The way in which the text volumes were arranged perhaps necessarily foregrounded the textual narrative of Roman expansion, a narrative derived from Dionysius of Halicarnassus, Livy and Polybius in large part. Just as the ancient narratives include an element of the destined evolution of Rome into a world power, so too the *Cambridge Ancient History* leads with Romans, having separated the Hellenistic world, whose period of flourishing is exactly contemporary with the 'rise of Rome' in the fourth to second centuries BC, into a separate volume. This wholly practical distinction nevertheless needs to be recognised for what it is, and not confused with any sense of the lived reality of the period. One of the very striking aspects of this volume is the degree of shared artistic experience across the western Mediterranean, much of it intimately connected with the lively transmission and transformation of Greek culture. From magnificent Iberian stone sculptures, through to Sicilian temple architecture, the development of Roman coin types, the intense trade with southern Gaul and back round to the fascinating amalgam of cultures represented in Carthaginian culture, we have to do here with an interconnected and interdependent world, and one which demonstrates repeated similarities with the eastern Mediterranean. Indeed we have chosen deliberately to complement the chapter on Sicily in *CAH Plates* VII.I with our own chapter, both to bring out some of the newer developments, but also to reinforce the connection with the east.

Moreover, material culture has a complex relationship with the textual evidence specifically in regard to the development of the Roman Empire. One can of course see the Roman Empire impinging on local culture in many instances, in terms of devastation and abandonment, both in parts of Italy and of course Carthage itself, destroyed after 146 BC, but also in the various ways in which the Roman impact is expressed through architecture, the traces of legal forms, especially in inscriptions, in language more generally and indeed in the reciprocal transformation of Rome itself.

Were the *Cambridge Ancient History* to be rewritten now, it is hard to imagine that the word Romanization would not have featured in the index, as it does not in either of the text volumes to which this volume relates. Of course, many of the characteristic processes which are gathered under that term are recognized and commented on in the text, and this is not the place for a discussion of the now enormous literature on the term, its history, its own archaeology one might say, its relationship with concepts of empire, colonialism and ideology, and the nuanced local responses which are now at least as prominent in the modern literature as the apparently inexorable top-down pressure the Romans were once thought to have exercised. Numerous examples could be given of where interpretations have been challenged, so for instance the key episode of the Bacchanalian conspiracy, and Roman responses to it, remains a site of contest between interpretative models of heavy-handed Roman repression, and indications of more pragmatic tolerance, and it is of course as salutary to see how archaeology has followed the texts perhaps against the grain of the evidence as it is to see the number of rather critical objects here whose authenticity is now denied, or whose date is questioned.

Presenting the local culture as we do here, one can also see good reasons to challenge the over-dependence on a Rome-centred model. The north African material in particular reveals the sophistication of the Carthaginian culture, and even the relatively less substantial remains of two other great foes of Rome, the Samnites and the Gauls, are still impressive, especially, and here perhaps unsurprisingly, in regard to their focus on the military. This volume displays with great clarity the consequences of the loss of all substantial accounts from Italy and the western Mediterranean except the Roman version, and serves both as the necessary corrective to a highly text-based narrative, and also as a demonstration of the relatively univocal account we have of a very rich, developed and differentiated group of cultures.

Each chapter of this account shows this tension between individuality and interdependence. Inevitably the two major vectors are artistic expression and economic or commercial activity. A less fragmented account than the format of the volume permits would spend more time on the mechanisms of these exchanges. Yet it is immediately clear that both examples involve a full range of society. The exchange of luxury goods to support an aristocratic lifestyle is evident. Artists and artisans were almost certainly highly mobile in this period. Agricultural produce, and, one has to assume, the means of such production on a relatively intensive scale, slaves, were also transported around the western Mediterranean as well as the eastern Mediterranean. All the evidence points to a ferment of commercial endeavour, and most of the chapters include illustrations of coinage too, some of which will have facilitated trade. At the same time, another function of coinage, and another driver of mobility on a micro-regional and macro-regional scale, is also abundantly evident: war. From the disputes arising from transhumant mobility through to the huge movements of armies and navies in the period of the Hannibalic War, from war as masculine competitive display to the organized deployment of massed forces, the material record is from the very beginning full of the evidence of conflict as a strong underlying motif of Mediterranean life.

Some level of religious or spiritual need is also clearly demonstrated. Funerary remains are exaggeratedly visible in the material record because of the privileged nature of their deposition and therefore survival, but we are reminded repeatedly of the amount of time, effort and imagination expended on the proper rituals for the deceased. In particular, the paintings which we see in funerary contexts remind us vividly that our picture of the ancient world is all too often far more monotone than the lively originals. Moreover, it is hard not to be impressed at the eschatological inventiveness of the western Mediterranean cultures, and the significance of cultic sites as markers of territory and prestige, of interaction between peoples, and of course between peoples and their gods, and of the susceptibility of these particular practices and places to external influence. Like agriculture, especially as revealed through several examples of Roman-influenced centuriation exposed by aerial photography, cult is an interesting barometer of the influence of Rome.

The volume ends, for all the western Mediterranean, at a point of transformation. The textual volume concludes in 133 BC, that watershed year of Tiberius Gracchus' tribunate and attempt both to transform Roman exploitation of Italian land, and to control the profits of a rapidly developing empire. By the time at which the next volume of the historical text draws to a close after Caesar's death, all of Italy will have been subordinated to Rome, granted Roman citizenship and implicated in the internal dissension of the Roman state. Rome's minor involvement in northern Italy and southern France will have been left far behind by Caesar's conquest of Gaul and incursion into Britain, an island scarcely known to the Mediterranean during the period of our volume. Spain and Africa will have seen devastating wars, both against the Romans, and of Romans fighting Romans, and Carthage will be rising again as a Roman colony. Local languages and coinages will be increasingly scarce. Romans will have come to see the Mediterranean as *mare nostrum*, their own sea.

1. EARLY ROME

CHRISTOPHER SMITH

It is arguable that of all the subjects treated in this volume, the one which has been transformed the most by recent archaeological discoveries since the publication of the second edition of *CAH* VII.II and VIII is the study of early Rome. In 1928, when the first edition of the relevant *CAH* volume (VII) appeared, Hugh Last could write only with caution about the potential of archaeology. There were no archaeological finds from the early period on either the Capitoline or the Quirinal, and nothing before the sixth century on the Palatine. The majority of that account was based on the literary evidence.

The second edition of *CAH* had somewhat more to say. Ogilvie, Drummond and Momigliano drew on the still slight evidence. Studies by Müller-Karpe and Gjerstad had placed the evidence on a more solid footing, even though Gjerstad's dating was already dismissed. Brown's vital work on the Regia and the continuing excavations at the Forum Boarium (S. Omobono) had provided very significant additional information about a building of central importance to the subsequent chapters on social and political institutions.

Nevertheless, it is notable that by 1989 the most significant archaeological developments had taken place not in Rome, but in the hinterland of Latium. The construction of the Grande Raccordo Anulare and a range of associated finds, together with the increasing amount of information from what would prove to be one of the most significant necropolis excavations in central Italy, Osteria dell'Osa, and work in southern Etruria (which Ridgway presented in *CAH Plates* IV in 1988), permitted a range of analogies to be presented which allowed some of the gaps in the Roman material to be filled. Ogilvie had written 'Rome itself is an impossible place to excavate: too many layers of priceless heritage have covered it' and described the excavation activity which had occurred thus far as 'trifling', though he acknowledged the profound importance of the results.

This situation has been completely overturned in the subsequent twenty years, and there is now a hugely significant set of new material emerging from the intersection between the Palatine and the Via Sacra; from the south-west Palatine; from the Capitoline and both the original and the imperial Forum area. The impetus for this development may be attributed in part to the enormous excitement generated by Coarelli's ground-breaking topographical studies of the Forum, Forum Boarium and Campus Martius, and Carandini's finds in the Palatine and Via Sacra area, which revealed the potential for new discoveries of great significance, and also by the massive spur to consolidation of knowledge begun by the Giubileo year 2000. Equally, the codification of information provided through such works as the *Lexicon Topographicum Urbis Romae* (*LTUR*) has been important.

We can now be far more confident about the significance and the extent of the settlement of Rome from the beginning of the first millennium BC, and we can begin to postulate exciting connections between the earliest phases and subsequent developments. In particular, the possibility for a more coherent and detailed account of the Palatine Hill is becoming very real. At the same time, there remain profound difficulties in terms of methodology in this area of study. Both the first and second editions of *CAH* spent a considerable amount of time on the problem of the source material, and this is one area where limited progress has been made, and where perhaps little can be made, since even the relatively improbable discovery of new sources in papyri is unlikely to overcome the difficulty of the chronological gap between the sources and the period they are describing.

Any new account of the city of Rome will therefore need to take account of the crucial archaeological evidence, but it must also be sensitive to the difficulty of forcing the sources to carry more weight than they may reasonably be expected to. It is remarkable that we have such a close connection between the eighth-century growth of Rome and the alleged date of Romulus, or between the sixth-century development of the city and the period of the Etruscan kings, but we must also remember that the emergence of this chronological schema was in part the result of scholarship of the third century BC and afterwards (Cornell 1995: 70–3). Furthermore, in a period so productive of new finds, we must acknowledge that we will need time fully to assimilate the information which has been provided and to arrive at fully tested conclusions. This chapter therefore presents a relatively conventional and conservative account of the most significant archaeological evidence from Rome and Latium.

The early evidence from most Latin sites is predominantly mortuary. For Rome, the Forum necropolis remains the most substantial collection of early material (1–2), but has been joined, very recently, by material from the Capitoline and the Forum of Caesar. There is a general pattern of cremation followed by inhumation across the region, and the pattern is most completely observable, and minutely documented, at Osteria dell'Osa (4). It is absolutely clear that there is evidence for role and gender differentiation, and, as elsewhere in Italy, the figure of the warrior is of early significance (13). We still have work to do to be sure of the nature of very early Roman warfare, but there are elements of a kind of heroic mentality, and of the sorts of commemoration we associate with heroes in the Greek world (*CAH Plates* III 244–7 for illustrations of Lefkandi).

Like Etruria, Rome and Latium were strongly influenced by the impact of Phoenician and Greek trading and colonization (see 7–8 for some examples). This can be seen in pottery, housing, social customs such as banqueting and the development of literacy (5, 9, 10, 15). In order to participate fully in the new trading networks, the elites of central Italy had to produce greater surpluses, and we can see evidence of intensification in settlement size and pattern, which was accompanied by the kinds of conspicuous display that both resulted from and reinforced an increasingly hierarchical society. The princely tombs of Praeneste (Palestrina) are the obvious Latin examples, and are striking both intrinsically and by the fact of their great similarity to specific Etruscan tombs; we can see the results here both of the trading network and the *koine* of artefacts for elite display, and the potential of horizontal social mobility, of marriage and movement between settlements (6). These general patterns across the period from the eighth to the sixth centuries differ slightly from site to site, of course. Castel di Decima and Osteria dell'Osa, important sites in earlier centuries, disappear, whereas Rome, Satricum, Tibur and Praeneste survived and grew (12, 15).

In terms of the settlements themselves, the three key features of their development in the sixth century are, first, the increasing monumentalization, visible in walls, temples and elite housing; second, the diminution of surviving burial evidence during the sixth century, which is so widespread a phenomenon as to be indisputable as a feature of the period and not a gap in the evidence; and, third, the creation of public space, most visible at Rome in the Forum (10, 11). Taken together, there is good evidence therefore for both a level of urbanization at this time, but also a discourse about the relative importance of public and private display and expenditure, which is inextricably linked with the political development of Rome, our best-known example, where powerful kings in the sixth century were replaced by a republic, and, as we shall see in Chapter 2, the archaeological record reflects this development. The development of the Forum at Rome in the sixth century is a vital piece of evidence for the interplay between individual power and communal identity in the archaic city.

GENERAL BIBLIOGRAPHY

Cornell has made substantial contributions to the debates about early Rome subsequent to the appearance of *CAH* VII.II; see T.J. Cornell, *The Beginnings of Rome: Italy and Rome from the Bronze Age to the Punic Wars (c. 1000 to 264 BC)* (London and New York, 1995), some of which reprises material in his chapters in the earlier work, but most of which is new, and fundamental. Other accounts include R. Ross Holloway, *The Archaeology of Early Rome and Latium* (London, 1994), T. P. Wiseman, *Remus: A Roman Myth* (Cambridge, 1995) and, most recently, G. Forsythe, *A Critical History of Early Rome: From Prehistory to the First Punic War* (Berkeley, Los Angeles and London, 2005). For the developments in and around the Jubilee year, see F. Filippi, *Archeologia e Giubileo: Gli interventi a Roma, e nel Lazio nel piano per il Grande Giubileo del 2000* (Naples, 2001).

On the archaeology, the most significant developments include the publication of Osteria dell'Osa (A. M. Bietti-Sestieri, *La necropoli laziale di Osteria dell'Osa* (Rome, 1992) and *The Iron Age Community of Osteria dell'Osa: A Study of Socio-political Development in Central Tyrrhenian Italy* (Cambridge, 1992)) and two major exhibition catalogues, *La grande Roma dei Tarquini* (Rome, 1990 – hereafter *GRT*) and *Roma: Romulo, Remo e la fondazione della città* (Rome, 2000). For a summary of the archaeological evidence up to and including the first two of these items, see R. Ross Holloway (above) and C. J. Smith, *Early*

Rome and Latium: Economy and Society c. 1000 to 500 BC (Oxford, 1995). Carandini's views are now extensively represented in *La nascità di Roma: Dei, Lari, eroi e uomini all'alba di una civiltà* (Turin, 2003) and *Remo e Romolo: Dai rioni dei quiriti alla città dei romani (775/750 – 700/675 a.C.)* (Turin, 2006).

Another important find, a villa beneath the new Auditorium of Rome, has been published in A. Carandini, with M. T. D'Alessio and H. di Giuseppe, *La fattoria e la villa dell' Auditorium nel quartiere Flaminio di Roma* (Rome, 2006); cf. N. Terrenato, 'The Auditorium site and the origins of the Roman villa', *JRA* 14 (2001) 5–32.

For the recent excavations on the south-west Palatine, see P. Pensabene and S. Falzone, *Scavi del Palatino I: L'area sud-occidentale del Palatino tra l'età protostorica e il IV secolo a.C. Scavi e materiali della struttura ipogea sotto la cella del tempio della Vittoria* (Studi Miscellanei, 32, Rome, 2001); for the northern side, see A. Carandini and P. Carafa, *Palatium e Sacra Via I: Prima delle mura, l'età delle mura e l'età case arcaiche* (Rome, 1994), and A. Carandini and E. Papi, *Palatium e Sacra Via II: L'età tardo-repubblicana e la prima età imperiale (fine III secolo a.C. – 64 d.C.)* (Rome, 2005).

For ongoing work in Latium, the important journal *Archeologia Laziale* has been replaced by *Lazio e Sabina*, and the Associazione di Archeologia Classica sponsors an online database of recent archaeological activity. For a massive summary of research, see B. Amendolea, *Un repertorio bibliografico per la Carta Archeologica della Provincia di Roma* (Rome, 2004).

1

1. The Forum necropolis. This aerial view of the Forum necropolis beside the temple of Antoninus and Faustina as it was being excavated by Boni from 1902 onwards shows some of the earliest-known burials in the city of Rome. Forty-one tombs were discovered in an area of 250 m^2, but which was nevertheless only a fraction of the whole. There is a mixture of cremation and inhumation, both of which styles are illustrated later. The cremations, from the late tenth and early ninth centuries BC, precede the inhumations, and it is usually thought that the necropolis precedes the necropolis found on the Esquiline Hill, which has predominantly inhumations. Other contemporary tombs are found elsewhere in the Forum, near the Arch of Augustus, and on the Palatine itself. Most importantly, there is new evidence for burials on the Capitoline Hill, and very recent finds have been made in the Forum of Caesar. There are no adult burials found in the Forum much after the end of the ninth century BC.

The Forum necropolis probably served the inhabitants of the Palatine and Velia Hills (the latter destroyed completely for the modern Via dei Fori Imperiali, built by Mussolini). It would originally have been outside the inhabited area of the city, but, as the settlement expanded, it was covered and abandoned, and burials increasingly are found further from the areas of housing, as is typical for the ancient world.

It has recently been suggested that the Forum necropolis may have been contemporary with the earlier phases of the Esquiline, which would indicate a larger burial population in Rome in the earliest phase. The idea that the shift from one burial site to another represented an immigrant population in Rome is now discounted. The grave goods found in the early tombs are very similar in style to those found in tombs in the Alban Hills. Traditionally, Rome had strong links with Alba Longa, which were preserved in ritual; the annual festival of Jupiter Latiaris, the Feriae Latinae, took place on the Mons Albanus (modern Monte Cavo), and all Latin peoples were represented there.

(Soprintendenza Archeologica di Roma E 2323)

Collection of evidence, with unreliable dating: E. Gjerstad, *Early Rome* (Skrifter utgivna av Svenska Institut i Rom, Lund, 1953–73) vol. II 13–161, vol. IV pt I 53–65; more recent accounts, *CLP* 103–43; Smith *Early Rome and Latium* 49–54; Ross Holloway *Archaeology of Early Rome and Latium* 20–36. For the Alban Hills, see P. Gierow, *The Iron Age Culture of Latium* (Lund, 1964–6), also with doubtful dating; *CLP* 68–98. Revised chronological account: M. Betelli, *Roma: La città prima della città: I tempi di una nascita. La cronologia delle sepolture ad inumazione di Roma e del Lazio nella prima età del ferro* (Rome, 1997).

2. Hut-urn burial. Cremations were interred in large holes in the tufa, with *dolia* or containers of pottery, within which were further finds.

Characteristic of some sites in central Italy are hut-urns, typically varying in height from about 20 to 35 cm; of some 200, those in Latium are the earliest and constitute 30 per cent of the total, and a further 33 lids in the shape of a roof have been found; there are also examples of bronze helmets surmounting pottery containers for the ashes. These urns and lids appear to mimic habitation, and can be used to reconstruct the huts whose post-holes we have found. The gradient of the roof, as well as the absence of tiles before the mid seventh century, indicates that roofs were thatched; some also have decorations in the form of horns or birds, or even humans. Circular urns are the most common in Latium.

(Photo C. J. Smith)

G. Bartoloni, F. Buranelli, V. D'Atri and A. De Santis, *Le urne a capanna rinvenute in Italia* (Archaeologica 68, Rome, 1987); H. Damgaard Andersen, in J. R. Brandt and L. Karlsson (eds.), *From Huts to Houses: Transformations of Ancient Societies* (Stockholm, 2001) 245–62.

3. Palatine hut. The post-holes which reveal a set of ninth- to eighth-century huts on the Palatine have been known since their first publication in 1947 and are dated by early Iron Age material found associated with them in that excavation. They were immediately associated with the hut-urns and a reconstruction made, based on that evidence. Further huts were alleged to have been found under the Regia, though there have been concerns expressed about whether these were intended for human habitation. The evidence from the Palatine was connected with the tradition of a hut of Romulus, first attested in Varro's account of the *Argeorum sacraria* (*de Lingua Latina* V.54) but allegedly preserved over time. Recent reconsiderations have developed the concept of the Palatine village. Perhaps the most certain and intriguing parallel is outside Rome: the discovery, and reconstruction, of a hut at Fidenae

3

4a

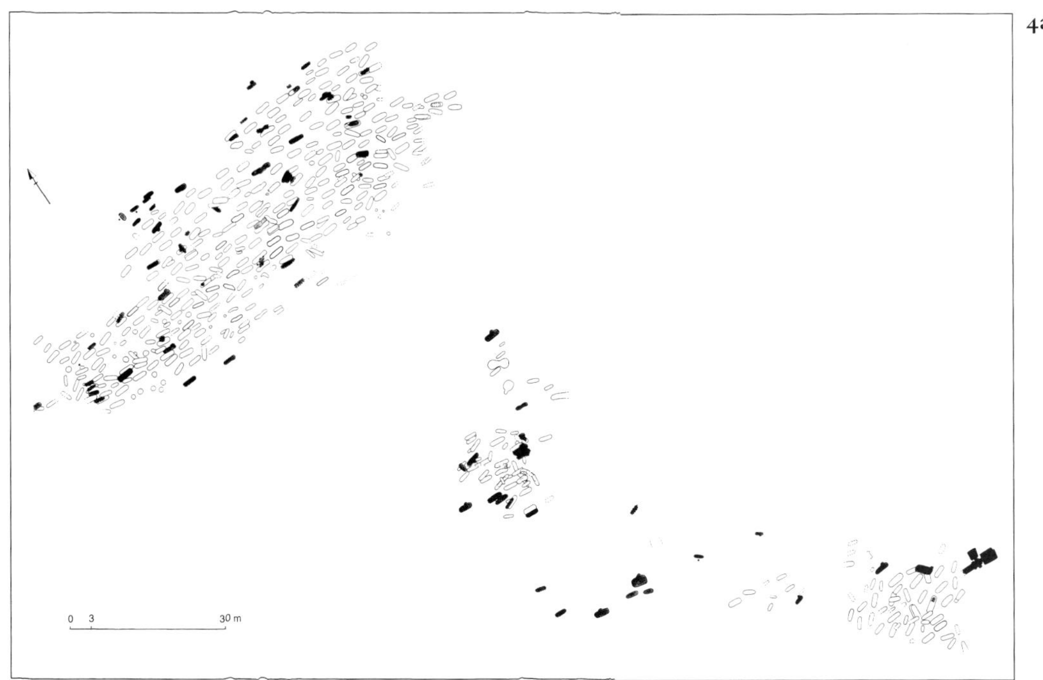

from the late ninth and early eighth centuries BC allows us to confirm the details of the Roman structures and to compare it with other examples at Ardea and Lavinium (Pratica di Mare), also sites with a clear early phase of occupation.

Hut A illustrated here and at *CAH* VII.II[2] Figures 19a and b (reconstruction) measured 4.9 m × 3.6 m; the majority of the rock-cut holes were 0.45 cm in depth and 0.42 m in diameter at the surface; the central hole supported the roof, and there was a hearth nearby; there were doorposts and a small porch, drainage channels for water, and the construction was wattle and daub.

(Photo C. J. Smith)

S.M. Puglisi, *Mon.Ant.* 41 (1951) 1–98; F.E. Brown, in L. Bonfante and H. von Heintze (eds.), *In Memoriam Otto J. Brendel: Essays in Archaeology and the Humanities* (Mainz, 1976) 5–12; A. Carandini (ed.), *Roma: Romolo, Remo e la fondazione della citta* (Rome, 2000) 283–7 and C. Angelelli and S. Falzone, *JRA* 12 (1999) 5–32 for modern debate. For Fidenae, A. De Santis, R. Merlo and J. De Grossi Mazzorin, *Fidene: Una casa dell'età del ferro* (Rome, 1998), with references.

4b

4. Osteria dell'Osa. Although cremations and inhumations are found at sites throughout Latium, no site has been published in such detail as Osteria dell'Osa. The first tomb was discovered at the site in the nineteenth century, but it was further explored from the 1970s, and fully published in 1992; the finds are now displayed superbly in the Museo Nazionale di Roma in the Baths of Diocletian. As such it is the only complete or nearly complete

4c

necropolis known from archaic Latium, and the combination of the relatively good preservation of the site and the detail attainable in modern excavations make it a uniquely significant contribution to our knowledge. Some 600 burials have been published.

The necropolis is situated about 24 km from Rome, and is one of a number of sites that surrounded an extinct volcanic crater (part of the same chain that formed the Alban Hills) which at some stage, probably after ancient times, flooded to form the Lago di Castiglione. All the sites here appear to have coalesced around 600 BC to create the important town of Gabii. Osteria dell'Osa itself has not produced any significant settlement evidence, and there is no reason to assume that in the period before the synoecism it was of particular wealth or importance, which makes the burial evidence all the more interesting, since it may justifiably be regarded as typical in its broadest features.

The necropolis begins around 900 BC with a series of cremations. These cremations form two groups, and around them cluster groups of later inhumations; thus it is conjectured that we have two descent groups from the early cremated individuals, or perhaps two communities using the same burial ground. It is very significant to note that there are distinctions between the pottery styles of the two groups that last for about a century, until the burying group changes its ritual and size. This shows that the production of pottery for the burials was tied to the expression of group identity, and the decoration may have held meaning that is largely unrecoverable by us today.

The cremations follow the form that is standard in Latium (see above). The move to inhumation is variously explained, but would appear to be a reflection of a cultural choice, since it occurs not only in Latium but also in Etruria at the same time. A similar range of objects are found with the deceased, though of increasing size, quantity and complexity through to the eighth century BC. Anthropological data from Osteria dell'Osa indicate that there was a tendency towards a gender differentiation in the goods deposited, with weaponry being more common for men, and the tools of weaving and the appurtenances of the cooking and distribution

4d

of food more common for women. The so-called weaver-sets are a very clear indication of what must have been one of the major products of Latium, textiles. The significance of weaving in antiquity is often underestimated because the product is not one which readily survives in the archaeological record. It must remain unclear whether this gender differentiation was strictly observed at all times in all Latin necropoleis.

Osteria dell'Osa unusually shows traces of the practice of reinterring an inhumed body some time after first burial. Some corpses have clearly been disturbed, and it is suggested that this represents the deliberate reopening of a grave, a practice which until recently was not uncommon in parts of rural Greece and southern Italy. This practice can mark the last act in a cycle of mourning.

The two groups that last through the ninth century seem to be replaced in the eighth century by a single, tightly defined group, presumably representing some shift in the burial population, or in rituals of deposition. It remains an open question whether any necropolis in Latium contains the burials of a settlement's whole population, or only a sample. From this eighth-century group has come the extraordinary discovery of an inscription on a pot buried in a woman's grave. The word has been interpreted as meaning 'good at weaving', but all interpretations must remain conjectural. What is certain is that the inscription is by far the earliest in Latium, and one of the earliest in the Phoenician-derived alphabet in the western Mediterranean, including Greece, which raises questions about our understanding of the spread and use of literacy in early antiquity.

In common with other necropoleis, Osteria dell'Osa sees fewer, wealthier burials in the seventh-century, before it closes. A votive deposit on the outskirts of the necropolis, with late seventh-century material, has been taken as a ritual marking of the closure of the necropolis before the synoecism of Gabii.

(**a** Plan of the Iron Age cemetery of Osteria dell'Osa (after Bietti-Sestieri *Necropoli*)

b The grave goods of cremation 357 (male adult, with hut-urn, stand, drinking set, knife, fibula and razor; and cremation 365 (female adult, with amphora urn, pots and fibula); ninth to early eighth century. (Soprintendenza Archeologica di Roma)

c The grave goods of inhumation 80 (male adult) and inhumation 471 (female adult, with set of weaving accoutrements). Mid eighth century. (Soprintendenza Archeologica di Roma)

d The grave goods of inhumation 235 (elderly female, with iron knife). Later eighth century. (Soprintendenza Archeologica di Roma))

Bietti-Sestieri *Necropoli*.

5. Ficana banqueting service. Excavations at Ficana (modern Monte Cugno) were begun as an Italo-Nordic project in 1976. A house here can be dated to the seventh century BC, making it one of the earliest stone-built houses with tiled roofs in Latium; it measures about 12 m × 6 m. Most of the material surviving from the house is ceramic, and it has been reconstructed as a banqueting service. The stand and cauldron in clay is almost 1 m in height and has precise parallels in bronze from other sites, including the griffin protomes; those at Ficana have decoration to denote the eyes. There is also a substantial number of drinking vessels in high-quality reddish-brown impasto of the chalice kind, and of impasto plates. Pyxides with clay balls in the lid which make a noise as it is moved have also been found, and a number of the types have holes which suggest that they may have been hung up for storage. Some pottery is found in nearby rubbish pits and may have been discarded after a fire. There may be evidence for some kind of metallurgical activity nearby. Whilst the finds at Ficana are not as spectacular as those at, say, Praeneste (see below) they nevertheless constitute a rich and valuable portfolio of evidence for daily life, and for the importance within it of communal feasting.

(After Rathje 1983)

A. Rathje, *Analecta Danici* 12 (1983) 7–30; J. R. Brandt, *Scavi di Ficana*, vol. II pt I *Il periodo protostorico e arcaico: Le zone di scavo 3b–c*, (Rome, 1996).

6. The Tomba Bernardini. The stunning finds from the Tomba Bernardini at Palestrina were made in 1876 and were soon brought to be displayed next to those from the Tomba Barberini, in the Villa Giulia in Rome. The tomb belongs to the early seventh century. At an early stage after the discovery, the so-called Manios fibula (illustrated at *CAH* VII.II^2 Figure 23) came to be associated with the finds, but it remains very uncertain whether this piece was original or a fake, and whether it was indeed ever part of this *corredo*. The finds are characterized by their extraordinary wealth, by the variety of provenances of the material and by the close relationship with material from Vetulonia and Caere, so close that it has been thought that they must have come

5
a
b
c
d
e
f
g
h
i
j
k
l

from the same shipment, or from immigrants from the east who have brought their skills into central Italy. The finds may even disclose a marriage connection between an Etruscan and a Latin, a position whose plausibility is strengthened but not proved by an, inscription with what may be a female name on one of the Praeneste bowls. Objects found include gold, silver, bronze and ivory, and the gilt-silver bowls at any rate have very close Phoenician ties and display the rich iconography of rulers in the east, with symbols of hunting prominent. There is therefore a complex mix of exotic foreign symbolism and wealth in a local context, which may yet be a potent example of the patterns of rulership in central Italy.

The shield (**a**) has a diameter of 1 m when reconstructed; bronze plate with decoration of animals, soldiers and cavalry.

The cauldron (**b**) is gilt silver, with birds, warriors, cavalry and a fight with a lion as decoration, and was probably imported from Cyprus; height 13.5 cm and 19cm with protomes; diameter 16 cm.

The gold belt-clasp (**c**, **d**) has 131 figures decorating it; chimaeras along the central cylinder; then rows of seated and standing lions, sirens and horses on the short outer edge; the two Janus-heads on one edge have associated remains of silver pins. The animals were made by soldering together two halves of stamped gold, with gold thread for claws and tails, and granulated gold decoration was then added. Manufacture may have been in Caere, with probably Syrian and Phoenician influence. Length 17.3 cm; width 10.3 cm.

6a

6b

6c

6d

(Soprintendenza Archeologica di Etruria Meridionale 38460, 61197, 20524, 90143)

CLP 221–46; F. Canciani and F-W. von Hase, *La Tomba Bernardini di Palestrina* (Rome, 1979); D. Neri, *Le coppe fenicie della Tomba Bernardini nel Museo di Villa Giulia* (La Spezia, 2000).

7. Hercules and Minerva statue, S. Omobono. This statue group, just short of life size, was found in 1937 in excavations by the church of S. Omobono in the region of the ancient Forum Boarium and can be dated to the second half of the sixth century BC. The excavations here are enormously significant because of the rich network of literary and archaeological material, and have been exhaustively studied by Coarelli. The area was in the third century the site of the temples of Fortuna and Mater Matuta, and we may assume that some elements of these cults date back to the sixth-century temple foundations, if not to the even earlier votive deposits. Servius Tullius fostered close links with Fortuna, according to the sources. Throughout this area and the analogous port areas of Pyrgi and Gravisca there are syncretizing cults related to Hercules and also to goddesses like Uni and Astarte, which seem to function both as ways of guaranteeing trade but also perhaps as indicators of the rich mix of peoples at these liminal port areas (the sacred boundary or *pomerium* of Rome does not include the Forum Boarium). An indication of this is the small ivory lion plaque found here which has the name of an Etruscan on the back, and perhaps indicating a dedication or some notion of mutual hospitality (*CAH* VII.II^2 79). In the statue group, Hercules is recognisable by his lion skin, whilst Athena wears an Ionic style helmet, and we might imagine her with some representation of the Gorgoneion. The most obvious parallels are with the ridgepole decorations at Veii, and there are also architectural friezes which can be compared with examples from Velletri. The rest of the decoration is too fragmentary to permit secure restoration, but it is at least worth pondering whether there is some kind of reference to Heracles' introduction to Olympus, and bearing in mind the story of Peisistratus, the Athenian tyrant, who appears in the city in a chariot alongside Athena. These types of analogies serve less to authenticate any given story in the sources than to indicate the kinds of identifications and the sort of metaphorical thinking that may have been available to those who were in a position to exploit the iconography of power in the archaic period.

(Musei Capitolini. Original height 145–50 cm)

A.M. Colini, *B.Com.* 66 (1938) 279–82; *GRT* 119–20; *LIMC* Herakles/Hercle 131 (+ Athene/Minerva 386); G. Bradley, in H. Bowden and L. Rawlings (eds.), *Heracles–Hercules* (Swansea, 2005) 129–51 with further references.

8. Spartan cup at Lavinium. The worship of the quintessentially Spartan heroes Castor and Pollux at Lavinium is attested by a sixth- to fifth-century

7

8a

bronze plaque with their names (*CAH* VII.II² 579 Figure 63). It is additionally interesting to discover imported Laconian pottery from the mid sixth century.

This example is badly damaged. It is a black-figure kylix from around 560 BC with a remarkably rich set of decoration; a continuous frieze of palmettes and lotus flowers, two lion-hunt groups and bird scenes on the outside; on the inside, two men recline at banquet, surrounded by a supporting cast of humans, winged figures and smaller animals, including snakes, lizards, dogs and birds. Below is a scene of satyrs, and the whole is surrounded by further decoration.

The kylix has been attributed to the Naukratis painter, and the two figures have been identified as the Dioscuri Castor and Pollux. This is supported, indeed suggested, by the inscription, but it fits with a picture of a strongly Hellenized sixth-century world in which Greek myth is adopted and adapted consciously and intelligently. It is therefore notable that the Dioscuri are the deities who announce to Rome their victory over the Latins at the battle of Lake Regillus early in the fifth century BC (Cic. *Nat. Deor.* II.6; III.11; Livy II.20; D.Hal. VI.13; Ovid *F.* 1.707–8; Pliny *NH* XXXIII.38 etc.); and that the temple of Castor can be securely dated to the early fifth century.

(Museo Nazionale di Roma inv. E. 1986; drawing after *GRT* 8.3.21. Height 11 cm; Diameter 22 cm)

GRT p. 188; C. Stibbe, *Lakonische Vasenmaler des sechsten Jahrhunderts v. Chr.* (Amsterdam, 1972–3) cat. 19;

8b

8c

8d

E. Paribeni, in F. Castagnoli (ed.), *Lavinium* II*: Le tredici are* (Rome, 1975) 362–8; on the Dioscuri, see G. Radke, *Enciclopedia virgiliana*, vol. II 88–91.

9. Palatine wall and houses. The rich set of finds from the slope of the Palatine as it descends towards the Via Sacra and the uppermost part of the Forum are genuinely challenging to many preconceptions of the city of Rome in its earliest phases. There are two main aspects. First, there is an eighth-century wall with what has been described as a foundation deposit on the lower slope of the Palatine, which has been identified with the *pomerium* around the Palatine which Tacitus mentions, and the ancient Porta Mugonia. This important discovery makes more likely the picture of an early Roman settlement spread across the hills and in that sense mirrors precisely the settlement pattern at Veii at this time, and also perhaps, and in a slightly different way, amongst the small communities around the Lago di Castiglione, of which Osteria dell'Osa was one, until they amalgamated into Gabii. One may well imagine small communities with some shared space and custom, but also a local identity, which were gradually coalescing across the period from the eighth to the sixth centuries.

The second major discovery is of domestic architecture around the Via Sacra, and one may imagine that on the lower slopes of the Palatine and the now lost Velia there were aristocratic houses of the kind which later Cicero and Metellus Celer lived in. The excavators claim for these houses an atrium and a complex internal organization which would make them extremely early predecessors of the subsequent atrium houses we find from the third century BC, but at the same time, if we believe that the chamber tombs of Etruria are a reflection of domestic architecture, then one can find examples of rooms gathered around a central space.

Moreover, the archaic cistern on the upper Palatine by the so-called House of Livia is another indication of the development of the settlement, possibly for domestic purposes. At Satricum and Lavinium (Pratica di Mare) there is evidence of settlement along roads within the centre of a settlement, and good evidence for the development of a significant extra-urban dwelling at the Auditorio villa. The sixth-century houses at Rome take their place therefore in the history of the development of habitation, and it is indeed interesting that there seems continuity into later periods, and that one persistent tradition about the later kings and the

9

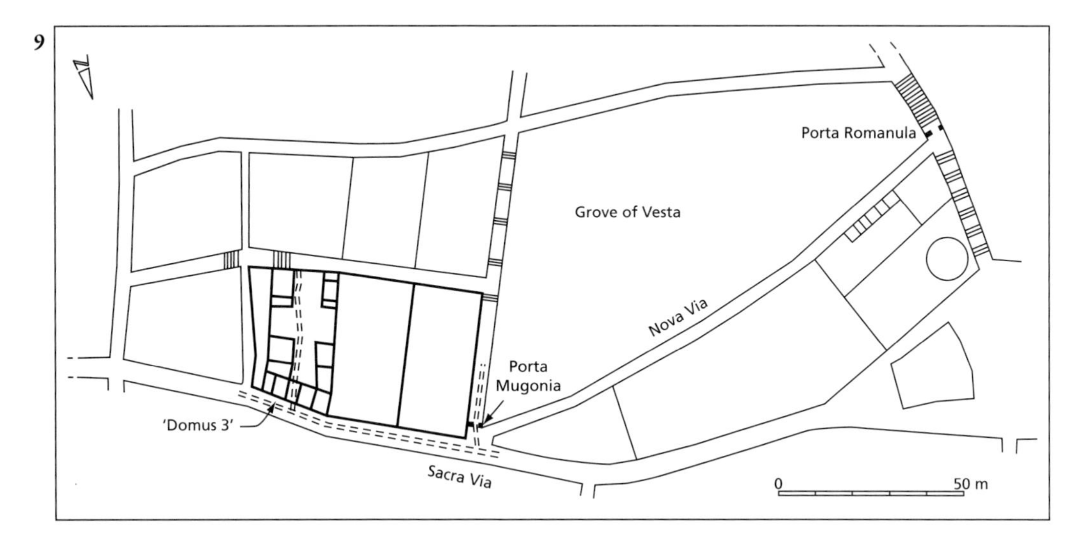

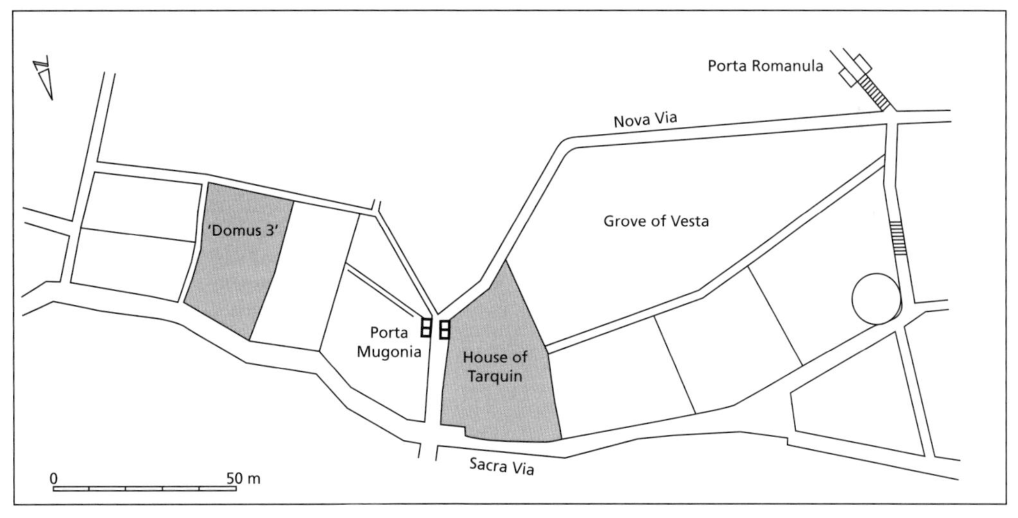

early Republic is about domestic architecture; indeed the house of Valerius Publicola at the foot of the Velia may be surmised to have been similar to those now available to study at the foot of the Palatine.

Having said that, as the plans shown here illustrate well, which are based on different reconstructions by Carandini, who excavated the area, we are still some distance from certainty as to the archaeology of the area. The finds are exiguous and whilst the dating seems secure the organization of the area remains unclear.

(After Wiseman 2008: 277; original drawing)

Carandini and Carafa, *Palatium 1*; T. P. Wiseman, *Unwritten Rome* (Exeter, 2008) 271–92.

10. Lapis Niger inscription. The survival of the Lapis Niger inscription tells us a great deal about what we can and cannot know about early Rome. Preserved at its original sixth-century level, whilst the pavement rose around it, it was eventually covered over in the Sullan period and its place marked by an irregular block of dark-grey stone, hence the name. The ancient sources preserved a confused memory of a tomb near the Volcanal and an inscription in Greek characters, thought to be an *elogium* (D.Hal. II.54.2; IV.26.4). Unless there is a very peculiar set of events, then, the inscription should be a sixth-century original of equivalent significance to the Satricum inscription (*CAH* VII.II^2 97). However, it is more or less incomprehensible,

and certainly not an *elogium*, and the best that one can do is to point to the appearance of a word which may be king, another possibly referring to a grove, and a third, perhaps the most intriguing, to a figure called a *kalator*; we know that the earliest assemblies were called *comitia calata* because they were summoned (*calare*). Given the appearance of this inscription in the Forum, along with the *REX* inscription under the Regia (*CAH* VII.II^2 25) and the identification of the Volcanal in the Forum we have good evidence for both the political institutions of the city-state as it develops through the sixth century, but no firm purchase on its meaning.

(Soprintendenza Archeologica di Roma 1877. Height 61 cm; base 47 cm × 52 cm)

CIL XII 4; F. Coarelli, *Il Foro Romano*, vol. I (Rome, 1984) 178–88; *GRT* 54–9; Cornell *Beginnings of Rome* 162–3 on Volcanal; *LTUR* 4.295–6 *sv* Sepulcrum Romuli.

11. Archaic walls of Rome and temple of Jupiter Optimus Maximus. The construction in large blocks of capellacio tufa of walls and podia in archaic Rome has long been clear and has positive confirmation from the substantial similar remains from elsewhere in central Italy. Grotta Oscura tufa from the other side of the Tiber has been assumed to be the marker of fourth-century work, since only after the conquest of Veii would Rome have access to this material – the long stretch in Piazza Cinquecento therefore appears below – but there may be elements of wall belonging to an early phase, such as this section (**a**) on the Capitoline Hill (also identified, however, with the Auguraculum or temple of Juno Moneta).

What is very clear is that the construction of the podium of the temple of Jupiter Optimus Maximus on the Capitol (**b**) was indeed of late sixth-century date, and we may add that finds at the base of the temple of Castor also support the dating of that temple. We can see a definite increase in the amount of temple-building at this period, as well as a number of destruction phases, and whilst one cannot rule out a sequence of unfortunate events, it is tempting to note the ancient accounts of the highly stressful and difficult transition from kingship, with the interlude of Lars Porsenna a notable potential interruption in the constitutional development of the Republic. Notwithstanding the difficulties indicated above, we must also retain a certain confidence in the construction of the Capitoline temple. The remains, included and now well displayed within the Capitoline Museum, give a sense of the very high podium on which it stood, and the temple dimensions of 62.25 m × 53.5 m and the temple area of 3,000 m^2 are outstanding. No known Italian temples outside Sicily match it. It is interesting that the temple is regarded in the sources as a building project of the regal period, even though it was dedicated in the early Republic.

(Photos C. J. Smith)

LTUR 3.319–23 for the walls; for the temple of Jupiter, *LTUR* 3.144–8; *GRT* 75–6; for the temple of Castor, *LTUR* 1.242–5; I. Nielsen and B. Poulsen (eds.), *The Temple of Castor and Pollux I: The Pre-Augustan Temple Phases with Related Decorative Elements* (Rome, 1992).

12. Temple decoration at Satricum and Lanuvium. Some temple decoration is monumental in scale, such as the Hercules and Minerva statue above; and some was mounted on the ridge-pole of temples, such as the famous Apollo from Veii across the Tiber. Other statues, such as that of Minerva at Lavinium (*CAH* VII.II^2 Figure 22) belonged inside sanctuaries. We also have relief terracottas,

11b

which are made in moulds used in various sites and have a combination of mythical scenes and possibly real processions (*CAH* VII.II[2] Figures 8, 11, 12), and these, interestingly, are found in both temple and elite domestic architecture. There is also a substantial amount of more generic sculpture, which has the dual function of decoration and masking architectural features such as gutters. Some of these antefixes, all datable to the end of the sixth century and early fifth century, are illustrated here and attest the considerable activity in temple-building of the time. The study of such decoration, when it is taken as part of a whole decorative system, hints at a rich world of symbolism, apotropaic figurines and repetitive invocations of tutelary deities, and whilst the influence of the Greek world is important, the Italic element remains profoundly significant.

12a

(a Satricum Typhon height 49.5 cm; Harpy height 47 cm; multiple examples of this symmetrical pair of figures with recognisable heads and monstrous lower bodies, the one ending in snakes and the other wings and claws. There are parallels in Campania and elsewhere in central Italy. (Soprintendenza Archeologica di Etruria Meridionale 4371)

12b

12d

12c

GRT 9.6.70

b Satricum Satyr and Maenad height 53 cm and 59.5 cm. There are two slightly different pairs from Satricum, equally impressive for the fluid movement and finely detailed heads. There is an ambiguity produced by the set between dance and assault, and it is interesting to find very similar motifs surviving in the later Praenestine ciste (below). (Soprintendenza Archeologica di Etruria Meridionale 103320)

c Lanuvium, temple of Juno Sospita. Satyr's head height 26.5 cm, width 19.2 cm, decorated with flowers and grapes, indicating the significance of the Dionysiac cult in archaic Italy, and associated with other indicators of the elite banquet. (Soprintendenza Archeologica di Roma 65168)

d Head of Juno Sospita? Height 40 cm. The type, with a decorated diadem, individualized hairstyle, distinctly modelled ears, and necklace, surrounded by a substantial halo, the whole richly decorated, may represent the tutelary deity of Lanuvium, Juno Sospita. (Soprintendenza Archeologica di Etruria Meridionale 160206))

GRT 196–200; A. Andrén, *Architectural Decorations from Etrusco-Italic Temples* (Lund, 1940); an important series of conference proceedings have been produced under the general title *Deliciae Fictiles* (Rome, 1990; Amsterdam, 1997; Oxford, 2006); for the importance of temples in the late sixth and early fifth centuries, see *Arch.Laz.* 6 (1984) 396–411. See now N. Winter, *Symbols of Wealth and Power: Architectural Terracotta Decoration in Etruria and Central Italy, 640–510 BC* (*MAAR* Supplementary vol. IX, Michigan, 2009).

13. Lanuvium armour. As indicated in the introduction, one characteristic of the fifth century is the reduction in the amount of private wealth visible in graves and other contexts, which has been

13a

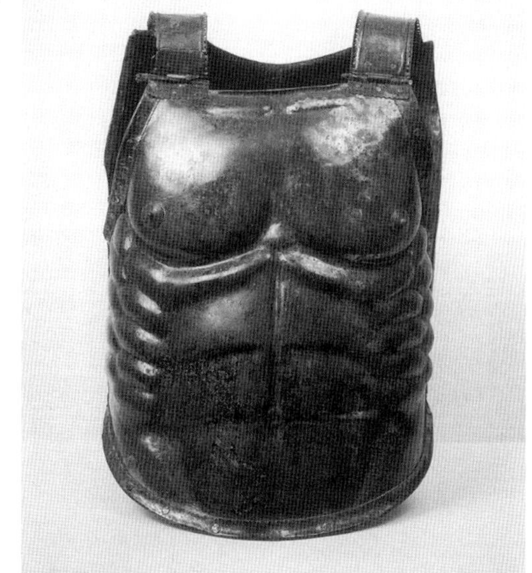

13c

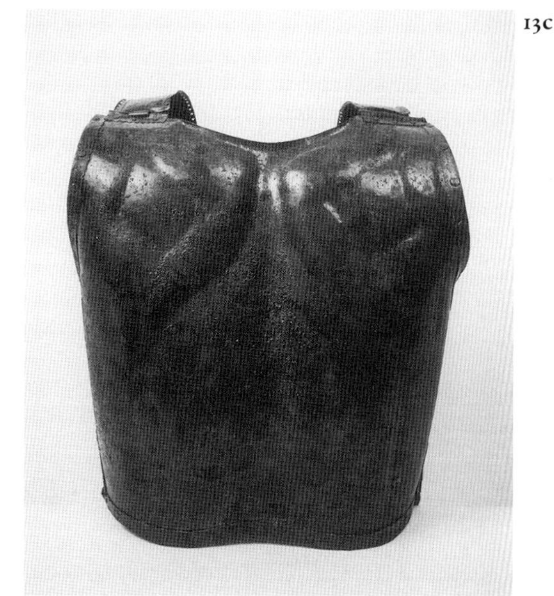

13b

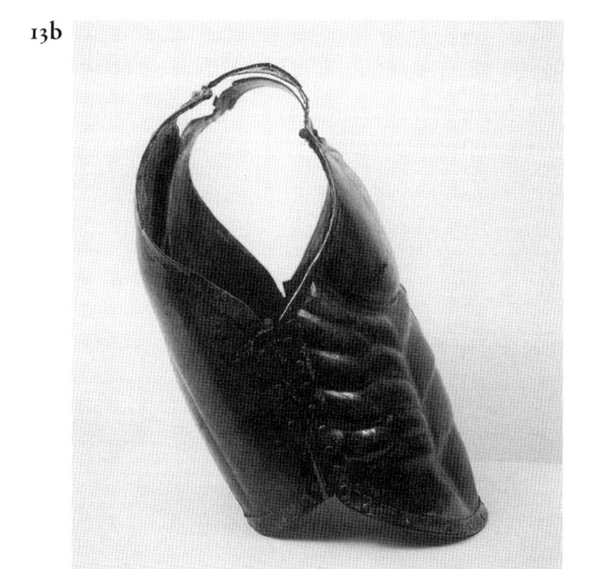

13d

thought to demonstrate an imposed or voluntary restriction of conspicuous consumption, perhaps associated with the problems posed by continuous warfare through that century (*CAH* VII.II[2] 274–94). However, there are exceptions to this pattern, which may itself indicate that there were individuals who chose to stand outside the discourse of community, something which is also mirrored in the literary record.

One example of military display is the lavish tomb of a warrior at Lanuvium. Discovered in 1934, it is datable to the early years of the fifth century BC. The beautifully constructed and shaped bronze cuirass (**a–c**) is of limited defensive use, and surely intended for display; the helmet has silver decoration, glass paste false eyes (**d**) with gold highlighting the iris, and would have been surmounted by a plume held in place by two horse-like figures, with wings on the side. Other elements found in the *corredo* include a discus and strigil which may imply the kind of athletic display we see in Etruscan tomb paintings, and which is very clearly linked to Greek practices. This tomb therefore participates in a whole discourse about male beauty, athleticism and military prowess, and must be read against the temple of Juno Sospita with her strong associations with the protection of cities.

(Soprintendenza Archeologica di Roma, Museo Nazionale di Roma 316936 (helmet); 316988, 316930, 316932 (cuirass)
Cuirass height (max.) 40.8 cm (50 with the straps); width 31 cm; depth 26 cm.
Helmet height 16.4; diameter 23.7 (max))
GRT 264–9.

14. Fidenae jewellery Similarly the late sixth century female grave at Fidenae contains a number of remarkable pieces, which are far richer than those expected at this period, or found elsewhere. Fidenae is an interesting site at the end of the sixth century, about which there is a tradition of violence and conflict with Rome, and which may have had close links with Veii across the river Tiber and with the Etruscan world. The deceased was placed in a sarcophagus of grey tufa (we know of one in Parian marble from Rome about the same time – again a surprising and isolated find). The assemblage included a pair of gold earrings (4 cm across) with rams' heads, and a necklace with gold and coloured paste beads, and

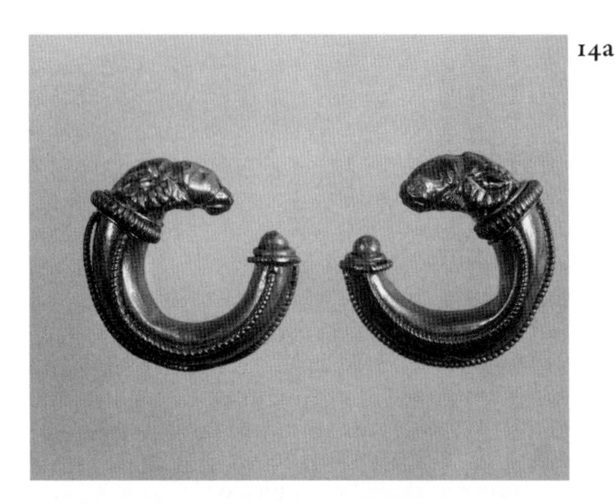

14a

14b

finely worked gold pendants. Parallels with items produced in Vulci have been identified. A silver fibula and a bronze mirror were also in the *corredo*, and are unusual in their own right.

(Soprintendenza Archeologica di Roma Museo Nazionale di Roma 335116; 361811)

GRT 260–2; L. Quilici, S. Quilici Gigli, *Fidenae* (Rome, 1986).

15. Satricum: Lead Axe-Head. According to Livy (II.39.1), the Volscians took over Satricum under Coriolanus' leadership in 489/8 BC, and it may be that it remained in Volscian hands until a Roman colony was sent there in 385 (Livy VI.16.5–8).

The south-west necropolis, which dates to the fifth century BC, is unique in Latium. Over 200 inhumations were found there, and grave goods of fairly low quality but high quantity occur in most of those which have been excavated. Compared with the almost complete absence of burial evidence from any other site in Latium, this is striking.

Grave 94 contained in its upper fill a miniature axe-head which had been pierced to be worn as a pendant. It bears a Sabello-Faliscan inscription, and the alphabet contains non-Latin elements; Colonna transliterates it as

iukus:ko:efiei:

where the lines of dots have a letter value. The meaning is unknown, but the inscription adds weight to the idea that this is a Volscian burial group. A recent intriguing suggestion produces a name (*Iukos Comius* or *Cominios*) and an office (*aedilis*); we find this office also in Arpinum, Formiae and Fundi. We should note that the famous Latin inscription to Publius Valerius (*CAH* VII.II[2] Figure 33) belongs to the beginning of the fifth century, but was placed in such a way that the inscription was invisible. Taken together we seem to have good evidence for some period of non-Latin, Volscian occupation but the latest interpetation suggests that the inscription is in Latin, in a Sabine script, and with an Umbrian or North Italic name.

Miniature lead objects are most commonly found in children's and especially boys' graves, but Grave 94 was unusually large; a possible explanation might be that it belonged to the son of the original owner.

(Dutch Institute in Rome and Soprintendenza Archeologica del Lazio V229; length 5.2 cm)

GRT I.13; M. Gnade, *The Southwest Necropolis of Satricum* (Amsterdam, 1992) 125–8, 274–6; Gnade, *Satricum in the Post-archaic Period: A Case Study of the Interpretation of Archeological Remains as Indicators of Ethno-cultural Identity* (Leuven, 2002) 124–34; M. H. Crawford *et al.*, *Imagines Italicae: A Corpus of Italic Inscriptions* (Bulletin of the Institute of Classical Studies Supplement) (London, 2011, 3 vols.) I.155–6.

15

2. THE CITY OF ROME IN THE EARLY AND MIDDLE REPUBLIC

CHRISTOPHER SMITH

The development of the city of Rome from the beginning of the Republic until the time of the Gracchi presents an interesting exercise in archaeological recovery. We know a good deal about the development of the city across this period through the literary sources; Livy in particular gives a substantial number of brief references to activity, for instance, by the censors in developing the civic amenities, and although we have lost the full text of his work from 167 BC onwards, the summaries and the text of Julius Obsequens together have allowed us to restore some sense of the immense building work of the second half of the second century BC. At the same time, there is an interesting and powerful discourse about luxury running through the ancient sources, which make claims for the austerity of the Romans, whilst revealing the actual development of a more luxurious lifestyle, at least from the fourth century on, in part based on the proceeds of Rome's Empire. The development of pottery forms, some of which imitate metal, shows to some extent both the luxury and the aspirational aspects of Roman consumption (18, 19). Meanwhile, war remained the absolutely central experience (19).

However, the early and middle Republic are genuinely rather difficult periods archaeologically. Whereas the earlier period has been the subject of intense recent scrutiny, and the late Republic and early Empire are both well attested in the sources and surviving material, the intervening period, of substantial duration, is relatively less well represented, and it is worth briefly asking why.

Part of the reason lies in the success of some of the building work of the sixth century; many of the temples, for instance, which were built then last with only minor repairs. The temple of Jupiter Optimus Maximus Capitolinus, for example, lasts until the disastrous fire of 83 BC. To some extent there is a retrenchment in the fourth century, and to an even larger extent a clearance of ground in the imperial period, removing Republican accretions from such areas as the imperial fora or the Campus Martius, and thereby denying us the opportunity to assess the scope and scale of the Republican achievement. Part of the reason lies in the essential but quotidian nature of some of the major contributions. The construction of aqueducts is an important part of the development of the late Republican city, but these were too important to leave alone, so few stretches remain simply Republican in date. The same can be said of roads: the Via Appia is endlessly renewed, but on the same track.

Taken together, though, the evidence is impressive. This is the period in which Rome develops the beginning of an infrastructure to support her steadily growing population. Perhaps the most impressive developments are precisely in this area – the aqueducts, the Porticus Aemilia (34, assuming it is this old), the walls (28), the road structure; the political structures (30). One might add the enormous rise in the number of temples built in the period (29, 32, 33); Ziolkowski catalogued around fifty from the period 396 to 219 BC. Smaller altars also abound (21, 22). We should not, however, dismiss the artistic wealth and achievement of the city, but this is where the most grievous losses have occurred. The problems of dating are profound, and it should be admitted that although there have been a number of attempts, the history of Roman art before the late Republic is extremely difficult to establish. What is striking is the Roman belief, which we find in Pliny the Elder *NH* XXXIV.52, that the art of statuary languished from the first Olympiad (295–292 BC) and only revived in the sixth (156–153 BC), a statement which is fascinating as a comment on Greek sculpture, but also notable because Pliny is not just discussing Greek art in the book, but includes a number of Roman examples, most of which fall either before or after this gap (an exception is Gaius Duillius' statue of 260 BC).

Yet it would simply be untrue to assume a cessation of art in general, in central Italy or Greece, and we must acknowledge a conundrum here that compounds the difficulties of the problematic material evidence.

We have both to reconstruct therefore the very old artistic material (bronze sculpture, terracotta decoration and so forth, **16**, **27**, **33**) which is largely or completely lost, and acknowledge the gaps in our knowledge; the barely legible fragment of painting from the Esquiline tomb (**24**) must stand for the paintings of Q. Fabius Pictor (ancestor of the historian) in the temple of Salus, dedicated in 303 BC, whose precise lines and pleasing mixture of colours were visible right through to a fire in the reign of the emperor Claudius (Pliny *NH* XXXV.19). The chronological issue then becomes profound, because it touches directly on our understanding of the degree to which Rome was open to Greek art in the period before the great conquests, and the consequent deluge of classical Greek sculpture and contemporary Greek artists which characterized the period after 146 BC. The recent demonstration that the Fortnum terracotta head in the Ashmolean museum is of modern date removes another potentially early and important piece of evidence for the development of Roman art; the dating of the Esquiline painting rests substantially on consensus rather than proof; and we have excluded the so-called Altar of Domitius Ahenobarbus, which was neither an altar nor anything to do with the Domitii Ahenobarbi, and would now appear to belong to at least the very late second century BC, or possibly the first century BC.

The chronological issue may mask a more complex problem, however, which is that the extent to which Romans acknowledged their Italic or their Greek connections may have been a specific point of concern, dissent and competition. In other fields such as literature, we can see imitation, emulation and rejection of Greek forms, and southern Italians such as Ennius are a key part of this process. At the same time Etruscan art develops its own trajectory, which, in the imagery that survives, is consciously Hellenizing (see next chapter). Some of the most famous pieces, the Cista Ficoroni (**23**) and the memorials of the Scipiones (**25–6**), are full of these contradictions. Romans will not have charted a single, simple course through this complex set of issues, just as the impact of Roman art and culture was by no means straightforward for the provinces.

GENERAL BIBLIOGRAPHY

Accounts of the art and archaeology of the Roman Republic tend to be slight until the later second century BC because of the scarcity of evidence. Some major publications show the potential of the subject; the exhibition *RMR* was followed by an important set of conference proceedings: P. Zanker (ed.), *Hellenismus in Mittelitalien* (Göttingen, 1976). I. Dondero and P. Pensabene (eds.), *Roma repubblicana fra il 509 e il 270 a.C.* (Rome, 1982) continued the arguments. F. Coarelli, *Revixit Ars: Arte e ideologia a Roma. Dai modelli ellenistici alla tradizione repubblicana* (Rome, 1996) is a major collection of articles with a broad coverage. See now for a major new assessment, F. Coarelli, *Le origini di Roma: La cultura artistica dalle origini al III secolo a.C.* (Milan, 2011).

For a general account of some of the issues, with a comprehensive bibliography, see T. J. Cornell, 'The city of Rome in the Middle Republic (*c.* 400–100 BC)' in J. C. N. Coulston and H. Dodge (eds.), *Ancient Rome: The Archaeology of the Eternal City* (Oxford, 2000) 42–60. Individual monuments can be studied through *LTUR*.

16. Capitoline wolf. This is one of the most famous and most argued-over pieces of Italian sculpture. We have records of a wolf statue at Rome from 296 BC, when the Ogulnii brothers added a pair of children (Livy X.23.11). This (or another) statue was struck by lightning on the Capitol in 63 BC (Cic. *Cat.* III.8.19; *De Div.* I.19.44, 47), and was visited by Dionysius of Halicarnassus (I.79.8). It is attested in the Piazza of the Lateran in a letter of Pope Leo IV, written in 853 AD, and appears in descriptions and drawings until Sixtus IV transferred it to the Campidoglio at the end of the fifteenth century. The figures of Romulus and Remus are Renaissance additions, possibly by Antonio Pallaiuolo. The sculpture has lost inlaid irises; the tongue and both hind legs are damaged.

The statue used to be considered a fifth-century Etruscan product, and in style is a curious mixture of naturalism and stylization. It seems that this or a similar statue was used as part of the complex effort to define and justify plebeian struggles against patricians in the middle Republic, and was a visual representation of the competing conceptions of the city and the citizen body. A recent attempt has been made to suggest that this sculpture is in fact medieval in date and this now appears to be winning general consent on the basis of scientific analysis. This statue was certainly used in the eighteenth century as a symbol of freedom, and in the nineteenth century and beyond as the emblem of Romanitas.

16

(Rome Palazzo dei Conservatori inv. S1181. Height 75 cm; legnth 136 cm; restoration on the tail and part of the chest)

M. Cristofani, *I bronzi degli Etruschi* (Novara, 1985) 1.1 54–63, 220–1, 290–1; S. Haynes, *Etruscan Civilization: A Cultural History* (London, 2000) 271–2, 166; C. Dulière, *Lupa romana: Recherches d'iconographie et essai d'interprétation* (Brussels and Rome, 1979) 21–43 and passim; T. P. Wiseman, *Remus: A Roman Myth* (Cambridge, 1995) 63–76; C. Parisi Presicce *La lupa capitolina* (Rome, 2000); A. M. Carruba, *La lupa capitolina: Un bronzo medievale* (Rome, 2007); C. Mazzoni, *She-Wolf: The Story of a Roman Icon* (Cambridge, 2010).

17

17. *Pocola.* One particular group of vessels which may have originated in Rome but spread through central Italy in small numbers are the *oinochoai*, cups and plates which have painted on them the word *pocolom* and the dedicatee. These inscriptions are significant evidence for some of the new cults which were arising in the fourth and third centuries BC, as well as the continuing importance of archaic cults. Deities mentioned include Vesta, Vulcan, Fortuna, Ceres, Saturn, Juno and Minerva of the older cults and Concordia (founded 367 BC), Salus (303), Bellona (296), Venus (Venus Obsequens in 295 is the first of the sanctuaries) and Aesculapius (291).

In addition, some of the dedicatees are unknown or unclear. Illustrated is a cup dedicated to Laverna, who gave her name to the Porta Lavernalis; but the location of her sanctuary is unclear. The cup has a picture of a winged Eros making an offering. Significantly, the cup was not found at Rome, but at Orte, and many of the other examples are found away from Rome. This is even true of a cup dedicated to Aesculapius, found at Chiusi, though the cult on the Tiber Island is the best known in central Italy. However, it has been suggested that there may be imitations at a few sites, which are, importantly, also the sites of Roman colonies (Ariminum, Caere).

The explanation for the distribution of these vessels then would seem to have less to do with patterns of dedication than with a habit of taking away vessels bought as souvenirs at the sanctuary as a reminder of the visit and of the deity, to be dedicated elsewhere perhaps, or buried with the pilgrim. The consequences of this are considerable for an understanding of habits of religious activity, and also for the economic significance of sanctuaries in Rome and other sites.

(Rome Musei Vaticani inv. AB3. Height 5.2 cm; diameter 13.8 cm.)

RMR nos. 57–68 (Coarelli, Morel); A. Franchi de Bellis, *Pro poplo arimenese* (Faenza, 1995) 367–92; F.M. Cifarelli, L. Ambrosini and D. Nonnis, *RendPontAcc.* 85 (2002) 245–325.

18. For early Rome, the ceramic remains are diverse, numerous and carefully studied. For the early and middle Republic, however, although the number of ceramic fragments is still high, they are less well studied. Imported Greek pottery tails off around the middle of the fifth century BC, an indication perhaps of the economic difficulties of Rome, and also the different priorities of the traders.

18a

18b

18c

Early accounts understated the extent of Roman, or at least Latin, manufacture of pottery, preferring to assign anything of quality to Campania. This is now less widely held, due to further discoveries, and increased attention is now being paid to the pottery of the early and middle Republic.

One may distinguish a series of waves of fashion, which are illustrated here. Scott Ryberg has suggested that we may fill the apparent fifth-century gap by assuming that there was little development in the shapes, fabrics and decoration of pottery at Rome during the fifth century. In the fourth century there is considerable influence from Etruria and the Faliscan region, though it is fair to say that the models of this pottery were ultimately Greek. It is hard to separate out the areas of artistic influence, and it appears that there is no evidence whatsoever for saying that Rome was in any sense isolated from the south in the fifth and fourth centuries BC, rather that the exigencies of her almost continuous warfare left little space for the dramatic artistic developments of either the sixth or the third centuries BC.

The first distinctively new form is the so-called Genucilia style, named after the inscription 'P. Genucilius' which appears on one example. All are characterized by the curling waves around the outside, surrounding a central space in which the most common themes are either geometrical or a female head. Some more elaborate decoration can also be found. They date to the late fourth century and the beginning of the third century BC. Most votive deposits before the Punic wars contain the typically Etrusco-Faliscan *oinochoe* (wine-jug) 'a cartoccio' Beazley shape VII.

A series of cups, identified as Form 96, are marked by the unevenness of their glaze, though despite their poor quality they are found in much of Latium and southern Etruria, including Aleria. Recently, it has been suggested that this form belongs to one workshop out of a number that were producing a form of pottery known as 'Petites Estampilles' because the decoration was punched into the clay before firing. This widespread pottery from the late fourth and early third centuries is particularly interesting because the method of decoration, and some of the motifs are reminiscent of coinage which was being produced at Rome for the first time at this period. As often, we see a cross-over of design and technique between different artisan activities.

The example illustrated (**a**) is a plate found in the Tiber; the external ring of stamps are geometric, the internal show a dolphin in relief. The dolphin is a common motif on Sicilian coinage and can also be paralleled on the Romano-Campanian bronze triens. Other stamp designs include a hand, palmettes, leaves and running figures.

There is also a significant amount of painted pottery from southern Italy coming into Rome, especially from Apulia (known as Gnathia pottery), and from Campania, where Teanum Sidicinum appears to be an important centre of production. Falerii north of the Tiber was also an important production site for red-figure pottery. All of this pottery takes its inspiration from earlier and contemporary Greek production, but as the import of Attic pottery falls away in the middle of the fifth century, the mixture of styles becomes more eclectic and more adapted to local requirements.

After the First Punic War, a distinctively Roman form is found called 'Heraklesschalen' which have a stamped Hercules at the centre of a fine, black-glazed, open-formed vessel (**b**). Only found in or near Rome, and dated to the second half of the third century BC, the stamps are reminiscent of (though not identical to) coins from Herakleia, and it has been suggested that the inscription AERAR on some is a misreading by the manufacturer of the name of the Greek town, which, if true, would be an interesting comment on degrees of literacy and bilingualism at this time in Rome. Also connected with the cult of Hercules are the vernice nera vessels which have a painted letter H for Hercules (and sometimes additional letters for cult titles, like V for Victor).

Some pottery deliberately and clearly imitates metal originals; the Malacena style of pottery from northern Etruria, which reaches Rome only in tiny quantities, is a good example. In addition, lamps with elaborate decoration may in fact have had a metal counterpart. The one illustrated shows a head of the Sun-god, Helios, with rays extending from his hair – a very appropriate deity for a lamp (**c**).

In general, the question of metal originals for pottery forms is one of considerable importance for the Republic. Much of the pottery is of a relatively low standard, mass-produced in a number of workshops, some in Rome and some in the Campanian and Etruscan areas. As an index of wealth they would be far less significant than the Greek imports which characterize the pottery remains in central Italy in the archaic period, which may have gained an additional value from their point of origin. However, references in the sources to metal statues, for instance, which have not survived, tend to indicate that we are only finding one part of the market with these specialist ceramics, and that metal was common for votive and luxury items, and was melted down for re-use. Its absence from votive deposits must indicate that if it was used at all it was seldom buried in the favissae, like the terracottas.

Throughout the Republic until the first century BC, vernice nera and red-figure decorated pottery are the most common ceramic finds, the former being found all over Rome, and being reliably diagnostic of a Republican phase. These types give way towards the end of the Republic to Italian terra sigillata production.

(**a** Petites Estampilles: *RMR* 46; Bernardini 1986: 44 no. 80; inv. 51249/1; neg. 178025L, 242828–9L; **b** Heraklesschalen: Bernardini 1986: 628; inv. 51246/1; neg. 179480L; 242783L, 5.1 cm across at foot; **c** Helios guttus: *RMR* p.71 no. 44 pl. XIV; Forum Antiquarium inv. 1025, from the Cloaca Maxima. Height 9.7 cm; diameter 9.5 cm.)

19

P. Bernardini, *Museo Nazionale Romano: Le ceramiche V.1: La ceramica a vernice nera dal Tevere* (Rome, 1986); J. P. Morel, *Céramique à vernis noir du Forum Romain et du Palatin* (Paris, 1965); Morel, *MEFRA* 81 (1969) 59–117.

19. This plate, found at Capena in chamber tomb 233 in the Necropolis delle Macchie, dates to the first half of the third century BC; inside the decorated rim, there is a picture of an elephant leading her baby, guided by a man with a whip, and carrying two warriors in some kind of tower. A very similar example has been found at Aleria in Corsica.

Romans first met elephants in the field in 280 BC when Pyrrhus brought twenty with him in his attempt to build an empire in Italy, and this plate may well reflect that first encounter, as is often suggested. In 279 BC Rome renewed her treaty with Carthage, which subsequently used elephants in the Hannibalic War.

As an intriguing addition, one may cite the unique votive offering at the sanctuary of Portonaccio at Veii of a pottery base, two elephants (one large, one small) and a three-headed dog (Cerberus), which may reflect a very individual soldier's response to these same events.

(Museo Nazionale Etrusco di Villa Giulia 23949. Diameter 29.5 cm)

M. Cristofani, in M. Martelli (ed.), *La ceramica degli Etruschi: La pittura vascolare* (Novara, 1987) 320; L. Ambrosini, in A. Comella and S. Mele (eds.), *Depositi votivi e culti dell'Italia antica dall'età arcaica a quella tardo-repubblicana* (Bari, 2005) 189–207.

20. In addition to the pottery dedications, the custom of dedicating terracotta models of parts of the body is characteristic of central Italy, and can be found in Rome particularly in connection with the Tiber river; the god Aesculapius was worshipped in a temple on the Isola Tiberina. The purpose is surely to ask for assistance with disease or infertility, and many models are of relatively poor quality and mass manufacture. Some of the items, such as the one illustrated in (**a**), which was found in the Tiber, suggest complex or vague medical problems. Others, such as breasts, penises, eyes, arms, hands and feet (**b**), are more precise. The heads, often of the young, present in a number of finds may stand for the individual.

We may return to the question of the status of the donor, which was touched upon above. This kind of votive deposit has been claimed as a

20a

20b

popular, peasant or relatively lower-class phenomenon. These terms are of course heavily loaded, but reflect the absence of higher-quality objects in the votive deposits. At the same time, their diffusion is striking; as it has recently been put, 'anatomical ex-votos are found, with a few rare exceptions, in all the votive deposits of central Italy, and, what is more, almost without exception, in those deposits only' (de Cazenove 2000: 75). In Southern Italy, they are present only in Roman colonies, and in this way present precisely the same issue as the *Pocola*, that is, whether we see here a direct reflection of Romanization. If the phenomenon could simply be connected to the introduction of Aesculapius to Rome in 293 BC, this might seem more plausible, but as it is, the dates do not appear to fit (votives start earlier, especially heads), and the connection with Aesculapius was not exclusive (dedications are made to a whole range of deities, and Aesculapius is quite rare). The anatomical dedications tend not to extend beyond the first century BC, and are replaced by common pottery vases and coins, and suggestions have been made that this reflects either the extension of *latifundia* and the disappearance of the peasant class or maybe even changes in the relationship between Rome and the Italians. What is striking, however, is that the simple act of dedication in the hope of, or as thanks for, good health is inextricably bound up with some of the most complex questions of the relationship between Rome and the Italians.

(a. Museo Nazionale di Roma inv. 14608; **b** University of Pennsylvania Museum of Archaeology and Anthropology (MS5756 male head; MS5757 female head; MS5752 head of swaddled infant; MS1630 bronze facial plaque; and feet L-64-551, L-64-478, L-64-553))

P. Pensabene and M. D. Gentili, in A. Comella and S. Mele (eds.) *Depositi votivi* 127–38, 367–78; O. de Cazenove, in E. Bispham and C. Smith (eds.), *Religion in Archaic and Republican Rome and Italy: Evidence and Experience* (Edinburgh, 2000) 71–6; *ThesCRA* Vol. I. 359–68 (J. Macintosh Turfa).

21. Arulae. These objects are believed to be miniature forms of altars. Their precise use is disputed; some have held that they had a role in the architectural decoration of tombs, temples and porticoes, others that they are small altars which had a real or symbolic use, and others again that, given the secure location of some in tombs and others in the disrupted strata of the Esquiline necropolis, they were part of funerary *corredi*. There are similar examples in Sicily from the sixth and fifth centuries, where they appear to have had a role in domestic cult; they are products of the Greek colonies there, and this suggests an artistic link. The Roman examples come mostly from the fourth and third centuries BC, and there are similar examples across central Italy from this period. Increasingly complex forms are found after our period; Verres steals some from a sanctuary at Heius in Sicily (Cic. *In Verr.* II.4.3), and they are found in temples, and domestic and burial contexts in central Italy. In our period, however, it may well be that the form was adopted for a specific funerary context, which would indicate the ways in which cultural forms were both adopted and adapted in central Italy.

The artistic link is borne out by the decoration which recalls various motifs of classical and Hellenistic Greek art. The first example (**a**) shows a Nereid swimming beside a dolphin, with a flowing mantle in her left hand, and a burning torch in her right hand; this comes from the Esquiline area.

The second example (**b**) shows a winged female holding two torches and standing between two Ionic columns; a feathered tail falls behind her. It has been suggested that she represents a siren, who, after leading men to their death, bewailed their fate. As in the first example, the torch may also be a part of the funerary symbolism.

The third example (**c**) shows a bull lifting its leg to trample the head of a snake that is rearing from the ground, an unusual motif amongst the plentiful examples of animals in combat. Lions and bulls are more common.

The fourth example (**d**) is decorated with a stage mask: a grotesque face with mouth wide open and a garland around his head, suggesting a satyr or something similar. The arula reminds us of the importance of theatre in the Greek world which was also impinging on Rome.

21a

21b

21c

21d

The arulae are made of terracotta and were produced in moulds, some of which have been recovered. Some have a depression in the top which may have been for burning incense.

(**a** *RMR* p. 84 no. 63 pl. XIX; E. D. Van Buren 1918: 31–2; **b** Ricciotti 1978: 97 no. 47; *RMR* no. 53; Rome, Antiquarium Comunale inv. 5142. Base 14 cm × 19 cm; height 11.5 cm; **c** *RMR* p. 93, no. 82 pl. XXI; E. D. Van Buren 1918: 23; **d** Ricciotti 1978: 100 no. 64: *RMR* no. 77; Rome, Antiquarium Comunale inv. 5122. Base 11.5 cm, height 11 cm)

D. Ricciotti, *Terrecotte votive dell'Antiquarium Comunale di Roma I: Arulae* (Rome, 1978) for a catalogue; E. D. Van Buren, *MAAR* 2 (1918) 15–53; I. Scott Ryberg, *An Archaeological Record of Rome from the Seventh to the Second Century BC* (University of Pennsylvania Press, 1940) 154–76; H. van der Meijden, *Terrakotta-Arulae aus Sikilien und Unteritalien* (Amsterdam, 1993).

22. Hercules dedication from the Tiber. Limestone statue base with two holes for the support; inscription reads:

M. C. Pomplio(s) No(vi) f(ili) | dedron | Hercole

The linguistic aspects suggest a late third-century date, and the position indicates a dedication to Hercules Invictus at the Ara Maxima. Earlier examples of dedications to Hercules can be found at Praeneste, and there are contemporary finds at Rome and elsewhere.

(Soprintendenza Archeologica di Roma neg. 231830. Height 8.6 cm; Width 14.2 cm; diameter 11.7 cm)

RMR p. 146 no. 183 pl. xxxi; *CIL* I^2 30 = VI 30898 = *ILLRP* 123.

23. Cista Ficoroni. The production of ciste at Praeneste and a few other sites began in the fifth century and was at its peak in the fourth and third. Ciste have a remarkably rich iconographic repertoire and in that sense imitate the bronze mirrors of the period. The date of this example is usually placed in the second half of the fourth century.

The Cista Ficoroni (**a**) was found in the mid eighteenth century, and we know little of its context. The handle has a youthful Dionysus supported by two ithyphallic satyrs. He wears shoes and a rectangular mantle with a criss-cross border. He has a *bulla* round his neck which has moved to the right, giving a sense of movement. The satyrs have tails; both wear lion or panther skins, and one has a drinking horn. The lid is decorated with an incised hunting scene.

22

The feet end in a small rectangular plinth, on which rests a clawed paw, and in between there is a frog. The claw opens into two volutes above, in between which is a group thought to represent Heracles and Iolaus with Hermes (or Eros?) in the middle. The feet may well be by a different artist – they are found in significant numbers attached to different ciste. Inside one of the feet is inscribed the name of the commissioner (**b**) – MAQVOVLNA (*CIL* I² 562).

The main body has inscribed on it a scene from the Argonautic saga, with specific reference to the Dioscuri. The core of the story is Pollux's defeat of Amycus, which grants the Argonauts, and those who come afterwards, access to his land and his water. Pollux is seen tying Amycus to a tree, while a winged Victory flies towards him bearing ribbons to crown the victor. This central scene happens under the gaze of various figures, including a winged old man, with sandals, and Athena/Minerva. The winged man may be the seer Mopsus, and he is looking down at a disembodied human head which may be predicting the future to him. As we move around we see the Argonauts making a leisurely descent from their boat into a landscape of plenty, with a Silenus, and water gushing from the head of an animal – a fountain ornament. One of them is drinking, and one is preparing for some kind of athletic activity; the Silenus comically imitates him. Bacchus reclines at ease, with ribbons, this time for the banquet perhaps. Finally, two men stand, one with his arm around the other in a very natural display of friendship. The quality of the work is very high.

The cista gains additional interest from an inscription on the attachment of the handle (**c**) to the whole: NOVIOS PLAUTIOS MED ROMAI FECID/ DINDIA MACOLNIA FILEAI DEDIT (Novios Plautios made me at Rome; Dindia Macolnia gave me to her daughter). It seems certain that this was a freedman of the Plautii; and the Macolnii reappear around 100 BC amongst the traders at Delos (*CIL* I² 2232). So we have important evidence for the commissioning of a cista by an originally Oscan freedman at Rome, given as a gift from mother to daughter, and demonstrating a close knowledge of a particular Greek myth in the fourth century BC, which was also found on a poorer-quality mirror, allegedly from the same find-spot. This mirror shows the

23a

goddess Losna or Luna, standing between Pollux and Amykos, so this must be a Roman variant.

(Soprintendenza Archeologica di Etruria Meridionale (Museo Nazionale Etrusco di Villa Giulia 24787). Height 74 cm; diameter 38.5 cm)

G. Bordenache Battaglia and A. Emiliozzi, *Le ciste prenestine* vol. I. pt II.2 (Rome, 1990) 11–26 (with extensive bibliography); T. Dohrn, *Die ficoronische Ciste in der Villa Giulia in Rom* (Berlin, 1970); T. P. Wiseman, *The Myths of Rome* (Exeter, 2004) 89–97.

24. This fragment of painting was found on the Esquiline Hill in 1875; it was the left-hand side of a wall painting, which probably went all the way around the inside of a tomb, and therefore was possibly as much as 20 m in length; the area of the Esquiline in the middle Republic may have had several substantial, rich tombs.

The top first register is missing; on the second on the left is the schematic outline of a tomb. The figures just visible on the rampart are in civilian dress. Outside, a warrior who may be wearing an anatomical corselet (above **13**) and gilded greaves, and has a large shield and helmet, extends a hand to a second figure who holds a spear vertically. There are letters above him which probably spell out a name, but the letters are hard to read.

The left-hand side of the next register has a figure in combat, though if this is the beginning of the painting there is no room for his opponent. Again we have a scene of a man holding out his hand to another, behind whom this time are three figures, in order of size. Above one of the men may be the letters M. FAN; above the other the letters Q. FABIO are clear. The lowest surviving register contains a fight scene; some of the combatants appear to be in Samnite armour. The painting was done swiftly, with sharp contrast of light and dark and highlights on key features like the helmet on the warrior on the lowest register. The use of foreshortening and perspective is highly advanced for its time.

Beyond this, we are to some extent speculating. It would be consonant with information about other paintings of roughly the same time, including those

23b

23c

of the Tomba Arieti nearby, to assume a historical depiction of military success, and opinion divides over whether it is that of Fabius or Fannius. Some connection with the Samnite Wars is required by the armour. The best context is the celebration of Roman *virtus* and military glory, but the scenes of apparent negotiation or congratulation add a more than purely martial tone, as does the presence of civilians overlooking the scene.

(Rome, Musei Comunali inv. 1025; photo Barbara Malter. Height 87.57 cm; width 45 cm)

RMR no. 283 (Coarelli); E. La Rocca, *Ricerche di pittura ellenistica: Lettura e interpretazione della produzione pittorica dal IV secolo a.C. all'ellenismo* (Quaderni dei Dialoghi d'Archeologia 1, Rome, 1985) 169–91; E. M. Moormann and A. Barber (eds.), *La peinture funéraire antique: IVe siècle av. J.-C. – IVe siècle apr. J.-C.* (Leiden, 1993) 99–107; P. J. Holliday, *The Origins of Roman Historical Commemoration in the Arts* (Cambridge, 2002) 83–91; on Samnite weaponry more generally, see S. P. Oakley, *A Commentary on Livy, Books VI–X, III* (Oxford, 1997–2005) 504–18.

25. Sarcophagus of P. Cornelius Scapula, Pontifex Maximus. Two sarcophagi were discovered in 1956 in the Via Marco Polo outside the Porta Ostiense. The sarcophagus illustrated has two pilasters at each end; and the characters suggest a third century date.

The identification of the individual is made easier when we accept that *cognomina* were fluid at this time. Hence it makes sense for this individual to be the same person as the Cornelius Scapula who was consul in 328 BC (Livy VIII.22.1), the Cornelius Scipio who was dictator in 306 (Livy IX.44.1) and the Cornelius Barbatus who was *pontifex maximus* in 304 (Livy IX.46.6).

This being so, the inscription is important as the earliest use of the *cognomen* attested outside the Fasti, but also problematic, partly because it raises the possibility of considerable confusion if *cognomina* were being used interchangeably, and partly because we have no good explanation for why Scapula was the *cognomen* chosen by this individual or his family for the tomb. Nevertheless, this is another indication of the complexity and sophistication of aristocratic self-presentation in the middle Republican period, which is even better represented by the following assemblage of tombs.

(Capitoline Museum: 2.09 m × 1.04 m × 0.9 m)

H. Blanck, *MDAIR* 73–4 (1966–7) 62–77; *AE* 1967; *RMR* pp. 240–1 no. 372 pl. LII; H. Etcheto, *Athenaeum* 91 (2003) 445–68.

26. Tomb of the Scipiones. Discovered first in 1614, and then more or less forgotten until 1780, the tomb of the Scipios is one of the most remarkable testimonies from Republican Rome, and yet remains in many ways elusive. Much destruction was caused both by the eighteenth-century intervention and much earlier when a large house was built on top of the tomb in the third or fourth century AD. Reconstruction took place in 1927–8, and that intervention remains crucial for our understanding of this monument, from which nine epitaphs have been discovered, from the earlier part of the third century BC to around 130 BC, with a gap, however, between 230 and 180 BC when the family of the Cornelii Scipiones were at their most famous.

The tomb is just by the old Porta Capena (as indicated by Cicero, *Tusc.* I.7.13), and is a largely

25

square area dug into the capellaccio tufa, with the sarcophagi in the niches of the corridor. This area could have taken some thirty sarcophagi. At a later stage, around the middle of the second century BC, another smaller area was created, and this contains the inscription of Cn. Scipio Hispanus, who died in the 130s. The outside of the tomb was probably decorated with columns, but may have passed through an initial phase to a reconstruction at the time the second chamber was added. The literary sources tell us of statues which were located here, including one of Ennius, which may have been part of a series added in the second century BC; it is tempting but possibly optimistic to associate this with the alleged statue of Ennius in the Vatican.

The sarcophagus of L. Cornelius Scipio Barbatus has floral decoration triglyphs and an altar-like form, and is the only decorated sarcophagus. There is a painted inscription on the cover : '[L. Corneli] o(s) Cn. f. Scipio'. The main inscription in terms of style and language seems later than the inscription on the tomb of his son, but there is also some deletion of lines before it begins. The most extreme hypothesis would date both the inscription and the sarcophagus to the second half of the second century BC, but current thought would accept an earlier date for the sarcophagus, and an original painted inscription with a subsequent elaboration. Although attempts have been made to claim an early date for sarcophagus and inscription, it is notable that the sources allege that the letter G was not in use before the 230s BC, and therefore the inscription would appear to be later than the death of its owner.

The main inscription, organized into Saturnian verse, reads:

> Cornelius Lucius Scipio Barbatus,
> Gnaivod patre | prognatus, fortis vir sapiensque,
> quoius forma virtutei parisuma | fuit;
> consol, censor, aidilis quei fuit apud vos;
> Taurasia Cisauna | Samnio cepit,
> subigit omne Loucanam opsidesque abdoucit.

Cornelius Lucius Scipio Barbatus, begotten son of Gnaeus, a brave and wise man, whose appearance was equal to his bravery; who was consul, censor, aedile amongst you; he took Taurasia and Cisauna from Samnium, and subjugated all Lucania, and took hostages from them.

One of the offices can be securely determined by reference to the historical sources – consulship

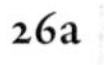
26a

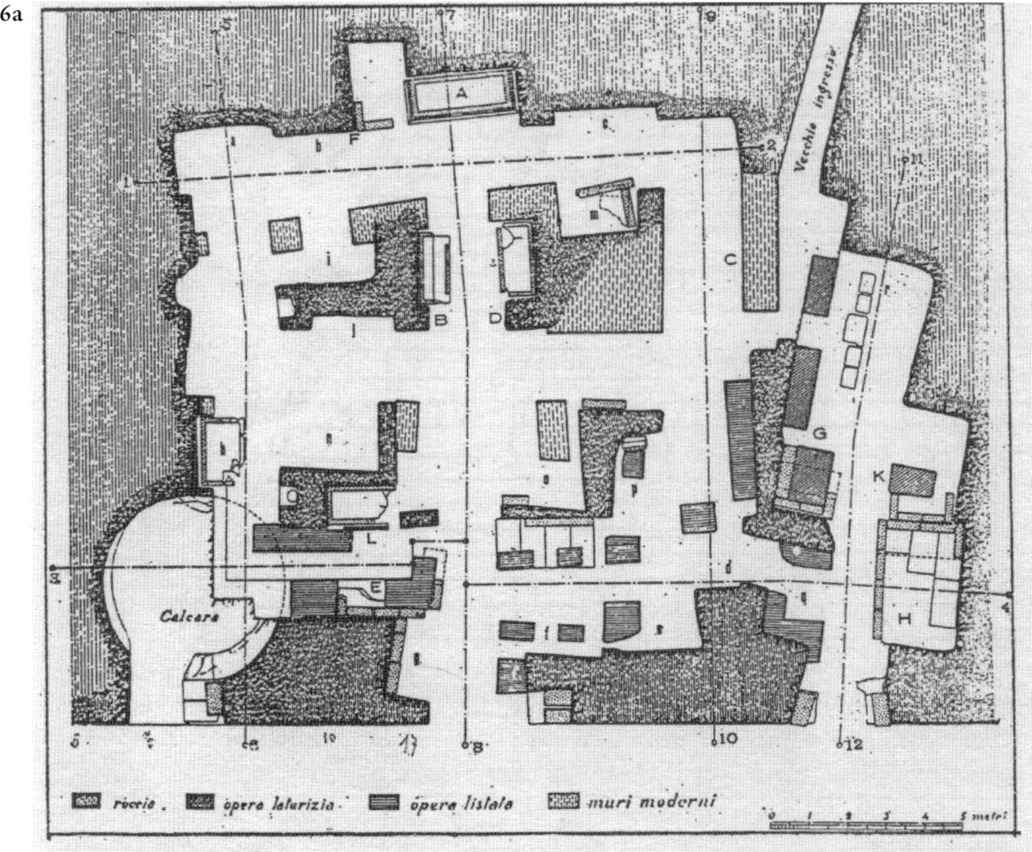
Vecchio ingresso
Calcara
riccio
opera laterizia
opera listata
muri moderni
5 metri

26b

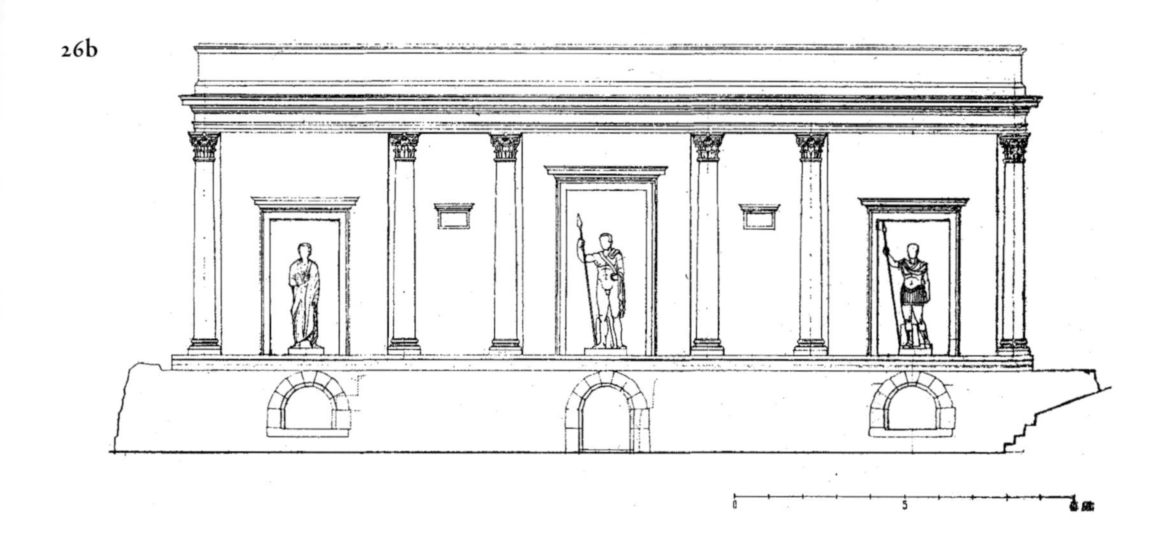

26c

298 BC (Livy X.11.10, though the reference to Lucania is only supported by Frontinus *Str.* I.6.1–2, 11.2); of the others, the censorship was perhaps in 280 BC (dependent on a restoration of Festus 270L); the aedileship is unknown.

The assemblage as a whole is testimony to the importance of a family unit (note, though, that this is the family of the Cornelii Scipiones, and not the whole *gens*); to the significance of funerary display and possibly to the use of the *elogium* in funerals; and to the persistence of this remarkable family at the heart of Roman affairs.

Interestingly, the last two inscriptions in the tomb belong to two members of the Cornelii Lentuli, who may have inherited the tomb, and, as Zevi suggests, in briefly re-using the tomb, in the archaizing period of the emperor Claudius, proudly affirmed their descent from such illustrious ancestors.

(**a** Tomb: 14.5 m × 13.5 m approximately; plan by Gismondi; **b** reconstruction after Coarelli; **c** sarcophagus: Musei Vaticani 1.42 m × 2.77 m × 1.1 m; **d** 'Bust of Ennius': Musei Vaticani inv. 1148, DAI 1993 Vat 0961)

LTUR 4.279–85 (Zevi) with full bibliography; V. Saladino, *Der Sarkophagus des Lucius Cornelius Scipio Barbatus* (Würzburg, 1970) for late date; Coarelli *Revixit Ars* 179–238.

26d

27. Via S. Stefano Rotondo Tomb, quadriga. This chamber tomb and perhaps three others were found on the Caelian Hill, near the Ospedale S. Giovanni.

27

They had been robbed out and damaged already in antiquity. The tomb contained one young man of about 1.9 m in height, with a small pottery *corredo*, including Genucilian ware.

The terracottas include two *quadrigae* driven by winged figures, another piece with a winged figure on an angle, an Eros crowned with ivy and a female head with a diadem. The piece above is 13 cm high in all, and the pair are identical in size, but one driver turns to the left and the other to the right.

La Rocca proposed a connection with the Greek idea of the transport of the dead across Ocean to the Isles of the Blest. Certainly the artistry is of the highest quality, and the pottery secures an early third-century date. Once again, we glimpse the extraordinary flexibility and originality of middle Republican art, but are deprived of a better understanding.

(Soprintendenza Archeologica di Roma neg. 177687)

RMR pp. 241–6, nos. 373–7 pl. LII–LV; V. Santa Maria Scrinari, *B.Com* 81 (1968) 17–24.

28. Whatever defences Rome had in the regal period, and it is clear there were some, these were improved substantially in the fourth century. The use of Grotta Oscura tufa, from across the Tiber, implies a date after the conquest of Veii, and it may well be that the construction was a response to the shocking invasion by the Gauls. It would appear that, perhaps for the first time, Rome gained a full enceinte wall, which may have been subsequently taken as regal – hence references to the Servian Walls may in fact be references to the fourth-century construction. This stretch was discovered as part of the construction of the railway station, and supported a large *agger*.

(Photo C. J. Smith)

LTUR 3.319–24 (Andreussi); S. Aurigemma, *B.Com.* 78 (1961–2) 19–36.

29. Largo Argentina. The four surviving Republican temples of the Largo Argentina, and the temple in the Via delle Botteghe Oscure, give a picture of the density of temple building and the complexity of the interplay between elite donors and their successors. Identification remains difficult but we at least know that the five temples must be from the six known in the area: Juturna, Feronia, Juno Curitis, Jupiter Fulgur, the Nymphs and the Lares Permarini.

The four temples in the Largo Argentina are conventionally known by the letters A–D and were

28

29a

29b

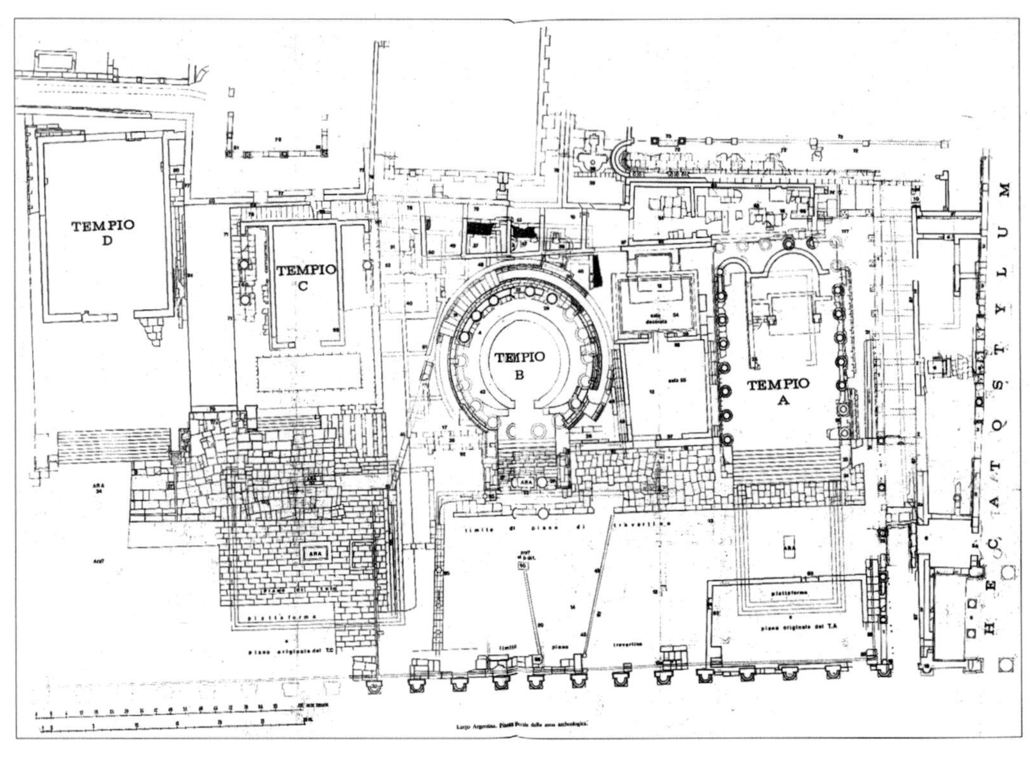

excavated, rather hastily, in the late 1920s. Temple A is rectangular with standing columns and a large tufa podium. The first temple belonged to the third century and was built on the natural clay, with a 4 m high podium, but the ground level was gradually raised. Temple B is circular and the youngest, and was set on a repaving of the whole area around 100 BC, and we can identify this one securely as that of Fortuna Huiusce Diei, dedicated by Q. Lutatius Catulus in 101 BC at the battle against the Cimbrians in Vercellae. There was a substantial cult image, and probably a good deal of statuary; certainly by Pliny the Elder's time the temple was known for its decoration of antique sculpture. Temple C, with its original tufa podium, is contemporary more or less with Temple A, and, similarly, repavings first raisd then buried the altar. The altar preserves an inscription (*CIL* I^2 2711) commemorating its restoration by one Aulus Postumius Albinus, son and grandson of Aulus. Temple D is the largest but largely hidden, and has two phases of a concrete podium, which puts it no earlier than the second century BC.

The colonnade on the east side of the area, now covered, and actually a Domitianic replacement of the earlier and original colonnade, has been argued by Coarelli above all to be that of the Porticus Minucia Vetus. This monument, raised by M. Minucius Rufus as a result of his victory over the Scordisci in 110, for which he triumphed in 106, included the temple of the Lares Permarini (Degrassi 1965 13.2.543, a calendar entry). We also have a fragment of the marble map (*FUR* 322) which helps locate the Porticus Minucia. On one reading, the Porticus Minucia Vetus is actually the Area Sacra of the Largo Argentina, and to it was added the Porticus Minucia, probably in the Domitianic period. This means that we must find the temple of the Lares Permarini in the Area Sacra. This temple was vowed by L. Aemilius Regillus during his naval battle in 190 BC with Antiochus the Great and built by the censor M. Aemilius Lepidus in 179, and Temple D is from the right period; the inscription is preserved imperfectly at Livy XL.52. The remaining two temples are identified most commonly as that of Juturna (Temple A, vowed probably by C. Lutatius Catulus in the first Punic War in 242) and Feronia (Temple C), who was one of the Di Novensiles introduced from the Sabina, probably by M. Curius Dentatus around 290 BC, and again the dates and the architecture of the two temples cohere. This leaves the temple on the Via delle Botteghe Oscure. The most common suggestion is the temple of the Nymphs, where census records were kept, so it ought to have been near the Villa Publica.

The arguments are complex, but the outcome the same – in this tightly packed area half a dozen temples can be found, and the Porticus Minucia, associated with the distribution of grain. Many are victory monuments, and the whole complex reflects the combative display and politics of the third to the first centuries BC. One can see Lutatius Catulus reprising the glory of an ancestor in his own monument in an area where the Aemilii and the Postumii Albini were also represented; then a Minucius enclosing the temples in a portico, which would be extended and itself in due course be outshone by Pompey's complex to the west.

(**a** Photo C. J. Smith; **b** plan after Coarelli 1997: Figure 57.)

F. Coarelli, *Il Campo Marzio* (Rome, 1997) 179–361 and individual entries in *LTUR*; A. Degrassi, *Inscriptiones latinae liberae rei publicae: Imagines*, vol. XIII. pt II (Berlin. 1965) 543

30. Comitium. The area of the *comitium* had been developed already in the archaic period, but received several interventions over the course of the middle Republic, which reflected both the political development of the city, and also the imperial expansion of Rome. Flanked by statues of Pythagoras and Alcibiades (Pliny *NH* XXXIV.26), the Comitium was close to the Rostra, and was an area in which treaties and other notices could be displayed (Cic. *Balb.* XXIII.53 for the *foedus Cassianum*; Diodorus Siculus XII.26 expresses amazement still to see the Twelve Tables on the Rostra).

A major renovation is conducted by C. Maenius, the consul of 338; the circular monument, which may be based on Greek models but is then exported across the colonies, was constructed in the mid third century; and part of the building is the Graecostasis to which foreign ambassadors to the Senate were invited. Up until the first Punic War, the consul declared mid-day when he saw the sun between the Rostra and the Graecostasis from the Curia (Pliny *NH* XXXIII.19). The construction of the Basilica Porcia in 184 may have limited space for the praetors' tribunal, which was subsequently moved. A generation later, either in 145 BC or slightly later, a tribune turned around to address the people gathered in the Forum, marking a shift in political culture.

(After Coarelli)

Coarelli *Il Foro Romano* vol. I; *LTUR* I.309–14.

30

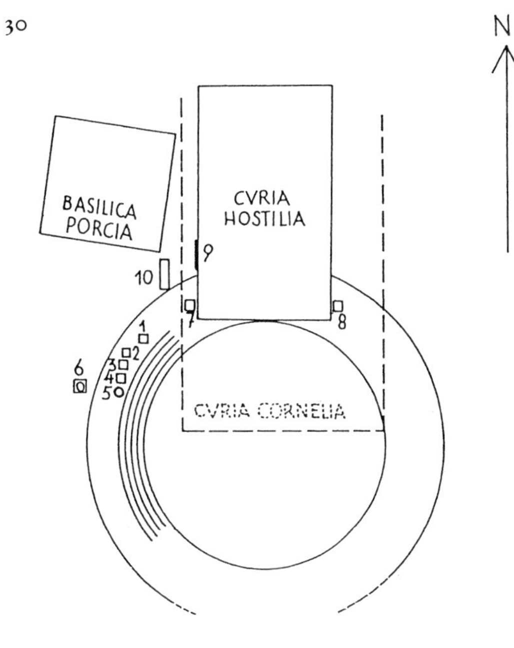

31. The votive deposit at the temple of Minerva Medica was found in 1887 during work on a new road and explored further later that century. The majority of the finds are from the third century BC, and presumably come from a favissa, an underground storeroom for old votives. It would appear that temples were occasionally cleared of previous dedications to make way for new ones.

The identification of the temple was made from a lamp inscribed '[Me]nerva dono de[det]'; there are also several representations of the goddess among the votives. Fourth-century AD catalogues of buildings and temples region by region place the temple of Minerva Medica in the Esquiline region (Augustan Regio V), and a nearby (and much later) temple of Isis, for which there is archeologial evidence. There are also anatomical votives in the deposit, which fits with the healing nature of the deity.

The finds include a variety of figurative representations: complete male and female figures, busts and statue groups, all in terracotta. As with other similar groups, there is a range of workmanship, some displaying clear debts to Greek sculpture, and others revealing an indigenous style with a greater degree of apparent realism.

The male statues illustrated were found in or near the other finds, both clearly from the same workshop and having significant parallels in Capua. The distribution of weight, the soft treatment of the curves of the body, and the classic lines of the face (**b**) reveal the Greek antecedents of these representations. The animal skin that one young man carries

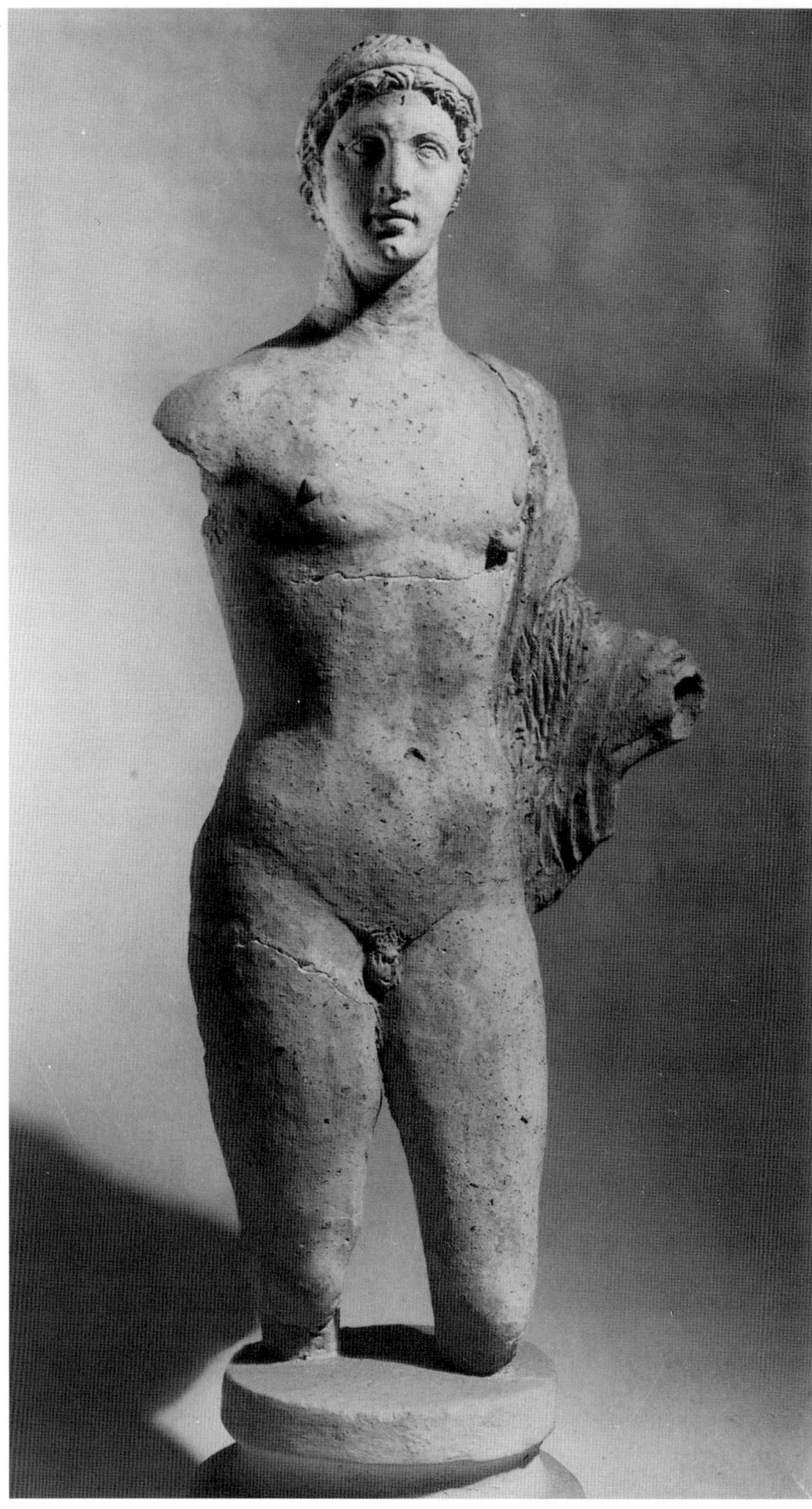

31b

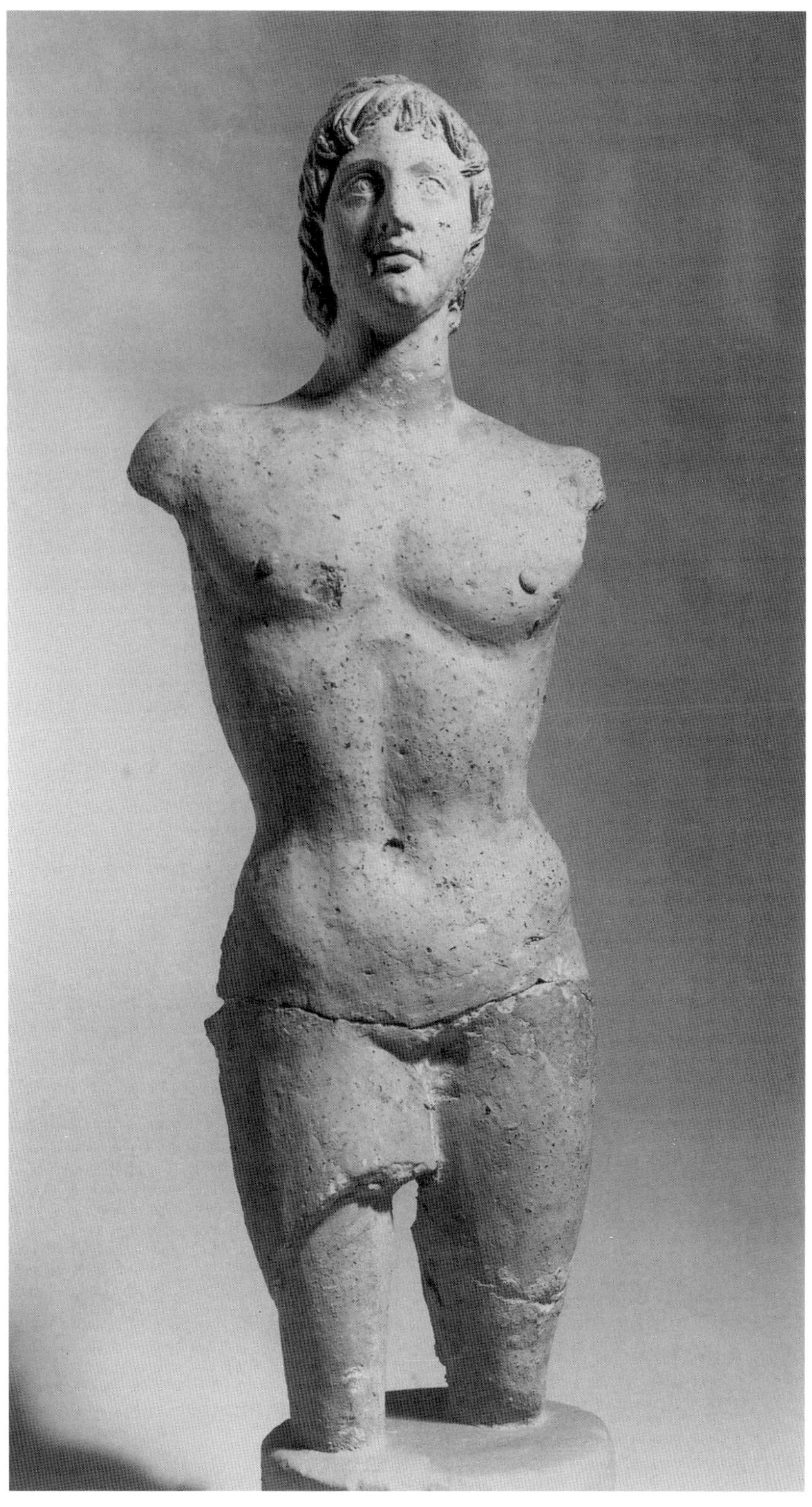

over his left arm (**a**) suggests a representation of a youthful Hercules.

(Rome Antiquarium Comunale inv. 2763, 2765. Height (**a**) 31.5 cm; height (**b**) 29.8 cm)

RMR pp. 186–7 no. 279 (Tav. XLIII) with reference.

32. Temple of Hercules Olivarius. We know from an inscription on the Caelian Hill that L. Mummius dedicated an *aedes et signum* to Hercules Victor from the spoils of his victory over Corinth (*CIL* 1^2.626 = VI. 331 = *ILLRP* 122); we know too that there were two such temples at Rome, one *ad portam Trigeminam* and one *ad Forum Boarium* (Macr. *Sat.* 3.6.10; cf. Serv. *Aen.* VIII.363), and this information seems to have come from Varro. The Porta Trigemina opened near the Forum Boarium. One source also tells of a temple of Hercules Olivarius, built by a merchant, Marcus Octavius Herrenus. This temple may also have been known as Hercules Victor.

One temple, long known and famous, is the round temple here illustrated; an inscription (*CIL* VI 33936) found nearby suggests that it housed a sculpture by the second-century BC artist Scopas, possibly a recumbent figure. We know that another round temple existed until the fifteenth century near S. Maria in Cosmedin. It is therefore difficult to be absolutely certain which the surviving temple is (it is definitely not a temple of Vesta as it is commonly described, solely on the basis of the familiar round shape). The surviving temple, with an inner round cella with Pentelic marble walls, an outer ring of twenty columns (some imperial in date) and wholly surrounded by steps, is 14.8 m in diameter and rests on a base of Grotta Oscura tufa. It has been suggested that this material is not used after about 100 BC, but the podium and temple are contemporary. Round temples of the late second century BC are also found in the Largo Argentina and at Tibur (Tivoli) outside Rome.

The complexity of worship of Hercules in the area of the Forum Boarium remains extraordinary and insoluble at present; we also have a reference in Festus 282L to a temple of Hercules near the shrine of Pudicitia in the Forum Boarium (but the text is difficult), and the Ara Maximi Herculis Invicti is in this area. If the round temple is second century BC in date, it would be, as Morel indicated (*CAH* VIII^2 506–8), our oldest surviving marble temple; and we know that the first marble temple

at Rome, Jupiter Stator in the Porticus of Metellus, was built after 146 (Vell. Pat. 1.11.5). What is undeniable is that this temple is part of the extraordinary development of the Forum Boarium area in the second century BC, which itself reflects Rome's economic growth and artistic development.

(Photo C. J. Smith)

LTUR 3.15–25; F. Rakob and W-D. Heilmeyer, *Die Rundtempel am Tiber in Rom* (Mainz am Rhein, 1973); F. Coarelli, *Il Foro Boario* (Rome, 1988) 98–103, 180–204; A. Ziolkowski, *Phoenix* 42 (1988) 309–33; R. E. A. Palmer, *JRA* 3 (1990) 234–44; G. Brands and M. Maischberger, *Rivista di Archeologia* 19 (1995) 102–20.

33. Architectural terracottas from the Via di San Gregorio. This splendid and well-preserved architectural frieze is probably from the mid second century BC. The fragments were discovered in 1878 in the region between the Palatine and the Caelian Hill, but languished for much of the subsequent period of time, until recently restored and displayed in the Capitoline Museum. The terracotta artistry is highly developed and retains traces of painting. Two female figures, one seated on an altar and one leaning on another, flank a standing figure, probably Mars, holding a spear and with cuirass, and sacrificial animals are being led from both sides. A jug stands on a table. On the acroterion can be seen images of Hercules with some kind of sea monster and a figure identified as Hesione. The standard interpretation, that of Strazzula, identified the temple with Fortuna Respiciens, which we know to have been in the vicinity; in an excellent publication of the fragments, Ferrea proposed that the temple be identified specifically with Mars, a hypothesis firmly rejected in a further treatment by Torelli. The specific identification appears likely to remain uncertain, another reminder of the depths of our ignorance of aspects of Roman topography, but also of the quantity of Roman temple building.

(Musei Capitolini: pediment *c.* width 2 m × height 1.8 m; acroterial figures *c.* height 0.5 m)

L. Anselmino, L. Ferrea and M. J. Strazzula, *RendPontAcc* 63 (1990–1) 193–62; L. Ferrea, *Gli dei di terracotta: La ricomposizione del frontone da Via di San Gregorio* (Rome, 2002); M. Torelli, *Ostraka* 13 (2004) 133–61.

34. Porticus Aemilia. Another building, the spectacular nature of which is hard to convey, is the Porticus Aemilia. In 193 BC, two Aemilii held the curule aedileship together and used money raised from fines to build a portico by the Tiber (Livy XXXV.10.12). This was paved and restored by the censors of 174 (Livy LXI.27.8).

The building is remarkable for its size and the way it coped with the slope down to the Tiber. It

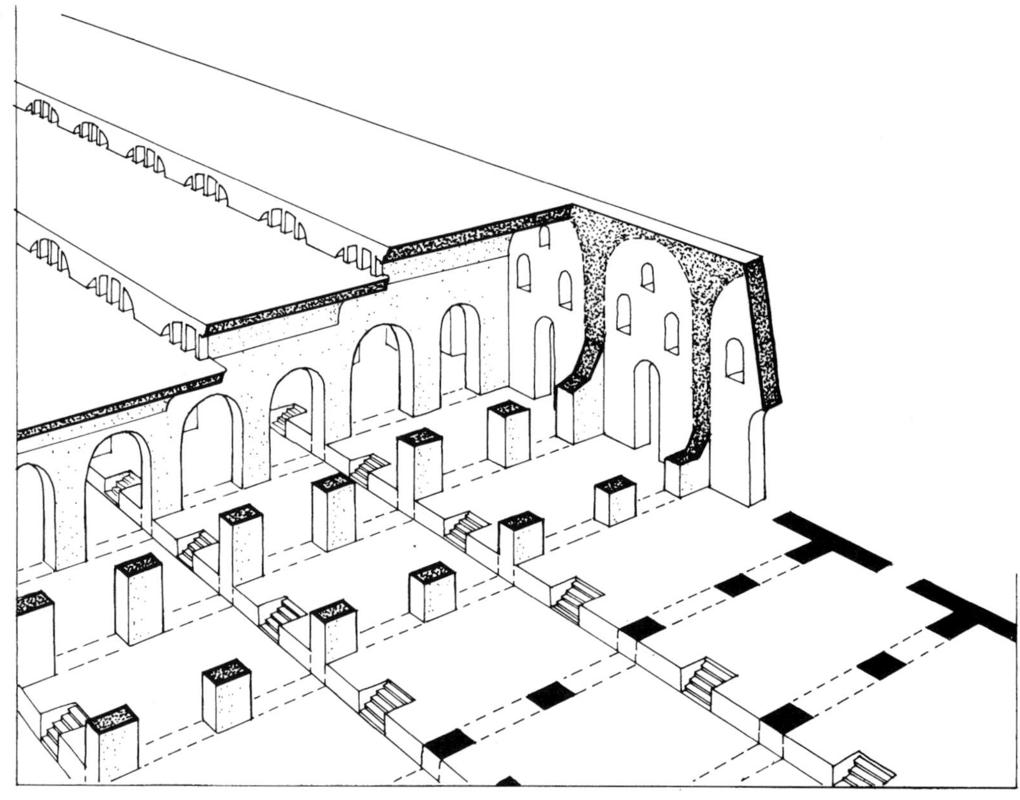

was 487 m long × 90 m wide in size, some 4.5 ha in area, with pilasters which supported arches, and at the ends arches and windows to provide light and access. The technique was *opus incertum*: irregularly shaped stones set into a concrete core. The building would therefore be a remarkable early experiment in the use of concrete for a building of this size, and attests Roman ambition and necessity. Such a large building, integrated into the developing urban fabric of the port area and sponsored by a family with a distinctive contribution to the building projects of this period, would demonstrate Rome's increasing need for a regular food supply and her reliance on external trade.

A recent article has put this all into question. The letters on the marble map, it was claimed, allow for an alternative reconstruction – *NAVALIA* – that is, the shipsheds of Rome, and there are arguments that this would permit a later date, which has attractions, given the otherwise very early use of concrete implied by the identification with the Porticus Aemilia, and that the architecture is at least as appropriate. This intriguing suggestion will, however, require further investigation, and recent research is moving back to the original identification.

(Plan after A. Boëthius, *Etruscan and Early Roman Architecture* (Harmondsworth, 1978))

LTUR sv Porticus Aemilia; G. Gatti, B.Com. (1934) 123–49; S. Tuck, *JRA* 13 (2000) 175–82; L.C. Lancaster, *Concrete Vaulted Construction in Imperial Rome: Innovation in Context* (Cambridge, 2005); L. Cozza and P.L. Tucci, *Arch.Cl.* 57 (2006) 175–202; F. P. Arata and E. Felici, *Arch. Cl.* 62 (2011) 127–54.

3. THE TRANSFORMATION OF CENTRAL ITALY

CHRISTOPHER SMITH

'The central issue in the development of Italy during the third and second centuries BC is without doubt that of its Hellenization; nevertheless, it would be a mistake to relate everything to this factor.' So Morel began his chapter on the transformation of Italy in *CAH* VIII, and this observation guides this chapter, which seeks to illustrate and comment upon his magisterial account. Since several of the other chapters in this volume also elucidate elements of this story, this chapter deals only with Etruria (42, 44, 47, 48), the Faliscans (49), Latium and Campania (50–2), but the proximity to Rome does not make the subject any the more simple, and only the briefest of introductions can be given to any part of it.

The issue of Hellenization has received sporadic attention, but there is no doubt that Romanization, especially in the context of the Empire, has been more seriously debated both in detail and in terms of methodology. There is also no doubt that we can learn from that debate, and from a more nuanced understanding of Romanization as a process and a complex mental phenomenon, and not merely an imposition of a foreign material culture. Hellenization in Italy differs because it had no military force behind it whatsoever, and there is no centre from which it can even potentially be said to come. Rome is not the leading force in the spread of Greek culture and lags behind some of its neighbours, even excluding those in the south of Italy who had the advantage of having Greek colonies in their territories. It would, however, be wrong to reduce the interest in Greek culture, and its adoption and spread, to a matter simply of style. Complex choices were made when Greek models were used, and such is the strength of the debate that one may suppose that complex choices were often being made when Greek models were not chosen. Indeed, one should add at this point that the distinction between Romanization and Hellenization is rather spurious. It would certainly not be appropriate or correct to see the first as taking up the entire range of political developments in the period, or the second to be the only relevant description of artistic development. They cannot be separated in time either, since one can see developments in the use of myth on Etruscan sarcophagi contemporary with the disappearance of Etruscan from inscriptions. As ever, we are dealing here with processes which are intimately bound up with major events such as conquest and war but not fully explained by them, and which admit of contradiction and complexity at every level.

Alongside the long and complex history of Hellenization, we must place the beginnings of an economic transformation, which would continue into the imperial period. As Morel makes clear, this is not a transformation which is confined to Rome, nor can it be said to be simply because of Rome, but one cannot extract the commercial and military power of Rome from any part of the picture. The impact of Roman power is ubiquitous, and yet it is also and obviously the case that the mechanisms by which Rome exhibited and extended that power were to some extent provided by her neighbours.

This process and this phenomenon are fascinating and of fundamental importance. Scholarship on the area has, however, been hampered by issues of insecure dating of key evidence and the staggering range of areas which need to be considered – language (38, 39), literature, high art (42, 43) and the most basic industrial products, such as amphorae (markers of their equally basic industrial contents) and coinage (56). Even the population figures for Italy are disputed, with at the extremes suggestions that the census figures reveal a decline in population from 225 to 28 BC from 4.5 to just 4 million, or a rise to about 11.5 million or maybe more.

The gap between these two interpretations gives some idea of the complexity of the problem which underlies the account of the transformation of Italy, and whilst it is the intention neither of this chapter nor of this volume to resolve this intractable argument, it is necessary to refer to it to indicate the level of uncertainty which underpins any historical account. It is true that archaeology may increasingly assist, and it is intriguing that the Tiber Valley Survey, which has reconsidered old data and generated new data, has tended to move away from earlier pictures of decline (**49**, and **54** for a different picture of land exploitation).

A key difficulty lies in understanding the massive impact on Italy of the import of slaves as a result of Roman expansion; another lies with the debate over the impact of the Second Punic War. Brunt rejected large parts of Toynbee's thesis on the devastating legacy of Hannibal's presence in Italy, but Cornell has suggested that it is Brunt's account that is at fault. Morley has suggested that the availability of land after the devastation of the Second Punic War may have encouraged population expansion in the relatively peaceful second century BC. Again it is hard to reconcile such very different pictures. One thing we can perhaps agree on is that the transformation of central Italy left some people very wealthy indeed. It is this wealth which drove some of the more spectacular artistic and architectural changes.

Finally, we must acknowledge the crucial role of the Roman colony in transforming Italy (**36**, **37**). The epigraphic and archaeological record of these colonies remains of central importance to understanding how Romans engaged with territory beyond their immediate hinterland, and the impact can be seen not only in the first moment of settlement, and derived from motives attendant on that moment, but also in the ongoing relationship between the colony and Rome on the one hand and the local population on the other. In this sense the revolt at Fregellae in 125 BC, with its strong Samnite presence, and the unexpectedly violent and destructive response of the Romans in destroying one colony and replacing it with Fabrateria Nova, constitute a moment just beyond our temporal limits, but illustrative of events and processes which are central to the history of the third and second centuries BC.

We are therefore at something of a crossroads in scholarship. We have an increasingly secure archaeological record, and a sophisticated theoretical debate on which to draw, and are in a better position to read across the artificial divides which are created either by events such as the Gracchan tribunates, or accident, such as the loss of Livy's history after 167 BC. It is beginning to be possible to contemplate new accounts of the transformation of central Italy, and it is likely that such an account will reinforce Morel's views; but there are fundamental areas where we need to make substantial progress before such an account can be written.

GENERAL BIBLIOGRAPHY

Some of the key works remain unsurpassed: *Roma medio Repubblicana* has much of interest outside Rome; and two major conferences, *Hellenismus in Mittelitalien* and *Les bourgeoisies municipales* are standard (see bibliography for Chapter 2).

For some reflections on issues of Romanization and Hellenization, see S. Keay and N. Terrenato (eds.), *Italy and the West: Comparative Issues in Romanization* (Oxford, 2001). An excellent overview has been provided by N. Morley, *Metropolis and Hinterland: The City of Rome and the Italian Economy, 200 BC–AD 200* (Cambridge, 1996).

For the problem of demography, see N. Morley, 'The transformation of Italy, 225–28 BC,' *JRS* 91 (2001) 50–62; L. de Ligt and S.J. Northwood (eds.), *People, Land, and Politics: Demographic Developments and the Transformation of Roman Italy 300 BC–AD 14* (Mnemosyne, Supplements; History and Archaeology of Classical Antiquity, 303, Leiden, 2008); for the debate over the Second Punic War, see Cornell in T. Cornell, B. Rankov and P. Sabin (eds.), *The Second Punic War: A Reappraisal* (London, 1996), 97–117.

For the Tiber Valley Survey, see H. Patterson (ed.), *Bridging the Tiber: Approaches to Regional Archaeology in the Middle Tiber Valley* (Rome, 2004).

35. Lavinium and its thirteen altars. Lavinium (modern Pratica di Mare) was, as we have seen, an important site in the early history of Rome (it was allegedly the site of Aeneas' landing in Italy and his burial place); it was also an important early port site (though changes in the coastline have left it inland today) and shared its religious cults with Rome (**8**). Antiquarian sources (Macrobius III.4.11, Serv. *Aen.* II.296) inform us that the chief Roman magistrates came there to sacrifice to the Penates and Vesta at the beginning of their term of office. In other ways, too, Lavinium may have served as a major federal cult centre; the sanctuaries of Minerva and of the Castores appear to have been less important.

Most significant of all is the expanding row of altars built at the site. There were at least thirteen in all (a fourteenth has recently been reported), though they were never all in use at any one time. The first three were built in the sixth century. Others were added by the mid fifth century, three built together on the same foundation, and a fourth abutting, and a fifth between these and the earlier

35

three. In the early fourth century two altars were added, and an extended foundation was inserted to join Altar 5 with Altars 4 and 8. At the end of the fourth century, Altar 13, the first of the series, was covered over; Altar 9 was moved closer to Altar 8, and three other tombs were added. All twelve altars were now joined; Altars 1, 2, and 8 were rebuilt before the end of the third century.

The altars, with their associated votive deposits, indicate the importance of the site, and tend to suggest a continuance of religious observance and expenditure after the sixth century and through the difficult period of the fifth and fourth centuries, when Latium suffered from continuing struggles with its neighbours and the invasion of the Gauls. The decline of the site as a whole through the third century, on the other hand, has been thought to be an indication of the deleterious effects of Rome's control over the Latins after 338 BC and her policy of religious imperialism. The site was briefly revived under Augustus, as part of the 'cultural heritage' programme reflected in Virgil's work.

As for the sanctuaries, that of Minerva was remarkable for the amount of terracotta statuary found there, apparently dumped when the sanctuary closed at the end of the third century BC. The statuary included images of the deity herself, and many representations of men and women, often extending a hand in offering.

(Castagnoli 1981: 171)

F. Castagnoli (ed.), *Lavinium I: Topografia generale, fonti e storia delle ricerche* (Rome, 1972); Castagnoli, *Lavinium II: Le tredici are* (Rome, 1975); Castagnoli, *Enea nel Lazio* (Rome, 1981), esp. 243–5 for statues; M. Torelli, *Lavinio e Roma: Riti iniziatici e matrimonio tra archeologia e storia* (Rome, 1984).

36. These tiny fragments of Attic red-figure ware were discovered in the area of the early castrum at Ostia. Beazley identified **b** as part of the production of the Black Thyrsus painter and suggested that it depicts a satyr wearing a panther skin.

Thanks to our ability to identify the date of Attic pottery with reasonable plausibility, we can assign these pieces to the fourth century BC, and, exiguous as they are, since they came from the lowest strata under the imperial forum, they may be taken as

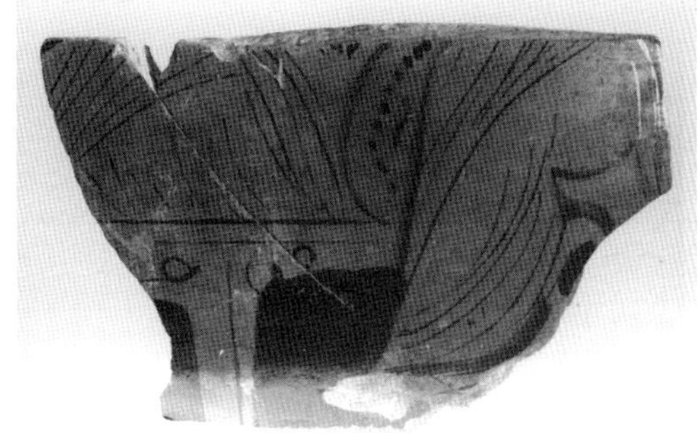

36a

36b

evidence for the new Roman settlement. Detailed study of walls at Ostia permits us to identify the rectangular structure of the early settlement, which looks very similar to later military camp layouts. Ostia was settled as a colony by the Romans precisely to fulfil this garrison function; we hear of plundering bands of Gauls, and a Greek fleet that ravaged the coast from Antium to the mouth of the Tiber (Livy VII.25.4).

(**a** Fragment of a red-figure *krater*, first half of fourth century BC. Width 6.3 cm × height 9.7 cm. (Ostia, Antiquarium inv. 16533)

b Fragment of a red-figure *krater*, attributed to the Black Thyrsus painter, second quarter of the fourth century BC. Width 10.1 cm × height 5 cm. (Ostia, Antiquarium inv. 16559))

Scavi di Ostia I. pl. 23; R. Meiggs, *Roman Ostia* (Oxford, 1970) 471; *RMR* pp. 343–61 nos. 449–523; B. Adembri, in A. Gallina and A. Claridge (eds.), *Roman Ostia Revisited* (London, 1996) 39–67.

37. Cosa. In 280 BC, at the same time as Pyrrhus was waging his war against the Romans in southern Italy, a second consular army defeated the combined levy of the towns of Volsinii and Vulci. The price of their defeat was an unequal alliance with Rome, and the loss of roughly one-third of their territory, an area including Vulci's fertile coastal plain. The colony of Cosa was planted here in 273 BC, and its careful excavation by the American Academy at Rome under Professor F. E. Brown and recent extensive publication have given a remarkably detailed picture of the development of a Roman colony. The preservation of more third- and second-century material than usual is due to the destruction and abandonment of the town around 70 BC after a major fire, which may have been the result of a piratical attack. There was only a partial revival in the Augustan period.

The colonies were vital defensive outposts for the Romans in their conquest of Italy, and the methods of their foundation were repeated up and down Italy both in our period and in the following period of agrarian unrest.

As with Paestum, Cosa occupied an important coastal position. It was situated on an uninhabited hill (though there was a town, Old Cosa, nearby), and it is clear from the plan of the colony that it was carefully laid out from the beginning; the territory was carefully delineated and divided, and the boundary of the town set out. The street plan was also orthogonal, determined by the position of the Arx at the highest point of a relatively flat hill, the forum (which clearly was marked out from the beginning) and the gates. The forum was naturally the central point and was provided with reserve water in the form of cisterns at the outset.

Permanent houses seem to have been laid out in the second quarter of the second century BC, but they will have been preceded by temporary structures. The majority of the colonists clearly lived in the countryside, and the colony itself was presumably a meeting place and place of refuge. The houses had cisterns within them fed by external conduits; stone, brick and beaten-earth floors; and a central hall with a *tablinum* or dining hall behind. They are perhaps related to the atrium style of house found at this time around the forum in their axiality.

It is notable that work proceeded on fortification, the monumentalization of the forum area and the first temple on the Arx before the development of private housing. An assembly area or Comitium, a large building that may have been a prison or a treasury and a temple, were all built before the second century BC (**a**, showing Rome top right, Cosa top left, Alba Fucens bottom right and Paestum bottom left; note the fundamental similarities). Eight large house-like buildings followed around the edges of the forum, which were probably used as shops, and from 180 BC onwards the inhabitants began to resurface and improve the area with a new Curia and repeated resurfacing of the square, a process similar to that which had been going on at Rome since the sixth century BC.

In the second quarter of the second century BC, porticoes were added in the forum, and a new temple, possibly of Concordia, which seems to have deliberately harked back to archaic Etrusco-Italic traditions in its severe architecture and its decoration with a pediment in the style of the Tarquinia workshop relating a scene from the Trojan cycle (**b**: A). The old altar was carefully preserved in the steps up to the new temple. We

37a

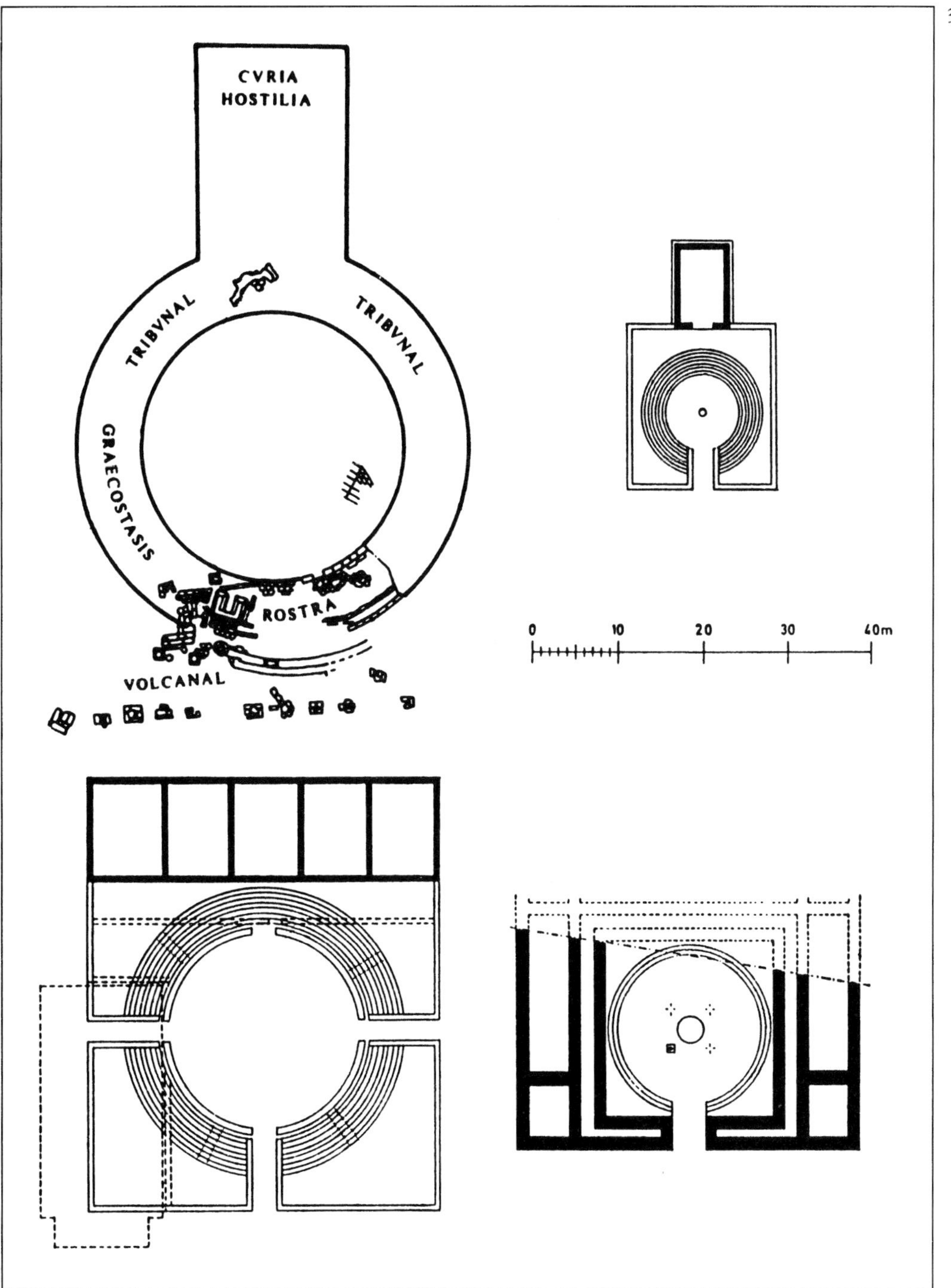

CVRIA
HOSTILIA
TRIBVNAL
TRIBVNAL
GRAECOSTASIS
ROSTRA
VOLCANAL
0
10
20
30
40m

37b

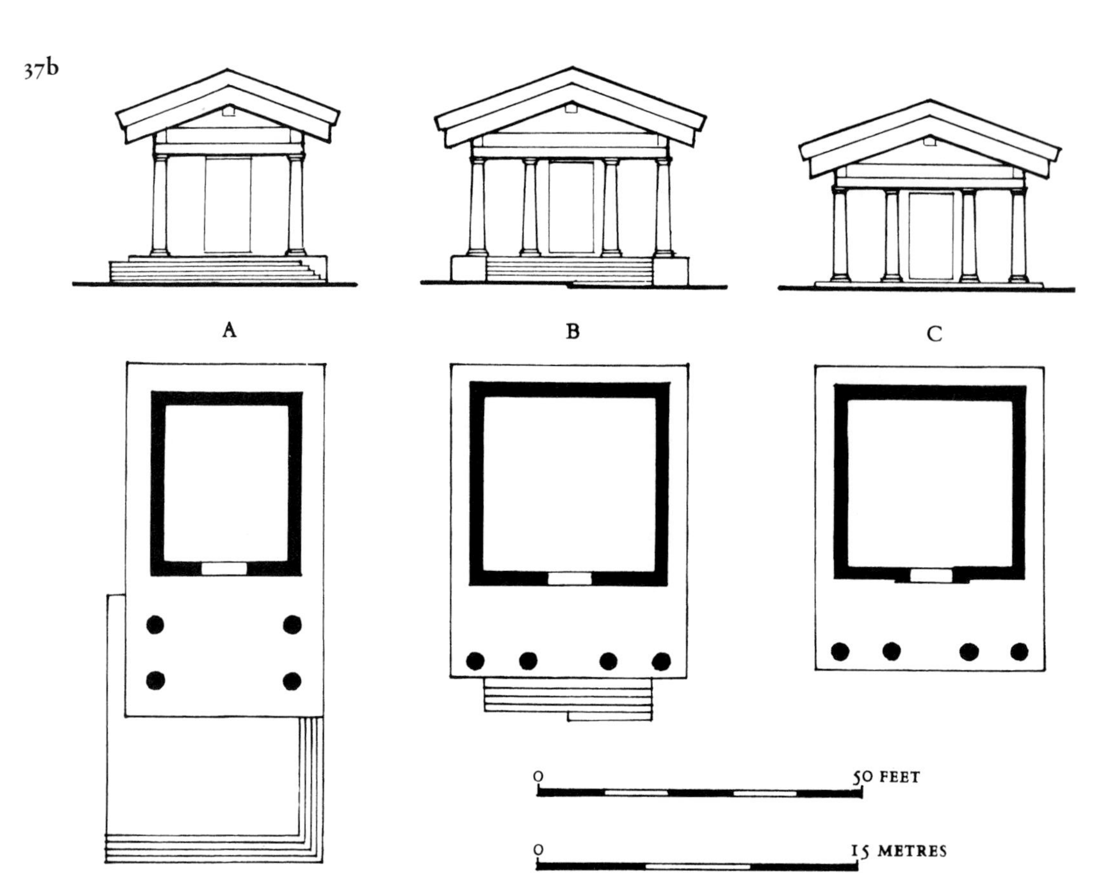

may suppose that this and the unusual houses reflect colonial decisions. On the Arx at about the same time a temple was built looking towards the sea; short and compact, with a perfectly square cella, it was highly regular and geometric in design. Within the altar a rough box contained ashes, perhaps from the inaugural sacrifice (**b**: B). Significant improvements were made to Cosa's port, inlcuding an identical and contemporary temple, subsequently extended in the first century BC (**b**: C). Brown identified these two temples as Mater Matuta and Portunus, but McCann has recently suggested Amphitrite and Neptune. A Capitolium was also built, incorporating the Latin Jupiter, the Etruscan Tinia or Jove (the deity of Old Cosa) and Hercules. The last remaining space in the forum was filled in the middle of the second century with a basilica similar to those developed in Rome a generation before.

As indicated earlier, the majority of Cosa's population did not live in the town but in the countryside, which had been divided into equal plots through centuriation. Around the turn of the first century BC, about 60 per cent of the land remained in these 2–ha plots; a further 25 per cent showed more solid occupation and improved housing; and some 15 per cent had become monumental villas. This situation indicates that in our period a steady process of accumulation of land through purchase, marriage, inheritance and so forth had been going on. The rise of the monumental villas will have occurred at the end of our period at the earliest.

(**a** After P. Gros, *L'architecture romaine* I (Paris, 1996) fig. 243; **b** after A. Boëthius, *Etruscan and Early Roman Architecture* (Harmondsworth, 1978) fig. 128)

F. E. Brown, *Cosa: The Making of a Roman Town* (Ann Arbor, 1980); A. M. McCann (ed.), *The Roman Port and Fishery of Cosa: A Centre of Ancient Trade* (Princeton, 1987) esp. 129–36; F. E. Brown, E. H. Richardson and L. Richardson Jr., *Cosa III: The Buildings of the Forum* (*MAAR* 37, Pennsylvania, 1993); V. J. Bruno and R. T. Scott, *Cosa IV: The Houses* (*MAAR* 38, Pennsylvania, 1993).

38. Inscribed on the bottom of a fifth-century BC Attic vernice nera kylix from Nola:

38

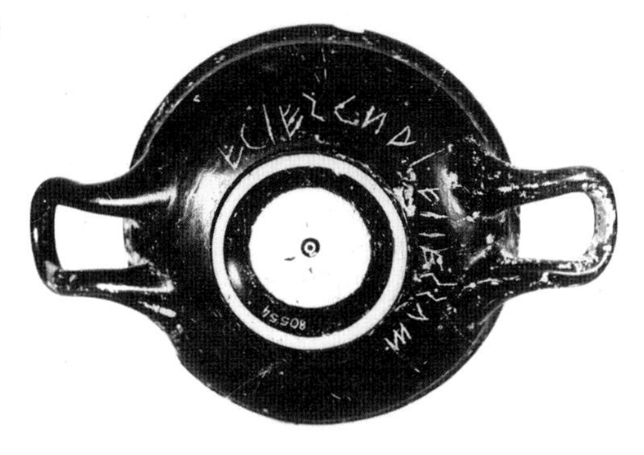

Luvkies Canaiviies sum

which is translated by some as 'I belong to Lucius Naevius.' The Naevii were a famous Campanian family; the inscription is in the Etrusco-Latin alphabet, but the Oscan dialect. It was found in a tomb at Nola in 1859. It is worth noting that many early accounts suggest that there were two such vessels with identical inscriptions; this has been shown to be an error of the nineteenth century.

The inscription is one of the very earliest Oscan inscriptions. If we are correct to see literacy as a relatively uncommon accomplishment, this and similar inscriptions where the object announces its ownership are part of the culture of an elite. The foreign origin of the vessel and its potential symposiastic use are further indications. On the other hand, the cup is not figurative, and not particularly uncommon, and might have had a more prosaic use and a more limited value, which might force us to reconsider our view of the social spread of literacy.

Morandi claims that the alphabet used is more Etruscan than other later inscriptions which have a modified version. A number of cultural choices would then be employed here; Etruscan alphabet, Oscan language, Greek vase.

(Naples inv. 80554. Height 5 cm; diameter 13 cm)

E. Vetter, *Handbuch der italischen Dialekte* (Heidelberg, 1953) 117; A. Morandi, *SE* 42 (1974) 391–2, pl. 71a; L. Agostiniani, *Iscrizioni Parlanti dell'Italia antica* (Florence, 1982) 158 no. 609; M.H. Crawford *et al.*, *Imagines Italicae: A Corpus of Italic Inscriptions* (Bulletin of the Institute of Classical Studies Supplement (London, 2011, 3 vols.) 2.870–1.

39. Velletri inscription. In a previous chapter we identified a possible Volscian occupation at Satricum by the language and script of an inscribed axe-head (**15**), but noted that the inscription also indicated a developed social system. By the fourth century, the Volscians had clearly adopted the Latin alphabet, as this inscription shows, but there are still surprises. This bronze tablet refers to the deity Declona, known only from this inscription, and two Volscian magistrates or *meddices*, Egnatius Cossutius, son of Sextus, and Maras Tafanius, son of Caius.

The date is uncertain; some authors place it before the decisive battle of the Astura, but Morandi dates it to the third century. It is interpreted as a requirement that a fine be paid by anyone who has taken anything from the goddess or committed any kind of sacrilege, and it would be

39

interesting if we can see the word *curia* underlying *co-uehriu*, which could indicate a senate or a curial group such as we see perhaps in the Iguvine Tables and certainly at Rome; Rix translates as 'assemblea comunale'.

Translation is insecure. The transliteration reads:

deue decline statom sepis atahus pis velestrom façia esaristrom se bim asif veseclis vinu arpatitu sepis toticu couehriu sepu ferom pihom estu ec. se. cosuties ma. ca. tafanies medix sistiatiens.

(Museo Nazionale, Naples inv. 2522. Length 23 cm × height 3.5 cm)

Vetter *Handbuch* 222; A. Morandi, *Epigrafia italica* (Rome, 1982) 151–3; H. Rix, *Quaderno di Archeologia Etrusco-italica* 20 (1992) 37–49; Crawford *et al. Imagines Italicae* 1.340–3.

40a

40. Cales votive deposits: terracotta heads. Like Capua and Cumae, Cales seems to have been a production centre for terracotta heads which were placed in votive deposits. These objects were mass-produced from the fifth century, but a particular impetus for expansion seems to have been given by the founding of a Roman colony at Cales in 335 BC (Livy VIII.16). Naples and Capua, larger centres than Cales, also benefited from the Roman presence, but all three retained the particularly Campanian combination of Hellenistic influences from the colonies of Magna Graecia, and local traditions. This may be illustrated for Cales by these two heads.

a is clearly influenced by an Alexander portrait. The treatment of the hair, the up-turned eyes and slightly parted, sensuous lips can all be paralleled in the portraiture of Alexander and of some of his successors. This type is found widely in central and southern Italy; Ciaghi suggests parallels at Civitella, Pesaro, Rome and Fratte, and relationships with Faliscan workshops.

b, undatable, and made by hand rather than in a mould, shows a completely different approach to portraiture. The man's eyes are simple triangles; his hair is represented by vertical incisions in the clay. His lips are parted and his teeth can be seen. As in much Italic sculpture, his ears are prominent. Although it has been suggested that the man is suffering from some sort of skin disease, it is perhaps more likely that the maker has chosen an unusual way of illustrating a beard. Some form of necklace or other ornament seems to be indicated around the man's neck.

40b

(**a** Museo Nazionale, Naples 22190. Height 26.5 cm; width 21 cm.

b Museo Nazionale, Naples 195081. Height 24 cm; width 14.8 cm)

S. Ciaghi, *Le terrecotte figurate da Cales del Museo Nazionale di Napoli: sacro, Stile, commitenza* (Rome, 1983) 146 and 253.

41. Terracotta and stone sculpture. We have already seen a substantial amount of outstanding terracotta sculpture in Rome (**31**, **33**), but the whole of central Italy produced terracottas, some at least for votive purposes, and they shared the fashions of the day, moving largely from idealizing to veristic presentation over time. The first of our group comes from a votive deposit at Falerii. The head (**a**) demonstrates a strong determined face, and the marks between the eyebrows almost suggest a frown. Dating is extremely difficult, but it may have predated the Roman conquest of 241.

The damaged figure of Orpheus in peperino (**b**) came from the Via Tiburtina by the Basilica of S. Lorenzo, where over 400 pieces were found, many reused as building material. Amongst other figures, there was a woman standing and nursing a baby, a most unusual pose, and the very rare representation of Orpheus, who is shown with animals at his feet and an owl on his thigh, and, probably, playing a flute; comparisons are often made between his head and the 'Ennius' bust in the Tomb of the Scipiones (**26**). Again, dating is difficult and varies from the beginning to the end of the second century BC, but it may be that there were a number of sculptural groups here, including perhaps scenes from the story of Jason and the Argonauts, amongst whose number was Orpheus, and a group of defeated Gauls. We know from Livy XXVI.10.3 that there was a temple of Hercules near here at the first mile, and we have a stone dedication to Hercules (*CIL* I^2 607; *ILLRP* 1.118) which shows that M. Minucius, as dictator in 217, made a dedication to Hercules – also one of the Argonauts. The head of Hercules in peperino now in the Ny Carlsberg Glyptothek is likely to be from the same group. This combination would seem to suggest the earlier date for the whole group, which, if true, would give us evidence of statue groups in stone, heavily influenced by Pergamene artistry, on the outskirts of Rome in the second century BC; notably the main cult at Tibur, at the other end of the Via Tiburtina, is Hercules Victor.

(**a** Soprintendenza Archeologica di Etruria Meridionale; Villa Giulia inv. 7311. Height 31 cm; *RMR* pp. 32–3 no. 2 pl. 11

b Musei Capitolini 1699. Height 0.9 m)

G. Colonna, *Sc.Ant.* 5 (1991) 209–32; M. Moltsen and M. Nielsen, *Etruria and Central Italy 450–30 BC* (Ny Carlsberg Glyptothek, 1996) 200–1 no. 88; *LTUR Suburbium sv* Herculis Templum (Via Tiburtina) (Z. Mari).

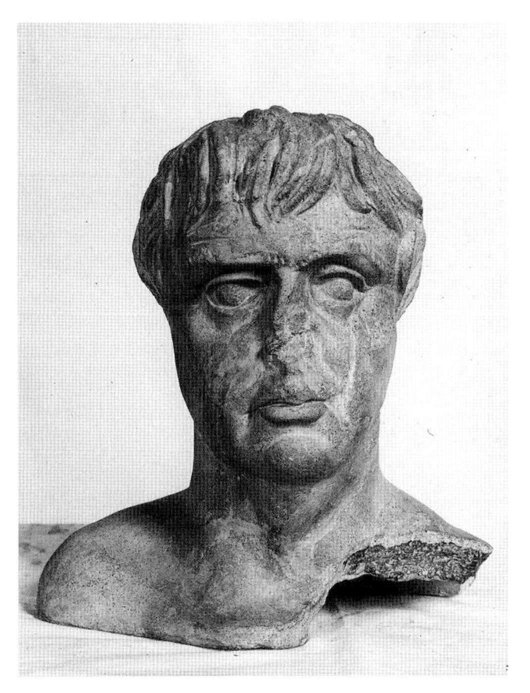

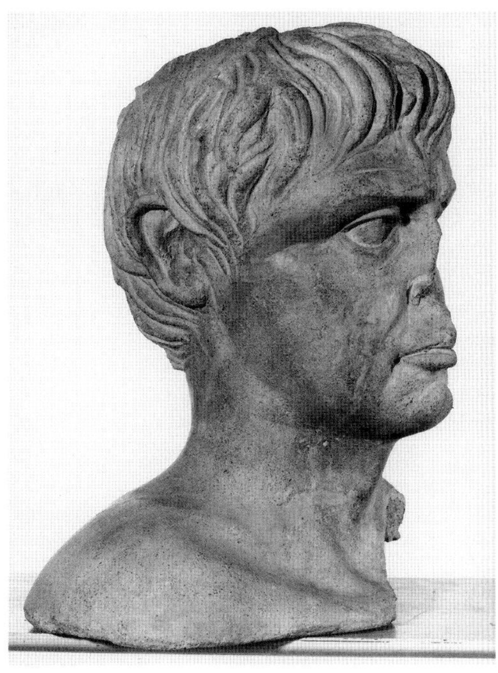

41a

41b

42. Hercules at rest. From a small walled defensive site in the Vetulonian territory. The hero, Hercle in Etruscan, stands at rest. He holds a drinking horn in one hand and an apple from the garden of the Hesperides in the other; and the lionskin that characterizes him flows down his back and across his left forearm. He is depicted with a fluid, easy anatomy, his weight resting on his right leg and his left leg slightly advanced and turned out. He is depicted as a young, lithe man, not as a muscle-bound hero. In his stance one can see clearly the influences of Greek sculpture. The piece is dated to the early third century BC.

Hercules was commonly represented from the sixth century BC as a Punic hero on the lines of Melqart; in the fourth century his image is less belligerent in Etruria. He retains, for the Sabellian and Samnite people, his military significance, but it has been suggested that this pose, with the cup and apple, has particular reference to his journey to the west in the cup of the Sun.

(Florence, Museo Archeologico inv. 5. Height 28 cm)

M. Cristofani, *I bronzi degli Etruschi* (Novara, 1985) 283; *LIMC sv* Herakles/Hercle 62.

43. 'Brutus'. This famous bronze head was originally from an over-life-size statue. His eyes dominate, with their perfectly preserved ivory eyeballs, and dark-brown and black paste with a ring of bronze for irises and pupils; one can still see eyelashes that have been cut from bronze sheet.

The head may have been discovered at Rome; it was drawn by Marten van Heemskerck between 1532 and 1536; it is clear that it did not have the bust at that time. Although the sixteenth-century identification with Junius Brutus, the first consul of Rome, is unfounded, the piece clearly shows a careful portrait that has gone beyond the purely generic and, in the pronounced forehead and intense eyes, reflects Early Hellenistic portrait sculpture. Every aspect of the sculpture deserves attention, from the hair and the modelling of the skin to the slight asymmetry which gives a tremendous sense of realism.

The date is disputed, and attempts have been made to push it down to the first century BC – Parisi Presicce claimed it as an Augustan original or copy of a not very old statue – but there are fair parallels from earlier contexts, such as an early

43

second-century terracotta head from the Ara della Regina deposit at Tarquinia, and painted figures in the middle to late fourth-century Tomba degli Scudi (Tomb of the Shields) at Tarquinia.

(Palazzo dei Conservatori, Rome inv. 1183. Height 32 cm (excluding later bust))

Colonna *I bronzi* 297–8; C. Parisi Presicce, *B.Com.* 98 (1997) 43–110; M. Papini, *Antichi volti della Repubblica: La ritrattistica in Italia centrale tra IV e II secolo a.C.* (*B.Com.* Supplement 13, Rome, 2004) 72–94.

44. Arezzo ploughman. The circumstances of the discovery of this group are uncertain. The findplace may have been Molino della Gagliarde, closely connected with the *cardo* of Arezzo and just on the transition between the urban and extra-urban area. The purpose of the group, which old engravings show with a woman with a diadem standing with her hands on her hips, may have been votive, but we cannot tell. A man is presented driving his two oxen, which pull what would have been a wooden plough with an iron ploughshare. The man wears a long tunic with the sleeves rolled up, an animal skin over that and some sort of cap; the clothes do not seem particularly appropriate to agriculture. The date would appear to be *c.* 430–400 BC.

The group most probably reflects some sort of prayer for agricultural prosperity, but the figure

44

of the ploughman, and the possible presence of a female (divine?) figure, has added interest, since it was such a man, Tarchon, who unearthed Tages, the figure who revealed Etruscan lore.

(Museo Nazionale Etrusco di Villa Giulia (ex coll. Kircheriana) inv. 24526. Height 10 cm)

Colonna *I bronzi* 270; F. Paturzo, *Arezzo antica: La città dalla preistoria alla fine del mondo romano* (2nd edn, Cortona, 1997) 187–90; for the myth of Tages, see J. R. Wood, *Latomus* 39 (1980) 325–44; for Tarchon, not including this type, see *LIMC sv* Tarchon.

45a

45. Praenestine *cippi* and bust. A distinctive characteristic of the dedication practices at Praeneste (Palestrina) are the *cippi*, shaped like pine cones (or eggs?) rising out of bases, some of which were inscribed, whilst some had figurative scenes; here we see a hunt. The inscriptions allow us to make some sense of Praenestine society; we can identify well over 100 gentilicial names. This practice lasts from the fourth to the first centuries BC. Also characteristic are the veristic and impressive busts in limestone, predominantly from the fourth and third centuries BC; the woman illustrated here typically has earrings and an impressive necklace. These busts and

45b

45c

cippi may have been on the outside of tombs, which inside often contained mirrors and ciste. Praeneste was a strong and independent city with her own territory; in the fourth century, she was one of the leading Latin towns to oppose Rome and maintained, despite defeat, a degree of individuality.

(**a, b** Rome, Palestrina Museo Archeologico inv. 100, 101. Height 65 cm and 48 cm; *RMR* pp. 298–9 no. 438 pl. XCVII **c** Palestrina Museo Archeologico inv. 18; inscribed *Graeca Vatronia* (= *CIL* I^2 336). Height 44 cm; max. width 31 cm; A. Giuliano, *MDAIR* 60–1 (1953–4) 172–83; *RMR* p. 303 no. 447 pl. C)

La necropoli di Praeneste: Periodo orientalizzante e medio repubblicano (Palestrina, 1992).

46. Sarcophagi: **a** mythical scene; **b** procession. These two examples stand for the extraordinarily rich and informative collection of Etruscan sarcophagi that have survived. Although there are a range of difficult issues in terms of dating, in terms of ensuring that the urn and its lid are correctly joined, and in terms of the loss of contextual information due to the fact that so much of this material has been robbed or unsystematically excavated, there is nevertheless enormous value in the study of these objects. They stand in their own right as works of art, and as indicators of a range of social, political and religious values. It is particularly unfortunate that it is rarely possible to gain a sense of the relationship between urns and the painted tomb in which they were deposited (see Ridgway *CAH Plates* IV 224–6).

The production of the sarcophagi can be traced back into the archaic period – the famous Sarcofago degli Sposi is a case in point. Broadly speaking, the north of Etruria cremated and the south inhumed (the ash-urns are about 0.6 m and the sarcophagi about 2 m long.). In both areas, the sarcophagi or ash-urns were often placed in familial chamber tombs. Some were relatively small, whilst a few contained over a hundred burials, and their duration varied too. We see a number of local traditions and local materials from the fourth century onwards; so, Volterra, from which we have about 1,100 examples, tends to use stone and then alabaster, whereas terracotta is more common at Chiusi. Many are plain, but some are highly ornate, with both mythical representation on the body and a portrait of the deceased. Not all were for the elite: at Chiusi there was a degree of mass production, and inscribed urns belonged also to the *lautni* class, which are sometimes thought to be equivalent to Roman freedmen. As regards the portraits, the focus is on the head rather than the body. Some figures are fully recumbent early on, but increasingly they are represented reclining as at a banquet, and some figures are shown garlanded and holding symposiastic cups. Some are highly individualized, and Volterran urns become veristic in the second

46a

46b

century BC. Some are inscribed. Production continues at least until the Social War, and in some instances longer, and we see an increasing use of Latin from the beginning of the first century BC.

Greek myth abounds on the sarcophagi. Most of the stories are fairly hackneyed, but it is interesting to see how many versions of the fratricidal struggle at the heart of the story of the Seven against Thebes can be identified. The question lies open as to the purpose of these representations; one interpretation would be to see it as a way of glorifying the deceased by association, but it may also carry meaning as a statement about the values of a civilized society. Etruscan politics was from time to time violent, and perhaps the myths warn against the dangers of this. Moreover, there seems every reason to suppose that the Trojan cycle held as much interest for Etruscans as for Romans, and that drama was also popular. Although the permanent theatre sites are mostly later (one exception is at Castelsecco near Arezzo), we know from Rome that theatrical performances could perfectly well take place in a temporary setting.

In the first example (**a**), the story is that of Odysseus and Philoctetes, who is sent away from the Greek army at Troy because of his festering wound, but whose presence (or at least the presence of his bow and arrows) is actually required for their ultimate victory; Odysseus is sent to persuade – or trick – him into coming back. In our version, Odysseus is holding Philoctetes' bandaged leg whilst, behind him, Diomedes is stealing the weapon; two figures holding horses flank the scene. As with many scenes, one is tempted to see the influence of drama, and since the urn is probably to be dated to the second quarter of the second century BC, we have a fairly precise parallel, since fragments survive of Accius' contemporary tragedy on the subject.

In the second example (**b**), we have a scene of procession; such scenes are often funerary and are typically found commemorating magistrates. The sarcophagus is in nenfro and dates to the mid third century; it was discovered in the nineteenth century between Tuscania and Tarquinia, and was said to have been found with three others, an elderly male, a younger man and a female in a chamber tomb, the interior of which was painted blue. Cups and vases hung on the walls, and there was a tripod in the middle of the room. On the sarcophagus, a beardless man reclines on two pillows and a coverlet with a scalloped edge. He wears a plaited wreath and a garment which partially clothes him. There is a ring on the third finger of his left hand. The flesh still showed signs of red paint, as did the chest beneath. A winged daemon leads the procession, followed by a two-horse chariot, inside which a pointing figure stands. Four attendants follow; three carry branches, (perhaps equivalent to the Roman *lictors* who carried the *fasces* as signs of authority) and the fourth a curved wind instrument. The inscription on the upper border of the chest (*CIE* 5755) reads:

atnas . vtẹl [.] larθal . clan . svalce . avil LXIII . zịt[lat]θ maruχva . tarilst . cepta . φeχucu

It is taken to refer to one Vel Atnas, who died aged 63, having been zilaθ or chief magistrate of Tuscania.

(**a**. Accademia Cortona inv. 1034 (Etr. 24). Length 0.52 m)

(**b**. British Museum D25–6; Cist length 2.13 m × height 0.64 m × width 0.62 m; lid length 2.13 m × height 0.63 m × width 0.74 m)

LIMC sv Odysseus/Uthuze 39; F.-H. Pairault, *Recherches sur quelques series d'urnes di Volterra à representations mythologiques* (Rome, 1972) 133–41.

F. N. Pryce, *Catalogue of Sculpture in the Department of Greek and Roman Antiquities of the British Museum* I. II: *Cypriote and Etruscan* (London, 1931) 193–6; R. Herbig, *Die jünger-etruskischen Stein Sarkophage* (Berlin, 1952) 38 no. 66; R. Lambrechts, *Essai sur la magistrature des républiques étrusques* (Brussels, 1959) 79–80, 133–4; G. Colonna, *SE* 50 (1982) 296 (inscription); Colonna, *SE* 46 (1978) 81–117 (discovery).

47. Terracotta frieze, Pyrgi. For the context and a general account of Pyrgi, see Ridgway, *CAH Plates* IV 227–31. The terracotta plaque at the back gable, illustrated here in its recently restored form, is the first of a series of terracotta decorations included in this chapter to demonstrate the richness of the tradition, and the local adaptation and reuse of Greek myth in an Italian context. The frieze is dated to about 460 BC and is in the forefront of artistic development anywhere in the Mediterranean – Spivey, for instance, compares the almost contemporary temple of Zeus at Olympia.

The event is taken from the Seven against Thebes saga, when Tydeus, wounded and enraged, bites into the head of Melanippus. Athena, who was going to save Tydeus, turns away in disgust, whilst Zeus intervenes across another warrior to destroy the braggart Capaneus with a thunderbolt. Spivey's commentary is to the point: 'it is a paradigm of hubristic impiety and its divine punishment. Picked out in polychrome, the tableau was a dense and furiously powerful piece of admonition.' Similarly, to the north and perhaps 200 years

47

later, at Talamone, Oedipus leans out in a gesture of helpless lament in the midst of the fratricidal carnage. In both instances Greek myth is deployed to striking effect in the civic context.

In the fourth century, the Pyrgi relief was replaced, perhaps with a representation of Herakles' arrival in Italy with Leucothea and Palaemon, which Ovid connects with Mater Matuta and Portunus. Links between Caere (of which Pyrgi was the port) and Rome were close after Caere sheltered Romans, including the Vestal Virgin, during the Gallic sack.

(Soprintendenza Archeologica di Etruria Meriodionale neg. 189718. Height (restored) 132.5 cm; width 137.5 cm; diameter 3–4 cm)

N. Spivey, *Etruscan Art* (London, 1997) 99–100; more generally F.-H. Pairault Massa, *Iconologia e politica nell'Italia antica: Roma, Lazio, Etruria dal VIII al I secolo a.C.* (Milan, 1992); new restoration and fourth-century material, G. Colonna, *L'altorilievo di Pyrgi: Dei ed eroi greci in Etruria* (Rome, 1996).

48. Tarquinia Ara della Regina horses. Tarquinia was one of the great Etruscan cities, and flourished in the sixth and fifth centuries BC. In the fourth century we know that the fortifications were renewed, some major tombs built and an extremely fine temple constructed. Some acknowledgement of the seismic change brought about by Rome's conquest of Veii may be felt here. The major temple site is dated by the evidence of the architectural terracottas to around the fourth century BC, though there appears to have been an earlier building on the same site, and two small buildings (x and y), looking rather like an altar and precinct, are preserved at a different alignment, suggesting some sort of commemoration. It was a Tuscan-style temple, the base of which is 77 m × 35 m, and on the south side there are 15 courses of tiered ashlar masonry over 7 m high. A cella anteroom and vestibule were placed between the *alae*, and a grand staircase led to an intermediate level, from which two more staircases and a ramp led to the main level.

The horses are particularly fine, and famous. Originally they were pulling a (lost) chariot, into which a deity may have been climbing (or on which he or she was already standing); some paint remains, and the harness would have been richly decorated. There are artistic parallels between the Ara della Regina terracottas and those from the Belvedere temple at Orvieto, reminding us of the possible movement of craftsmen, or artistic ideas, across Etruria.

A nearby deposit contained a variety of statues, anatomical votives and coins from the fourth to the second centuries BC. The deity worshipped at the temple remains unknown.

(Soprintendenza per i Beni Archeologici dell'Etruria Meridionale Foto 207270. Height 114 cm; Length 124 cm; heavily restored)

M. Bonghi Jovino (ed.), *Gli Etruschi di Tarquinia* (Modena, 1986) 355–76; A. Comella, *Deposito votivo presso l'Ara della Regina* (Rome, 1982); M. Y. Goldberg, *MDAIR* 92 (1985) 107–25; R. Leighton, *Tarquinia: An Etruscan City* (London, 2004) 172–5.

49. The Faliscan territory. The Faliscans occupy an interesting position between the Etruscans and the Sabines on the north side of the Tiber (**a**). The Ager Capenas, focused on the Lucus Feroniae federal sanctuary, is different again. The Faliscan territory sees a development of aristocratic behaviour in the eighth century BC, and some unusual local forms in pottery and jewellery. We find a number of inscriptions, which suggests that literacy was seen as a desirable elite activity. Falerii Veteres is very much the centre of economic and political developments, and right through the fifth century, the Faliscan territory is open to strong Greek influence, as well as its own native traditions (**b**). Examples of this include the amount of Greek pottery found in burial deposits, and the spectacular architectural terracottas from the temples of Mercury and Apollo at Sassi Caduti, of Minerva and of Apollo at Scasato, and of Apollo at Vignale. There were also cults of Juno Curitis, perhaps the most important, and Janus Quadrifons.

The destruction of Veii and the Roman colonies at Nepi and Sutri left Falerii isolated, and there is a long story of resistance, culminating in a rebellion in 293 BC (Livy X.45) and another, final rebellion

49a

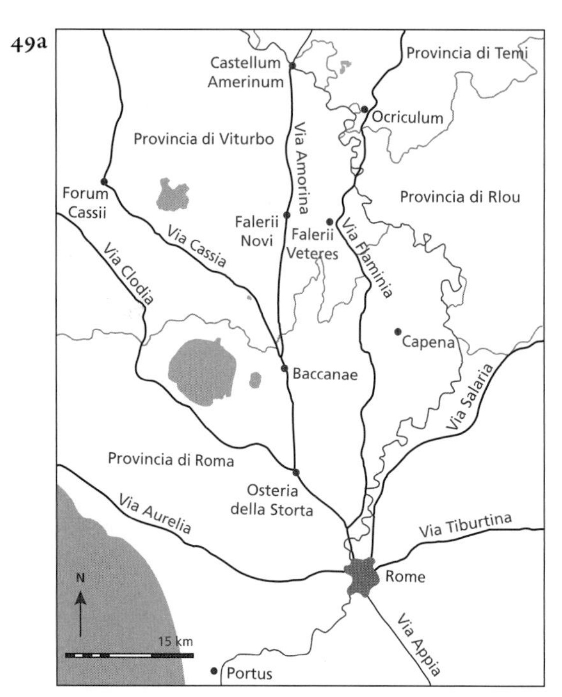

in 241 BC. According to a late source, the city was destroyed and 15,000 Faliscans killed. We do know that Falerii Novi was founded a few kilometres away (**c**), and it is now well known through recent survey and geophysics, with a very clear forum and temple complex, and a road network, part of which connects up to the continuing cult-site of Juno Curitis at Falerii Veteres. We can see evidence that the Roman road network through the area profoundly affected the local settlement pattern, and set up dislocations and transformations; Falerii Veteres and Novi are thus key sites in the debate about the nature of Roman imperial expansion.

(**a.** Faliscan territory, British School at Rome; **b** Falerii Veteres; Vignale plateau (photo S. Keay); **c** Falerii Novi, Porta di Giove (photo S. Keay))

T.W. Potter, *The Changing Landscape of Southern Etruria* (London, 1979) 93–137; A. Comella, *Le terrecotte architettoniche del santuario dello Scasato a Falerii: Scavi 1886–1887* (Naples, 1993); S. Keay, M. Millett, S. Poppy, J. Robinson, J. Taylor and N. Terrenato *PBSR* 68 (2000) 1–93; S. Keay, M. Millett, S. Poppy, J. Robinson, J. Taylor and N. Terrenato in Patterson (ed.) *Bridging the Tiber* 223–36.

50. Pompeii – Sanctuary of Dionysus 'S. Abbondio' pediment (**a**); plan (**b**); Bolsena throne (**c**). Less than 1 km south-east of the amphitheatre at Pompeii, this small sanctuary has an inscribed altar in front of a Doric temple with strong Hellenistic architectural influences. The pediment was originally thought to depict Dionysus with a bunch of

49b

49c

grapes and cup, and other figures associated with him, including a panther and a female (Semele, Aphrodite or Ariadne). The cult was set up by town magistrates, and on the original interpretation seems to have been unaffected by the decree against the Bacchanalian cult passed in 186 BC, and attested both in Livy (XXXIX.8–18) and in an important inscription found near the colony of Vibo Valentia at Tirioli (*CIL* I^{2}. 581). More recently the temple has been dated to later in the second century BC, attributed to the more acceptably Roman pair of Liber and Libera, and construed as a response to

50a

50b

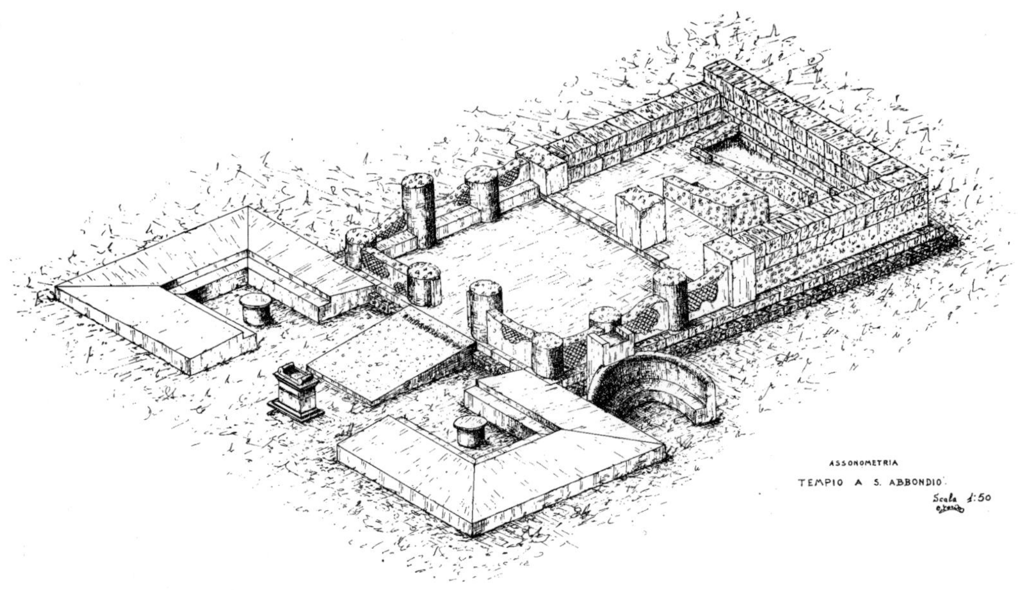

the Dionysiac interdict. The temple was extensively redeveloped in the Flavian period.

North of Rome at Bolsena (Volsinii) an attempt has been made to identify an initiation site with a throne, with a representation of a panther, and to claim that it was destroyed as a result of this decree in 186 BC or thereabouts. A recent interpretation suggests first that the S. C. de Bacchanalibus only affected Roman colonies or land under Roman control, and only the most recently established cults at that; and, second, that what we have at Bolsena is a cistern, not an initiation site, and that we should be more cautious about connecting the destruction to the specific decree. That Bacchus was important in an Italic context is undeniable; that Rome violently intervened to suppress his cult is less certain.

(**a**, **b**. after Elia and Caratelli 1975; **c**. École française de Rome, neg. BOL4500G (O. Savio))

Sanctuary of Dionysus: O. Elia and G. Pugliese Carratelli, *Orfismo in Magna Grecia: Atti del XIV Convegno di Studi sulla Magna Grecia* (Naples, 1975) 139–53; Elia and Pugliese Carratelli, *PdP* 34 (1979) 442–81; A. Cooley, *Pompeii* (London, 2003) 124; A. Cooley and M. G. L. Cooley, *Pompeii: A Sourcebook* (London, 2004) 11–12; M. Wolf, *MDAI(R)* 113 (2007) 277–316; R. Bielfeldt *MDAI(R)* 113 (2007) 317–71.

Bolsena: J. M. Pailler, *MEFRA* 83 (1971) 367–403; F.-H. Pairault-Massa and J. M. Pailler, *La maison aux salles souterraines I: Les terres cuites sous le péristyle* (Rome, 1979); O. de Cazenove, *Athenaeum* 88 (2000) 59–68; de Cazenove, *AC* 69 (2000) 237–53.

51. Pompeii – early houses. The antiquity of settlement at Pompeii, even before the settlement of the Sullan colony, can now confidently be demonstrated as far back as the sixth century. There was an Etruscan presence from the beginning. This may be reflected in the contemporary decline of some nearby villages, suggesting a process of concentration of settlement. Moreover, it would appear that one can assign both the settlement of the Altstadt, which is slightly differently aligned from the rest of the site, and the perimeter wall, to this early phase, so that questions arise about the area outside the Altstadt, where archaic finds have been made. Arguably, there may have been more and even earlier settlement at Pompeii.

At the same time, work on dating the use of Sarno limestone, hitherto regarded as 'archaic', suggests that this was in use longer and later, thus disrupting some chronological conclusions; and whereas the original picture was of an expansion in the fourth century, it is now thought that Pompeii developed rapidly at the end of the third century, which again is intriguing, given the allegedly disrupted nature of conditions in Italy under Hannibalic occupation. Nevertheless, the late fourth and third centuries seem still to be the period when the organization of territory and some internal areas took place, and it has been suggested that there was a strong correlation between the axes of development of the town and of the centuriated territory outside.

50c

51

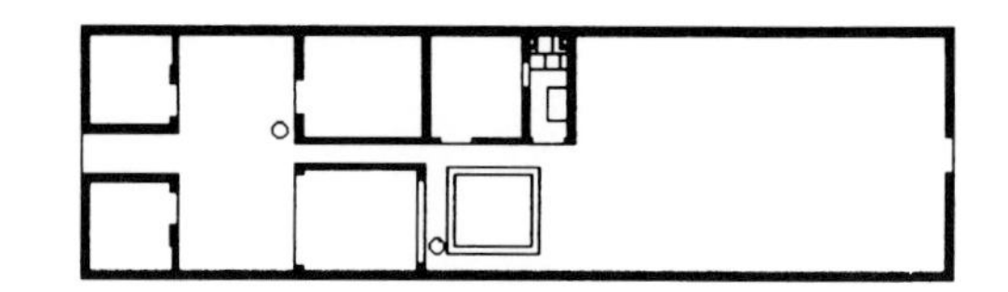

tipo n.1

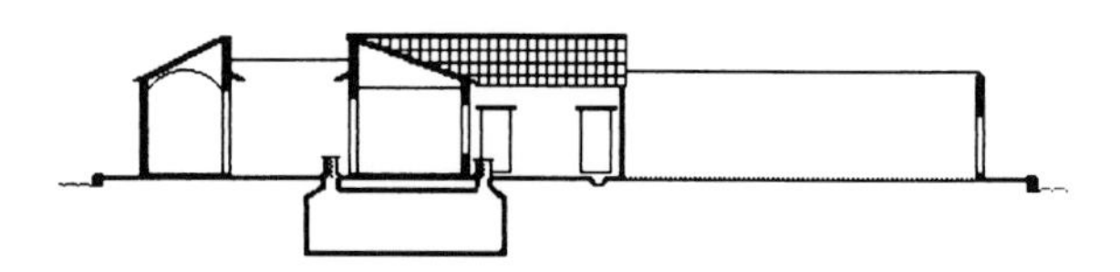

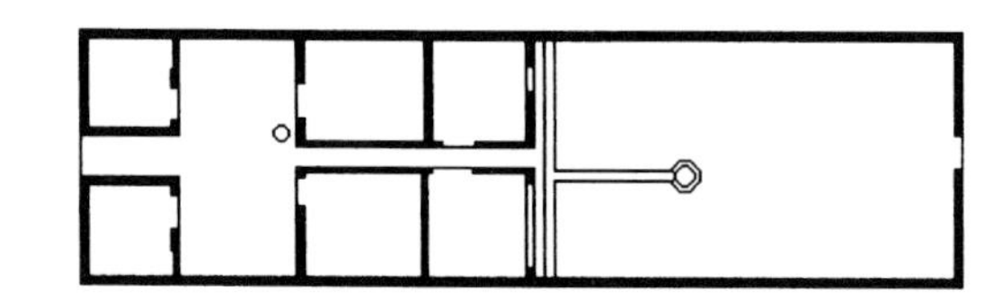

tipo n.2

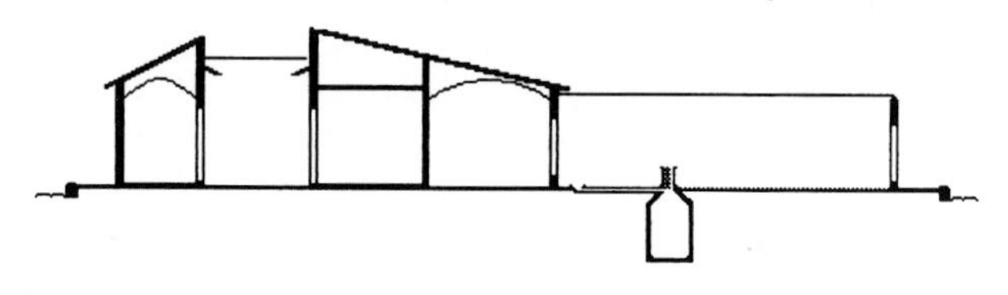

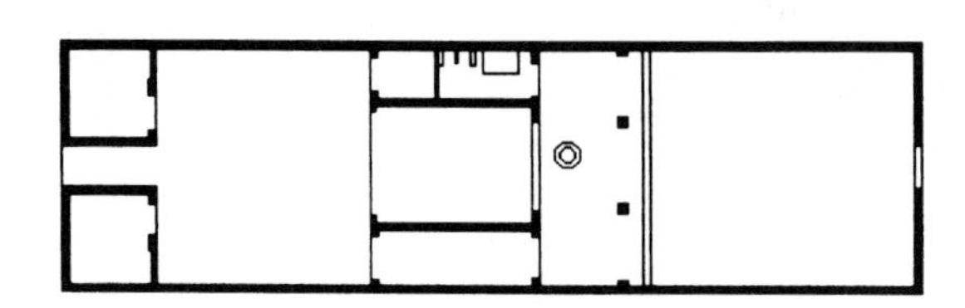

tipo n.3

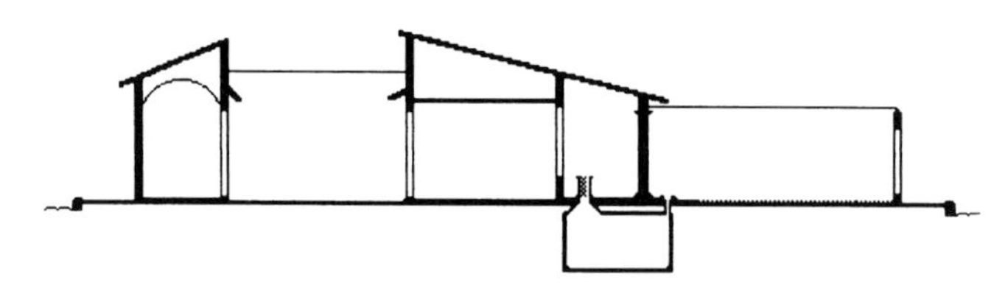

By the end of the third century BC the layout of the city was set, and the landscape divided into *insulae*. These *insulae* were further subdivided into houses, and where we can see the earlier layout it appears to be of simple, modest houses, relatively homogeneous in building material, with an open courtyard and a garden, and largely single-storey in height. If this reconstruction is correct, it has profound implications for what is happening at this phase of construction. An earlier account suggested a prosperous middle class occupying rather grander buildings. But this account suggests a rapid development of much smaller units, and this may tie in better with the influx of people into Pompeii as a result of the destruction of neighbouring towns such as Capua and Nocera.

This rise in population and in urban development is followed in the second century by a phase of urban remodelling, with particular emphasis on the forum. The old forum, with a beaten-earth floor, a temple of Apollo and shops, was replaced by a paved area with a portico, basilica and a temple of Jupiter, and this required additional work on the temple of Apollo, and in the second half of the second century BC a *macellum* was added.

This new picture of the development of Pompeii, from its earliest phases, through a period of slow growth up to the Hannibalic War, and, as a result of that difficult period, a rapid growth in population from immigration which would lead to a significant rise in prosperity and public magnificence, is a good indication of the kinds of factors which transformed individual settlements in central Italy.

(After Nappo 1997, illustrating three different types of relatively modest housing within *insula* blocks)

S.C. Nappo, in R. Laurence and A. Wallace-Hadrill (eds.), *Domestic Space in the Roman World: Pompeii and Beyond* (*JRA* Supplement 22, Portsmouth, 1997) 91–120; M. Fulford and A. Wallace-Hadrill, *PBSR* 67 (1999) 37–144; R. I. Cooley, *Pompeii* 113–25.

52. Teanum fibulae. The fibulae came from T62 in the Hellenistic necropolis at Teanum, excavated in the late nineteenth and early twentieth centuries. The tomb was particularly wealthy, even in this rich burial area; it contained gold, silver, bronze and

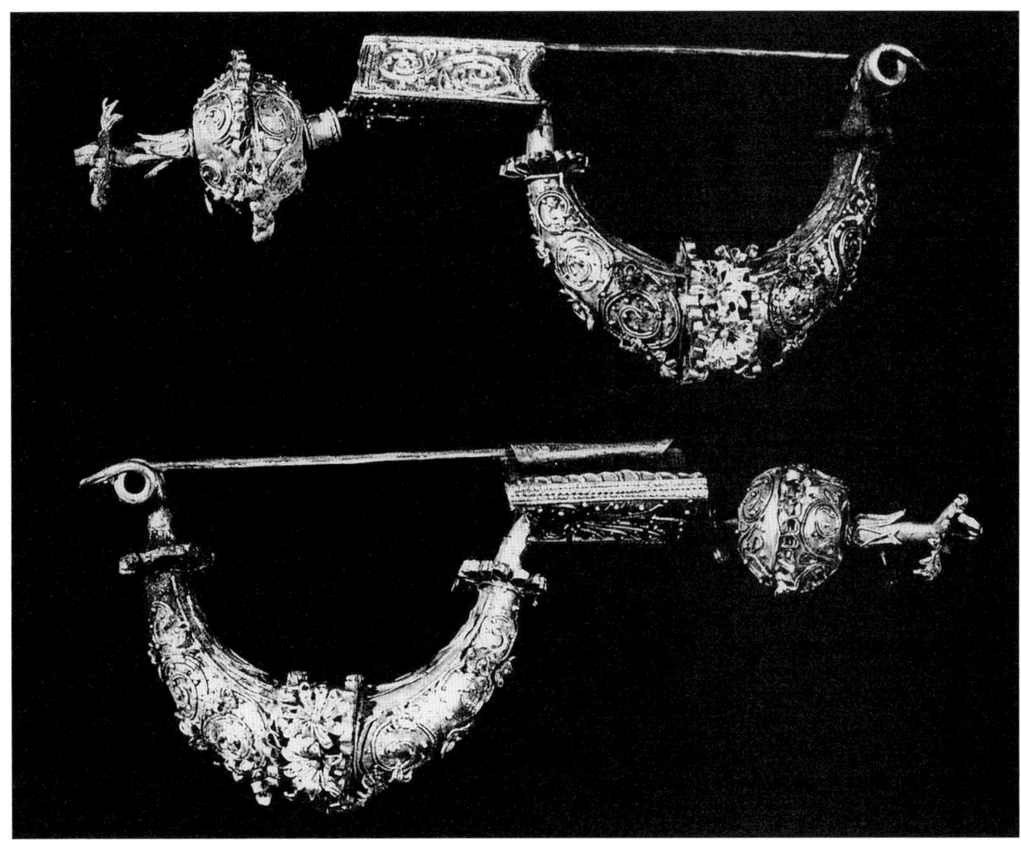

52

ivory decorations, and a considerable amount of red-figure and vernice nera pottery. Teanum itself was the major Campanian site on the Via Latina, and its wealth seems to have derived at least in part from the major sanctuary area, which has produced architectural terracottas from the sixth century, and no fewer than four temple podia from the fourth to third centuries BC.

This pair of fibulae are remarkable for the amount of detailed granulated decoration; one scholar speaks unkindly of a 'barbaric sense of horror vacui'; others see the fibulae as the finest product of one of Italy's best workshops.

(Museo Nazionale, Naples, neg. 144392. Length 9 cm)

E. Gabrici, *Mon.Ant.* 20 (1910) 8–151; A. Gramiccia and F. Pagnotta, *Le collezioni del Museo Nazionale di Napoli: La scultura greco-romana 1: Le sculture antiche della collezione farnese, le collezioni monetali, le oreficerie, la collezione glittica* (Rome, 1989) 211 no. 39.

53. Chalchas mirror. This mirror from Vulci from the late fourth century BC is in the tradition of classicizing Etruscan art and shows an intriguing attempt to marry Etruscan practices with the Trojan legends. The figure is winged and shown leaning over the liver of an animal in an act of haruspicy, the form of prognosticism of the future and ascertaining of divine will characteristic of Etruscan discipline.

He is shown as a daemon or genius, a kind of figure frequently found in Etruscan representations, and similar to the seer Mopsus on the Cista Ficoroni (above). An inscription beside him reads 'Chalchas'. Now Chalchas was the great seer of the Greek expedition to Troy, though he is specifically introduced at *Iliad* I.69 as an *oionopolos*, a diviner by bird flight, or an augur in Roman terms, and haruspicy was foreign to the Greeks. There is perhaps a deliberate ideological statement underlying this artistic rapprochement of something singularly Etruscan with someone quintessentially Homeric.

53

Etruscan *haruspices* were prominent in the historical records: in 340 they indicated that the voluntary death of one or other commander would settle the war between Rome and the Latins, and P. Decius Mus devoted himself (a form of self-sacrifice); they resolved the omens before the battle of Sentinum (when there was another Decian devotion); and in 276 they proposed an alteration to the ritual of the Lupercalia to resolve an epidemic of miscarriages and still-births.

(Vatican, Museo Gregoriano Etrusco inv. 12240. Height 18.5 cm; diameter 14.8 cm)

LIMC sv Kalchas 1; T. P. Wiseman, *The Myths of Rome* (Exeter, 2004) 149–52.

54. Terracina centuriation. Terracina, conquered by the Volscians and renamed Anxur in the fifth century, was retaken by Rome in 406 BC (Livy IV.59) and definitively submitted to Roman rule when a maritime colony of 300 was established there in 318 BC (Livy IX.20.6). The Via Appia was constructed through the settlement in 312 BC and probably determined the layout of the forum area, though we only have the late first-century phase, which also follows the road. The road gave additional commercial importance to the site, which already had a favourable position as a port and expanded significantly in the early Empire.

When founding a colony, the Romans divided the land into equal plots, in this case of 2 *jugera*, as we know from the very precise information given by the sources (Livy VIII.21.11; Vell. Pat. I.14.4). These plots of land were often retained in that form for many centuries, though their ownership changed considerably. Centuriation seems to have been used from an early period, and it was the method that would be used later by the Gracchan land commission, so it is not always easy to date. Continuing use of field divisions makes it possible in some instances for us to see them from the air; this photograph, taken by the RAF during World

War II, clearly shows the centuriation pattern near the colony.

(The Aerial Reconnaissance Archives, Keele)

M. di Mario, *Terracina, urbs prona in paludes: Osservazioni sullo sviluppo urbanistico della città antica* (Terracina, 1994); P. Longo, in M. Pasquinucci, E. Roffia and A. Tamassia (eds.), *Misurare la Terra: Centuriazione e coloni nel mondo romano. Città, agricoltura, commercio: Materiali da Roma e dal suburbia* (Modena, 1985) 40–4; G. Chouquer, M. Claudel-Lévêque and J.-P. Vallat (eds.), *Structures agraires en Italie centro-méridionale: Cadastres et paysages ruraux* (Rome, 1987) 105–9.

55. Villas and agriculture. There is still considerable debate about the agricultural developments in the middle Republic, which led to the unrest that is symbolized by the tribunates of the Gracchi. A key text has always been Cato the Elder's handbook on agriculture, and naturally archaeologists have sought to find examples of villa agriculture

55a

in the second century BC. In fact most of the surviving examples are either too small to have the productive capacity which Cato required or too luxurious for his taste, but that may simply reinforce the point that Cato's work has a strong literary element.

The earliest rural settlements are identifiable only by remains of artificial terracing in brick, and then *opus incertum*, and these can be found in Latium. There are hints of the sorts of settlement which might demonstrate the kind of mixed economy which characterizes the literary accounts of a villa, with a strong dependence on slave labour and a highly efficient and organized management of production; some of these show the beginnings of peristyle architecture, for instance at Blera in Etruria. The most exciting discovery, however, was the villa uncovered in rescue archaeology at the Auditorio site in what would have been the outskirts of the city, pictured here. Its earliest phases are sixth to fifth century, and it was radically restructured in the third to second centuries BC, but even in its earliest phases it shows the kind of luxury associated with the palaces of Etruria. A transition from austerity through Catonian productivity to luxury does not fit here, but the capacity for intensive and productive agriculture is demonstrable.

(**a**. C. J. Smith; **b**. after Carandini 2006: fig. 41, reconstruction of villa plan *c*. 550–500 BC; **c** after Carandini 2006: fig. 71, reconstruction of villa plan *c*. 500–300 BC)

N. Purcell, in T. Cornell and K. Lomas (eds.), *Urban Society in Roman Italy* (London, 1995) 151–80; A. Carandini, in AA. VV., *Storia di Roma*, vol. IV (Rome, 1989) 101–99; Carandini, *MDAIR* 104 (1997) 117–48; N. Terrenato, *JRA* 14 (2001) 5–32; P. Gros, *L'architecture romaine* II: *Maisons, palais, villas et tombeaux* (Paris 2001) 271–88; A. Carandini, with M. T. D'Alessio and H. di Giuseppe, *La fattoria e la villa dell'Auditorium nel quartiere Flaminio di Roma* (Rome, 2006).

56. Money and coinage. The history of money and coinage in central Italy begins with Greek influence and ends with Roman domination. The vast majority of coins before about 300 BC are Greek and belonged to, and stayed in, the colonies, though through the fourth century we do see increasing evidence of the penetration of coinage into the Italic tribes of the south, who may have controlled some of the mineral resources. There was some gold and bronze coinage, but most was silver.

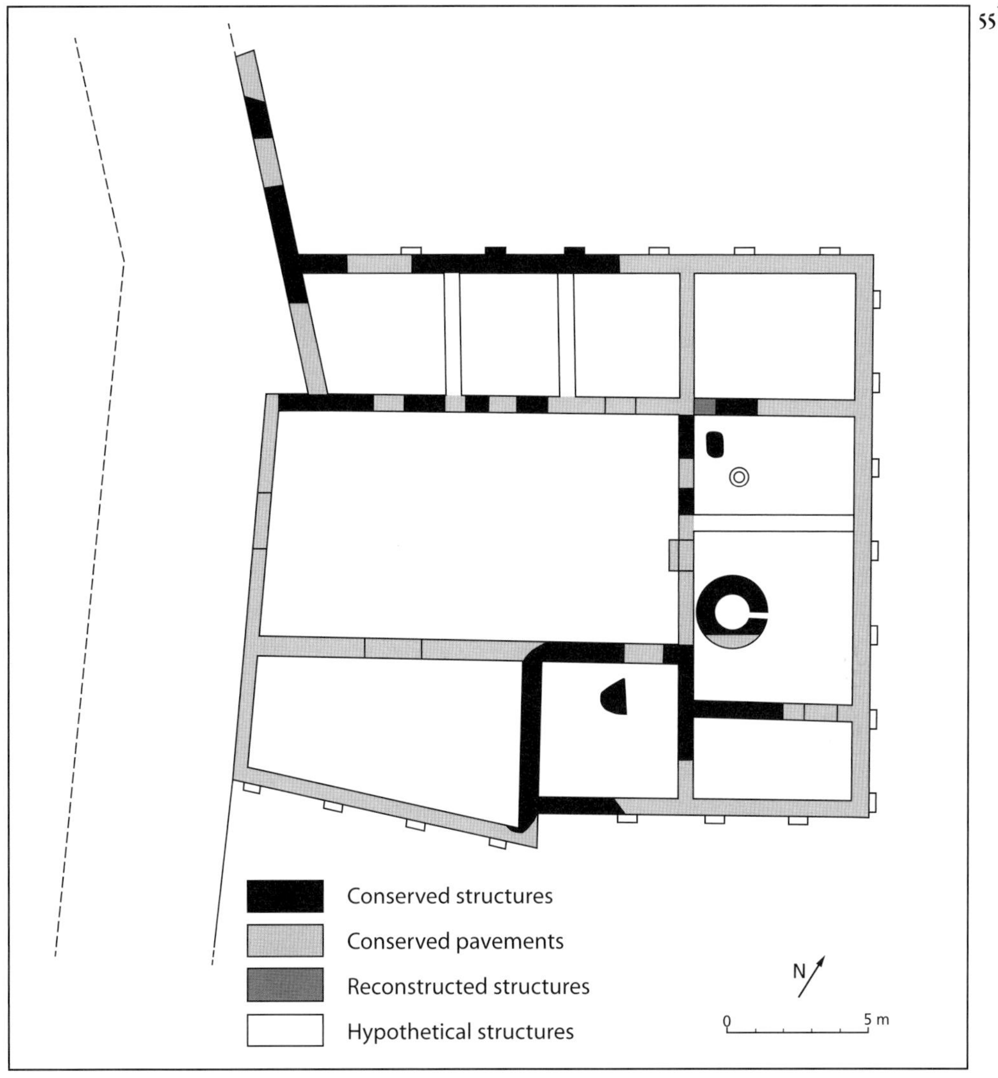

Early Roman coinage has been divided into four kinds; aes signatum, aes grave, silver and struck bronze, and the relationship between them is illustrated in the table below. The large bronze bars resemble some other Italian forms, but they are of a standard weight, though the designs differ; the one illustrated at *CAH* VII.II² 477 shows an elephant, another reminiscence of the Pyrrhic War. From about 300 BC there is a small issue of silver didrachms from Rome, and this is clearly based on Greek examples and largely circulates in the Greek south of Italy, especially Campania. Naples was an important centre and may have minted the example shown here (**a**). The Roman didrachms, with the legend ROMANO and a picture of Mars and a horse's head, may have been precisely intended to match the artistic achievements of southern Italian coinage. This would imply an occasional and improvised coinage, like the later production of silver denarii with either Apollo and a horse, or Hercules and Romulus and Remus, in the aftermath of the import of plundered silver from Magna Graecia in 269/8 BC. Bronze was issued either in large cast discs (aes grave) (**b**) or struck bronze, and both tended to circulate in central Italy.

The silver coinage was intermittent until the middle of the third century, when the bronze issues became lighter and a degree of integration between

55c

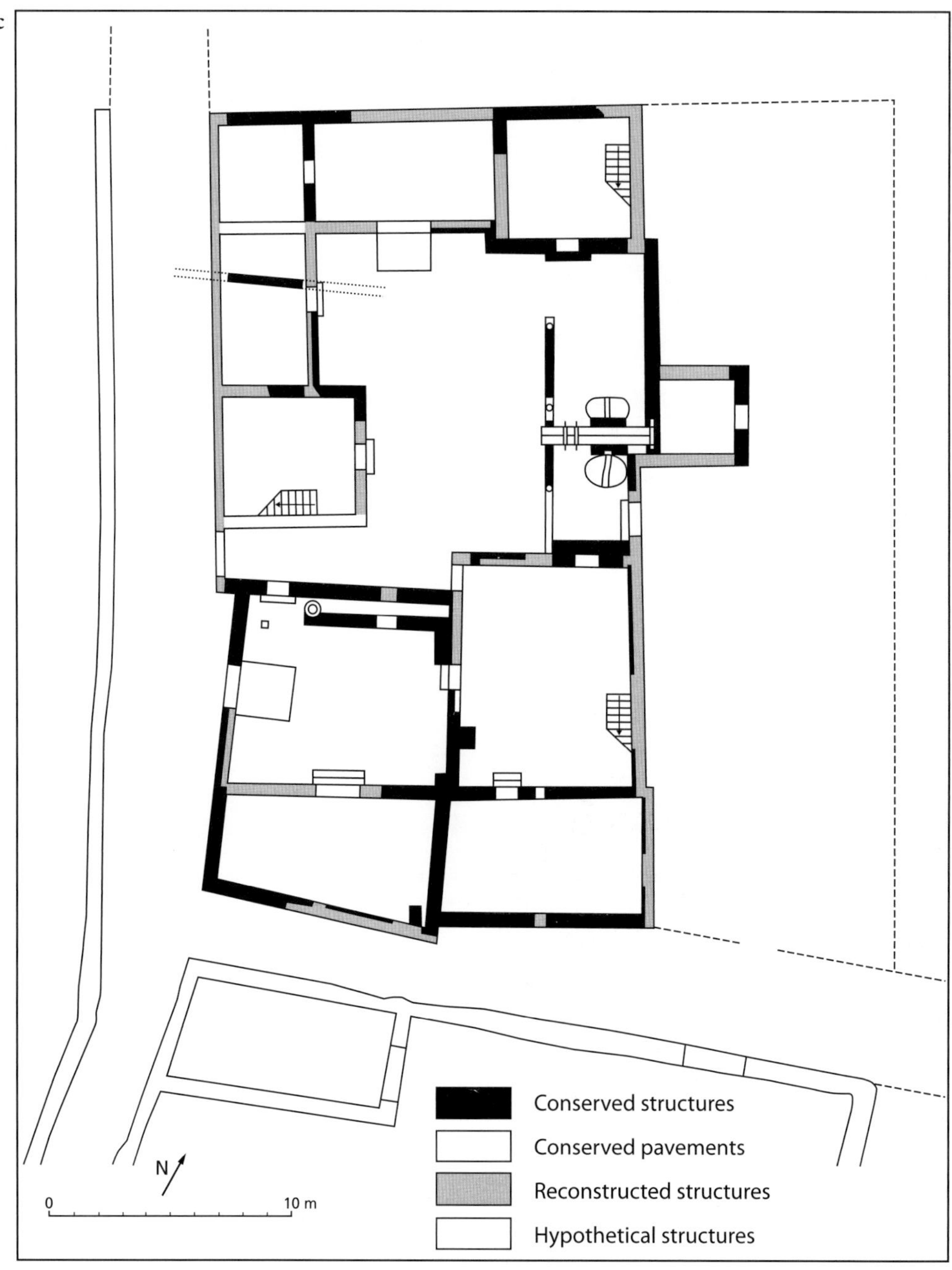

the different systems was introduced, this time with the mark ROMA (**c**). At the same time the amount of bronze coinage and the number and geographical spread of mints increased greatly.

The Second Punic War put this system under huge pressure. Independent minting resumed in Italy during the presence of Hannibal in, for instance, Capua, Tarentum, Metapontum and Bruttium, perhaps as a sign of claims for autonomy. In the first part of the war, metal was scarce, and the production of coinage may have ceased briefly, but from around 212 BC a steady flow of bullion was available from Syracuse and then Spain, and the Roman authorities reformed the coinage into

56a

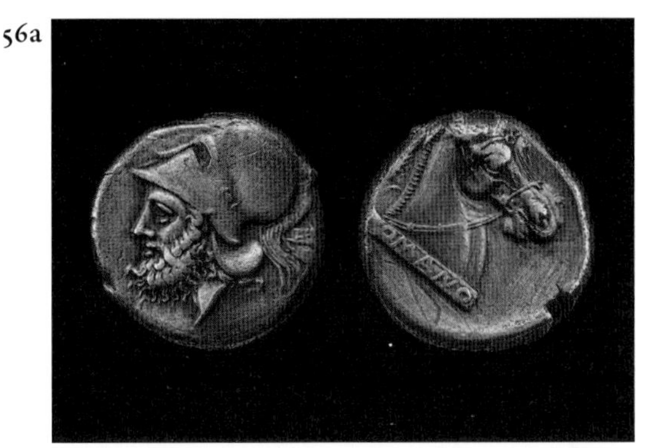

56e

56b

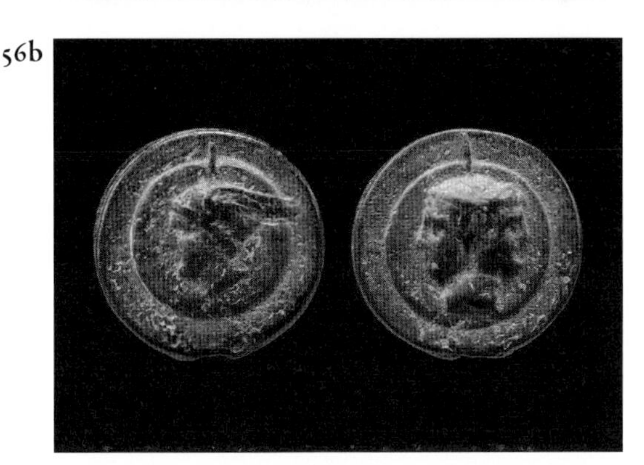

56c

56d

a unified system that lasted until the third century AD, one of the great achievements of the period. The basis was the bronze *as*; the relative value, originally based on the intrinsic value of the metal content was as shown in the table below.

Silver	denarius	10 *asses*	(**d**)
Quinarius	5 *asses*		
Sestertius	2.5 *asses*		
Bronze	*as*		(**e**)
	semis	half *as*	
	triens	third *as*	
	quadrans	quarter *as*	
	sextans	one-sixth *as*	
	uncia	one-twelfth *as*	

This had the effect, however, of suppressing local coinages, and even though Rome minted far more bronze than gold or silver until the second half of the second century BC, Roman coinage dominated the whole of Italy, and was influential on local eastern and western coinages. Even the brief revival of local minting by the rebels in the Social War (*CAH* IX^2 118) was based on the Roman weight standard.

(British Museum: **a** Mars horse's head ROMANO didrachm BM 1949–4–11–967 (obv); 1946–1–1–33 (rev); **b** aes Grave *as* BMC Italy p48, 1 = RRC 14.1; **c** BMCRR Romano-Campanian 68 = RRC 26.1; **d** BMCRR Rome 448 denarius = RRC 114.1; **e** BMCRR Rome 451 *as* = RRC 114.2)

M. H. Crawford, *Coinage and Money under the Roman Republic: Italy and the Mediterranean Economy* (London, 1985) and A. Burnett, *Coinage in the Roman World* (London, 1987) give helpful introductions; *RRC* and *HN*^{2} are essential works of reference.

4. UMBRIA AND PICENUM

GUY BRADLEY

The close relationship between the regions of Umbria and Picenum makes a unified treatment of them sensible. Both regions had separate peoples, with a sense of their own identity, although their boundaries must have been imprecise for much of their history. The definition of Picenum, though fragile and ambiguous, can be characterized in part by the use of the South Picene language, which is believed to be related to Sabine and Umbrian. The existence of North Picene as a distinct language group is uncertain, as the authenticity of the inscriptions where it occurs has been doubted. Picene culture is manifested to us mostly through the accumulated grave goods of the local elite, rather than through monumentalized sanctuaries and settlements on the lines of Etruria and Latium. Wealthy Picene burials are marked by their high concentration of ornamental objects, weaponry, and extensive Greek and other foreign imports. There is notable local production of objects in amber and metal, and in stone statuary.

Umbria is marked by the use of the Umbrian language, which is at first written in two separate Etruscan alphabets, hinting at independent transmission (rather than a unified, shared culture). Umbria's material culture blended into neighbouring regions, especially in frontier sites like Tuder, closely linked to the Etruscan cities on the other side of the Tiber. The Umbrians extended to the Adriatic coast according to ancient authors, and held northern cities such as Ariminum and Ravenna.

The development of both regions is linked to the impact of the changes of the Orientalizing period on Italy as a whole, from the late eighth century BC. Trade expanded between Etruria and Picenum, which by necessity had to cross Umbria. Picenum came into contact with the increasingly vibrant Greek trade along the Adriatic in the sixth and fifth centuries BC, especially with the flourishing of the ports of Spina and Adria in the north. Picene elites also benefited from links with northern European cultures, manifested in the amber trade and in the similarities between Picene sculpture and the statuary of central Europe in the sixth and fifth centuries, such as the Hirschlanden warrior (dell'Orto 1999: 23–9). In both Picenum and Umbria traces of monumental urbanism before the Roman conquest are rare. But there were some significant developments in Umbria in the fourth century BC, by which time most future Umbrian city sites were settled, and there is evidence for temples before the Roman conquest at Arna, Mevania, Tuder, Ocriculum and perhaps also Iguvium and Ameria.

Roman involvement in Umbria predated that in Picenum. Umbria was a more critical theatre of Roman intervention because it was linked with Etruria both geographically (the route through Umbria led to northern Etruria, especially Perusia) and politically (as Umbrian cities seem often to be in alliance and religious association with their Etruscan counterparts). The conquest of Umbria began in 308 BC, saw the decisive battle at Sentinum in 295 BC (a Roman victory that in fact sealed the fate of the whole peninsula) and ended around 266 BC with the suppression of the north Umbrian Sassinates. Picenum was apparently conquered after 300 BC. After an initial alliance with Rome in 299 BC, the territory of the Praetuttii (a group in southern Picenum) was seized by Curius Denatatus in 290 BC and more of Picenum with the capture of Asculum in 268 BC, when the Romans celebrated a triumph. The aftermath of this Picene defeat saw the deportation of an unspecified number of Picentes to the district around Paestum on the Tyrrhenian coast, probably with the intention of preventing future resistance in their homeland. Picenum was made almost wholly Roman in status after the conquest, meaning that virtually all the territory, with the exception of Asculum and Ancona (which became allied) and various Latin colonies, was now technically part of the Roman state. There was a more complex outcome in Umbria, where a patchwork of different statuses was imposed by the Romans on conquered communities. The *ager Gallicus* along the Adriatic coast of Umbria became Roman territory when the Senones were expelled (Appian, *Samn.* 13–14, Polybius II.21.7), as did swathes of southern Umbria (probably including Interamna Nahars and Fulginiae). Colonies were established at Spoletium and Narnia. The majority of communities probably became allied in status. The existence of treaties mostly cannot be documented, but must surely have governed Roman–Umbrian relations.

After the conquest, both Roman and allied communities had to supply troops for the Roman army. Hannibal marched through Umbria on his way south after his victory at Lake Trasimene (217 BC), but according to Livy he was repelled from an advance on Rome by the resistance of Spoletium (XXII.9). He turned aside to plunder Umbria and Picenum, and failed during the course of the Second Punic War to entice any ally in these districts over to the Carthaginian side.

The third and second centuries BC saw a complex series of changes, often subsumed under the term 'Romanization'. Roman influence rapidly became apparent in colonial and Roman areas, where immigration probably took place from Rome and Latium on a large scale (see, for instance, the early Latin *lex sacra* from Spoletium). Latin was not adopted so quickly in allied communities, but the Latin alphabet seems in many cities to have replaced the Umbrian one in the course of the second century BC. Other evidence for Roman influence on allied communities comes in the form of the adoption of magisterial titles (such as the Roman quaestorship, evident in the Umbrian-scripted Iguvine Tables, for which see below). We also have evidence that the Latin language was used by the second half of the second century BC in Asisium, Ameria and Mevania, probably alongside Umbrian. Urbanism developed rapidly under local initiative but with Roman and Etruscan models, and by the later stages of the second century BC many features of the distinctive civic identity of Umbrian cities seems to be present.

GENERAL BIBLIOGRAPHY

For an overview of Umbria in this period, tracing the long-term impact of Roman control, see G. Bradley, *Ancient Umbria: State, Culture, and Identity in Central Italy from the Iron Age to the Augustan Era* (Oxford, 2000); a more recent study is P. Amann, *Die antiken Umbrer zwischen Tiber und Apennin* (Vienna, 2012). For more detailed pictures of the conquest and aftermath, W. V. Harris, *Rome in Etruria and Umbria* (Oxford, 1971) is still worth consulting, and see also S. Sisani, *Fenomenologia della conquista: La romanizzazione dell'Umbria tra il IV sec. a.C. e la guerra sociale* (Rome, 2007). Sisani covers pre-Roman Umbria in *Umbrorum gens antiquissima Italiae: Studi sulla società e le istituzioni dell'Umbria preromana* (Perugia, 2009). There are specific studies of the western Umbrian communities in G. M. Della Fina (ed.), *Gli umbri del Tevere: Atti dell' VIII Convegno Internazionale di Studi sulla Storia e l'Archeologia dell' Etruria* (Annali per la Fondazione per il Museo Claudio Faina 8, Rome, 2001) and G. Cifani, *Storia di una frontiera* (Rome, 2003). There are many useful studies in G. Bonamente and F. Coarelli (eds.), *Assisi e gli umbri nell'antichità: Atti del Convegno Internazionale, Assisi (18–21 dicembre 1991)* (Assisi, 1996) and P. Fontaine (ed.), *L'Etrurie et L'Ombrie avant Rome: Cité et territoire* (Louvain-la-Neuve, 2010).

On Umbrian epigraphy, see A. L. Prosdocimi, *Tavole Iguvine* I (Florence, 1984), G. Rocca, *Iscrizioni umbre minori* (Florence, 1996), H. Rix, *Sabellische Texte: Die Texte des Oskischen, Umbrischen und Südpikenischen* (Heidelberg, 2002) and M. H. Crawford *et al.*, *Imagines Italicae: A Corpus of Italic Inscriptions* (London, 2011). For the archaeology of Umbria, the series of *Gens antiquissima Italiae* catalogues (*Vaticano, Budapest e Cracovia, Leningrado* and *New York*) and the *Catalogo dei beni regionali dell'Umbria* series are fundamental. Important specialist contributions include P. Fontaine, *Cités et enceintes de l'Ombrie antique* (Brussels and Rome, 1990), C. Malone and S. Stoddart (eds.), *Territory, Time and State* (Cambridge, 1994) and S. Sisani, *Tuta ikuvina: Sviluppo e ideologia della forma urbana a Gubbio* (Rome, 2001). The current state of archaeological knowledge is summarized in S. Sisani, *Umbria Marche* (Guida archeologica Laterza, Bari, 2006) and F. Colivicchi and C. Zaccagnino, *L'Umbria: Archeologia delle regioni d'Italia* (Rome, 2008).

For overviews of Picenum before the Roman conquest, see C. Riva, in G. Bradley, C. Riva and E. Isayev (eds.), *Ancient Italy: Regions without Boundaries* (Exeter, 2007) 79–113 and E. Naso, *I Piceni: Storia e archeologia delle Marche in epoca preromana* (Bari, 2000). There are important studies of new evidence in L. Franchi dell'Orto (ed.), *Piceni: Popolo d'Europa* (Rome, 1999) and *I Piceni e l'Italia medio-adriatica: Atti del XXII Convegno di Studi Etruschi ed Italici* (Florence, 2003). For south Picene epigraphy, see A. Marinetti *Le iscrizioni sudpicene I: Testi* (Florence, 1985), Rix *Sabellische Texte* and Crawford *et al.* *Imagines Italicae.*

57. An aerial view of part of the cemetery at Campovalano. This site is in the southern area of Picenum, attributed by ancient authors to the Praetuttii, and in archaeological terms displaying a mixed Adriatic culture, with some elements typical

of Picenum and some of Samnium to the south. This very large and significant cemetery was in use from the eleventh to the second centuries BC, with some 605 graves excavated since 1964. The most important phases are the orientalizing and archaic (eighth to sixth century BC), and the Hellenistic (mid fourth to second century BC).

The cemetery was at its most flourishing in the orientalizing and archaic periods, from when 250 tombs have been excavated, arranged along a road. The burials consist of inhumations in trenches, the majority marked by a stone circle containing a tumulus, many of which have been ploughed out. The tumuli range in size from 4 to 25 m across; the largest is Tumulus 2, containing a chariot burial signifying particularly elevated status (four others were also found). The graves display a complex burial symbolism. Many have considerable quantities of bronze and ceramic vases used in banqueting. Male graves have weaponry in addition, and female graves ornaments, such as shells worn by younger women and neolithic axe-heads worn by older women.

After a period of apparent hiatus from the early fifth century, probably related to a change in funerary custom, burials are again evident in large numbers (some 300) in the Hellenistic period. They are now arranged more tightly along the sides of the road and have a very different tomb structure from earlier burials, often with quadrangular cordons of stones. Weaponry is much rarer than in the earlier era, though there is a wealth of female ornamentation and the continued representation of banqueting as a status symbol through the presence of *kraters*, amphorae and *skyphoi*, if on a smaller scale than in the archaic era.

(Ancona, Museo Archeologico Nazionale)

V. d'Ercole, in Franchi dell'Orto (ed.) *Piceni* 81–3; C. Chiaramonte Trere and V. d'Ercole, *La necropoli di Campovalano: Tombe orientalizzanti e arcaiche Pt 1* (BAR International Series, Oxford, 2003).

58. Attic red-figure volute-*krater* from Numana. Greek figured pottery is typical of the contents of wealthy graves from Picenum in the classical period (sixth and fifth centuries BC). Such monumental vases, named after the volutes (scroll-like decoration) on Ionic columns, were used as mixing vessels in banqueting settings. This example comes from the Giulietta-Marinelli tomb in Numana Sirolo

57

(*c.* 460 BC), which produced a collection of the highest-quality Attic red-figure pottery, as well as an Etruscan candelabrum. The mythological scene visible on this side of the *krater* shows a female deity (perhaps Demeter) departing on a chariot, accompanied by other gods. It is attributed to the Bologna painter 228, and dates to *c.* 470 BC. The larger-than-average size of the piece reflects its particular prestige, and it may have been specifically produced for the Picene market.

Numana developed as an emporium on the coast, plugging into the very active trade during the classical era in the Adriatic between Greece and the Greek settlements at Spina and Adria in the north at the mouth of the Po. It now seems likely that Numana had its own direct connection with Greek traders, given the tailored selection of Greek material that occurs there in comparison with the northern Adriatic emporia. Over 1,500 graves from the sixth and fifth centuries BC have been excavated in Numana. Attic pottery imports are especially striking in the second quarter of the fifth century BC, when monumental volute-*kraters* are also found inland at Pitino and Pianello.

(Ancona, Museo Archeologico Nazionale, inv. 3122. Height 88 cm)

M. Landolfi, in Franchi dell'Orto (ed.) *Piceni.* 147–50, 227–8; B. B. Shefton, in *I Piceni e l'Italia* 315–37.

59. Large piece of amber carved into a representation of a mating lion and lioness, designed to decorate a fibula (first half of the sixth century BC). Amber was an exotic material generally used for decorative purposes, on fibulae, pendants and rings. Amber is typical of Picenum, which was a centre for its trade, particularly from the ninth to the fourth centuries BC. Picenum operated in the middle of the trade route from the original sources in the Nordic regions between the North Sea and the Baltic, through the Alps and down into the Adriatic, and from there to Greece and the Aegean. This is clear from objects such as the amber pendants and the amber and bone fibula from a votive deposit in Ephesus, perhaps made in Verucchio.

The carved piece comes from Tomb 72 of Belmonte Piceno, one of the wealthiest Picene cemeteries, where more than 300 tombs have been excavated (though many of the contents were lost in the bombing of Ancona during World War II). The object is typical of local tombs and shows the local production of amber items in the area.

58

59

This particular example provides one of the most sophisticated uses of the material from Picenum, and stylistic considerations (its combination of eastern influence with a typically local 'baroque' form) suggest that it may have been produced by a craftsman from Magna Graecia.

(Ancona, Museo Archeologico Nazionale, inv. 11014. Length 10.5 cm)

N. Negroni Catacchio and also M. Landolfi, in Franchi dell'Orto (ed.) *Piceni* 100–3, 231; Naso *I Piceni* 92, 200.

60. A bronze disc-cuirass from Pitino di San Severino Marche, a cemetery of the orientalizing period in the upper Potenza valley which was used from just after the mid seventh to the early sixth centuries BC. This example comes from Tomb 17, one of the earliest graves, consisting of a large trench (2 × 4 m) lined with stone. The grave can be dated to *c.* 650–625 BC by the presence of four protocorinthian vessels. The elevated social rank of the tomb's occupant is suggested by its precious contents, including this disc-cuirass and the remains of a possible sceptre and chariot.

Disc-cuirasses were worn as a pair over the shoulder for chest protection, but the thinness and unusual size of this example implies that it was parade armour. Produced locally from the late eighth to the early fifth centuries BC, they seem to be prestige items, judging from their representation on large statues like the Capestrano warrior and the Guardiagrele stele, and their appearance in wealthy male graves. This is a fine example of the figured type of disc-cuirass, and there is also a pair of the other 'geometric' type in this grave, more typical of the Fucine area. The fantastical horse-like animals with conjoined bodies are typical of figurative examples, although not the two human figures, one ithyphallic, the other perhaps riding the horse-like creature. The intended symbolism has generated a variety of different interpretations, with the strange animals, like the Chimera, perhaps having magical, apotropaic significance, and the figures indicative of equestrian and warrior prowess (often associated with sexual potency), common themes in the local elite funerary ideology.

(Ancona, Museo Archeologico Nazionale, inv. 43560. Diameter 31 cm)

R. Papi, in *La Tavola di Agnone* (1996) 119–21; R. Papi, in Franchi dell'Orto (ed.) *Piceni* 120–2, 253; Naso *I Piceni* 109–20; G. Tagliamonte, in *I Piceni e l'Italia* 540.

60

61. Stele with a South Picene inscription from Penna Sant'Andrea. The South Picene language is known from twenty-three inscriptions from the mid Adriatic area, inscribed using an alphabet similar to that on a *cippus* from the Sabine town of Cures, and ultimately derived from Etruscan models. The language is linked to Umbrian and unrelated to 'North Picene' found on inscriptions from Novilara, whose authenticity is now doubted (see Agostiniani, 'Le iscrizioni di Novilara' in *I Piceni e l'Italia* 115–25). The South Picene inscriptions date from the mid sixth century to the end of the fourth/start of the third century BC, with the Latin alphabet used in this area after the Roman conquest. The inscriptions are most commonly found on monumental stele, although there are also some inscribed movable objects.

Penna Sant'Andrea lies in the Vomano valley in the south of Picenum. The stele was found by chance together with two others of similar type, but more fragmentary state, in a cemetery area in 1974. The stele is 2.18 m high, with the lower part left clear for fixing in the ground. The inscription is four lines long, running up and down the stele in boustrophedon fashion (changing direction at the end of each line). The text cannot be fully understood, but it refers to a community of Sabines or Samnites (*safinas tútas*) and their elite leaders (*safinúm nerf*). This is the earliest mention of the ethnic *safin-*, and suggests that the population of

this area had a common identity with the Sabines attested to the west (and from where the Picenes are said to have originated in ancient myth). The inscription dates to the first half of the fifth century BC.

(Chieti, Museo Archeologico Nazionale, inv. 10016/17/18)

Marinetti, *Le iscrizioni sudpicene* 218–19; A. Marinetti, in Franchi dell'Orto (ed.) *Piceni* 134–9; R. Papi, in Franchi dell'Orto (ed.) *Piceni* 242–4; L. Agostiniani, in *I Piceni e l'Italia* 115–25.

62. Crested helmet from Tomb 12 of the Gallic cemetery at Santa Paolina di Filottrano, in the hinterland behind Ancona and Numana. Literary sources describe this as an area of the Senones, the last of the Gauls to enter Italy, who lived between the Utis and the Aesis (Livy V.35.3). It was this group that arrived at Clusium and sacked Rome in 390 BC, but Livy is uncertain whether other Gauls were present as well. The Senones also served as mercenaries for Dionysius of Syracuse, recruited through the Syracusan settlement at Ancona.

The archaeological evidence from this area goes some way towards confirming the reputed military ethos of the Senones. There are a high proportion of arms in Senonian tombs and links with Gaul in the form of torques which parallel examples from Champagne (and nowhere else). The so-called Waldalgesheim Style of La Tène culture used on gold torques, with stylized vegetal motifs, may originate from this area. La Tène objects are also found in local tombs. The helmet here is bronze with incised decoration, and the plume-holder iron. It was locally made and dates to the mid fourth century BC. This cemetery is one of several in Picenum showing close links to Transalpine Gallic areas. Unlike the La Tène graves of Gaul proper, helmets are more widely distributed. There is thus good reason for believing that these graves are Gallic in some sense, although identifying the ethnicity of individual burials is often complicated by the mix of materials with different origins, and the presence of items like torques in earlier graves as well.

(Ancona, Museo Archeologico Nazionale, inv. 3793)

M. Landolfi, in Franchi dell'Orto (ed.) *Piceni* 278; V. Kruta, in Franchi dell'Orto (ed.) *Piceni* 174–6; C. Riva, in G. Bradley, C. Riva and E. Isayev (eds.) *Ancient Italy* 105–7.

62

63. Tomb 176 from Plestia (modern Colfiorito), second half of the sixth century BC. Plestia was positioned on a pass over the Apennines from the Adriatic to the Tyrrhenian zone.

The cemetery at Plestia was used from the early ninth century until the third century BC. In the seventh and sixth centuries the burials became more differentiated in terms of the quality and quantity of grave goods. Tomb 176, a male grave with the deceased laid supine in a trench of 1.8 m × 1.1 m, is one of the most ostentatious burials, with a notable accumulation of imported and locally produced objects (shown in **a** as deposited). Typical features are the weaponry (spear, no. 8, and mace head, no. 10) and the banqueting equipment. This latter includes an iron spit (no. 19), bronze cauldron (no. 9), pearl lipped bronze basin (no. 11 – **c**), and impasto pottery, demonstrating the importance of feasting. Other vessels include stamnoid *ollae* (lidded jars), locally produced in black impasto, such as no. 3 (**b**) decorated with four bands of incised triangular motifs.

The burial evidence can be set alongside the appearance of a sanctuary and hillforts in the surrounding territory, beginning in the

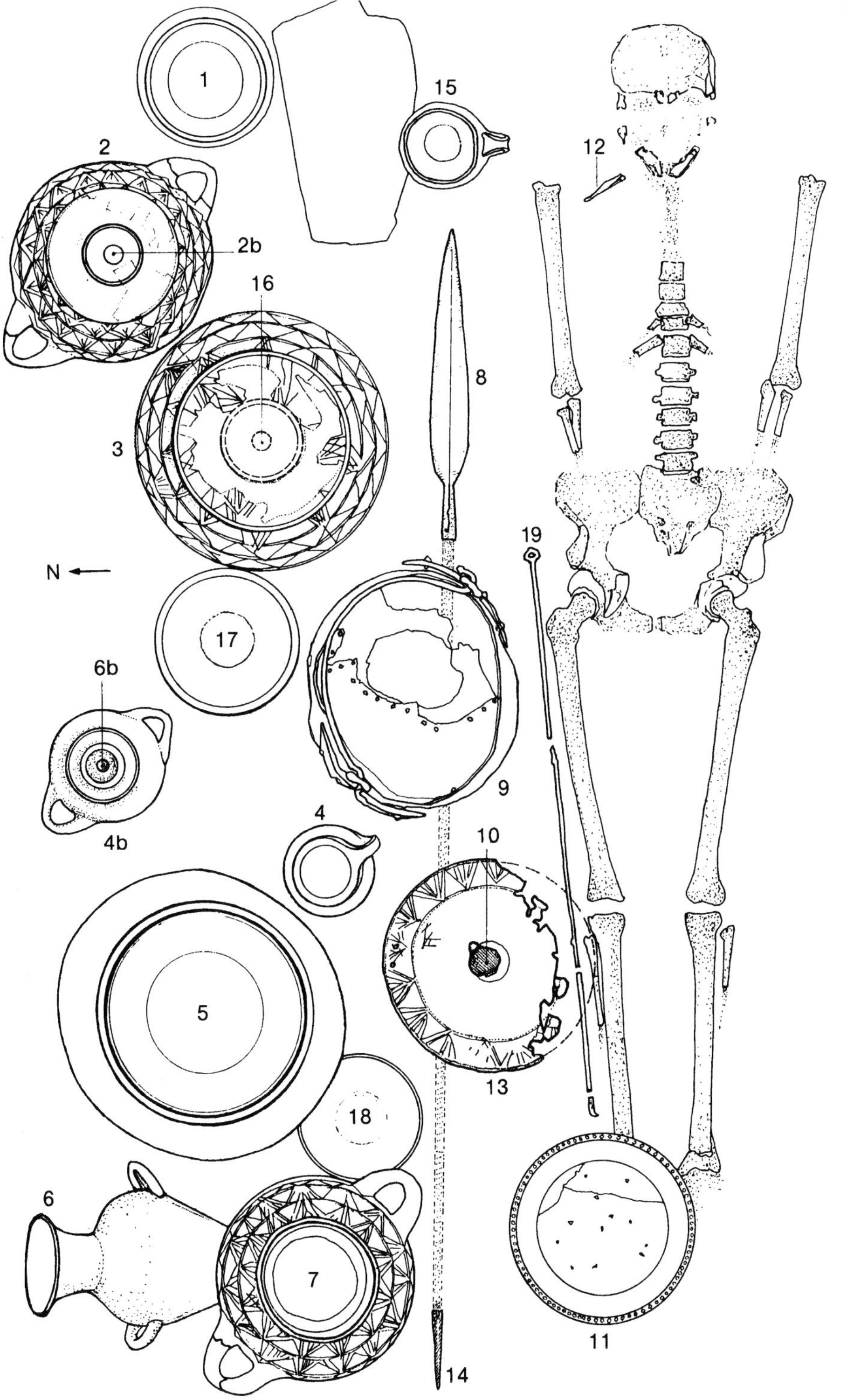
1
15
2
12
2b
16
8
3
N
19
17
6b
9
4
4b
10
5
13
18
6
7
11
14

63b

63c

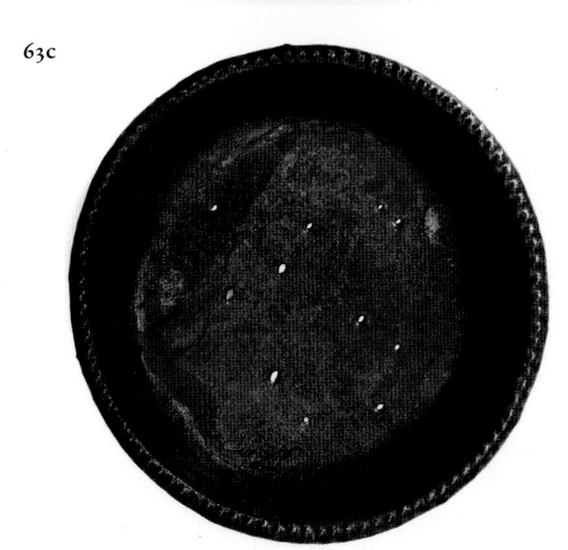

sixth century BC. The evident investment in fortifications and weaponry (displayed in burials) suggests that warfare was an important occupation of the male elite; rich female graves are found as well as male. Displays of burial wealth, particularly from the sixth century, probably relate to the control of the community over the significant trade between Tyrrhenian Etruria and Adriatic Picenum, that would need to use this or other comparable passes: hence the presence of imports such as bronze items from Volsinii and Attic pottery (most probably obtained from Numana on the Adriatic coast).

(Soprintendenza per i Beni Archeologici dell'Umbria)

L. Bonomi Ponzi, in F. Roncalli and L. Bonfante (eds.), *Gens antiquissima Italiae: Antichità dall'Umbria in New York* (Perugia, 1991) 151–64; L. Bonomi Ponzi, *La necropoli plestina di Colfiorito di Foligno* (Collana di Studi di Storia e Archeologia dell'Umbria Antica 2, Perugia, 1997) 348–60.

64. Umbrian bronze statuette, representing the goddess Minerva, in the Villa Giulia museum. The statuette has an elongated, stylized body, and a face portrayed with a severe, stylized expression. The goddess wears a helmet (crest restored), a cuirass decorated with an incised pattern and a relief of a Gorgon's head, and a chiton underneath the armour, visible around the legs. There are tangs on the feet for fixing the statuette into a surface. On stylistic grounds Colonna classified the statuette as part of the 'Fossato di Vico' group (named after the find-spot of one of the group), and dated it to the second half of the fifth century BC.

This statuette is in the larger size bracket of Umbrian figurines typically found in the sanctuaries of the region before the Roman conquest. Such bronze figurines, often very schematic, are found in their hundreds and sometimes thousands. Manufacture was by casting then filing, and a variety of types was produced. Some represented gods, such as Hercules or, as here, Minerva; others are more difficult to determine, but seem to be worshippers, posed with arms outstretched and open palms for offering. Male hoplite warrior figures are also common, and could represent either Mars or the dedicants themselves. The types are generally derived from Etruscan examples and stylized in various ways by Umbrian metalworkers.

These offerings were collected and buried when they became too numerous for the sanctuary space. The huge quantities of figurines even in plundered deposits show that these were (at least in the simple versions) not expensive, complex objects and were in effect mass-produced. This implies that all but the poorest classes were able to dedicate such objects, which reflects on the role of archaic Umbrian sanctuaries as important places of community activity and identity before the development of true urbanism.

(Museo Nazionale Etrusco di Villa Giulia, inv. 24551. Height 32.5 cm)

G. Colonna, *Bronzi votivi umbro-sabellici a figura umana I: Periodo 'arcaico'* (Florence, 1970) 42, 44–5; G. Bradley, *Cahiers du Centre G. Glotz* 8 (1997) 111–29.

65. The 'Mars of Todi', a near life-size bronze statue of a warrior (141 cm high). This is one of the greatest works of classical bronze statuary surviving in Italy. It was found in 1835 on Monte Santo, a hill to the west of Tuder (modern Todi). Votive bronze statuettes attest the presence of an extra-urban sanctuary on this site in the archaic period, which was then monumentalized in temple form, judging by the architectural terracottas recently recovered. The statue is in an exceptional state of preservation as it had been buried in a pit lined with travertine slabs during the second or first century BC, perhaps after being knocked down by a lightning strike.

The statue was cast in pieces by the lost-wax method and then soldered together. The figure is in a typically classical pose, making a libation from a *patera* in his right hand whilst leaning on a spear (now lost) held in his left. It has been interpreted as representing a departing warrior. It dates to the late fifth century BC and has been attributed to a central Etruscan workshop, perhaps operating in Volsinii. An Umbrian inscription in the south Etruscan alphabet on the cuirass records its dedication by 'Aha. Trutitius L. (f.)' or 'Ah. Trutitius Al. (f.)'. Although the gentile name is similar to that on a Celtic/Latin bilingual inscription from here of a much later date, the name of the dedicator of the statue is probably Italic rather than Celtic.

This is an exceptional gift for this sanctuary, especially when considered against the small statuettes typical of most Umbrian sanctuaries (see previous item). It demonstrates the particularly cosmopolitan and wealthy status of Tuder, and is a clear sign of the strong links of this centre with southern and central Etruria.

(Musei Vaticani, Museo Gregoriano Etrusco inv. 13886)

F. Roncalli, *Rend Pont Acc* ser. III vol. II, 2, (Vatican, 1973); Rocca *Iscrizioni umbre minori* 111–116; F. Buranelli, in M. Corbucci and S. Pettine (eds.), *Gens antiquissima Italiae: Antichità dall'Umbria in Vaticano* (Perugia, 1988) 64–5; P. Bruschetti, in Della Fina (ed.) *Gli Umbri* 155.

66. Jewellery from a female burial in Tuder, dating to the second half of the fourth or early third century BC. The tomb was discovered casually in 1886 in the Peschiera locality, and its equipment is now preserved in the Villa Giulia museum. The grave goods are representative of the very prestigious objects deposited in the cemeteries on the southern slopes of the hill of Tuder, which were in use from the late eighth to the second century BC.

As with many other graves from the area, the deceased was buried in an ornamented wooden

65

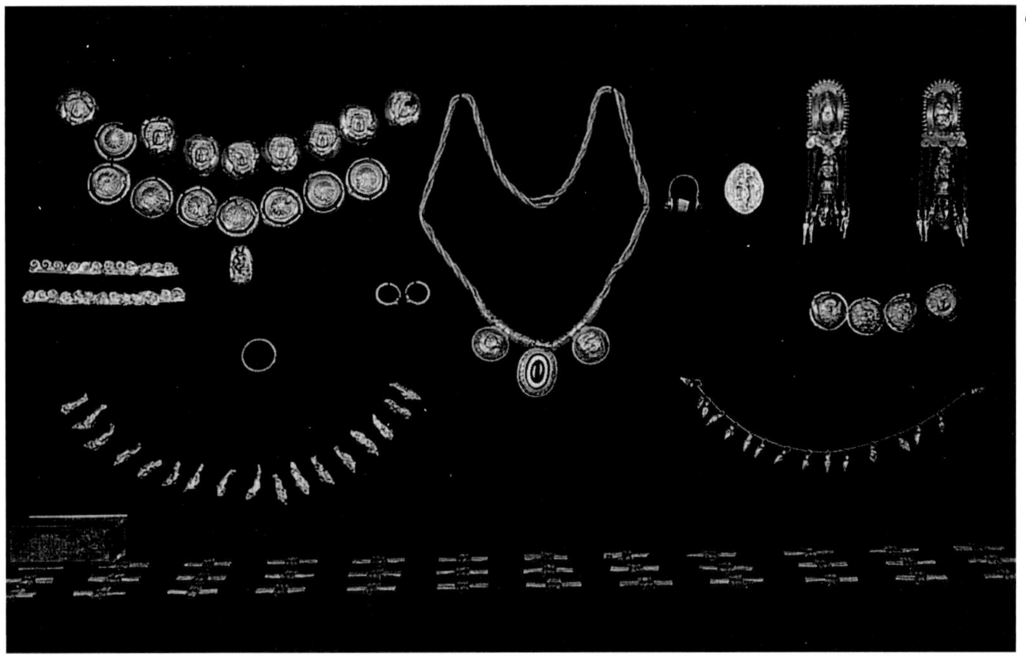

66

casket within a large trench. Few tombs were monumental in structure, as adequate local building stone is lacking, and the slopes of the hill, where the cemeteries developed, are unstable. The deceased wore fine clothing, of which some decorative gold thread and metal ornaments are preserved. There was a very striking accumulation of jewellery in the tomb, consisting of a necklace with *bullae*, the probable remains of another necklace, two pairs of ear-rings (one very elaborate), three rings, and numerous other ornaments, all in gold. Most of this material is of Etruscan production of the second half of the fourth century, and shows the influence of Greek craftsmanship from southern Italy and Sicily. The tomb also has very significant bronze and ceramic assemblages.

Tuder was one of the most sophisticated centres of ancient Umbria in the fourth century, closely linked to powerful cities of central inland Etruria like Perusia, Clusium and Volsinii, and was developing an urban aspect through the monumentalization of its sanctuaries (see next item) and the fortification of the site (in the fourth or third century). The autonomy of the city in the period of its alliance with Rome was manifested in the emission of bronze coinage (it is one of only two Umbrian cities to have done so, the other being Iguvium).

(Museo Nazionale Etrusco di Villa Giulia)

P. Bruschetti, in Roncalli and Bonfante (eds.) *Gens antiquissima Italiae* 354–69; M. Bergamini Simoni, *Todi: Antica città degli Umbri* (Assisi, 2001) 88, 207–17.

67. Architectural terracotta from the church of S. Maria in Camuccia, Tuder, third century BC. This is a terracotta revetment plaque that would have covered a horizontal beam on the outside of a temple. It preserves the nail-fixing holes, is largely complete and would originally have been painted in vivid polychrome. This example is one of a group. It dates to the third century BC and was found together with material from a votive deposit, itself largely datable from the third century BC to the fifth/sixth century AD. It is possible that the terracottas and votive material relate to a sanctuary on this site. But a dump of very similar architectural terracottas was also found nearby at the Porta Catena in 1925, including antefixes, plaques and figures in relief, which must be related. They date to the end of the fourth to the third century BC, so it is likely that a temple with associated votive offerings was positioned somewhere in the vicinity, in the south-east corner of the city.

Architectural terracottas are often our only remaining evidence for temples in the urban areas of Umbrian cities, whose continuous occupation

67

has generally obliterated more substantial traces of the building itself. They begin to be found in western zones of Umbria from the fourth century BC (with some isolated earlier examples), as monumental sanctuaries were created. Stylistically the terracottas generally show connections early on with Etruria (particularly Volsinii), demonstrating the impact of Etruscan centres on Umbria, and later with Rome and Latin colonies.

(Soprintendenza per i Beni Archeologici dell'Umbria)

E. Fabbricotti, *Ritrovamenti archeologici sotto la chiesa della visitazione di Santa Maria 'in Camuccia'* (Res Tudertinae 10, Todi, 1969) 11–16, 131–2; Bergamini Simoni *Todi* 81–6.

68. Fortifications at Ameria. Ameria was an important city in southern Umbria. Its cemeteries show close Etruscan links in the sixth to fifth centuries BC, and the wealth of its inhabitants is demonstrated by their use of chamber tombs and prestige grave goods such as Attic pottery. There is a sanctuary of the sixth and fifth century in the same area as the cemetery.

The walls of Ameria are some of the best-preserved fortifications in Umbria, and ring the site, which is atop a hill with steep slopes on all but

68

the southern sides. The stretch shown is in the south east, where a particularly impressive section protects the least defensible part of the site. The technique used is refined polygonal masonry, with local limestone blocks up to 3 m across fitted very tightly together to give a smooth finish. Other stretches of the wall around the north-east part of the site are in *opus quadrata* (rectangular blocks) of local travertine. Recent excavations have suggested that the two sections of wall were joined together, and are thus contemporary. This provided a unified circuit of some 2,150 m, enclosing around 20 ha, probably dating to the third century BC. The close echoes of its technique with the walls of the late fourth- and early third-century Latin colonies at Alba Fucens, Cosa and elsewhere, combined with the contemporary provision of drainage (and hence a broad conception of urbanistic requirements), have been taken to suggest Roman involvement. This could have been in connection with the creation of the Via Amerina, which led here from Rome, although this type of intervention would be very unusual in an allied centre at this time.

(Soprintendenza per i Beni Archeologici dell'Umbria)

Fontaine, *Cités*. D. Monacchi, C. Angelelli and S. Zampolini Faustini, *Journal of Ancient Topography* 11 (2001) 69–114.

69. The 'Lex Luci' from Spoletium, *CIL* I² 366, found in the wall of S. Quirici, near Montefalco, in the 1870s, now in Spoleto museum. This is one of the earliest Latin inscriptions from Umbria, and the find-spot near Montefalco suggests that it originated in part of the low-lying Valle Umbra that was in the territory of the Latin colony of Spoletium, founded by Rome in 241 BC.

The inscription records a religious law concerning a grove sacred to Jupiter. It is one of a pair of near-identical texts, probably relating to the same sacred grove. The law prohibits the cutting of trees in the grove, except on the day of public festivals to the god. It institutes a penance of an ox sacrifice to be enacted by whoever cuts wood unaware of the sacred status of the grove; if knowingly done, then the guilty party is to be fined 300 *asses* in addition. These measures are to be enforced by a *dicator*. This is an official with religious competence, but it is unclear whether the office also has magisterial functions on the lines of the Latin dictator. The palaeography of the inscription suggests it dates to c. 180–150 BC. A similar law is known from the Latin colony of Luceria in Apulia (*CIL* I² 401, late fourth or early third century BC), protecting a sacred grove against the dumping of dung or a corpse, or the holding of a funeral.

The use of Latin is not surprising: the majority of the settlers of Spoletium were probably from Rome and Latium, and Latin was the official language of colonies. It also shows how the creation of colonies might promote the spread not just of the Latin language but also of Roman and Latin customs and cult practices, such as the inscription of sacred laws, to other areas of Italy.

(Soprintendenza per i Beni Archeologici dell'Umbria)

B. Vine, *Studies in Archaic Latin Inscriptions* (Innsbruck, 1993) 289; S. Panciera, in AA. VV., *Monteluco e i monti sacri* (Spoleto, 1994) 25–46.

70. Iguvine Tables, side Vb. The Iguvine Tables are a set of seven bronzes inscribed with a long Umbrian text. They were discovered in Iguvium (modern Gubbio) in 1444, in the vicinity of the Roman theatre, and bought by the Comune of Gubbio in 1456. The Tables record the rituals and regulations of a priesthood known as the Atiedian Brethren. The Tables vary in size and content, and were inscribed in different hands. Tables I–IV and most of V are in an Umbrian script derived from the Etruscan alphabet of Perusia. Table Vb lines 8–18 and all of VI–VII are in Latin script. The Table illustrated, side b of Table V, seems to mark a transition between the Umbrian script, used for the first seven lines, and the Latin script, employed for the next ten. It has three holes, made before its engraving, to allow hanging or handling. The text of Table Va–b 7 (Umbrian script) has been interpreted as resolutions concerning compensation and fines of the Atiedian Brethren, and Vb 8–18 (Latin script) as regulations involving exchanges between districts of the territory and the Brethren.

The Umbrian script used in Va–b 7 seems to date from the late second century, based on comparisons with Etruscan archetypes; the Latin script is likely to be soon after, and no later than the Sullan period. This Table thus illustrates the spread of Roman practices, in this case the Latin alphabet, in Umbria in the second century BC, which is also attested in other Umbrian cities like Asisium. Roman influence on Iguvium, one of the most important Umbrian cities in the period before the Social War, is also evident through the adoption of the quaestorship, a Roman magistracy.

69

(Soprintendenza per i Beni Archeologici dell'Umbria)

A. L. Prosdocimi, in Prosdocimi, *Lingue e dialetti nell' Italia antica* (*Popoli e Civiltà dell'Italia Antica* VI, Padua, 1978) 585–787; Prosdocimi *Tavole Iguvine* I 151–61; Sisani *Tuta Ikuvina* 237–45.

71. The 'Ponte Augusto' carrying the Via Flaminia over the river Nera. The Via Flaminia was the most important land route to northern Italy from Rome, running for much of its course through Umbria from Ocriculum in the south to Ariminum on the Adriatic coast in the north. It was created in 220 BC by C. Flaminius as censor (Paulus-Festus 79.16–17L; Livy *per.* 20; Plut. *Quaest. Rom.* 66). It is likely to have been built for a military purpose, given that Flaminius had been campaigning in Gallic northern Italy in 223 BC. Flaminius' road must also have been linked to his political programme, providing good communications between the *ager Gallicus*, which he had divided up for settlers in 232 BC, and Rome, where he could benefit from their support. The road must soon have been used for other purposes

71

as well, and it became a conduit for cultural ideas and Roman influence into Umbria. Writing in the Augustan era, Strabo (V.2.10) describes the region in terms of its orientation around the road. Very little trace of Flaminius' original road survives. The oldest archaeological remains, a polygonal bridge foundation of the third century BC, are at Valle Petrosa on the western branch of the road, which went through Carsulae, as opposed to the eastern branch through Spoletium. Most bridges and paved stretches along the route belong to the restoration by Augustus in 27 BC. One such example is the great bridge of Augustus at Narnia, built to carry the road across the Nera (only one of the four original arches survives).

(Soprintendenza per i Beni Archeologici dell'Umbria)

M. Gaggiotti, D. Manconi, L. Mercando, M. Verzar, *Umbria Marche* (Guida archeologica Laterza, Rome and Bari 1980), 297–300.

5. SAMNIUM AND THE SAMNITES

S. P. OAKLEY

The Samnites occupied a land that has always been remote and unfashionable: perhaps only to a few professional ancient historians and to students of the Latin classics of a certain age, among whom the historian Livy's eloquent account of their victory over Rome at the Caudine Forks in 321 BC gives them fame, are they much more than a name. Yet in the last thirty-five years of the twentieth century a series of remarkable topographical and archaeological discoveries, rivalling any others in the study of ancient settlement, has established the Samnites and their neighbours in the Italian mountains as a subject worthy of serious study.

Who were the Samnites? In 1967 E. T. Salmon used the term in much the same way as Livy, that is, to denote the people living in some of the mountainous parts of the modern provinces of Abruzzi, Molise, Campania and Puglia who fought Rome in the Samnite Wars. These included the Hirpini of Beneventum and the lands to its east (a tribe that perhaps later distinguished itself from the Samnites) but excluded tribes such as the Volsci, Marsi, Paeligni and Marrucini to their west and north and (more importantly) the Sidicini, Campani and Lucani to their south, closely related though these latter tribes may have been as regards their use of the Oscan language (72) and (perhaps) their genetic descent. Today questions of ethnic identity seem more complex and less precise: scholars have argued recently that the name 'Samnite' gained currency because of its use to define a large number of dwellers in the Apennines against the Greeks, Latins and other dwellers on the plain, and that, as the power of Rome advanced and that of the mountain-dwellers waned, so the number of those eligible to be called 'Samnite' contracted; but no one has demonstrated that for the period *c.* 300 BC Salmon's usage was fundamentally wrong.

Still more important than asking who the Samnites were is to explore how over the last four millennia their rugged and forested land has been exploited increasingly by its inhabitants: in Samnium, as elsewhere in pre-industrial Italy, the physical environment was the most important factor in determining the pattern of settlement and way of life. Samnium lies either side of the watersheds that divide the rivers which flow to the Tyrrhenian and Adriatic coasts. It is dominated by mountains – high, inhospitable, snow-clad in winter, thickly wooded in many places today and doubtless more so in antiquity, home to wolves and wild boar, and yet also providers of secure fastnesses, of upland pasture surprising in its extent, of cool in the dusty Italian summer, and, paradoxically, of roads and tracks that unite the dwellers on their differing faces. From these mountains flow six important rivers: to the east the Sangro, Trigno, Biferno, Fortore and Ofanto, to the west the Volturno. The steep valleys of these rivers and their numerous tributaries make communication across them or down them extremely difficult; and in the manner in which they interlock they defy concise description, just as years ago they defied the Roman legions.

Systematic archaeological survey has transformed our knowledge of how land was settled and farmed in the Mediterranean basin in prehistory, classical antiquity and the Middle Ages; and in the 1970s and 1980s Samnium was an early beneficiary of this work, when Professor Graeme Barker led his survey of the Biferno valley, the publication of which in 1995 marks the single most important event in recent study of the Samnites. Unfolded in these pages is the great theme of man's attempt to eke out a living from the mountainous environment and of the profound changes which he has wrought in that environment.

Throughout the period with which we are concerned the dominant pattern of settlement was 'dispersed', a pattern common in antiquity in many of the mountainous zones of the Mediterranean basin, in which one finds few or no towns, some larger villages (often on hills, and sometimes fortified), fortified refuges, smaller villages, hamlets, isolated farmsteads and some rural sanctuaries.

By 300 BC Larinum (modern Larino) just outside Samnite territory may have acquired some quasi-urban trappings, some large hill-forts with stable populations had been established (e.g. at Monte Vairano) and some settlements on the plain had begun to grow (e.g. at Saepinum); but until the Romans founded three colonies on Samnite territory between 313 and 263 BC (see below), there was no proper town in Samnium itself. By the end of our period some other settlements were beginning to look more like towns (see below), and land use had become more intensive; but throughout antiquity genuine urbanization was always rare in the region.

Greek and Latin writers refer several times to this dispersed pattern of settlement, and its later reflexes may be seen in medieval and modern times; but for the most part physical remains of ancient settlement survive in only three forms. Most important is the faunal and floral evidence and the sherds and other artefacts that have been recovered in excavation and in field survey, especially in the Biferno valley (74–6). These have provided proper physical documentation of the pattern described above and have allowed developments and changes in the pattern to be identified.

Dominant among the visible remains for the Samnite pattern of settlement is a remarkable series of hill-forts (77–9). In 1960 the number of known Samnite fortified sites was very small. Now, thanks to the work of such pioneers as La Regina, Conta Haller, De Benedittis and Caiazza, more than eighty are known, and in many other parts of the central Apennines similar sites have been discovered in equal profusion; these discoveries constitute another very important area in which progress has recently been made. Difficulties and uncertainties still bedevil the study of these sites: very few have been excavated, and only one extensively; their size varies from the minute to the vast; and the date of most is unknown, although the available evidence makes it a reasonable conjecture that many were in use *c.* 300. Yet amid all these difficulties one fact shines forth: where there was a fort there must have been associated settlement in the vicinity, and therefore the discovery of these sites has added local colour and detail to the model which intensive archaeological survey has allowed us to establish; and if many of these forts were indeed in use *c.* 300, they provide striking physical evidence of the great series of wars between the Samnites and Rome.

Sanctuaries, too, survive: at Campochiaro, Pietrabbondante, Pratella, Quadri, San Giovanni in Galdo, Schiavi di Abruzzo and Vastogirardi. Splendid testimony to an important later historical process, too few of these are known for the place of the sanctuary in the Samnite pattern of settlement securely to be established. Yet here too recent scholarship has made progress: the site at Campochiaro was identified as a sanctuary only in the 1970s, that at Pratella was found only in the 1980s and architectural terracottas found in the Biferno valley survey showed that at Colle Sparanise (80–1), where structures have been largely destroyed by the plough, there must have been a sanctuary. On the basis of the function of sanctuaries in the Greek world, about which we are far better informed, it is legitimate to conjecture that many Samnite sanctuaries must have been founded on sites at which deities had been worshipped for centuries; that they served to propitiate the gods who were believed to control a harsh physical environment; that they marked out the boundaries of territories; and that they provided focal points at which diverse rustic communities could meet for religious rituals and festivities, and for exchange at fairs.

The archaeological survey of the Biferno valley has shown that the Samnites of the classical period grew barley, wheat, peas, beans, grapes and olives, and kept pigs, cattle, sheep and goats. Pastoralism must have been important to all Samnite communities, and in some areas agriculture must have been quite difficult. Yet it would be wrong to underestimate the importance of Samnite agriculture (as some scholars used to do), which is more extensive than has sometimes been realized: for the Samnites dwelling on the Tyrrhenian side of the watershed there was some land excellent for farming in the Volturno valley, on the borders of Campania, and around Beneventum; and in the mountains steep valleys often open out to reveal basins of land ripe for tilling.

One of the most notable features of southern Italian pastoralism in the centuries before the advent of transport by railway and motor-vehicle was the extensive network of drove-roads or *tratturi* used for transhumance, that is, by shepherds taking their flocks from the mountains (where in summer the pastures are rich and cool but in winter too cold) to the plains (where in summer the pastures are too hot and desiccated but in winter more lush and hospitable) and vice versa. Whether transhumance along these or similar *tratturi* was possible before the Romans united Italy and hence whether it was a feature of Samnite social and economic life *c.* 300 BC, is disputed; but Varro's treatise *De re rustica* (*On farming*) leaves no doubt that *tratturi* existed in the first century BC, and probably they were coming more extensively into use at the end of our period.

To this story of dispersed settlement in the harsh environment of the Apennines the Samnites who dwelt in the lower valley of the Volturno and on the fringes of Campania provide something of an exception. Here, as we have observed, the agricultural land is finer than elsewhere in Samnium, and throughout our period proximity to Campania made for a richer and more sophisticated way of life, influenced strongly by the urban culture of that region. For example, tombs with Greek vases dating from the early sixth to the late fifth century have been found in cemeteries at several sites (e.g. Caudium, Trebula (**82**) and Sant'Agata dei Goti (probably ancient Saticula)), and *c.* 400 BC Allifae produced coins very similar in style to those of Neapolis (where they were perhaps minted), Nola and other Campanian towns, a very clear sign that it regarded itself as belonging to the world of Campania (**83**). However, in the end the Samnites had an even more profound influence on the Campanian way of life: by the end of the fifth century they controlled Acerrae, Nola, Pompeii, Nuceria and Capua (together with its satellites), and the Greek city of Cumae; and although Neapolis managed to remain Greek, it was forced to absorb Samnite insurgents. Yet once they had adapted themselves to the easier agricultural conditions of Campania, the Campani (as the new rulers of Capua had come to be termed) themselves were exposed to pressure from other Samnites in the mountains who envied their land; and their weakness in the face of this pressure led to the appeal to Rome in 343 BC from which the First Samnite War began. Therefore Samnite communities which were on the fringes of Campania – Allifae, Cubulteria, Telesia, Caudium and others – look two ways: in part towards the mountains which come down to the edge of their territory, but also towards the Campanian plain.

From patterns of settlement and of economics we may turn to people and events. Archaeological evidence allows us to document the emergence of elites who lived and were buried with more style than their fellow peasants; but how these elites established chiefdoms, how these chiefdoms related to each other, how and when the individual tribes of the Samnites were formed, how these tribes related to each other, how and when they began to form part of a Samnite state (if there was indeed such a thing), and how recruiting for troops was carried out – these are important questions for which we have no sure answers. Our literary and epigraphic sources mention four tribes, the Carricini, Caudini, Hirpini and Pentri. It is a reasonable conjecture that these four tribes had come into being by 350 BC; but there may well have been many more tribes, and that the tribe may not have been a particularly important unit is suggested by the fact that a town like Allifae could mint coinage on its own. For the cooperation of these tribes as part of a Samnite confederation in 343 BC, the date at which the wars with Rome began, may seem a clear *terminus ante quem*; but the physical diversity of the region should make one suspicious of the unity with which our literary sources allege that the Samnites operated against Rome.

Of the later political history of Samnium we are a little better informed, although what we know derives almost entirely from Greek and Roman sources. At first, in the fifth and fourth centuries BC, it is a story of expansion, a time in which bands of Samnites, aggressive for land, killing and plunder, threatened not just the towns of Campania (see above), but also Apulians in the area of Luceria. From the mid fourth century onwards the story becomes one of a retreat in face of that remarkable advance which between 366 and 264 gave Rome hegemony over all of peninsular Italy and dominion over much of it. Yet the Samnites stood more firmly and obdurately in Rome's way than even the Greeks, Etruscans or Gauls. The struggle between the two powers lasted seventy years, with wars from 343 to 341, and 327 to 304 (perhaps with a break from either 321 or 319 until 316), 298 to 290 and 282 to 269.

Tales of battles are the principal monuments of these years – of that great day in 321 when the Samnites humiliated the Romans in the Caudine Forks; but also of the crushing defeats – at Sentinum in 295 at the hands of Q. Fabius Rullianus, and at Aquilonia and Cominium in 293 at the hands of Sp. Carvilius Maximus and L. Papirius Cursor. For much of these wars Rome was on the offensive, and no part of Samnium escaped her legions. This was the time when the great series of Samnite hill-forts had its most urgent use – and often was found wanting. For visual images of these wars that shaped the future of Roman Italy we have to rely largely on our own imaginations; but the striking and evocative pass of Arpaia, the likely site of the battle in the Caudine Forks, can still be visited (84), and there are several settlements known to have been captured by Rome at which Samnite fortifications may still be seen, including the splendid Terravecchia, Samnite Saepinum (77).

Our dearth of literary sources for the years between 293 and 219 may encourage the notion that defeat by Rome led swiftly to friendship and integration with Rome. On the contrary: although they suffered from confiscation of land, most of the Samnites survived as states independent of Rome (albeit with a range of political activity very heavily circumscribed by Rome's mastery) and probably resentful towards their unwanted mistress. It is no surprise that in the Second Punic War large numbers of Samnites joined Hannibal in a doomed bid to regain their liberty. No isolated aberration in 178 years of Roman control of central Italy, this should be seen as a long-delayed southern Italian rebellion: we should not forget that boys of 16 who fought the Romans in that last campaign in 269 BC could still have been alive at 69 when, in 216 BC, Rome's power wavered after Cannae.

The Romans controlled their defeated foes by confiscating land from them and settling colonies of Latin-speakers on it. Three such colonies were established in Samnium – at Saticula (probably Sant'Agata dei Goti) in 313, at Beneventum (Benevento) in 268 and at Aesernia (Isernia) in 263; and one was placed on its north-east border, at Luceria (Lucera) in 314. To this day all survive as towns, and at Luceria and Beneventum there are significant remains from the late Republic and high empire; but only at Aesernia are remains of the original Latin colony visible, in the form of defensive walls and the podium of the principal temple (85).

The long series of wars with Rome almost certainly brought some changes to settlement and society in Samnium: groves of olives and other trees must have been ravaged, settlements destroyed, new fortified settlements constructed and perhaps some land deforested. More fundamental changes, however, are likely to have come only with the increasing integration into the wider economy of Italy that finally began with the end of the Second Punic War in 202. The archaeological evidence does not always allow the precise dating of such matters but at best encourages, and at worst is compatible with, the view that this period saw more intensive exploitation of agrarian land, further clearing of woods, the abandonment of some sites on the top of hills and, at least at southern Samnite sites such as Allifae, Combulteria and Telesia, a movement towards larger urban or quasi-urban settlement.

From the Second Punic and to the Social War and beyond, Rome's rapid conquest and exploitation of large tracts of the Mediterranean basin made many Italians richer. At Rome the social and political effects of this wealth are well known (see Chapter 4); about the rest of Italy we are less well informed, but we have evidence for some parallel phenomena: the towns of Italy saw expansion, monumentalization and beautification, a process that was to quicken with the municipalization that came in the aftermath of the Social War.

Apart from its Latin colonies, Samnium had no large towns; but a remarkable analogue to this urban patronage may be seen in the beautification and monumentalization of several sanctuaries, at which temples were built in the most refined Hellenistic style. The excavation and study of these important sites is another area in which recent scholarship has made very substantial progress. The glory of the phenomenon lies at Pietrabbondante. Here there was already a hill-fort and had probably been a sanctuary from time immemorial; and already around the time of the Second Punic War a small temple had been constructed. Then, *c.* 110, a large temple was built, probably modelled on the now destroyed temple at the Fondo Patturelli at Capua, with a theatre and associated buildings on the slopes of the hill below it. Of ancient sites in the mountains of central Italy none is more beautiful, none more important; and none offers such a splendid vista to either eyes or imagination (86). Around the same time another large temple was constructed at Campochiaro, and smaller temples are known from San Giovanni in Galdo, Schiavi di Abruzzo (where, in a reversal of the pattern found at Pietrabbondante, an earlier and larger temple was built around the time of the Second Punic War), and Vastogirardi; and proper excavation may reveal that the temple at Quadri dates from this time (87).

Here we take our leave of the Samnites, still independent of Rome, still largely living in a land of dispersed settlement of Rome, but now with an elite increasingly involved in Roman affairs, wealthier than ever before, and ready to spend that wealth for their own prestige and for the public good. With the Social War and the consequent arrival of Roman citizenship and municipalization changes would come swiftly, but few were of a fundamental nature: it would take the industrial revolution to loosen the grip that the mountains and river valleys of Samnium held over the lives of the men and women who dwelt among them.

GENERAL BIBLIOGRAPHY

E. T. Salmon's *Samnium and the Samnites* (Cambridge, 1967) was the first general study of the Samnites ever written and helped to inspire the extraordinarily productive period of Samnite studies at the end of the twentieth century; it remains an attractive first port of call for anyone seeking basic knowledge about the Samnites. Some aspects of Salmon's treatment of the literary evidence for the Samnite Wars (pp. 187–292) have not worn well; but since in 1967 most of the sites now known had not been mentioned in print, it is in matters topographical and archaeological that his book now seems most dated. It has been replaced as the standard work on the subject by G. Tagliamonte *I Sanniti: Caudini, irpini, pentri, carricini, frentani* (Milan, 1996), which gives the archaeological evidence proper weight. Another attractive introduction to the subject is provided by E. Dench's *From Barbarians to New Men: Greek, Roman, and Modern Perceptions of Peoples from the Central Apennines* (Oxford, 1995); as her title suggests, Dench devotes much space to studying the Samnites from the perspective of modern theories of ethnicity, but she also provides an introduction to the archaeology of Samnium. A third attractive introduction to the subject is A. La Regina, 'I Sanniti' in AA.VV., *Italia* (Milan, 1989) 301–432 and 697–700, even though some of La Regina's interpretations of the literary evidence for the Samnites are speculative and controversial. Notwithstanding this, most of the major modern advances in the study of the northern territory of the Samnites received their impetus from La Regina, whose other notable publications include 'Le iscrizione osche di Pietrabbondante e la questione di Bovianum Vetus', *Rheinisches Museum* 109 (1966) 260–86, 'Cluviae e il territorio carecino', *Rendiconti dell'Accademia dei Lincei* 22 (1967) 89–99, 'Note sulla formazione dei centri urbani in area sabellica' in AA. VV., *Atti del Convegno di Studi sulla Città Etrusca e Italica Preromana* (Bologna, 1970) 191–207, 'Centri fortificati preromani nei territori sabellici dell'Italia centrale adriatica', *Posebna Izdanja* 24 (1975) 271–82, 'Il Sannio' in P. Zanker (ed.), *Hellenismus in Mittelitalien*, vol. I (Göttingen, 1976) 219–48, and two co-authored volumes: *Culture adriatiche antiche d'Abruzzo e di Molise*, vol. II (Rome, 1978) (edited with L. F. Dell'Orto) and *Abruzzo Molise* (Guida archeologicha Laterza, Rome and Bari, 1984) (written with F. Coarelli). There are stimulating general essays in AA.VV., *Sannio: Pentri e Frentani dal VI al I sec. a.C.: Atti del Convegno 10–11 Novembre 1980* (Rome, 1980) and up-to-date essays on a variety of topics connnected with the Samnites in AA.VV., *Studi sull'Italia dei Sanniti* (Rome, 2000). The best starting-points for the detailed study of Samnite artefacts and evidence from excavation, especially that gleaned from the modern province of Molise, are AA.VV. *Sannio* and S. Capini and A. Di Niro (eds.), *Samnium: Archeologia del Molise* (Rome, 1991).

For the survey of the Biferno valley and the pattern of settlement in Samnium, see now above all G. W. W. Barker, *A Mediterranean Valley* (London and New York, 1995) and Barker (ed.), *The Biferno Valley Survey* (London and New York, 1995). The first volume, in which much of the chapters concerned with the Samnites was written by J. A. Lloyd, presents an historical and archaeological interpretation, easily accessible to the non-specialist reader; the technical evidence on which it is based is published in the second volume.

For Samnite fortified sites, see the synthesis in S. P. Oakley, *The Hill-Forts of the Samnites* (Archaeological Monographs of the British School at Rome 10, London, 1995), in which virtually every site known in 1995 is discussed; but three publications above all others have advanced our knowledge of the subject: La Regina's 1975 article (see above), G. Conta Haller, *Richerche su alcuni centri fortificati in opera poligonale in area Campano-Sannitica* (Naples, 1978) and D. Caiazza, *Archeologia e storia antica del mandamento di Pietramelara e del Montemaggiore I: Preistoria ed età sannitica* (Pietramelara, 1986). Note too M. Pagano and M. Raddi, *Atlante delle cinte murarie sannitiche* (Campobasso, 2006). Monte Vairano is unique among the forts in that it has been excavated and the results of the excavations have been published: see numerous publications by G. De Benedittis, of which *Il centro sannitico di Monte Vairano presso Campobasso* (Documenti di Antichità Italiche e Romane 5, Campobasso, 1974) and *Monte Vairano: La casa di 'LN': Catalogo della mostra* (Campobasso, 1988) are the most substantial.

The archaeological and cultural context in which the Greek vases recovered from Caudium and elsewhere should be placed is most conveniently studied in pp. 38–77 of Tagliamonte's book.

Samnite coinage is assessed briefly in *HN*[2] 58–74. N. K. Rutter, *Campanian Coinages 475–380 BC* (Edinburgh, 1979) is a very full study of the Campanian context into which the first issues of Allifae and Phistelia must be placed.

For the Roman conquest of Samnium the literary sources are fullest for the period 343–293, for all of which Livy (VII.29–X.47), and for some of which Diodorus Siculus (various passages in Books XIX and XX), provide a full narrative. These sources are discussed at length in S. P. Oakley, *A Commentary on Livy, Books VI–X* (Oxford, 1997–2005). Up-to-date narrative of the Samnite Wars is provided by T. J. Cornell in *CAH* VII.II[2] 351–91 and more briefly in his *The Beginnings of Rome: Italy and Rome from the Bronze Age to the Punic Wars (c. 1000 to 264 BC)* (London and New York, 1995) 345–68 and G. Forsythe, *A Critical History of Early Rome: From Prehistory to the First Punic War* (Berkeley, 2005) 281–368. More extended narratives are provided by G. De Sanctis, *Storia dei romani,* vol. II (1907–64) 266–429 (later reprinted with changes of pagination but no other changes) and Salmon (discussed above). For Roman and Latin colonization, E. T. Salmon, *Roman Colonization under the Republic* (London, 1969) remains the easiest introduction.

For urbanization in Italy after the Second Punic War the classic study remains E. Gabba, 'Urbanizzazione e rinnovamenti urbanistici nell'Italia centro-meridionale del I sec. a.C.', *Studi Classici e Orientali* 21 (1972) 73–112 = *Italia Romana* (Como, 1994) 63–103. For the growth of Larinum, see Barker *A Mediterranean Valley* 185 and 197.

For the monumentalization of the rural sanctuaries in Samnium, see especially La Regina's 1976 article. The site at Pietrabbondante is discussed in virtually every work listed in the first paragraph of this bibliography; for Campochiaro, see the numerous publications of S. Capini, especially *Campochiaro* (Campobasso, 1982).

72. Oscan and Latin both belong to the Italic branch of Indo-European, but the two languages were not mutually intelligible. Most of our very imperfect knowledge of Oscan comes from inscriptions, of which the most famous is perhaps the so-called 'Agnone Table', now in the British Museum. Found in 1848 near Fonte Romita in the Comune of Capracotta (which borders on that of Agnone), where remains of a Samnite sanctuary have since been uncovered, this bronze tablet is very small in size (just 28 cm × 16.5 cm) and is inscribed in Oscan on both sides. It dates perhaps from the second century BC, and the inscription (the precise interpretation of which is disputed) records rules for the conduct of sacrifices at the sanctuary.

(**a** Front; **b** reverse. British Museum PS220340, PS220341)

For up-to-date text, translation, and interpretation, see M. H. Crawford *et al.*, *Imagines Italicae: A Corpus of Italic Inscriptions* (Bulletin of the Institute of Classical Studies Supplement) (London, 2011, 3 vols.); this includes also a full account of the circumstances in which the table was found. A large number of essays centred more or less closely on the Table are collected in L. del Tutto Palma (ed.), *La tavola di Agnone nel contesto italico* (Florence, 1996).

73. Amidst the mountains of Samnium there are some large upland pastures. The most extensive, partly illustrated here, surround Rivisondoli on the edge of the Sangro valley.

(Photo S. P. Oakley)

74. The archaeological survey of the Biferno valley organized by Professor Graeme Barker in the 1970s made important and decisive advances in our knowledge of the pattern of settlement in Samnium. Fundamental to much archaeological survey in Italy is the recording of scatters of ancient tile and pottery in ploughed fields. This picture, taken in the lower valley of the Biferno, well illustrates such a scatter.

(Photo G. W. W. Barker)

75. The survey of the Biferno valley revealed the existence of a farmstead at Matrice. This was later excavated and found to have been occupied in the mid Republican and imperial periods. The existence of farms of this kind is a good illustration of the progressive 'opening-up' of the countryside after the Samnite Wars had finished.

(Photo J. A. Lloyd)

76. Survey and limited excavation revealed that the ancient terracing near Vinchiaturo illustrated in this photograph served as the platform for a villa occupied in the mid Republican and imperial periods.

(Photo G. W. W. Barker)

Barker (ed.) *Biferno Valley* 90–1 (where this photograph was mistakenly inverted).

77. Of the great series of hill-forts that have been found in Samnium, the best known is that at Terravecchia, Samnite Saepinum. Here, on a hill of 953 m, the remains of Samnite fortifications can be traced with ease; notable is the well-preserved Postierla del Matese, which is illustrated in this picture. However, what gives this fort its particular interest is the fact that Livy (X.44.9, XLV.12–14) refers to an assault on Saepinum in 293 BC by the Roman consul L. Papirius Cursor: it is very rare for us to be able to connect a Samnite hill-fort with the events of the Samnite Wars, but beyond any reasonable doubt these were the walls which Cursor attacked.

(Photo S. P. Oakley)

A. Maiuri, *NSc* (1926) 244–51; G. Colonna, *Archeologia Classica* 14 (1962) 80–107; E. Paoletti, *Storici campi di battaglia nel glorioso Sannio antico ovvero la battaglia di Aquilonia* (Trivento, 1982) 54–5; Coarelli and La Regina (eds.) *Abruzzo Molise* 209–28; E. Martino, *Almanacco del Molise* 24 (1992) 29–38; Oakley *Hill-Forts of the Samnites* 69–71, and (for the Roman campaign of 293 BC) *Commentary* IV 379–457.

72a

72b

73

74

75

76

77

78

78. This photograph illustrates part of the polygonal walling surviving at Monte della Foresta, a hill of 994 m that dominates the upper valley of the Volturno close to the source of the river. The construction in dry stone and the varying size of the blocks used may also be seen. The study of hill-forts in Samnium has been advanced as much by amateurs as by professional historians and archaeologists: standing on the wall is dott. D. Caiazza, who has found more new Samnite hill-forts than anyone else; below it is dott. M. Raddi, who discovered this site in the early 1990s.

(Photo S. P. Oakley)

Oakley *Hill-Forts of the Samnites* 21–2; Pagano and Raddi *Atlante* 35–47.

79. When the ancient walls have collapsed or been robbed, or when later farmers have constructed agricultural terracing, the identification of Samnite hill-forts can become difficult and uncertain. This wall, never previously mentioned in print, was discovered recently by dott. Raddi at the Serra d'Ambla at Pantaniello, near Pettoranello del Molise. It is imperfectly preserved and cannot now be traced around all the summit of the hill, but the size of some of the boulders used in its construction suggests that probably it should be distinguished from the agricultural terracing found on the lower slopes of the hill and be regarded as a Samnite site. As this picture shows, an added difficulty for those searching for new Samnite sites is that many hilltops are now wooded.

(Photo S. P. Oakley)

80. The sanctuary at Colle Sparanise, with material dating from the third century BC, was one of the most important sites discovered by the Biferno valley survey. This photograph illustrates limited trial excavation of the site.

(Photo G. W. W. Barker)

Barker *A Mediterranean Valley* 49 and 192; Barker (ed.) *Biferno Valley* 87–9, 102.

81. This picture illustrates how at Colle Sparanise the collapsed roof made of tile presented itself in excavation.

(Photo G. W. W. Barker)

79

80

82. Greek vases have been recovered from several Samnite graves. **a** is of Carlo Nolli's engraving after a drawing by Giuseppe Bracci, of a tomb at Trebula, which is famous for having been studied by both Winckelmann and Sir William Hamilton; **b** is of the grave goods found in the tomb. Note in particular the red-figured bell-*krater* of *c.* 430 BC.

(**a** British Museum 295454; **b** British Museum 298107)

For the discovery of this tomb, see P. F. Hugues d'Hancarville, *Antiquités étrusques, grecques et romaines, tirées du cabinet de M. Hamilton, envoyé extraordinaire et plenipotentiare de S. M. Britannique en cour de Naples*, vol. II (Naples, 1766–7) 74, and I. Jenkins and K. Sloan, *Vases and Volcanoes: Sir William Hamilton and his Collection* (London, 1996) 141–3. For the bell-*krater*, see J. D. Beazley, *ARV*[2] 1045 no. 8.

83. The Samnites produced coins in two periods. Around 400 BC Allifae and the unidentified community of Phistelia produced didrachms which were perhaps minted at Neapolis and certainly take their place among the Campanian coinages of the period. Around 300 BC they produced obols; these again take their place among the Campanian coinages, which now included the first issue of Roman coins. Around 260 BC several other Samnite communities – Caiatia, Combulteria, Telesia – produced coins but as part of a phenomenon which had spread further afield: for example, they were joined by Aesernia, Aquinum, Cales and Teanum Sidicinum. Illustrated in this plate are coins of Allifae (**a**, **b**), Combulteria (**c**, **d**) and Phistelia (**e**).

(British Museum: Alliba 1946–1–1–50; Compultina 1841–4–3–35; 1902–5–6–6; Phistelia 1946–1–1–86; 1946–1–1–88)

Rutter *HN*[2] 62, 59, 72.

84. The most famous battle between the Samnites and the Romans took place at the Caudine Forks in 321 BC. The precise location of the site is disputed, but the ancient sources, unreliable though they

81

82b

83a

83b

are for most details of the battle, are likely to be right when they state that the Roman legions were trapped in a defile; and in the region of Caudium (modern Montesarchio) the only plausible site for this defile is between Arienzo and Arpaia. This picture, taken from the flank of Monte Tairano to the north of Arpaia, illustrates the narrow eastern exit of the defile.

(Photo S. P. Oakley)

P. Sommella, *Antichi campi di battaglia in Italia* (Rome, 1967) 49–68; N. M. Horsfall, *PBSR* n.s. 37 (1982) 45–52; Oakley *Commentary* III 52–60.

85. Aesernia, modern Isernia, was colonized by the Romans with a Latin colony in 263 BC, and the site has been occupied ever since; today it is one of the two provincial capitals of the region of Molise. The colony lay in the centre of the basin formed by the upper valley of the Volturno, and its presence will have done much to ensure the peaceful behaviour of the Samnites who lived in the region. The only significant visible remains of the ancient town are part of the walled circuit and the podium of its principal temple (doubtless dedicated to Jupiter). This was probably established at the time of the

83c

83d

foundation of the colony; like many pagan sites, it was taken over for Christian worship and now serves as the foundation for the *duomo*. This photograph shows a detail of the podium.

(Photo S. P. Oakley)

Dell'Orto and La Regina *Culture adriatiche antiche* II 535–8.

86. Between about 110 and 90 BC the Samnites constructed a new temple and a theatre at Pietrabbondante and thereby made the sanctuary, which already contained a significant temple built *c.* 250 BC, a place of the most exquisite Hellenistic refinement. This picture shows how the new temple and theatre were integrated into one complex. The moulding on the podium and on the backs of the seats in the theatre may also be discerned.

(Photo S. P. Oakley)

For plans of the site and the basic facts, see M. J. Strazzulla and B. Di Marco, *Il santuario sannitico di Pietrabbondante* (Chieti, 1973). Syntheses of scholarly work and of the extensive bibliography may be found in Dell'Orto and La Regina

83e

84

85

Culture adriatiche antiche II. 449–89, AA.VV. *Sannio* 129–96, Coarelli and La Regina (eds.) *Abruzzo Molise* 230–57, and by S. Capini, in Capini and Di Niro (eds.) *Samnium* 113–14.

87. Underneath the ruins of the medieval church of the Madonna dello Spineto near Quadri (probably known in antiquity as Trebula) there is the podium of an ancient temple. Much less well known than the sanctuary at Pietrabbondante, although built in a position hardly less evocative and beautiful, this site awaits proper excavation. However, it is a reasonable conjecture that the temple dates from the second century BC and resembled other small rural temples in Samnium, such as those found at Vastogirardi and San Giovanni in Galdo. This photograph shows the ruins of the medieval church, which includes some ancient blocks in its walls.

(Photo S. P. Oakley)
Dell'Orto and La Regina *Culture adriatiche antiche* II. 499.

86

6. SOUTHERN ITALY

ALASTAIR SMALL

Southern Italy in the fourth and third centuries BC was a mosaic of different ethnic and sub-ethnic groups, distinguished by language, customs and material culture. The Greek city-states on the coastal plains still used the dialects (Doric (cf. 93), Achaean and Ionic) of their original settlers, practised their traditional cults and asserted their political autonomy, though they were able from time to time to band together in an Italiote league to defend their territories against attack by the Syracusans or by the Italic peoples in their hinterland. At the beginning of the fourth century the most vigorous of the Italic peoples in the south of the peninsula were the Oscan-speaking Lucanians, who had emerged as a powerful new *ethnos* and were expanding outwards from their homeland in the Apennine mountains, impinging on their neighbours in the coastal plains. In the cities they captured, such as Poseidonia-Paestum, they cohabited with the Greek population and created a vibrant new syncretistic culture (98, 101). Around the middle of the fourth century the Bruttians (or Brettians) separated from the Lucanians and formed another *ethnos* which overran most of what is now Calabria. The area that later came to be known as Apulia, including the Salentine peninsula and the plains and plateaux to the east of the Apennines, was occupied predominantly by Messapic-speaking peoples. Nineteenth-century scholars distinguished three principal subdivisions of their material culture which they correlated with the main ethnic categories known from the literary sources: Daunians in the north, Peucetians in the centre and Messapians in the south. These terms are still of some use and will be followed here, but since other names are also found in the written sources for the Italic peoples in Apulia (Poediculi in the centre, Iapyges, Sallentini and Calabri in the south), the ethnic categories were probably rather fluid and may have changed over time. The archaeological evidence shows that there were numerous local variations within the regional cultures which reflect the growing importance of the larger settlements and therefore of political rather than ethnic units. The ethnic structures remained, and were reinforced by cult practices (108), but they gave way increasingly to new political institutions based on the territorial city (cf. 91c, 91d, 105, 106). In peacetime, the primary loyalty of most Italic individuals during this period was probably to their community rather than to their *ethnos*, although men and women continued to assert their ethnic identity in their burial rituals (99, 100), hair-style (102), dress (98, 102) and military apparatus (99–101), and no doubt in other ways.

The ethnic structures also retained their importance in time of war, since they formed a basis for constructing military leagues (91e). The ancient writers view the conflicts between the Greeks and the Italic peoples in ethnic terms: in their eyes it is the Lucanians or Bruttians (less frequently the Messapians) who threaten the Greek cities, and it is probable that most of these conflicts involved the armies of several communities. The causes of the wars were complex, but population increase is apparent all over southern Italy in the fourth century BC (110, 111, 118), and shortage of land was probably the most important single factor driving the expansion of the Oscan-speaking peoples from the mountains towards the coastal plains.

Victory in these wars was impossible without intensive training, physical fitness, and skills in weaponry and tactics. The Greek cities came to depend more and more on mercenaries – professional soldiers, many of whom, like the Mamertines, or the Italic warrior buried at Metapontum (100) must have been drawn from the native peoples in the hinterland. Mercenary soldiers needed professional commanders, and to control them the Tarentines had recourse to high-ranking Greek *condottieri*. The first in a notable series, King Archidamus III of Sparta (89) fought against the Messapians (or perhaps Lucanians) from 343 until his death in battle in 338 BC; Alexander of Epirus (or Molossus) campaigned against the Lucanians from *c.* 334 to 331 and also died in battle; the last, Pyrrhus (**90**), waged war between 280 and 275 BC against the Romans who had invaded southern Italy several times in the Samnite Wars, impinging on the Tarentine sphere of influence. To meet the cost of these wars the Tarentines minted special issues of gold and silver coins (**91a, b**).

Another aspect of the intensification of warfare was the development of artillery, in which Syracusan engineers played a leading role. Those cities which had the expertise and resources of manpower built new walls fortified with high towers which could house counter-artillery able to out-perform hostile siege engines on the ground. The new machinery led defenders to adopt offensive tactics, and towers were also built to control postern gates, through which a besieged army could make surprise sorties against the enemy. The development is well illustrated by the city walls of Hipponium (**92**), which were reconstructed around the end of the fourth century, most probably by Agathocles after he had captured the city with the use of catapults.

The Heraclea Tablets (**93**) provide an unusual glimpse of the effects of prolonged war on the administration of a Greek city-state. They show the city taking steps to re-appropriate temple lands that had been illegally occupied by private individuals in time of war (perhaps the wars of Alexander of Molossus). The city authorities laid out procedures to be followed in renting out the lands that had been recovered. New tenants were required *inter alia* to plant vines and olives where the land was suitable, and to replace old vines with new. The measure suggests that Heraclea, like other Greek cities in southern Italy, was participating in the expansion of the wine industry. The analysis of MGS amphorae (**94**) made in Magna Graecia and Sicily to contain wine for export helps to fill in the picture. Already in the late fifth century some cities were producing a surplus of wine and were using locally made amphorae in which to export it. Production grew throughout the fourth and third centuries, and reached increasingly distant markets.

In agricultural and economic development and in many aspects of daily life the Italic peoples willingly adopted (and adapted) ideas from the Greeks. Hellenization was not just the result of interaction with the Greek cities on the coast. There was also direct influence from mainland Greece, especially Corinth and Athens. A remarkable number of Attic red-figure pots found in central Apulian sites suggests that the Athenians developed commercial contacts directly with the Peucetian peoples of this area. They were probably interested in it as a source of grain. Some of the imported pieces are of the highest quality, such as the name-vase of the Talos painter (**95**). Athenian imports dried up before the middle of the fourth century, but the vacuum was filled by goods imported on an increasing scale from Magna Graecia in spite of (or perhaps because of) the frequent wars recorded by the literary sources (**94, 102**). Innumerable Greek artefacts deposited in native tombs, such as strigils (as in the burial at Laus, **99**) for use in the palaestra and *kraters* for the symposium, show that the Italic elites had adopted some of the most characteristic elements of Greek culture. The area continued to be open to Greek influence even after the Roman conquest. The bronze skeleton (*larva*) (**96**) from a simple tomb of the second century BC near the tip of the Salentine peninsula shows that this symbol of popular Epicureanism caught on among the Messapians long before it is attested in Roman society.

Other grave goods and tomb furnishings, however, illustrate the militaristic character of the Italic peoples and point a contrast to the Greeks, who did not bury weapons or armour with their dead. Italic warriors were buried with symbols of their military valour – with weapons and armour worn by themselves (**99, 100**) or won in battle (**97, 99**). In Lucanian Paestum the graves themselves were painted with scenes that emphasize the military values of the society. The elites fought with spear and javelin on horseback wearing a full panoply; those lower down the social scale wore less body armour and fought with spears in hoplite fashion or as light-armed javelineers. As the fourth century progressed the role of the foot-soldier grew in importance, due in part to the need for better-trained infantry to match the Roman legions; but the traditions of the society continued to encourage acts of individual valour (**101**). The military ethos is captured in some Campanian vase paintings and in a notable series of frescoes on the sides of tombs at Capua and Paestum, many of which show the role played by women in supporting male warriors in life and death (**98**). In the indigenous Apulian cities, more exposed to the influence of Tarentum, the heroic role of the warrior was expressed in painted images on Apulian red-figure column-*kraters* made by Greek artisans for burial in native tombs (**102**).

The need for secure defence in this period of intense warfare was a powerful factor leading to the consolidation of the Italic communities and the beginnings of urbanization. Numerous indigenous settlements were fortified in the last half of the fourth century and during the course of the third. Monte Sannace (103), for example, built a circuit of walls in the fourth century and added others in the third to meet the new emergencies of the Pyrrhic and Hannibalic Wars. Italic fortifications were mostly massive but simple constructions, which took no account of the developments in artillery that were transforming warfare in this period. There were, however, some exceptions: for example, the inhabitants of Pomarico Vecchio (104) in the late fourth century built walls with projecting towers on the Greek model, controlling postern gates.

The construction of such vast settlement defences required a highly organized labour force and political direction. In Lucania this was supplied by *meddikes*, who were probably elected annually from the leading families of the community to carry out public policy. One *meddix*, Mais Arries, recorded the construction of walls under his magistracy in an Oscan inscription at Raia S. Basile (105), while another, Nummelos (106), recorded the construction of walls under his rule at Serra di Vaglio. His name is Oscan, but he used the Greek language, addressing a public of Greeks or Hellenized Lucanians.

Within their walls many Apulian and Lucanian communities restructured the fabric of their cities in the fourth and third centuries. Sometimes, as at Laus or Pomarico Vecchio (104), a new start was made and the roads and housing blocks were laid out on Greek principles with a broad main street, the *plateia*, intersected at right angles by narrower *stenopoi*. The oblong blocks created by the streets were subdivided into smaller lots for houses. Such schemes suggest that there was a citizen body able to share the advantages of membership of the community on more-or-less egalitarian principles, whatever its relationship with the ruling elites. Elsewhere, as at Roccagloriosa (107), there are indications of greater social differentiation, with houses of varying size arranged in groups according to Greek principles, but without the overall cohesion of a Greek city plan.

Among the Oscan-speaking Lucanians (but less so among the Apulians) the house was also a focus of religious cult. The deity worshipped was usually female, if we may judge by the votive offerings of terracotta figurines of an enthroned goddess, and can probably be identified with Mefitis, the chief female divinity of the Oscan-speaking peoples, who was honoured with such votives in the great Lucanian sanctuary of Macchia di Rossano (108). In the small farm at Montegiordano (112) the focus of the cult was in the main work-room of the house, which was probably the women's quarters. At Roccagloriosa (107) the rituals were carried out in the courtyard, and may have involved a wider community than the immediate household, at least in the case of the largest house, which must have belonged to one of the leading members of the community. At Pomarico Vecchio (104) there was a separate cult building with a courtyard for sacrificial rituals, and a room adjacent to it for feasting. There were also shrines associated with springs outside the city walls, or located at territorial boundaries. The pre-eminent example is the sanctuary at Macchia di Rossano near the Apennine watershed, which appears to have been a cantonal centre for a sub-group of the Lucanians called the Utiani. It had a great double-altar in the centre of a courtyard, flanked by treasuries and other cult buildings.

Several field surveys, such as that in the Basentello valley (110) or in the Messapic settlement at Muro Tenente (111) show that the number and size of settlements expanded markedly in the territories of the Italic peoples in the fourth century, just as it did among the Italiote Greeks. To feed the growing population, small farms, modelled on Greek prototypes, were founded in the open countryside, always within easy range of a walled site where refuge could be found if necessary. The farm houses were simple structures in which domestic and agricultural functions were organized around a single courtyard. Some, like the farm at Montegiordano (112), were equipped with wine-presses and produced an exportable surplus of wine. It was transported in MGS amphorae (94), which began to be produced on some 'native' Italic sites (including Montegiordano) from the middle of the fourth century onwards and which are practically indistinguishable from amphorae of the same type produced in the Greek city-states.

In the last half of the fourth century BC the larger Italic communities were evolving into city-states in which civic institutions replaced kinship groups as the principal form of social and political organization. An effective symbol of this was coinage. In the late fourth and third centuries, numerous Italic cities in southern Italy minted their own coins in bronze or silver, especially in Apulia. They bore legends or symbols to identify the city, and frequently the name of the chief magistrate under whom they were minted. Two examples are illustrated here, both of the late fourth or early third century BC. One is a bronze coin of Laus (91c) stamped with the name of one of the city's *meddikes*; the other a silver coin of Arpi with the name Dazos (91d). Since the same name is also found on coins of Salapia and Ruvo, it is possible that he controlled some form of league between the three cities. Some cities coined only rarely and in small quantities to meet particular emergencies. In the war with Hannibal, both his Lucanian and Bruttian (91e) allies (but not the Apulians) issued a common coinage.

Most communities which minted coins before the Hannibalic War did so under Roman hegemony as more or less willing allies of the Roman Senate and people. The instruments of Roman control, the Latin colonies and roads (88), were developed in the Latin and Samnite Wars. The earliest of the colonies in the south, at Luceria and Venusia (113), lie under modern cities, and the grid plan of *decumani* and *cardines* of the original foundations can only be reconstructed in part; but both cities had ample space within their walls to shelter refugees from the countryside in an emergency. The arable land surrounding the colonies was centuriated and divided into small lots for the colonists: traces of the earliest centuriation at Luceria, contemporary with the foundation of the colony in 314 BC, are clearly visible on early aerial photographs (114). The first Roman road across southern Italy, the Via Appia, linked the Latin colonies of Beneventum, Venusia and Brundisium. It was built primarily for military reasons, and to give access to the eastern Mediterranean through the port at Brundisium, but it brought economic benefits to the interior. In the Basentello valley, in the second century BC, settlement survived best in the vicinity of the road (110).

In general the first episodes of Roman hegemony were not immediately harmful to the economy and culture of the new, largely forced, allies. A few communities, however, like Silvium (110), which had stood siege in the Samnite or Pyrrhic Wars and had been punished in the aftermath, never regained their previous prosperity. Yet Tarentum (117) survived defeat in the Pyrrhic War, and continued to produce gold and silver work of marvellous quality (115) down to the end of the third century BC.

The consequences of the Hannibalic War were much more drastic, though far from uniform. Some cities, including Herdonea (Ordona) (116), are known to have been destroyed in the war. Many more seem from archaeological evidence to have been abandoned around the end of the third century, and may have been destroyed either by the Romans or the Carthaginians. They include Laus (91c), Silvium (110) and Pomarico Vecchio (104). Generally, the fate of communities was determined by their behaviour in the war. Most of those which had supported Hannibal were allowed to continue, but forfeited large parts of their territories to the Roman people. With the economic base of the community destroyed and part of the population no doubt enslaved, the city was often doomed to decline. This must be the case with Muro Tenente (111) and Monte Sannace (103), where a marked reduction in the inhabited area indicates a drastic fall in the population. Tarentum (117), which had been captured by Hannibal and then sacked by the Romans, also shrank, and part of the city was left abandoned until the foundation of the Gracchan colony. Metapontum, which had sided voluntarily with Hannibal, appears to have been abolished as a city-state and declined drastically in the second century. Its rural population was greatly reduced, but part of the arable land continued to be cultivated from a much smaller number of farms (118). Heraclea, Rome's earliest ally among the Greek cities, had also sided with Hannibal, but under duress, and was treated more leniently. The city continued to develop down to the time of the Principate (119). The few cities which had remained constant to Rome throughout the war fared much better, especially Daunian Canusium, which had taken in the Roman fugitives after the battle of Cannae. The city flourished after the war was over, as the rich grave goods of members of a princely family interred in the Tomba degli Ori show (115). It maintained trading contacts with the Greek East, and probably attracted Greek artisans from Tarentum. Some may have worked on a magnificent new temple built in a cosmopolitan Hellenistic style incorporating elements from all three orders of Greek architecture (109).

The scale of population displacement and economic disruption involved in this process is gradually being revealed by archaeological field surveys. A key factor in the analysis is the presence or absence of grey-glaze pottery (120) which came into vogue in Apulia in the second quarter of the second century BC. It was produced in many of the larger settlements and practically replaced other forms of table ware in sites within easy range of the production centres, so that in much of south-east Italy it provides an easy means of identifying sites of the Late Hellenistic period. In the Basentello valley (110) the distribution pattern of this pottery, compared with that of black glaze of the preceding period, reveals a drastic reduction in the number and location of occupied sites, which must imply that large areas which had once been arable were given over to forest or rough grazing for transhumant sheep. Other field surveys confirm that over much of southern Italy the number of inhabited sites fell markedly, and nucleated settlements shrank in size. All of this points to a demographic collapse which finds an echo in the literary tradition of the decline in Italian manpower in the period before the Gracchan reforms.

The new landlords of the post-Hannibalic era, whether they were Romans, Campanians or local grandees who supported the Roman regime, were able to profit from these changes by developing estates for the production of cash crops for export by sea. New and larger types of amphora were produced to contain the oil and wine, such as the so-called Brindisine amphorae (121), which appear first in contexts of the second quarter of the second century. They were made in various centres in the vicinity of Brundisium and were mainly used to transport the oil produced in the Salentine peninsula. They were followed later in the century by Lamboglia 2s on the Adriatic coast, and Dressel 1s on the Tyrrhenian (*CAH* VIII^2 497–8).

Demographic decline and economic change contributed to a loss of cultural identity among the southern Italian peoples. One aspect of this is the decay of many of the religious cults which had sustained the cultural life of the Italiote Greeks. The process was aggravated by the policies of the Roman state and the wilful behaviour of some of its magistrates. The decree of the Senate abolishing Bacchic rituals (186 BC) outlawed a cult which had been immensely popular. In 173 BC the censor Q. Fulvius Flaccus stripped the marble tiles from the ancient sanctuary of Hera on the Lacinian promontory (122) to roof his new temple of Fortuna Equestris in Rome. The Senate intervened and voted unanimously to perform expiatory rituals and restore the tiles, but no skilled artisans could be found to replace them.

Another aspect of change was the deliberate adoption of a Roman lifestyle and Roman cultural symbols, exemplified by the atrium house built at Civitá di Tricarico in this period (123), or the temples of Romano-Campanian type erected there and at Herdonea (116). Rome was now the main source of cultural innovation, as well as the distant focus of political and economic life.

GENERAL BIBLIOGRAPHY

The best bibliographical resource for the archaeology and history of southern Italy in the period of the Greek city-states is the *Bibliografia topografica della colonizzazione greca in Italia*, begun in 1977. Several volumes list works of a general character; others deal with sites throughout Italy and Sicily.

Also indispensable are the *Atti del Convegno di Studi sulla Magna Grecia*. In addition to the thematic studies, the *Atti* include the summary reports of excavations presented each year by the archaeological superintendencies.

A major exhibition series on the theme of *The Greeks in the West* (*I Greci in Occidente*) was organized in 1996 by the Ministero per i Beni Culturali e Ambientali, which issued six interpretative catalogues in conjunction with the exhibitions. The primary one is *The Western Greeks: Classical Civilisation in the Western Mediterranean* (ed. G. Pugliese Carratelli); others are *Arte e artigianato in Magna Grecia* (ed. E. Lippolis); *Greci, Enotri e Lucani nella Basilicata meridionale* (ed. S. Bianco *et al.*); *La Magna Grecia nelle collezioni del Museo Archeologico di Napoli* (ed. S. Cassani); *Poseidonia e i Lucani* (ed. M. Cipriani and F. Longo); and *Santuari della Magna Grecia in Calabria* (ed. E. Lattanzi *et al.*). The exhibitions were intended to illustrate aspects of the culture of Magna Graecia which are documented primarily by archaeological discoveries, and especially the cultural synthesis which resulted from the interaction of Greeks and natives.

Two regional histories contain important sections relevant to this period, namely S. Settis (ed.), *Storia della Calabria antica* II: *Età italica e romana* (Rome, 1994) and D. Adamesteanu (ed.), *Storia della Basilicata* I: *L'antichità* (Rome and Bari, 1999).

Several volumes focus on the native Italic peoples and their interaction with the Greeks. M. Tagliente (ed.), *Italici in Magna Grecia: Lingua, insediamenti e strutture* (Venosa, 1990) contains a number of detailed studies of Italic communities in various parts of southern Italy. Other books deal with different tribal groups. The Lucanians have a large role in two of the volumes of *I Greci in Occidente* cited above and are the subject of a number of studies by A. Pontrandolfo Greco, whose book *I Lucani: Etnografia e archeologia di una regione antica* (Milan, 1982) remains the standard introduction. Also noteworthy are H.W. Horsnaes, *The Cultural Development in NW Lucania c. 600–273 BC* (Analecta Romana Instituti Danici, Copenhagen, 2002) and E. Isayev, *Inside Ancient Lucania: Dialogues in History and Archaeology* (*Bulletin of the Institute of Classical Studies* Supplement 10, London, 2007). Two volumes entitled *I Brettii* contain papers by various authors which deal with aspects of Bruttian culture: see *Tomo* I: *Cultura, lingua e documentazione storico-archeologica* edited by G. De Sensi

Sestito, and *Tomo II: Fonti letterarie ed epigrafiche*, edited by M. Intrieri and A. Zumbo, with indices and bibliography (Soveria Mannelli, 1995).

Within Apulia, the Messapians have been particularly intensively studied. *I Messapi* provide the theme of the thirtieth volume of the *Atti del Convegno di Studi sulla Magna Grecia* (1990), and they are the subject of several books, including F. D'Andria (ed.), *Archeologia dei Messapi* (Bari, 1990), in which a wide range of material is published for the first time, and J.-L. Lamboley, *Recherches sur les messapiens, IVe–IIe siècles avant J.-C.* (Paris, 1996), which contains a comprehensive catalogue and discussion of Messapian sites with full bibliography.

E. M. De Juliis gives an overview of the development of Peucetian pottery in *La ceramica geometrica della Peucezia* (Rome, 1995), but no recent monograph deals with broader aspects of Peucetian culture in the pre-Roman period, although there have been several studies of individual Peucetian settlements such as Monte Sannace (103) and Botromagno near Gravina (110). Neither is there a recent monograph (since the publication of *CAH* VII.II^2 and VIII^2) that deals comprehensively with the Daunians, though in their case too there have been numerous detailed studies, for example of Canosa (97, 109, 115), Ordona (116) and Arpi (91d). These make it clear that the Daunian culture was locally focused on large settlements, and that the differences between them became increasingly pronounced.

Numerous recent studies deal with the impact of Roman conquest on the Italic peoples of southern Italy. Particularly notable among these is G. Volpe, *La Daunia nell'età della romanizzazione* (Bari, 1990); also useful are L. de Lachenal (ed.), *Da Leukania a Lucania: La Lucania centro-orientale fra Pirro ed i Giulio-Claudii* (Rome, 1993); M. Salvatore (ed.), *Basilicata: L'espansionismo romano nel sud-est d'Italia. Il quadro archeologico* (Venosa, 1997); and J. Mertens and R. Lambrechts (eds.), *Comunità indigene e problemi della romanizzazione nell'Italia centro-meridionale (IV°–III° sec. av.C.)* (Brussels and Rome, 1991), which ranges rather more widely, but includes several papers on the progress of Romanization in Apulia and Lucania.

The impact of Rome on the Greek communities is studied by K. Lomas in *Rome and the Western Greeks 350 BC–AD 200: Conquest and Acculturation in Southern Italy* (London and New York, 1993). In *Fra Taranto e Roma: Società e cultura urbana in Puglia tra Annibale e l'età imperiale* (Taranto, 1997), E. Lippolis discusses the effects of Roman conquest on the economic development of Tarentum and Apulia in general, and notes that it brought considerable benefits in some areas.

Important work has been done recently on the typology and chronology of artefacts of the Hellenistic period in southern Italy. The study of tomb groups from Tarentum, many of which contained datable coins, has led to some significant revisions. These can be found in E. Lippolis (ed.), *Catalogo del Museo Nazionale di Taranto, III.1: Taranto, La necropoli: Aspetti e problemi della documentazione archeologica tra VII e I sec. a.C.* (Taranto, 1994), and in K. G. Hempel, *Die Nekropole von Tarent im 2. und 1. Jahrhundert v. Chr. Studien zur materiellen Kultur / La necropoli di Taranto nel II e I sec. a.C.: Studi sulla cultura materiale* (Taranto, 2001).

D. Yntema, *South-East Italy in the First Millennium* BC, completed but not yet in press at the time of writing, should shortly make much recent scholarship available in English.

88. Map of southern Italy *c.* 400–133 BC, showing places mentioned in the text.

89. Herm-portrait in white marble of Archidamus III, king of Sparta, from the Great Peristyle of the Villa of the Papyri at Herculaneum, copied from an original of the late fourth century BC. The portrait is identified by the name ΑΡΧΙΔΑ[μος, which was painted below the right shoulder strap of his cuirass. His military role is emphasized by the cuirass and sword belt, and his kingship by a narrow diadem high on his head.

Archidamus was the first of the mercenary generals called on by the Tarentines to campaign against the Italic peoples in their hinterland. He arrived in Tarentum in 343 or 342 BC and died in battle in 338 BC. According to Diodorus (XVI.62–3) he was campaigning against the Lucanians, but his Italian wars have probably been confused with those of Alexander of Epirus, and an alternative tradition transmitted by Plutarch (*Agis* 3.2), in which he died fighting against the Messapians, is to be preferred.

(Museo Nazionale di Napoli, inv. 6156. Archivio Fotografico Pedicini MN 416. Height 55 cm; height of head 32 cm)

A. Gramiccia and F. Pagnotta, *Le collezioni del Museo Nazionale di Napoli: La scultura greco-romana I: Le sculture antiche della collezione farnese, le collezioni monetali, le oreficerie, la collezione glittica* (Rome, 1989) 124–5 no. 143; M. R. Wojcik, *La Villa dei Papiri ad Ercolano: Contributo alla ricostruzione dell'ideologia della nobilitas* (Rome, 1986) 61–2 no. B8, pl. XXXVII.

90. Herm-portrait of Pyrrhus in white marble from the Great Peristyle of the Villa of the Papyri at Herculaneum, copied from an original of the early third century BC. He is shown wearing a helmet of Macedonian type, garlanded with an oak-wreath, alluding to the sacred tree of the oracle of Zeus at Dodona in Epirus, his homeland. A royal diadem emerges below the helmet at the back of his head. His stern expression matches Plutarch's description of his frightening face (*Pyrrhus* 3.4).

Pyrrhus campaigned on behalf of the Tarentines against the Romans, winning inconclusive victories at Heraclea in 280 and Ausculum in 279 BC, but he was defeated at Beneventum in 275 BC and withdrew to Epirus, leaving Tarentum to be captured by the Romans in 272 BC.

88

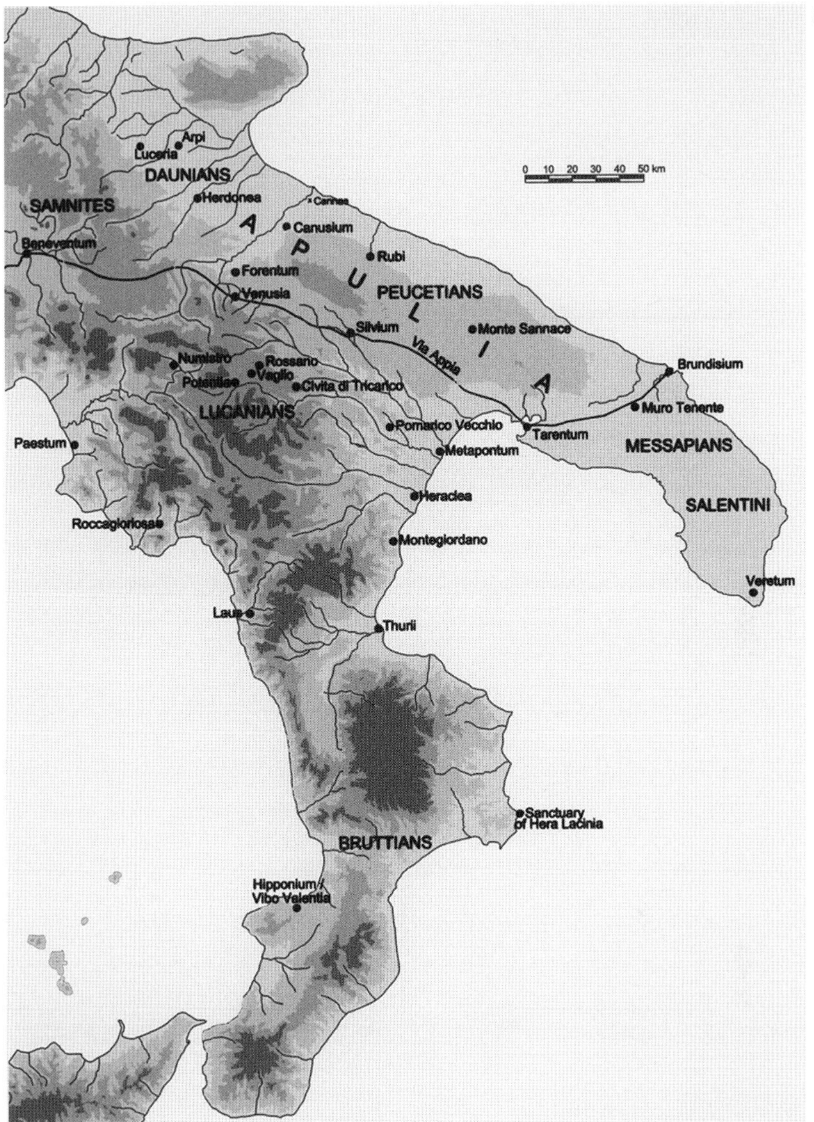

(Museo Nazionale di Napoli, inv. 6150; photo courtesy of Mario Adda Editore. Height 46 cm; height of head 24.5 cm)

Gramiccia and Pagnotta *Le Collezioni del Museo Nazionale di Napoli* 124–5 no. 141; Wojcik *La Villa dei Papiri* 61–2 no. B10, pl. XXXIX.

91. Coinage.

a Reverse of gold stater of Tarentum, 334–332 BC, showing Taras, the eponymous hero of the city, as a boy, raising his hands in supplication to Poseidon; a star; four letters of uncertain significance; and the legend 'Of the Tarentines'. This issue of gold coins was one of several minted to pay for the campaigns of Alexander of Molossus.

(*HN*[2] no. 901)

b Reverse of a silver nomos of Tarentum, showing a young hero (Taras or a local hero, Phalanthus) riding a dolphin and holding bow and arrow; below him the letters Δ I, probably the beginning of the name of the senior magistrate of the year. The small elephant alludes to the use of these animals by Pyrrhus in the war of 280–272 BC, when war-elephants were seen for the first time in Italy. The coin was minted on a reduced-weight

89

90

91a 91b 91c

91d 91e

standard (6.6 g down from 7.9 g) introduced by the Tarentines during the war.

(*HN*[2] no. 999)

c Reverse of a bronze coin of the Lucanian city Laus, datable to the second half of the fourth century BC, showing a bird and the legend ΣΤΑ ΟΨΙ. The Greek letters are abbreviated forms of the Oscan name latinized as Statius Opsius. They indicate the magistrate under whom the coins were minted, possibly the same *meddix* who is consigned to the Underworld in the lead curse-tablet found in the chamber tomb at Laus (**99**).

The city of Laus was refounded on an orthogonal plan around the middle of the fourth century and was abandoned around the end of the third century, probably in the Hannibalic War.

(*HN*[2] no. 2306. Weight 1.77 g; diameter 12 mm)
R. Cantilena, in E. Greco, S. Luppino and A. Schnapp, *Laos I: Scavi a Marcellina 1973–1985* (Taranto, 1989) 25–37.

d Reverse of a silver coin (didrachm) of the Daunian city Arpi, late fourth or early third century BC, showing a horse prancing, a star with eight rays and the legend ΔΑΖΟΥ – 'of Dazos', the magistrate under whom the coin was minted. The name of the community – ΑΡΠΑΝΩΝ – 'of the people of Arpi' – is given on the other side. Dazos was probably an ancestor of the man called by Appian Dasios, who claimed to be descended from Diomedes, and who persuaded the people of Arpi to defect to Hannibal after the battle of Cannae and then tried unsuccessfully to re-ingratiate himself with the Romans (Appian, *Hannibalic War* 7.31).

(*HN*[2] no. 633)
M. Mazzei, *Arpi: L'ipogeo della Medusa e la necropoli* (Bari, 1995).

e Reverse of a bronze coin minted by the Bruttian League *c.* 211–208 BC during the Second Punic War, showing Athena moving to the right with spear over her shoulder and grasping her shield with both hands; a racing torch; and the legend ΒΡΕΤΤΙΩΝ – 'of the Bruttii'.

(Weight *c.* 17.4 g; diameter 25 mm)
HN[2] no. 1987.

92. The walls of the Greek city of Hipponium provide an outstanding illustration of the development of fortification between the classical and Hellenistic periods. The city controlled an important natural harbour on the Gulf of S. Eufemia, easily accessible from Sicily. In the fourth and third centuries it came under attack from the Bruttii in the interior and from the Syracusans, who used the city as a springboard for the invasion of southern Italy. Dionysius I sacked the city in his Italian campaign of 388 BC, and the Bruttii appear to have captured it around the middle of the fourth century. They were driven out by Agathocles, who took the city by storm with the use of catapults, but they recovered it again after Agathocles had returned to Sicily. The territory of the city was ravaged by the Carthaginians in 218 BC, but nothing else is heard of it during the Second Punic War. It must, however, have suffered at the hands of one or other of the combatants, because it was refounded by the Romans in 192 BC as a Latin colony with the name of Valentia, which was subsequently given the prefix Vibo, the Oscan equivalent of Hipponium.

The city was defended by steep slopes on most sides, but needed a strong land wall to prevent attack across relatively level ground to the north. Five main phases of fortification have been distinguished in this area. The late archaic walls of Phase 1, which had no towers, have left few visible traces. The wall of Phase 2 was a curtain wall with occasional rectangular towers projecting inwards which served as observation platforms but offered little possibility for counter-attack. It can be dated to the fifth century. It was probably damaged in the siege by Dionysius, but was repaired and strengthened with additional towers in Phase 3 (fourth century), only to be destroyed again, most probably by Agathocles,

92

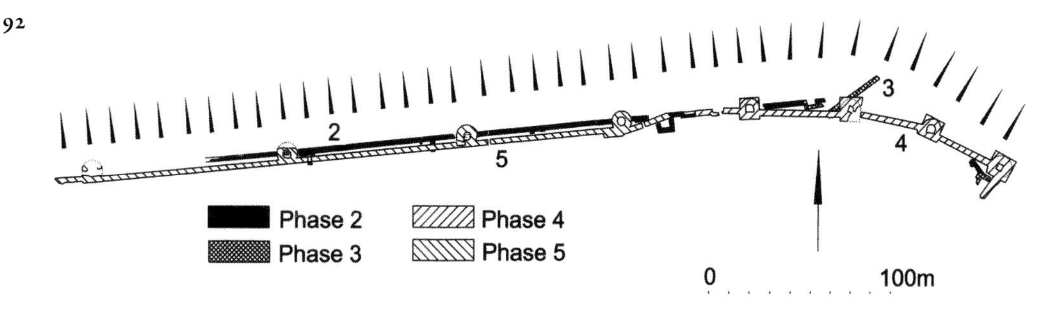

who may have built the massive new wall of Phase 4 (late fourth or early third century). It had round towers, designed to house artillery, built on square bases and projecting forward from the curtain wall. The wall of Phase 5 must have followed soon afterwards, perhaps in a later phase of the same building programme. Its towers project still further from the wall face. Several towers control sally ports through which the defenders could launch surprise assaults on an enemy attempting to attack the wall.

(Adapted from Aumüller 1994: fig. 6)

G. Säflund, *Opuscula Archeologica* 1/2 (1935) 87–119; T. Aumüller, *MDAIR* 101 (1994) 241–78.

93. The beginning of the first Heraclea Tablet. The two bronze plaques known as the Heraclea Tablets were found in 1732 in the river Cavone near the northern boundary of the territory of Heraclea. They have long inscriptions in Doric (the dialect of Heraclea) recording measures taken by the city to recover lands belonging to the temples of Dionysus (Tablet 1) and Athena (Tablet 2) that had been illegally occupied by private individuals. They are generally dated to a period shortly after the wars of Alexander of Molossus or of Pyrrhus on the assumption that the abuses took place in time of war, but there is no evidence to confirm either date. The tablets provide a wealth of information on the organization and land use of the countryside at a time when the city's institutions were in full vigour, especially Tablet 1, which is practically complete. The temple of Dionysus owned 3,320 *schoinoi* (approximately 350 ha) of land on either side of the road to Pandosia west of the city. A little more than one-third was arable, the rest being scrub and oak forest. A commission of five *horistai*, set up by decree of the city's assembly, surveyed the land, set up new boundary stones to mark the individual lots and started proceedings against illegal occupants. The land recovered was leased out in heritable life rents which brought in 300 *medimnoi* (nearly 16 kilolitres) of barley per annum into the granaries of the city-state. The new tenants were required to plant vines and olives where the land was suitable, and to replace old vines with new.

The Tablets were reused after the Social War, when a draft of a Roman municipal law was inscribed on the reverse.

(Museo Nazionale di Napoli, inv. 2480. Fotografia della Soprintendenza Archeologica della Provincia di Napoli e Caserta – Napoli neg. C700. Height 1.81 m; width 0.39 m)

A. Uguzzoni and F. Ghinatti, *Le tavole greche di Eraclea* (Rome, 1968); F. Sartori, in B. Neutsch (ed.), *Herakleiastudien* (*MDAIR* Ergänzungsheft XI, Heidelberg, 1967) 16–95.

94. Amphorae of types MGS I–VI were produced in Magna Graecia and Sicily between the mid fifth and mid second centuries BC. They were used to transport wine to increasingly distant markets, mainly by sea. The earliest, of type MGS I, were made in the second half of the fifth century at several centres on the Gulf of Taranto and on the Tyrrhenian coast of (modern) Calabria. Type MGS II was produced in the late fifth and fourth centuries in various Greek cities on the Italian coast between Naples and Heraclea, and in Sicily. Types MGS III–V date mainly to the fourth century. They were made at first in the territories of the Greek cities, but after the middle of the century they were also produced on some Italic (Lucanian and Bruttian) sites. Type MGS VI (Greco-Italic), which develops from Type MGS V, is the typical amphora type of the third century, lasting in some places into the second century BC. It was made in various production centres on the Tyrrhenian coast from Cosa southwards, and in southern Italy and Sicily. Some amphorae of Types III–VI were stamped with the potter's name, and the analysis of the stamps helps to determine centres of production and patterns of trade. They show that MGS VI amphorae were widely distributed, being found in considerable numbers along the Italian coast from Apulia to Elba, in Sicily, and in north Africa from Carthage to Cyrenaica. A few examples reached the south coast of France, the east coast of Spain, the Aegean and Alexandria.

(After Vandermersch 1994: 63, 66, 70, 74, 77, 82)

C. Vandermersch, *Vins et amphores de Grande Grèce et de Sicile, IVe–IIIe s. avant J.-C.* (Études, Centre Jean Bèrard 1, Naples, 1994).

95. Attic red-figure volute-*krater*, the name-vase of the Talos painter, probably found in a tomb at Ruvo (Roman Rubi). The main scene shows the Cretan bronze giant Talos (in white), who had opposed the landing of the Argonauts on his island, beginning to collapse, drained of his blood by the spell cast upon him by Medea (shown on the left). The Dioscuri grasp him. On the far right a female figure, Europa or Crete, runs away in alarm. Above her, Poseidon, and Amphitrite contemplate the scene. In the neck zone there is a Dionysiac procession. End of the fifth century BC.

The volute-*krater* is one of many fine Attic vases imported into central Apulia in the late fifth and

93

94

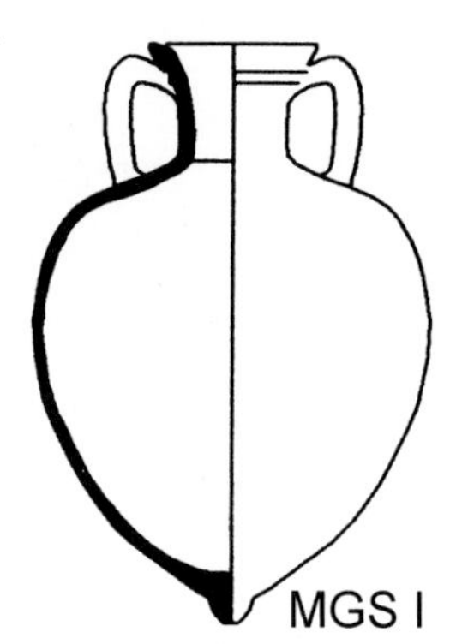

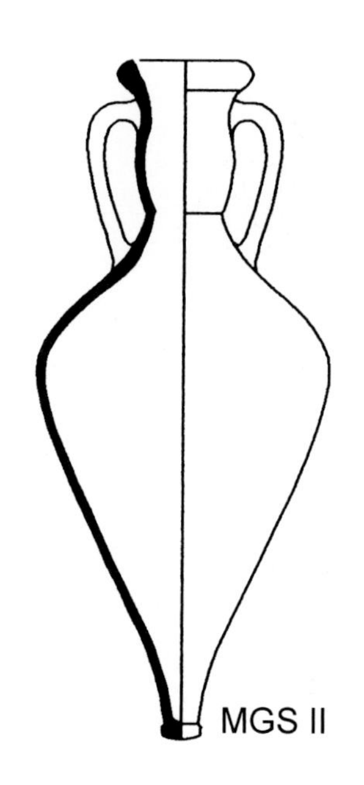

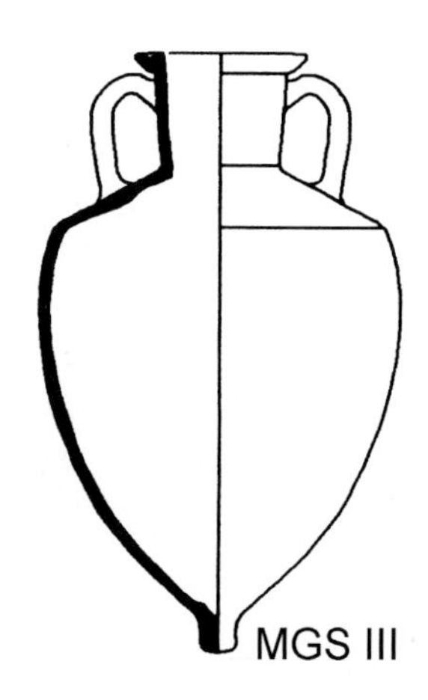

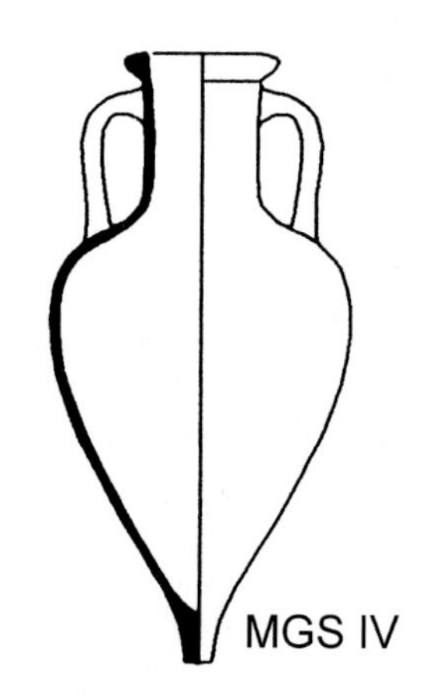

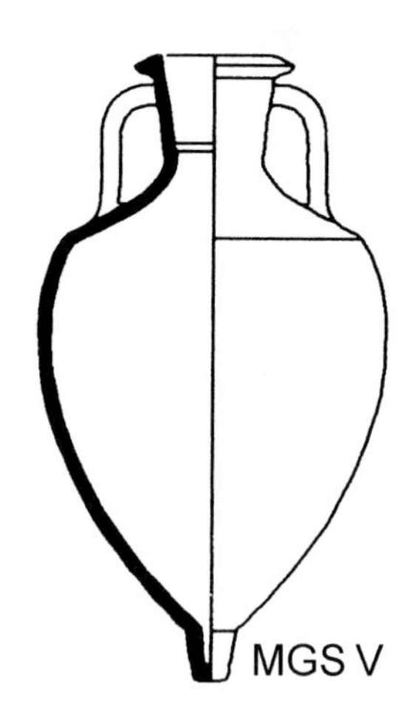

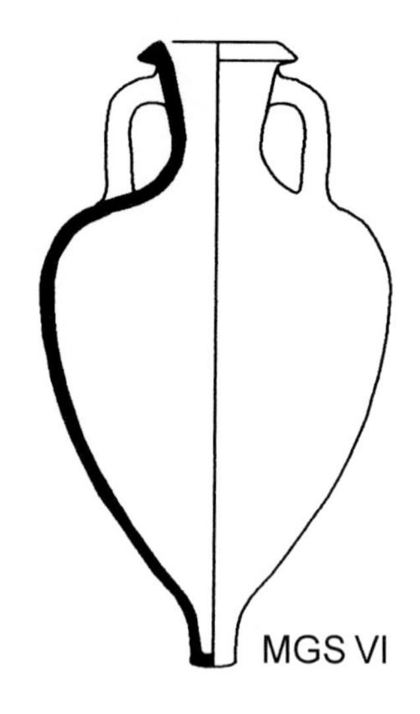

early fourth centuries to meet the demands of the Italic elites. They were highly valued. Another vase by the same painter has been found in a dump of waste material associated with a public building at the great Lucanian site at Serra di Vaglio. It was restored in antiquity and was kept for a hundred years before being broken and discarded around the end of the fourth century BC.

The concentration of Attic vases of the last half of the fifth and beginning of the fourth century BC in central Apulian sites such as Botromagno, Ceglie, Monte Sannace, Rutigliano and especially Ruvo suggests that there were direct commercial connections between Athens and these Apulian settlements. Since much of Apulia is well suited for cereal production, it is probable that the Athenians were interested in this area primarily as a source of grain.

(Museo Nazionale Jatta di Ruvo, inv. 1501; photo H. Koppermann, DAIR neg. 64.1045. Height 75 cm)

ARV^2 1338, Talos Painter no. 1.

H. Sichtermann, *Griechische Vasen in Unteritalien* (Tübingen, 1966) 23–4 no. 14 and pl. 1, 24–34; K. Mannino, *Ostraca: Rivista di antichità* 6.2 (1997) 389–99. A. Ciancio, in R. Cassano (ed.), *Andar per mare: Puglia e Mediterraneo tra mito e storia* (Bari, 1998) 62–86; G. Greco, *Rivista dell'Istituto Nazionale di Archeologia e Storia dell'Arte* ser. 3, 8–9 (1985–6) 5–35; K. Mannino and D. Roubis, in B. Sabbatini (ed.), *La céramique attique du IVe siècle en Méditerranée Occidentale* (Naples, 2000) 67–76.

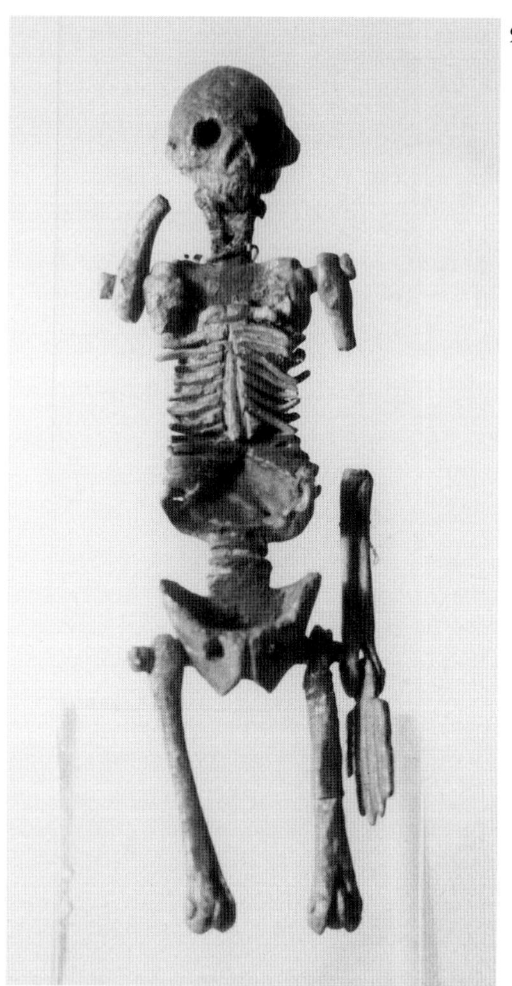

96

96. Bronze skeleton (*larva*) from a Messapian tomb of the third quarter of the second century BC excavated at Patù (Roman Veretum) near the south end of the Salentine peninsula. It was found with a black-glaze lamp, several plain-ware vases, four unguentaria for perfumed oil and an amphora of Brindisine type. The *larva* is the earliest datable example of a motif commonly associated with popular Epicureanism which invited the banqueter to eat, drink and be merry before death intervenes. Its use in a funerary context transfers the idea of the banquet or symposium to the after-life.

(Museo Provinciale Castromediano di Lecce, inv. 5159. Length 10.7 cm)

G. Delli Ponti, in C. Marangio and A. Nitti (eds.), *Scritti vari di antichità in onore di Benita Sciarra Bardaro* (Fasano, 1994) 47–52; K. M. D. Dunbabin, *JDAI* 101 (1986) 185–255.

97

97. Celtic helmet from the Scocchera hypogeum A in Canosa (Roman Canusium). The helmet has an inner cap of iron, clad externally with an upper cap and a broad lower band of bronze which is decorated in repoussé with complex scroll patterns typical of La Tène B1. The gaps between the scrolls are inlaid with coral, and an exposed band of iron between the two bronze parts was perhaps covered with gold leaf. Two vertical bronze tubes originally held plumes. The moveable cheek pieces present at the time of discovery are missing.

A drawing made soon after the excavation of the hypogeum in 1895 shows three skeletons lying side by side. The helmet was set beside the central burial, which was also provided with a bronze anatomical cuirass and four javelins or spears. Two horse bits indicate that the individual was a mounted warrior. The burial can be dated by red-figure vases to the last quarter of the fourth century BC.

The helmet was perhaps a trophy won from a Gaul in one of the numerous Celtic incursions into Italy in the fourth century, such as that recorded by Livy (VII.26.9) under 348 BC when the Gauls, defeated by the Romans in the Pomptine plain, crossed into Apulia.

(Antikensammlung, Staatliche Museen zu Berlin – Preussischer Kulturbesitz (L.80); photo Ingrid Geske/bpk. Height 25 cm; max. diameter 23.3 cm)

E. M. De Juliis, in R. Cassano (ed.), *Principi imperatori vescovi: Duemila anni di storia a Canosa* (Venice, 1992) 225–30 and 549; R. and V. Megaw, *Celtic Art from its Beginning to the Book of Kells* (London, 1989) 111.

98. Wall painting of the middle of the fourth century BC from the Vannullo cemetery at Paestum, Tomb 4, west wall, showing a Lucanian cavalry warrior returning from battle to be greeted by his wife. He wears a plumed helmet, a cuirass of three discs and a broad Italic belt over a white tunic with red border. He probably also had greaves, but the damage in this part of the painting leaves this uncertain. He carries a spear over his left shoulder, from which are slung his shield and a second belt, presumably captured from a defeated enemy. The warrior holds the horse's reins loosely in his right hand and looks fixedly at the woman, who wears a veil fringed with purple (held in place by a headband ornamented with beads), a long white dress with purple stripe down the front, and black sandals. She extends her right arm to pour a libation from a *skyphos* in thanksgiving for his return – or as an offering to his departed spirit.

(Museo Nazionale Archeologico di Paestum, inv. 31737. Height of figured panel *c.* 46 cm)

A. Pontrandolfo and A. Rouveret, *Le tombe dipinte di Paestum* (Modena, 1992) 286–7, 396–7.

99. Armour of a Lucanian cavalryman buried at Laus. Italic aristocrats in the fourth century BC were frequently buried with grave goods which

98

99a

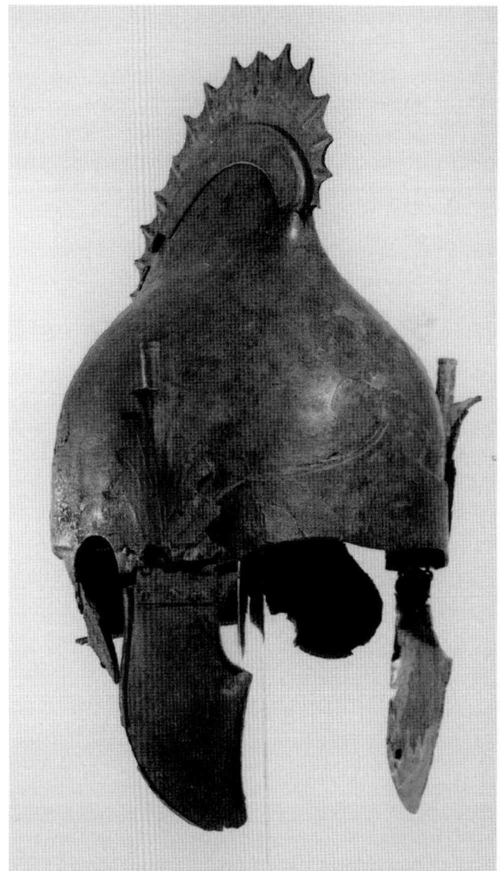

attested to their prowess as cavalrymen, their wealth and their absorption of Hellenic culture. A chamber tomb excavated at Laus in 1963 provides a spectacular example. The warrior was buried with his horse and a lavish array of grave goods: spear and javelin, bronze helmet (**a**), ornamental cuirass (**b**), greaves (**c**), fragments of at least three belts (some of them perhaps trophies and including one (**d**) decorated with silver figurines in relief), a gold wreath, a bronze spur, a strigil, numerous vases (including many with red-figure decoration), several terracotta figures and various other objects. Several iron spits had probably been used in the funeral feast. Some of the grave goods may have been deposited with a woman who was also buried in the tomb. Both burials can be dated to *c.* 330 BC and are therefore roughly contemporary with the refoundation of the city of Laus on an orthogonal plan inspired by Greek models.

A lead curse-tablet was also found in the tomb, inscribed on both sides with an Oscan text in Greek letters. It gives the names of thirteen individuals to be consigned by magical power to the Underworld. Four of them are identified as magistrates (*meddikes*). They include (in the Oscan accusative case) Statin Opsion (Statius Opsius),

99b

99c

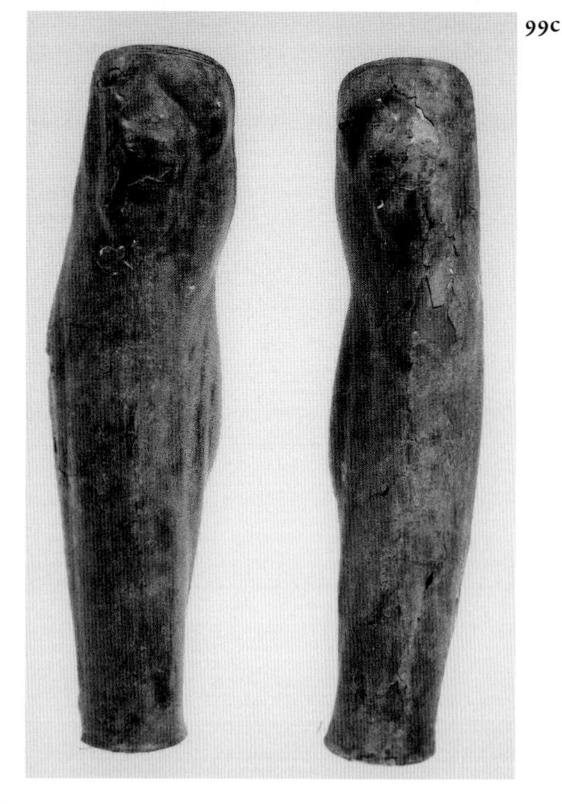

99d

a name which recurs on coins of Laus of approximately the same period (**91c**). Such lead tablets are likely to have been deposited surreptitiously in tombs by someone who wished to use the power of the dead person to put a curse on an enemy.

(Museo Nazionale di Reggio Calabria, inv. 11803–11808)

E. Greco and P. G. Guzzo (eds.), *Laos II: La tomba a camera di Marcellina* (Taranto, 1992); G. Pugliese Carratelli, in Greco and Guzzo (eds.), *Laos I: Scavi a Marcellina 1973–1985* (Taranto, 1989) 17–19.

100. Tomb group of the last quarter of the fourth century BC from the Urban necropolis at Metapontum, containing a bronze belt of Italic type, three iron spear heads, an iron javelin head, four strigils, several other metal objects and three black-glaze pots.

Since weapons and armour were not normally deposited in Greek tombs of this period, and since the bronze belt is the characteristic item of dress of an Italic warrior, the individual buried in this tomb was in all probability Italic. The fact that he was buried in Metapontum suggests that he was employed by the Metapontines as a mercenary.

A. Bottini, (ed.), *Armi: Gli strumenti della guerra in Lucania* (Bari, 1994) 181–6.

100

101

101. Painting from the north wall of Tomb 114 in the Andriuolo necropolis at Paestum, *c.* 330–320 BC. Two rows of warriors with large round shields and several different types of helmet face each other across the battle line, holding long spears at the ready. A herd of cattle, half hidden by a mountain, suggests the booty that is at stake. In the middle, a warrior, naked except for his plumed helmet and small round shield, has advanced from the battle line on the right and is about to hurl a javelin at the line on the left, using a throwing strap wrapped around the wrist and index finger of his right hand. The warrior's helmet marks him as Lucanian, but the mode of fighting recalls that of the twenty elite young men, armed only with spears and heavy javelins, who fought in advance of the main lines of the maniples according to Livy's account of the organization of the Roman legion in 340 BC (VIII.8.3–14). The painting suggests that the best and most agile young Lucanian warriors had a similar heroic role.

The javelin has a thin iron shank which extends as far as the warrior's thumb and an iron *sauroter* (rather than feathers) to balance it at the butt end. It is therefore an early version of the *pilum* which, by the time of Polybius (VI.23.11), had become the standard weapon of the Roman legionary. Javelin heads of comparable length have been found in tombs of the fourth century BC at Lavello, which has been identified with Forentum, captured by the Romans from the Samnites in 318–317 BC (Livy IX.20).

(Museo Nazionale Archeologico di Paestum, inv. 24316. Height of figured panel 42 cm)

Pontrandolfo and Rouveret *Le tombe dipinte di Paestum* 66–7, 174–5 and 344–5; A. Small, in F. R. Serra Ridgway, M. Pearce, E. Herring, R. D. Whitehouse and J. B. Wilkins (eds.), *Ancient Italy in its Mediterranean Setting: Studies in Honour of Ellen Macnamara* (London, 2000) 221–34, at 229–30.

102. Apulian red-figure column-*krater* by the Prisoner Painter, *c.* 370 BC. One warrior armed with hoplite shield and spear attacks another, who is falling to the ground and raises his hand in supplication. A third warrior sits naked on the ground with his hands bound, despoiled of his shield and spears, which the victorious warrior has placed against the tree. It is possible that the scene represents two different moments in time, and that the

102

captive is to be identified with the warrior appealing for mercy. The scene represents a battle between native Apulians. All three have the characteristic Apulian hair-style of pony-tail and coiff; and the two to the right wear the elaborately decorated tunics favoured in central Apulia, and the typical belt of Italic warriors.

The vase is one of a large number of column-*kraters* made by Greek artisans, probably in Tarentum, for the indigenous market. They were especially in demand as grave goods in central Apulia (Peucetia).

(British Museum inv. F173. Height 52 cm)

RFAp I p. 76 no. 73. E. Herring, in Herring, I. Lemos, F. L. Schiaro L. Vagnetti, R. D. Whitehouse and J. B. Wilkins (eds.), *Across Frontiers: Etruscans, Greeks, Phoenicians and Cypriots. Studies in Honour of David Ridgway and Francesca Romana Serra Ridgway* (London, 2006) 225–35; T. H. Carpenter, *MAAR* 48 (2003) 1–24.

103. The walls of Monte Sannace (unexcavated sections in thin line). Monte Sannace, the largest indigenous (Peucetian) settlement in central Apulia, was urbanized in the second half of the fourth century BC. Two wall circuits were erected soon after the middle of the century. One (no. I on the plan), 1,400 m long, enclosed the acropolis; the other (no. II), attached to it, 1,700 m long, encompassed the lower part of the city to the west. Various tombs and houses of the previous period were obliterated in the construction. The walls varied in thickness from 6.3 to 8 m and, like others of the time, had an external face of large cut-stone blocks and an inner one of irregular masonry. The two faces were linked at intervals by cross walls and the intervening spaces filled with rubble. A projection in the wall on the north-west side defended the adjacent gate. These fortifications were strengthened early in the third century by the construction of another wall (no. III), 1,300 m long, protecting the acropolis on the east side; and towards the end of the third century yet another wall (no. IV), 3,900 m long, was built which encircled all the existing circuits, leaving a large open space to the east of the acropolis as a refuge for people and animals from the country-side. This wall shows signs of hurried construction, suggesting that it was built in an emergency. There are some traces of a fifth wall, not yet fully analysed, beyond it. None of these walls shows any knowledge of the advances in fortification seen, for example, at Hipponium (**92**). The city was

103

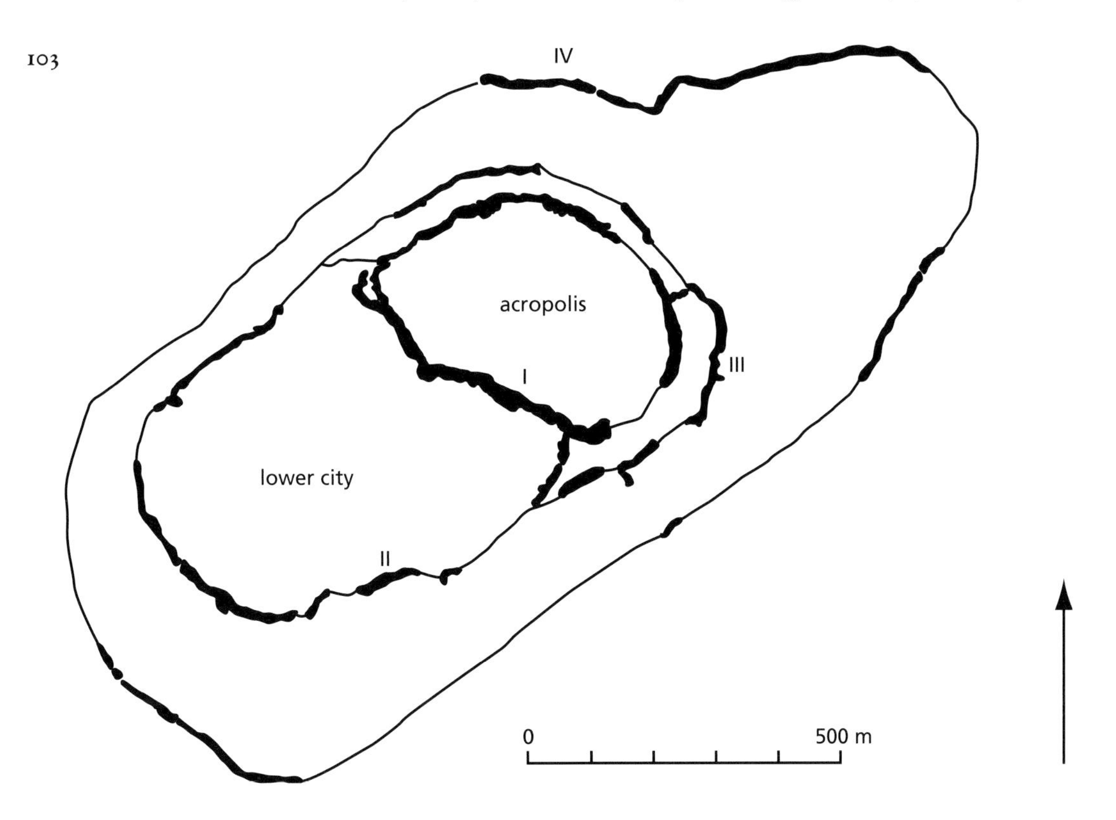

destroyed at the end of the third century, no doubt in the Second Punic War. The lower part of the city was then abandoned, but the acropolis continued to be inhabited at a lower economic level down to the first century BC.

(Based on a revised plan provided under concession from the Ministero per i Beni e le Attività Culturali – Soprintendenza per i Beni Archeologici della Puglia)

F. Radina and A. Ciancio, *Monte Sannace: Gli scavi dell'acropoli (1978–1983)* (Galatina, 1989) 221–5; B. M. Scarfì, *NSc* (1962) 1–288, esp. 25–96.

104. The settlement at Pomarico Vecchio occupies a small plateau defended by steep scarps 23 km inland from Metapontum. It was reorganized on a Greek model in the second half of the fourth century BC, with a broad street (*plateia*) on the main axis, intersected at right angles by another *plateia* and by several alleyways (*stenopoi*) which create housing blocks *c.* 10 m wide. An open space in the south-east quadrant was probably the agora. The large, almost square building on the south-west side of the main *plateia* was a cult centre: it had

104

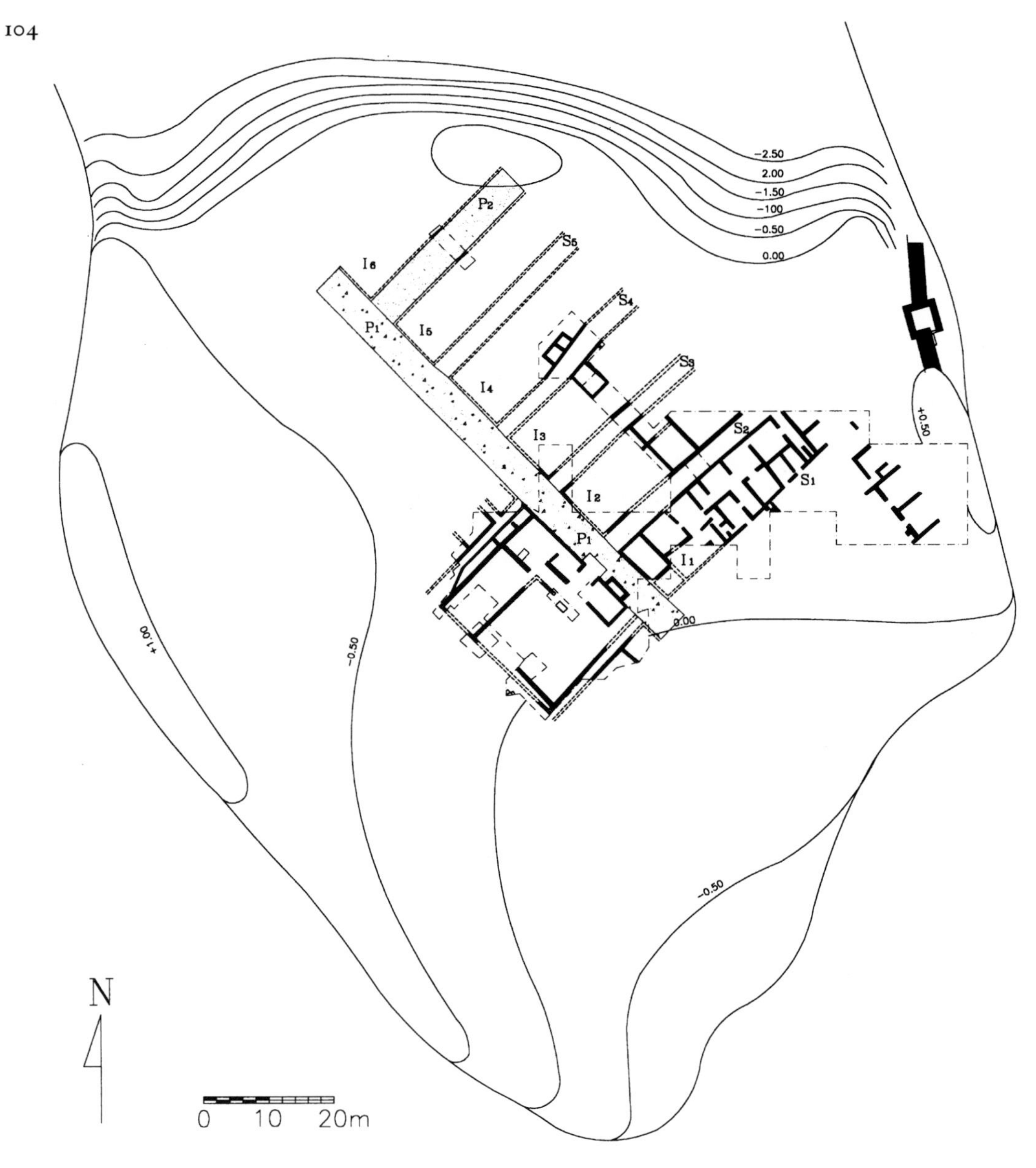

105

three rooms, apparently used for feasting, arranged around a courtyard where an altar and statue base were found. A defensive wall encircled the hill top, punctuated at frequent intervals by towers controlling postern gates. One of these is visible at the east side of the plan. The settlement was abandoned late in the third century, perhaps in the Second Punic War. Although the plan of the settlement and the design of its walls are typically Greek, the burials of the period are of native Apulian type, with the dead laid in the foetal position.

(Plan courtesy of Marcella Barra Bagnasco)

Marcella Barra Bagnasco (ed.), *Pomarico Vecchio I*, vol. II (Galatina, 1997).

105. Squared sandstone block 0.54 m high and 0.62 m wide found in 1981 in the excavation of the city wall and adjacent buildings in the Lucanian hill settlement at Raia S. Basile near Muro Lucano. The block, broken into two joining parts, is inscribed in the Oscan language in Greek letters:

ΜΑΙΣΑΡΡ/ΙΕΣΣΟΥFΕΝ/ΜΕΔΔΙΚΕΝ

i.e. Mais Arries during his term as *meddix*. The *meddikia* was the chief magistracy in Lucanian as in Samnite communities. The block, which can be dated by archaeological context to the early third century, evidently records the construction (or reconstruction) of the city wall under this magistrate. Raia S. Basile can be identified with Numistro, near which the battle between Hannibal's forces and the Romans under Marcellus was fought in 210 BC (Livy XXVII.2.4–10).

(Museo Nazionale Archeologico di Muro Lucano, inv. 67206. Height of slab 0.54 m)

A. Capano and L. Del Tutto Palma, in Tagliente (ed.) *Italici in Magna Grecia* 105–10, pl. XXXVII; M. C. Crawford *et al.*, *Imagines Italicae: A Corpus of Italian Inscriptions* (Bulletin of the Institute of Classical Studies Supplement), vol. III (London, 2011) 1360–1.

106. Squared sandstone block 1.23 m high and 0.59 m wide found in about 1960 in excavations along the outside face of the west part of the main fortification wall at Serra di Vaglio, one of the largest settlements in the interior of Lucania, occupying a strategic position near the Apennine watershed. It is inscribed in Ionic or Attic Greek:

ΕΠΙ ΤΗΣ ΝΥΜΜΕ/ΛΟΥ ΑΡΧΗΣ

i.e. in the magistracy of Nummelos. The block is similar to others still *in situ* in the wall face and must have been built into the wall to record its construction, which can be dated archaeologically to the third quarter of the fourth century BC. The use of Greek in the inscription may indicate that a Greek architect was involved, but it also points to a high degree of Hellenization among the local Lucanian population to whom the inscription must have been directed. The Ionic / Attic dialect shows the influence of Thurii or Athens rather than Doric Tarentum or Achaean Metapontum.

The word *arche* (rule) has been seen as referring to the special form of kingship (equivalent perhaps to the Roman dictatorship) which, according to Strabo (VI.1.3), the Lucanians resorted to in time of war; but the word is frequently used to refer to the regular magistracies of Greek cities, and comparison with the inscription from Raia S. Basile suggests that it is merely the Greek rendering of the Oscan *meddikia*.

(Museo Nazionale Archeologico di Potenza. Height of slab 1.23 m)

106

M. Lejeune, *REL* 45 (1967) 210–11 and pl. 1; D. Adamesteanu, in H. Daicoviciu, *In memoriam Constantini Daicoviciu* (Cluj, 1974) 9–21.

107. Complex A at Roccagloriosa. The Lucanian settlement of Roccagloriosa was founded in the fifth century BC on a hilltop site defended by steep scarps on the north and east sides. The vulnerable west and south sides were fortified by a defensive wall in the first half of the fourth century. In the last half of the fourth century and beginning of the third, several clusters of houses were built in planned units on the more level parts of the site both inside and outside the walls. Complex A is the largest and best preserved of a group of houses situated inside the walls near the centre of the site, on the east side of a broad street. At its centre was a paved courtyard, flanked on two or three sides by porticoes. The domestic rooms were to the north-east and south-west. One in the corner contained a tank which was perhaps a rudimentary bath. The largest room on the north-east side, with a rectangular platform in the centre and walls decorated with red and white plaster, has been interpreted as a room for banqueting. Near the north-east corner of the courtyard there was a small shrine, inside which were found numerous terracotta figurines of a seated goddess, miniature votive pots and the remains of about ten sheep or goats. They had presumably been sacrificed at an altar formed by a limestone block in front of the shrine. Further evidence for domestic cult was found in House B to the south and in another group of houses excavated outside the walls.

The settlement declined drastically in the second half of the third century BC and barely survived into the second century.

(Plan courtesy of Maurizio Gualtieri)

M. Gualtieri and H. Fracchia, *Roccagloriosa I: L'abitato: Scavo e ricognizione topografica (1976–1986)* (Naples, 1990) 63–77, 101–50; M. Gualtieri, in F. D'Andria and K. Mannino (eds.), *Ricerche sulla casa in Magna Grecia e in Sicilia* (Galatina, 1996) 301–20.

108. The sanctuary of Mefitis at Macchia di Rossano was founded in the second half of the fourth century in a well-watered area high in the Lucanian Apennines. The two large altars date to the time of the foundation. They were set in the middle of a paved area surrounded by buildings which were extensively reconstructed around the end of the third century BC. Shortly afterwards

107

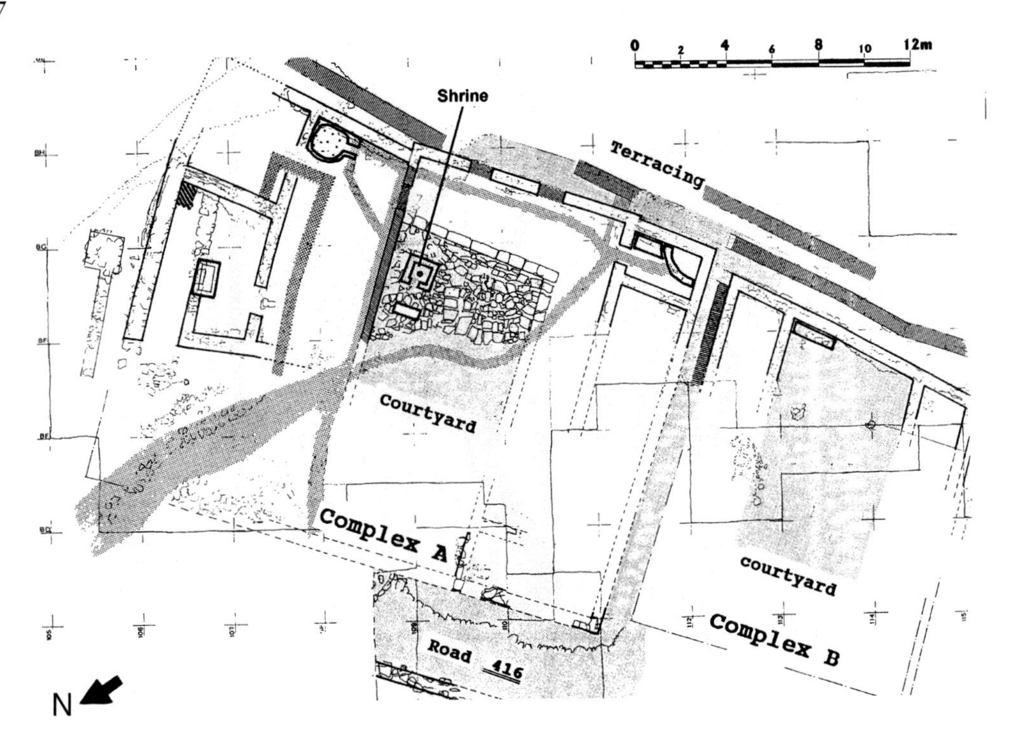

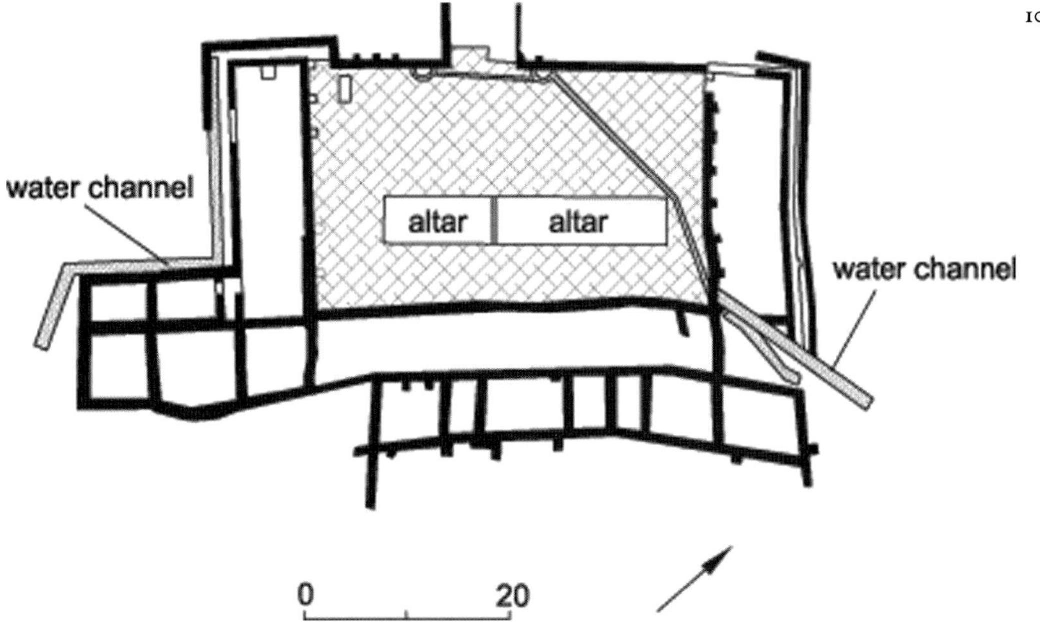

the sanctuary was embellished with statues of gods in Greek marble. The complex was restored for the last time early in the first century AD, but was abandoned soon afterwards. In its most developed form the altars were enclosed in a rectangular precinct with long colonnaded rooms on three sides and several subsidiary buildings. That on the west side contained the largest deposit of votive offerings. Numerous Oscan inscriptions show that the main cult was that of Mefitis, the principal female goddess of the Oscan-speaking peoples, often connected with springs, who in one inscription is said to own the lands and waters. Other inscriptions show that she was worshipped in conjunction with Mamertius, the god of war, and the military ethos of the sanctuary is confirmed by numerous spear heads and items of armour which must have been deposited as votives. The two altars probably belonged to these two gods, although other divinities, including Jupiter, Juno and Venus, are also attested.

Rossano is the largest Lucanian sanctuary. Its size, its central position in Lucania and the fact that it is connected by hill-tracks with a number of large settlements (including Serra di Vaglio, no. 19 on 88) suggests that it served as the cantonal sanctuary for a group of Lucanian peoples known from inscriptions as the Utiani. An Oscan inscription of the end of the second century BC which records the restoration of statues of kings suggests that they had a tradition of a period when they had had a common monarchy.

(After D. Adamesteanu, in de Lachenal (ed.) *Da Leukania a Lucania* 63 fig. 111)

D. Adamesteanu and H. Dilthey, *Macchia di Rossano: Il santuario della Mefitis. Rapporto preliminare* (Galatina, 1992); M. Denti, *Ellenismo e romanizzazione nella X Regio: La scultura delle élites locali dall'età repubblicana ai Giulio-Claudii* (Rome, 1991); M. Lejeune, *Méfitis d'après les dédicaces lucaniennes de Rossano di Vaglio* (Louvain-la-Neuve, 1990).

109. Reconstruction of a column with Corinthian figured capital from a Hellenistic temple at Canusium. The temple, buried below the palaeochristian church of S. Leucio, was the largest cult building put up by an Italic community in southern Italy. Its architectural motifs were inspired by buildings from various parts of the Hellenistic world, especially Tarentum, and were drawn from all three orders. The surviving elements are on a large scale, and include triglyphs and metopes and giant *telamones* of Doric type, as well as Ionic volute capitals and Corinthian figured capitals. The date and form of the temple have been much debated, but the most recent study leaves little doubt that it was erected in the first half of the second century BC. In ground plan it was probably of Greek type, but not enough remains for the walls and placement of the columns

109a

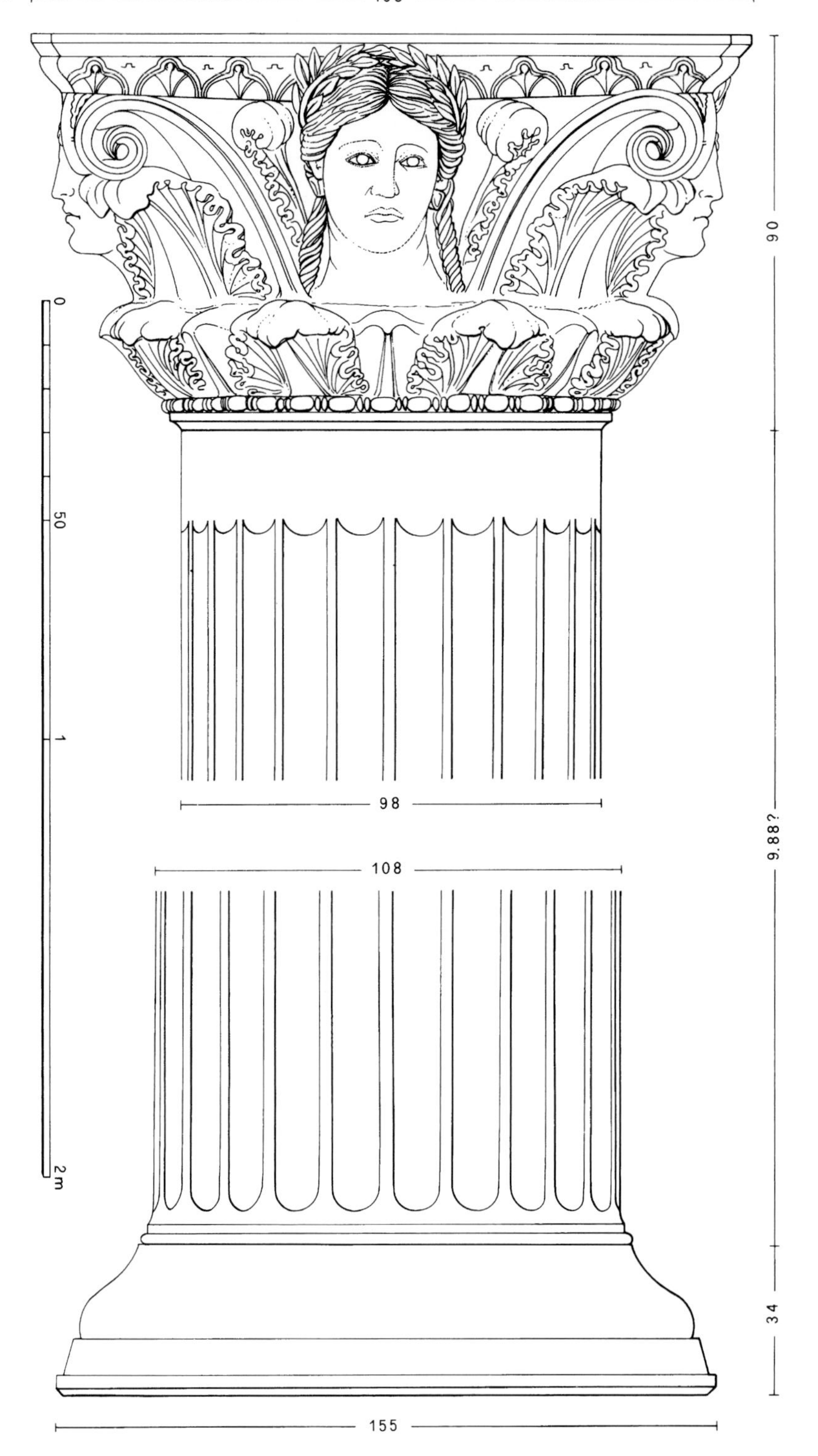

109b

to be reconstructed reliably. The building of the temple illustrates the prosperity of Canusium after the Second Punic War (in which it had continued to support Rome even after Hannibal's victory at nearby Cannae), and the architectural elements point to the continuing influence of Greek cultural models in the second century BC, and the far-reaching contacts of Canusium in this period. The temple was probably dedicated to Athena, but inscriptions show that the deity was venerated as Minerva when the city became a *municipium* after the Social War.

(After Pensabene 1992)

P. Pensabene, in Cassano (ed.) *Principi imperatori vescovi* 620–54; O. Dally, *Canosa, località San Leucio: Untersuchungen zu Akkulturationsprozessen vom 6. bis zum 2. Jh. v. Chr. am Beispiel eines daunischen Heiligtums* (Heidelberg, 2000).

110. Field survey in the Basentello valley. Intensive archaeological field survey over an area of nearly 100 km^2 in the Basentello valley, *c.* 60 km upriver from Metapontum, has shown that a drastic change occurred in the pattern of settlement in this area during the period of Roman conquest. The settlement pattern of the fourth and third centuries BC

110

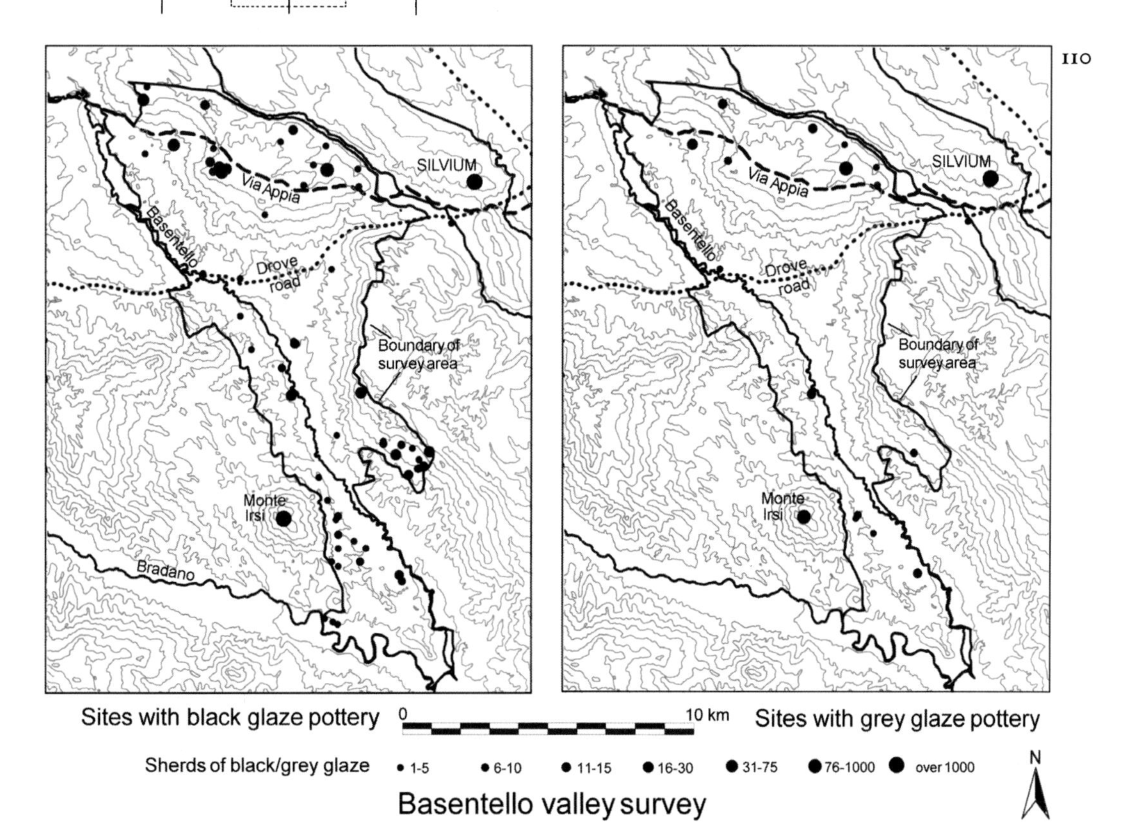

can be illustrated by the distribution of black-glaze pottery (left-hand map in 110). The main site in the area was Botromagno (*c.* 140 ha within its walls built in the late fourth century BC), which can be identified with the Peucetian city of Silvium. On the hilltops on the east side of the river there was a string of smaller (3–15 ha) settlements with natural defences augmented by walls, and another large site, Monte Irsi (*c.* 32 ha), on the west side. In the last half of the fourth century numerous small farms were established in the open countryside around these settlements: a total of sixty-three sites within the survey area have yielded black-glaze sherds mostly datable between the fifth and third centuries BC. The distribution of grey-glaze pottery shows a marked contrast. Only twenty-two sites have produced sherds of grey-glaze pottery datable to the second and first centuries BC, mostly located within a short distance of a road which can probably be identified with the Via Appia. Large areas where there had previously been settlement were abandoned. A swathe of land *c.* 5 km wide was left unoccupied on either side of a drove road leading to the high Apennines, probably to be used as grazing for transhumant flocks.

The impact of Roman conquest was felt early in this area, which straddles the route from central Italy to Tarentum. Although Silvium was an Apulian (Peucetian) city, it had a Samnite garrison in the late fourth century. According to Diodorus (XX.80), the Romans took it by storm in 306 BC and carried off 5,000 prisoners and a large amount of booty. Excavation has shown that the lower part of the settlement was abandoned at about this time, and that the upper part was destroyed at the end of the third century BC, presumably in the Second Punic War. It was replaced after an interval by a villa and adjacent village. The field survey shows the effect of these events on the surrounding countryside.

(Maps by Carola Small)

A. Small, in E. Lo Cascio and A. Storchi Marino (eds.), *Modalità insediative e strutture agrarie nell'Italia meridionale in età romana* (Bari, 2001) 36–53.

111. The Messapian settlement at Muro Tenente 18 km south-west of Brindisi was surrounded by a defensive wall 2.7 km long enclosing 52 ha. Surface survey carried out within units of *c.* 25 × 25 m has shown how the site developed over time. After a long period of thin occupation from the eighth to the fifth centuries BC, the settlement expanded markedly in the fourth and third centuries. The main tableware of the period, black-glaze pottery, is scattered across the site, with several large concentrations where occupation must have been particularly dense (**a**). By contrast, the grey-glaze pottery of the second and first centuries BC is thinly distributed, with only one nucleus continuing (**b**). Comparison is complicated by the fact that the grey-glaze pottery, unlike the black, may not have been produced locally; nevertheless, the change in distribution within the site shows that the settlement had shrunk. By the imperial period it was confined to a small part of the central nucleus which can be identified with the road station of Scamnum on the Via Appia.

G.-J. Burgers, *Constructing Messapian Landscapes: Settlement Dynamics, Social Organization and Culture Contact in the Margins of Graeco-Roman Italy* (Amsterdam, 1998).

112. A small Lucanian farmhouse datable to *c.* 350–280 BC excavated at Menzinaro near Montegiordano. The building, made of mud brick on a socle of river stones, was well laid out in a square with sides of approximately 22 m. Seven rooms were arranged around a central courtyard, entered from a door in the west wall by way of a narrow passage. The domestic rooms were on the north and west sides: Room 1 appears to have been the women's quarters with a hearth, and at least one loom (indicated by a large number of loomweights). Several terracotta statuettes of an enthroned goddess must come from a household shrine. Room 2 was the kitchen and living-room, with another hearth in the south-west corner. Room 7, which contained two terracotta washbasins, part of a red-figure *krater*, and numerous fragments of pots for eating and drinking, must have been used for banqueting. The rooms to the south and east were probably intended for storage and agricultural processing. This was certainly the case with Room 4, which contained the base of a wine press and the remains of at least two large terracotta jars (*pithoi*) set in the floor to hold the fermenting must. A narrow space between rooms on the south side probably held a wooden stair which led to an upper storey or loft. A small group of ten coins was found on the north side of the courtyard. Outside, to the south, there was a terrace protected by a lean-to roof, with a kiln apparently used for firing MGS amphorae (**94**). Two graffiti on the bottom of plain vases probably give the name of the owner: NOVIOS OPSIOS.

The house was evidently the centre of a working farm, small enough to be managed by the owner himself with his family, but producing a surplus of wine for export. It appears to have been abandoned suddenly, perhaps in the Pyrrhic War.

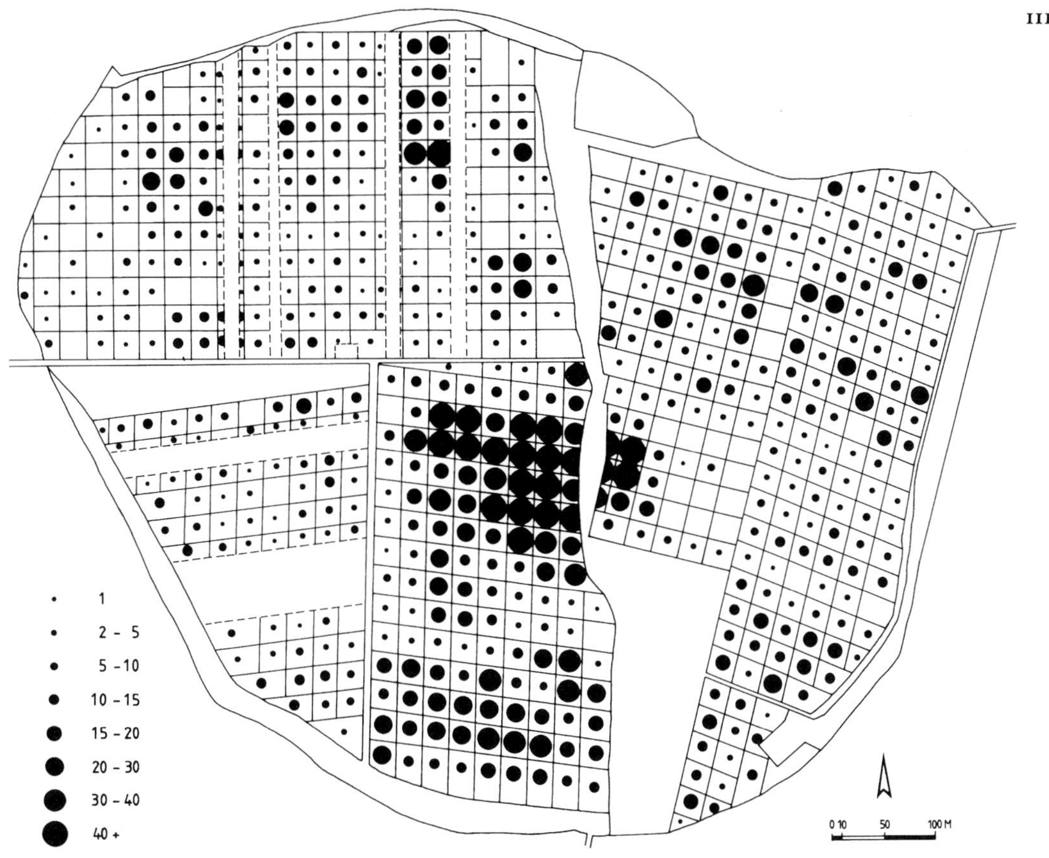

E. Lattanzi, *Atti del XXI Convegno di Studi sulla Magna Grecia* (Taranto, 1982) 220–2; S. Luppino, *SE* 49 (1981) 495–6; A. Russo Tagliente, *Edilizia domestica in Apulia e Lucania: Ellenizzazione e società nella tipologia abitativa indigena tra VIII e III secolo a.C.* (Galatina, 1992) 183–6; Vandermersch *Vins et amphores* 100.

113. The Latin colony of Venusia was founded in 291 BC on a projecting tongue of an extensive plateau with steep scarps on three sides. The ancient city is buried under the medieval and modern town, but some elements of the original urban plan survive in the present-day road system, and others are known from excavation. The main axis of the colony, the *decumanus maximus*, ran south-west to north-east across the site, with a second *decumanus* not quite parallel to it to the north, adjusted to fit the available space. Numerous *cardines* intersected the *decumanus maximus* at right angles at intervals of 1.5 *actus* (*c.* 53 m). The forum was probably situated on the north side of the *decumanus maximus* towards the west end.

At the extreme east end of the settlement there was an industrial quarter where there were numerous kilns. The city was defended by a massive wall faced with large squared blocks, parts of which survive where it crossed the plateau on the exposed west side.

M. L. Marchi and M. Salvatore, *Venosa* (Rome, 1997).

114. Centuriation connected with the Latin colony of Luceria founded in 314 BC. Luceria (modern Lucera) is situated on the western fringe of the North Apulian plain. The arid conditions of the area are particularly conducive to the study of crop marks by aerial photography, and analysis of aerial photographs taken during World War II before the advent of mechanized agriculture has revealed traces of several systems of centuriation in the vicinity of the city. One, which extends *c.* 9 km to the north-east, probably dates to the time of the foundation of the colony. The framework was formed by seven roads (*decumani*) flanked by

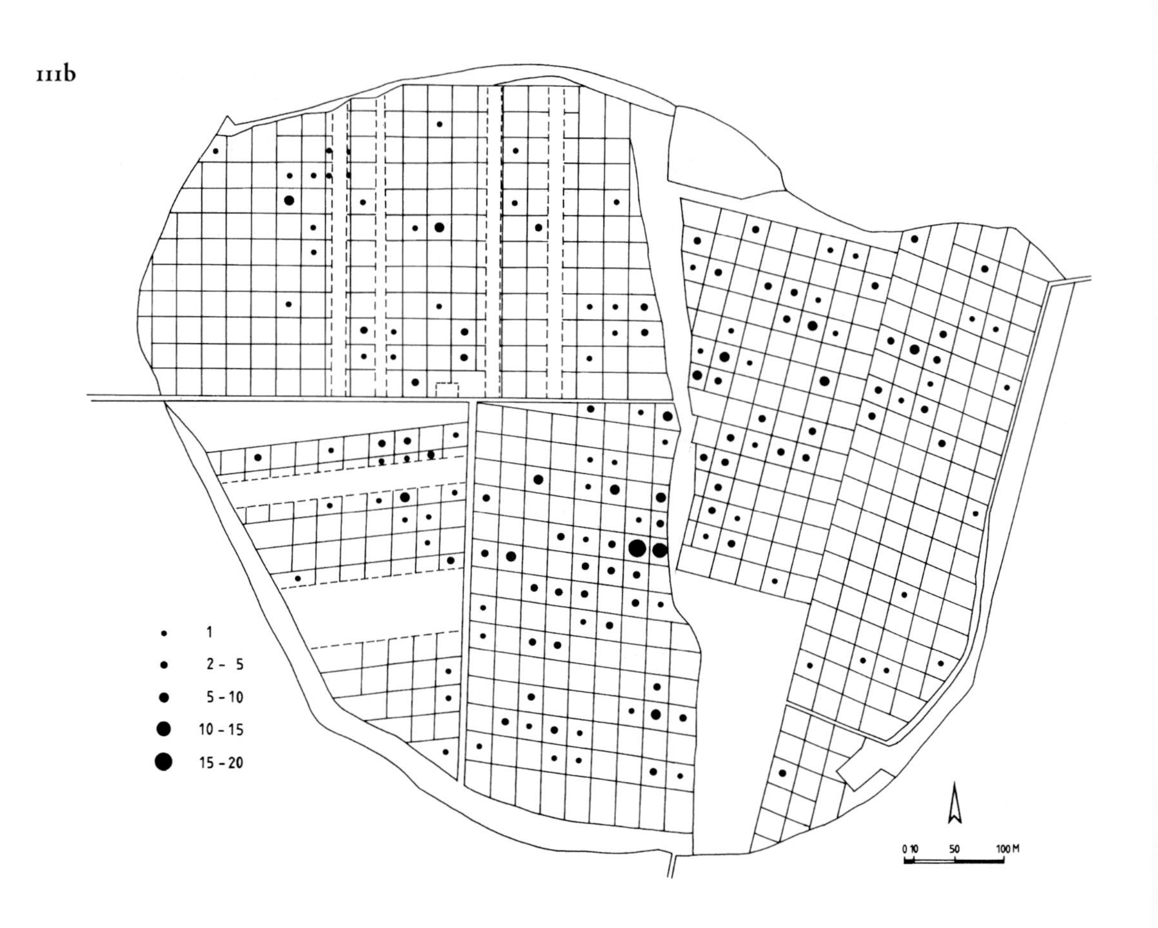
111b
1
2 - 5
5 - 10
10 - 15
15 - 20
0 10
50
100 M

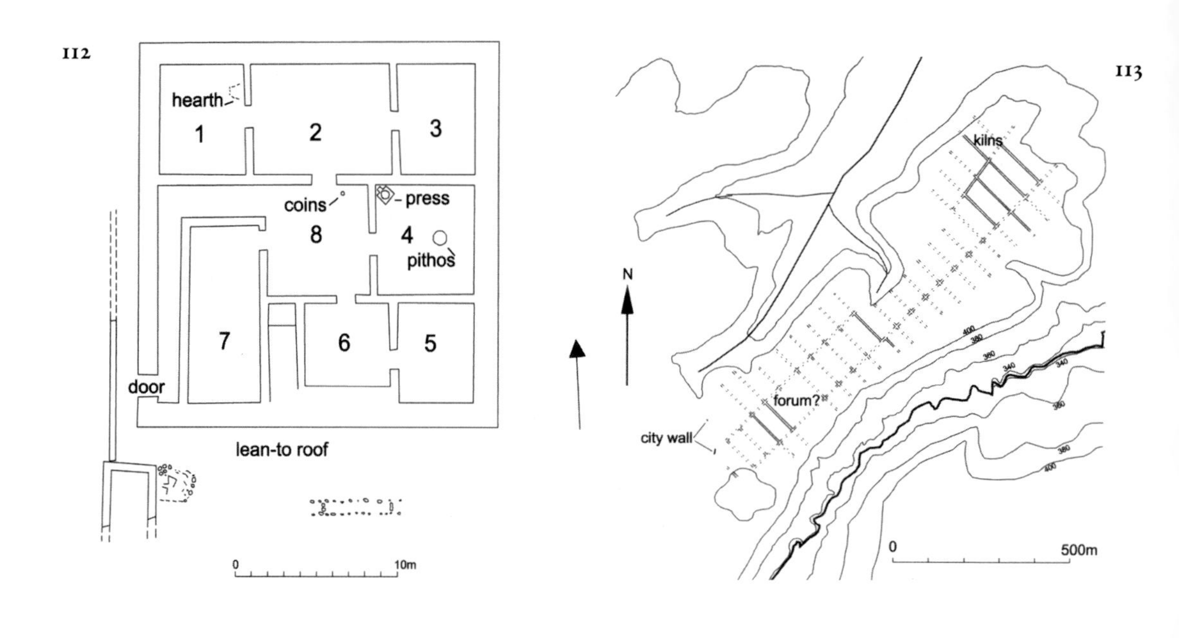
112
hearth
1
2
3
coins
press
8
4
pithos
7
6
5
door
lean-to roof
0
10m
113
kilns
N
400
380
360
340
forum?
city wall
0
500m

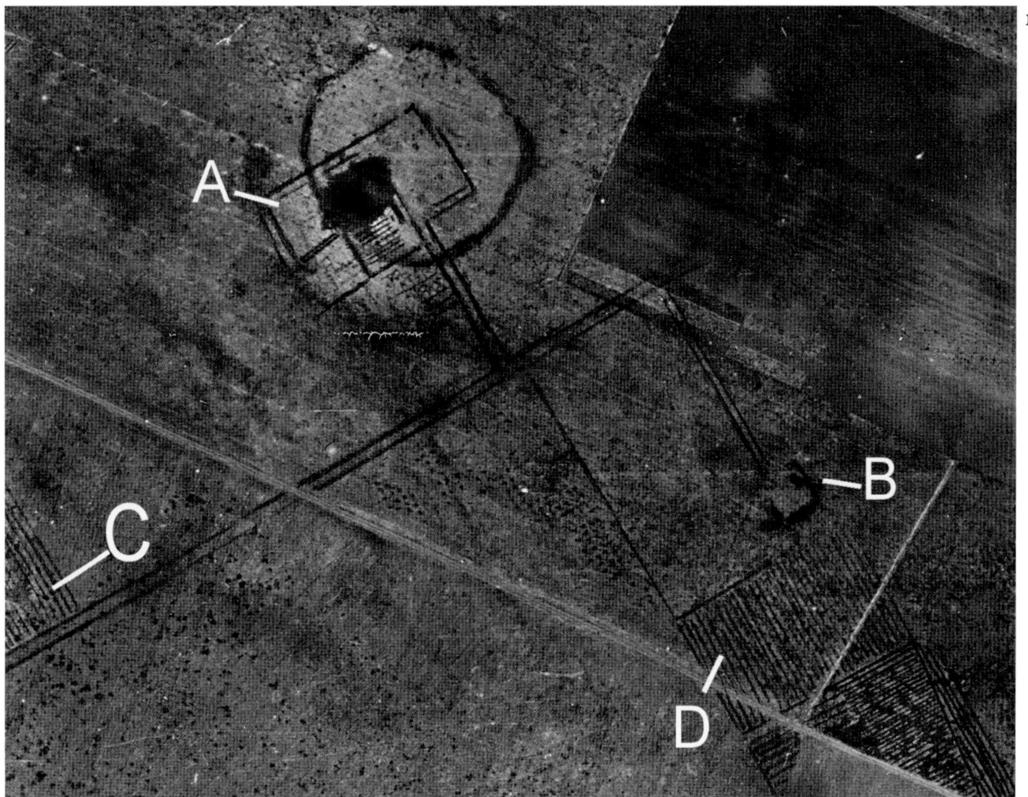

ditches, laid out parallel to each other and *c.* 550 m (15.5 *actus*) apart on a NW–SE axis, and the strips of land defined by the roads were divided into small rectangular lots for the 2,500 settlers.

A small part of the scheme can be seen in this wartime photograph of fields near the modern Masseria Villano which shows two small farm buildings at A and B, set in rectangular enclosures and linked by short roads to one of the *decumani*. The roads are flanked by ditches which appear as black lines in the photograph. The farm at A overlies a circular ditch of the Neolithic period. Close to C and D there are parallel cultivation trenches for vines, and in the plot between B and C there are rows of pits for planting fruit trees or olives. In addition to their small-holdings, the colonists would also have had the use of communal grazing on unallocated land for their animals, principally sheep and goats.

(Pitt Rivers Museum, Bradford Collection, neg.1988.296)

J. Bradford, *Antiquity* 23 (1949) 66–8 and pl. 3A; Volpe *La Daunia* 46–7, 209–13.

115. Silver cosmetic box with gilded decoration from the Tomba degli Ori in Canusium. The lower half of the box is in the form of a scallop shell. The lid, which was attached by a hinge, has an applied *emblema*, with a female figure riding a sea monster. The scales of the monster, the woman's hair and mantel, and some of the waves are gilded, as are alternate rays around the circumference. A second *emblema* on the inside of the lid also shows a woman riding a sea monster. The name of the owner, Opaka Sabaleida, is inscribed in Greek letters imprinted in small dots on the back of the hinge. The box was most probably made in Tarentum in the late third century BC and imported to Canusium to be deposited together with many other precious objects in a female burial in a side room of the chamber tomb. The tomb was partially excavated in confused circumstances in 1928. New excavations in 1991 revealed the remains of a rich warrior burial in another side room of the tomb. The latest objects, including several glass vessels imported from Alexandria, date the burials to the end of the third or beginning of the second century BC.

(Museo Archeologico Nazionale di Taranto, inv. 22429–22430. Width 16 cm)

E. M. De Juliis (ed.), *Gli ori di Taranto in età ellenistica* (Taranto, 1984) 58–62, 447–52; Cassano (ed.) *Principi imperatori vescovi* 337–45 (Corrente), 530–1 (Guzzo), 550–1 (Santoro).

116. Temple of Romano-Campanian type adjoining the forum at Herdonea (modern Ordona). In its original form, it stood on a high podium (16.25 m × 13.50 m × 1.9 m high at the front) approached by a single flight of steps. The cella was flanked by two aisles, but the form of the *pronaos* is uncertain: it may have had two columns between projecting walls (*in antis*) or four columns across the whole of the front (prostyle). A fragment of a Doric frieze with triglyphs and metopes may come from the temple.

The building was probably erected soon after the middle of the second century BC when the city was rebuilt after its destruction by Hannibal in 210 BC.

(Photo and plans by F. Van Wonterghem, in J. Mertens and G. Volpe, *Herdonia: Un itinerario storico-archeologico* (Bari, 1999) 63 fig. 72; reproduced by permission of the author)

F. Van Wonterghem, in J. Mertens (ed.), *Ordona VI: Rapports et études* (Brussels, 1979) 41–81, pl. 21–38.

117. Hypothetical plan of Tarentum in the Hellenistic period. The Greek city of Taras, Roman Tarentum (modern Taranto) occupied a strategic position on a wedge-shaped strip of land that separates the lagoon of the Mare Piccolo from the wide bay of the Mare Grande. The Mare Piccolo, which is entered by a narrow inlet, is the safest harbour on the Italian coastline. Most of the ancient city lies under modern buildings, but casual finds and the discoveries of rescue excavations have revealed some of the main features of the ancient city. A low hill near the western tip of the wedge formed the acropolis of the city, where the main temples were situated. There were some houses in this area, but most of the domestic buildings and the main public spaces lay further east, with the necropolis beyond them. In the fifth century BC the whole of this area, including (unusually) the necropolis, was enclosed by a massive city wall 4.2 m wide and *c.* 4 km long,

116a

116b

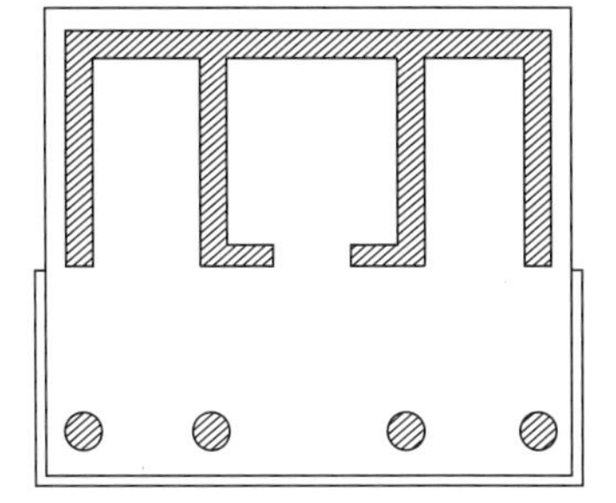

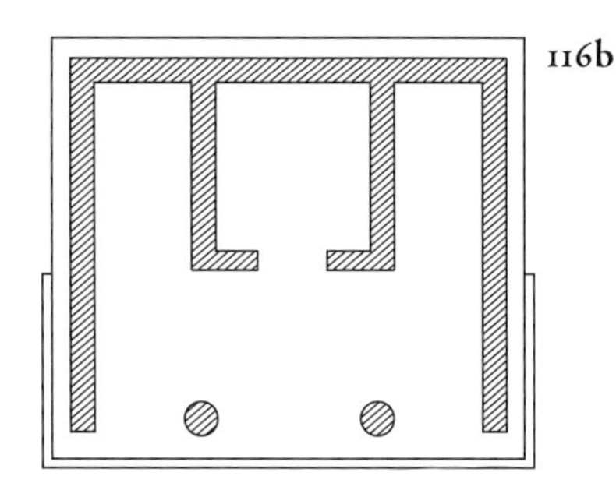

117

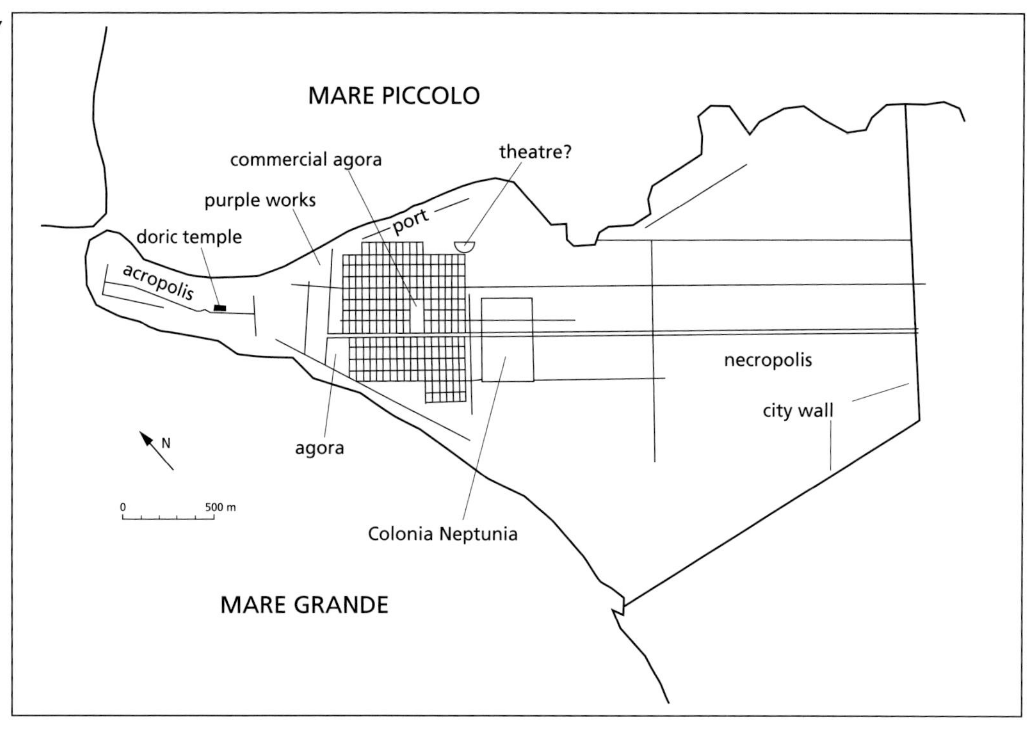

faced on both sides with squared stones; and streets were laid out on a grid system to the east and north of the agora, forming blocks of *c.* 30 × 54 m. Some of these were assigned to workshops while others were subdivided for houses. The main axis was a broad west–east road (*plateia*) which linked the agora with a gate in the wall and led to the countryside. In the fourth century BC the city wall was strengthened by a ditch 11 m wide and 3.5 m deep, excavated *c.* 10 m in front of it to fend off siege engines. It was widened to 19 m at the vulnerable south-east angle. As the population expanded in the late classical period new housing areas were laid out over part of the earlier necropolis. There were extensive commercial and industrial areas along the shore of the Mare Piccolo, including shipyards and a dye works for producing purple from the murex shellfish. In the crisis of the Hannibalic War the city wall was breached, not to be rebuilt, and the city outside the acropolis was largely destroyed. Much of it remained abandoned until the reorganization of the city as Colonia Neptunia, promoted by Gaius Gracchus.

(Adapted from E. Lippolis, in C. D'Angela and E. Lippolis, *Gli scavi dell'Arsenale e l'archeologia tarantina* (Taranto, 1989) 25)

P. Wuilleumier, *Tarente des origines à la conquête romaine* (Paris, 1939); Lippolis *Fra Taranto e Roma* 39–55; E. M. De Juliis, *Città della Magna Grecia: Taranto* (Bari, 2000) 51–71.

118. The territory of Metapontum. Archaeological field survey carried out over 42 km² of the agricultural plain in the hinterland of Metapontum, combined with the excavation of selected sites, has yielded much information on the changes in settlement and land use in this area in the period of Romanization. In the late fourth century the plain was intensively cultivated (**a**), with nearly 200 small farms and a few small villages distributed more or less uniformly between the Bradano and Basento rivers. The principal crops were cereals (especially barley) and legumes, although olives and vines were gaining in importance. In the second century BC the number of occupied settlements shrank to one-sixth of its previous level (**b**). Large areas were abandoned altogether, but there was a slight increase in the average size of the remaining farms. Analysis of animal bones from two sites of the period shows that oxen and horses of large size were being raised, presumably as draught animals for ploughing and hauling goods to market; and excavations in the site of Pantanello between Metapontum and the

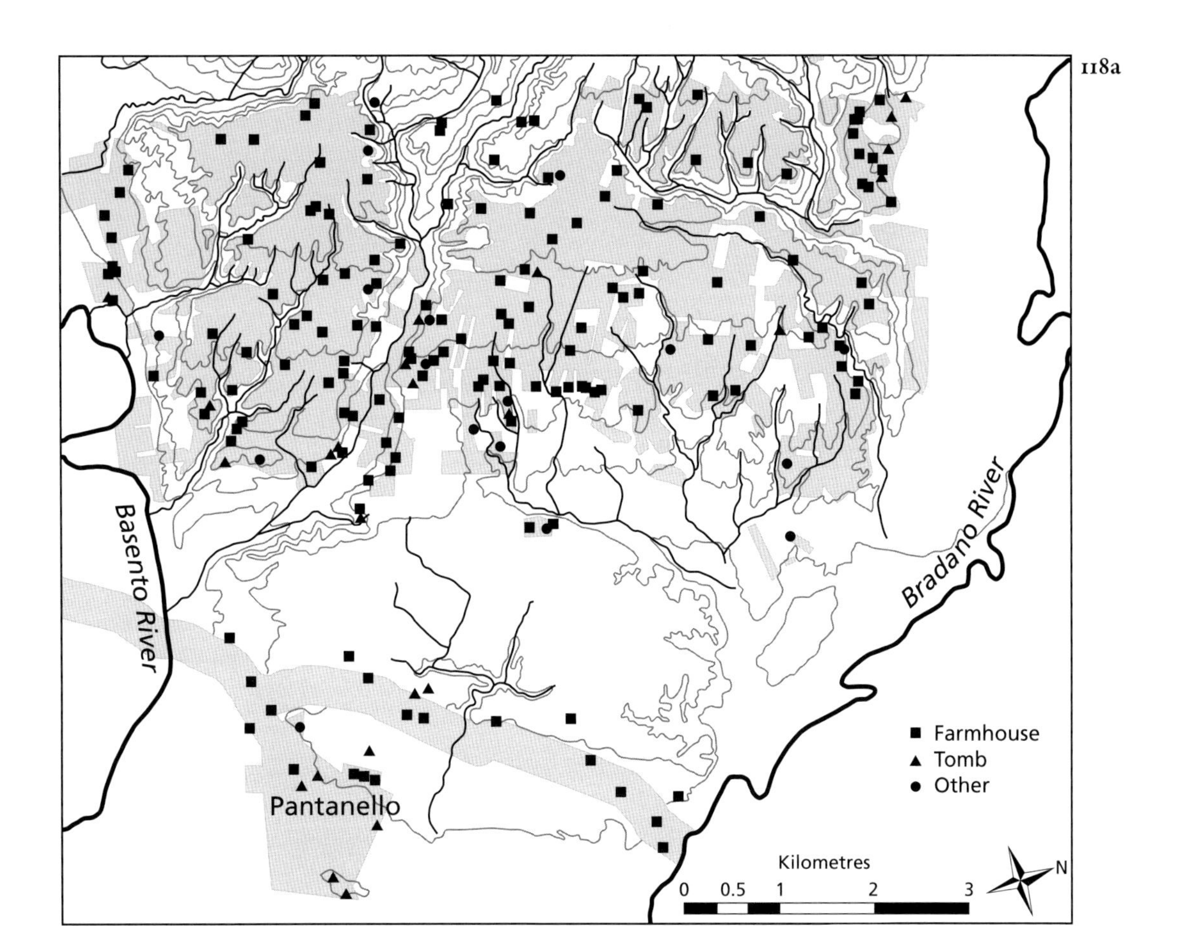

southern limit of the survey area show that MGS VI amphorae (**94** above) were being made there, evidently for the export of wine produced in the territory. It seems probable that the farms of the second century were exploiting larger areas of land for more productive agriculture.

(Updated plan, courtesy of Carter and Prieto: 2011)

J. C. Carter and A. Prieto (eds.), *The Chora of Metaponto* III*: Archaeological Field Survey, Bradano to Basento* (Austin, 2011); see also esp. vol. II, 785–922.

119. The northern part of the city of Heraclea (see *CAH plates* VII.1 no. 89) was laid out in the third century BC with a single broad street (*plateia*) 10 m in width, joined at right angles by narrower *stenopoi* which defined and served the housing blocks. Eight have been excavated. Each was subdivided by a single wall, perpendicular to the *plateia*, and by several transverse walls, to create modest houses of 200–300 m^2. Most had rooms ranged round a central courtyard. Kilns and moulds for terracotta figurines found in some of the courtyards show that this quarter was inhabited partly by artisans who had their workshops inside the houses. Later in the third century a few richer inhabitants built larger houses with peristyles which extended beyond the limits of the original buildings: two can be seen at A and B on the plan. At the end of the third or beginning of the second century BC the houses facing onto the *plateia* in block I were replaced by a complex of six shops (the western two were subsequently combined), with other spaces for storage and domestic life behind. The Pyrrhic and Hannibalic Wars left little or no mark on the city, and these houses continued to be occupied, with various modifications, down to the beginning of the Augustan Principate.

(After L. Giardino in Andria and Mannino (eds.) *Ricerche sulla casa* 143 fig. 6)

L. Giardino, in Adamesteanu (ed.) *Storia della Basilicata* 295–337.

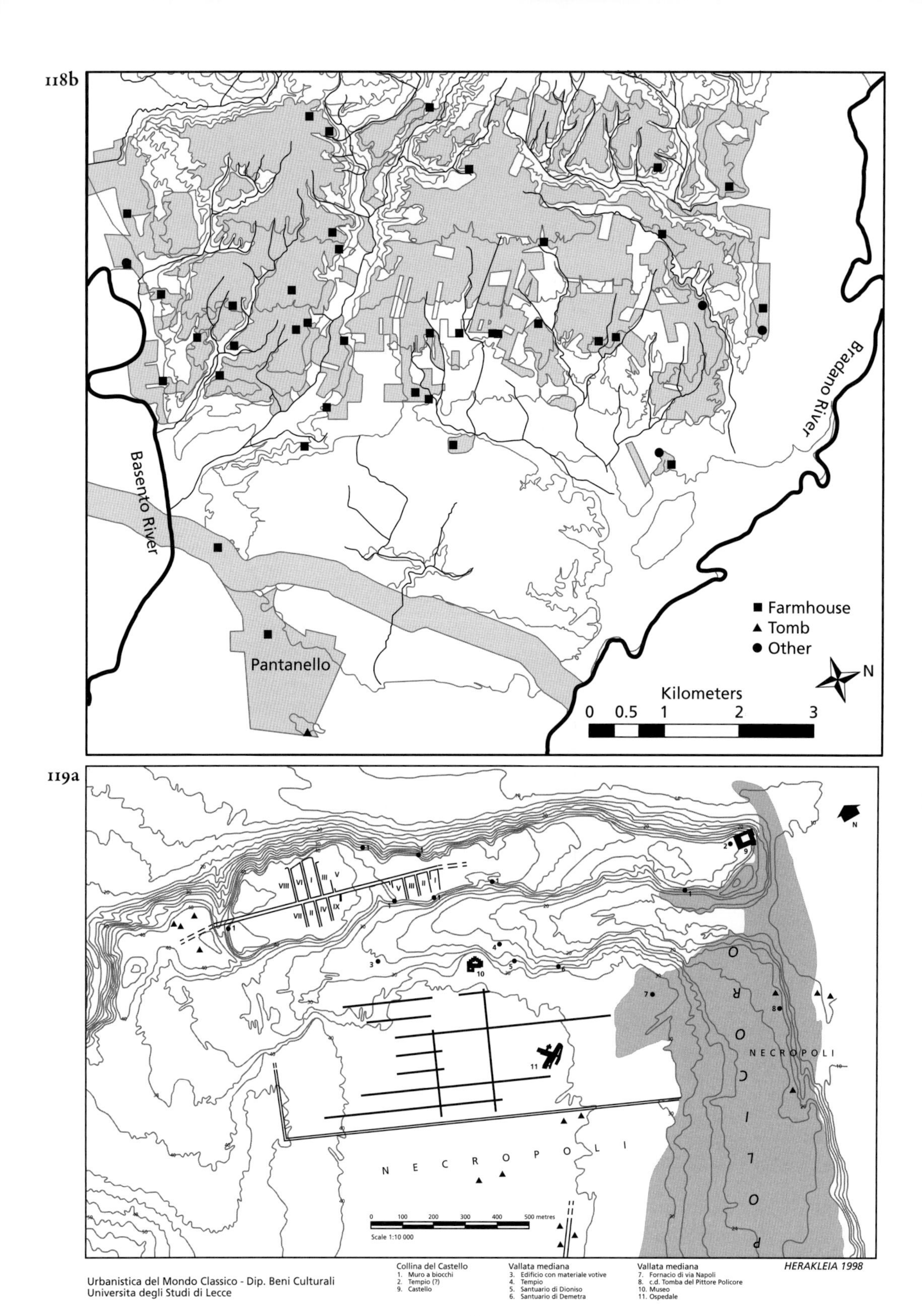
118b
Basento River
Bradano River
Pantanello
Farmhouse
Tomb
Other
N
Kilometers
0 0.5 1 2 3
119a
N
NECROPOLI
NECROPOLI
0 100 200 300 400 500 metres
Scale 1:10 000
Collina del Castello
1. Muro a biocchi
2. Tempio (?)
9. Castello
Vallata mediana
3. Edificio con materiale votive
4. Tempio
5. Santuario di Dioniso
6. Santuario di Demetra
Vallata mediana
7. Fornacio di via Napoli
8. c.d. Tomba del Pittore Policore
10. Museo
11. Ospedale
HERAKLEIA 1998
Urbanistica del Mondo Classico - Dip. Beni Culturali
Universita degli Studi di Lecce

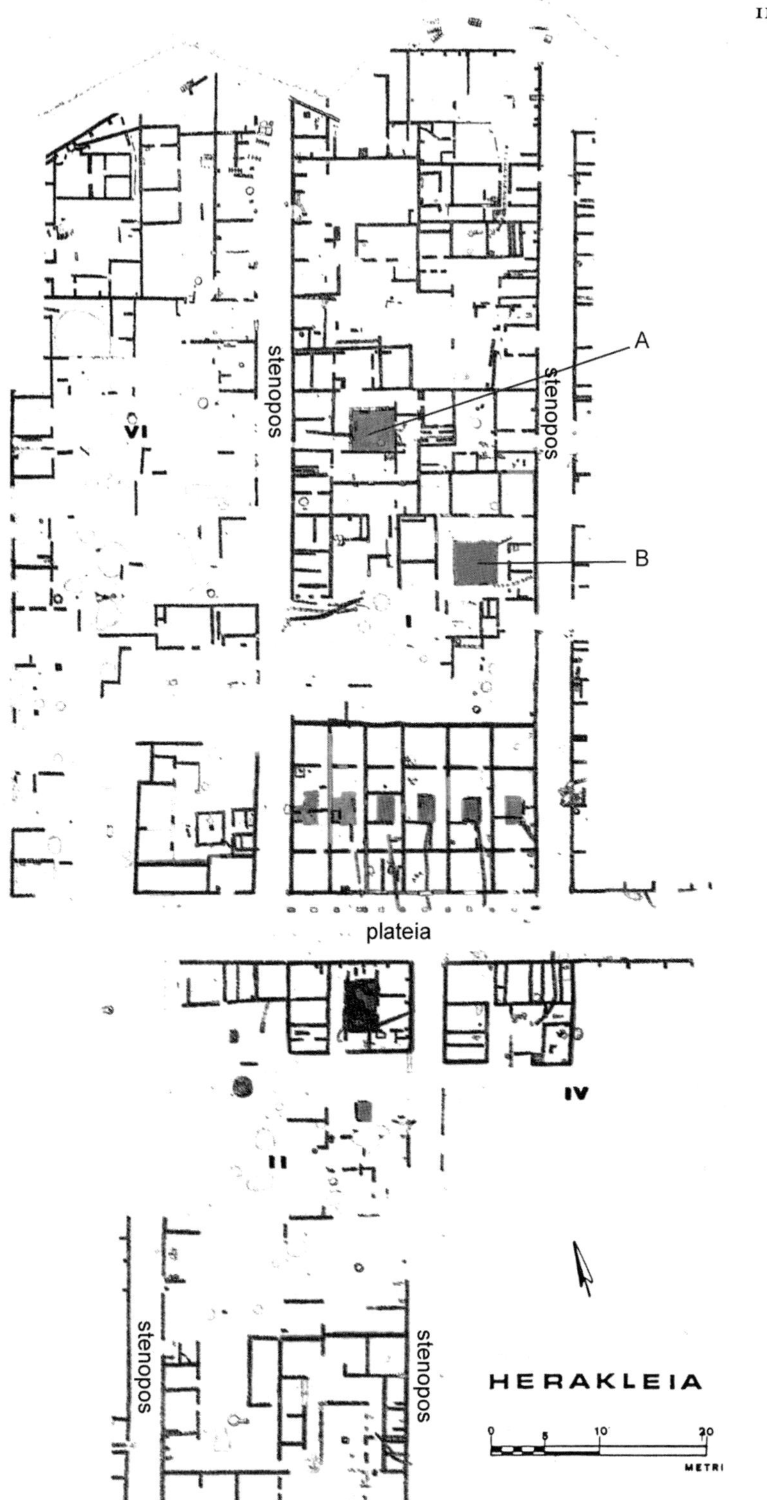
A
B
stenopos
stenopos
VI
plateia
IV
II
stenopos
stenopos
HERAKLEIA
0
5
10
20
METRI

120. Grey-glaze (or grey-gloss) pottery was the standard tableware used in much of Apulia in the Late Hellenistic period. A limited range of shapes, principally bowls and plates, was made in this ware, which, when fired, had hard grey clay covered in whole or in part with a moderately lustrous grey slip. The effect was intended to imitate silver. Shapes with distinct feet, such as the plate (**c**), were frequently partially dipped in the wet slip by the potter, who held the pot by the foot and then set it upright to dry before firing, allowing the slip to dribble down the outside. The ware was produced in many of the larger settlements between the middle of the second century BC and the beginning of the Augustan Principate, and is a useful means of dating archaeological contexts of a period when the traditional economic and social structures of southern Italy were undergoing profound changes. The examples shown come from the Hellenistic settlement on Botromagno (Silvium) reconstructed around the middle of the second century BC (110).

D. Yntema, *Conspectus Formarum of Apulian Grey Gloss Wares* (Amsterdam, 2005); A. J. N. W. Prag, in A. M. Small (ed.), *Gravina: An Iron Age and Republican Settlement in Apulia*, vol. 1 (London, 1992) 134–62.

120a

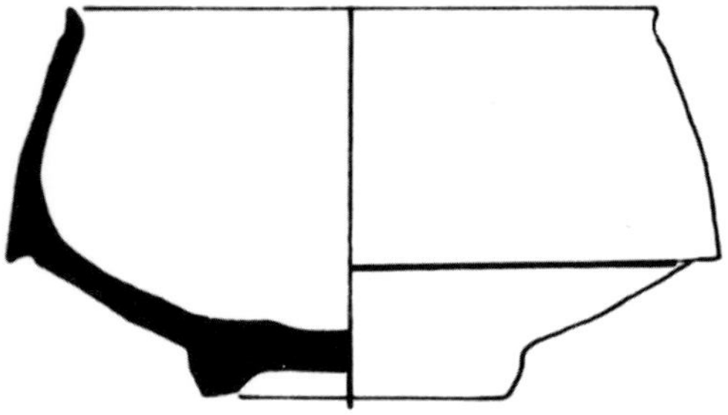

120b

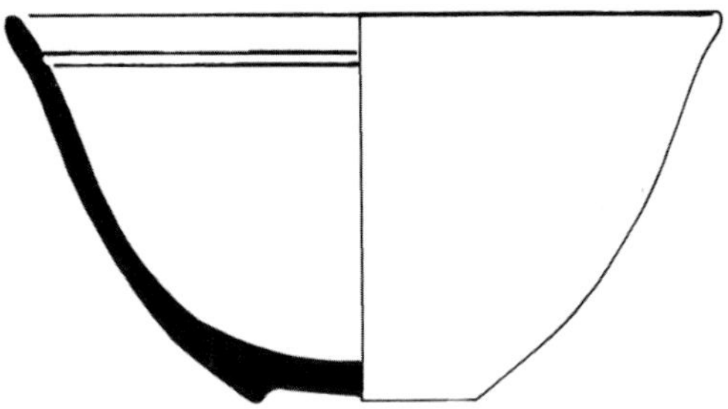

120c

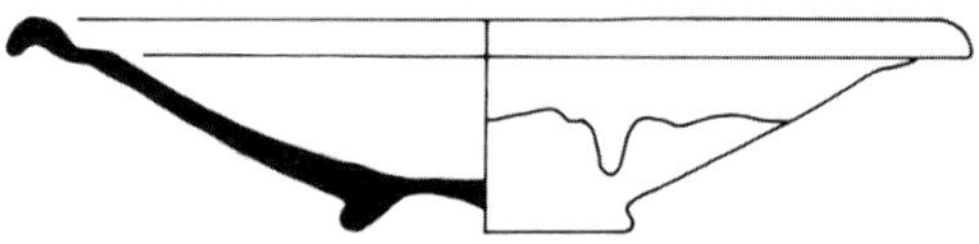

121. Brindisine amphorae. The dry climate of the Salentine peninsula was well suited to the cultivation of olives, and in the second and first centuries BC large quantities of olive oil were exported through Brundisium (Brindisi), which developed as a major port after the foundation of the Latin colony in 244 BC. Shortly before the middle of the second century new types of amphora began to be produced on coastal sites in the territory of the city to contain the oil and other products of the region. They were exported to many parts of the Mediterranean world, including Carthage, Athens and Delos, and a few were transported north of the Alps. They were frequently stamped on the handles with the names of the slaves who made them, and of the owners of the workshops. The forms of the amphorae varied considerably, even within the same workshop. The four types shown here were all produced at Apani near Brindisi, where two kilns and their associated workshops have been excavated, one belonging to Gaius Aninius and the other to Gaius Vehilius. Production of Brindisine amphorae continued down to the end of the Republic.

(After Palazzo 1989: fig. 1)

P. Palazzo, in *Amphores romaines et histoire économique: Dix ans de recherches* (Rome, 1989) 548–53; Volpe *La Daunia* 225–50; D. Manacorda and S. Pallecchi (eds.), *Le fornaci romane di Giancola (Brindisi)* (Bari, 2012).

122. Marble tiles found by Paolo Orsi in 1910–11 in excavations in the temple of Hera on the Lacinian promontory near Croton. The temple, surrounded by a grove of firs which sheltered herds of wild cattle dedicated to the goddess, was one of the most sacred shrines in Magna Graecia. It was built in the Doric order early in the sixth century BC and largely reconstructed in the second quarter of the fifth century. One column survives *in situ*, and much of the stylobate. The temple was spared by Pyrrhus and Hannibal, but was despoiled in 173 BC by the censor Q. Fulvius Flaccus, who removed its marble roof tiles to adorn the temple of Fortuna Equestris in Rome which he had vowed during the Celtiberian War in Spain. When the Senate heard of the sacrilege it voted unanimously to authorize a contract for transporting the tiles back to the temple and ordered expiatory offerings to be made to Hera. The contractors subsequently reported that they had left the tiles in the sanctuary, since they were unable to find skilled workers to replace them (Livy XLII.3.1). The task would have been

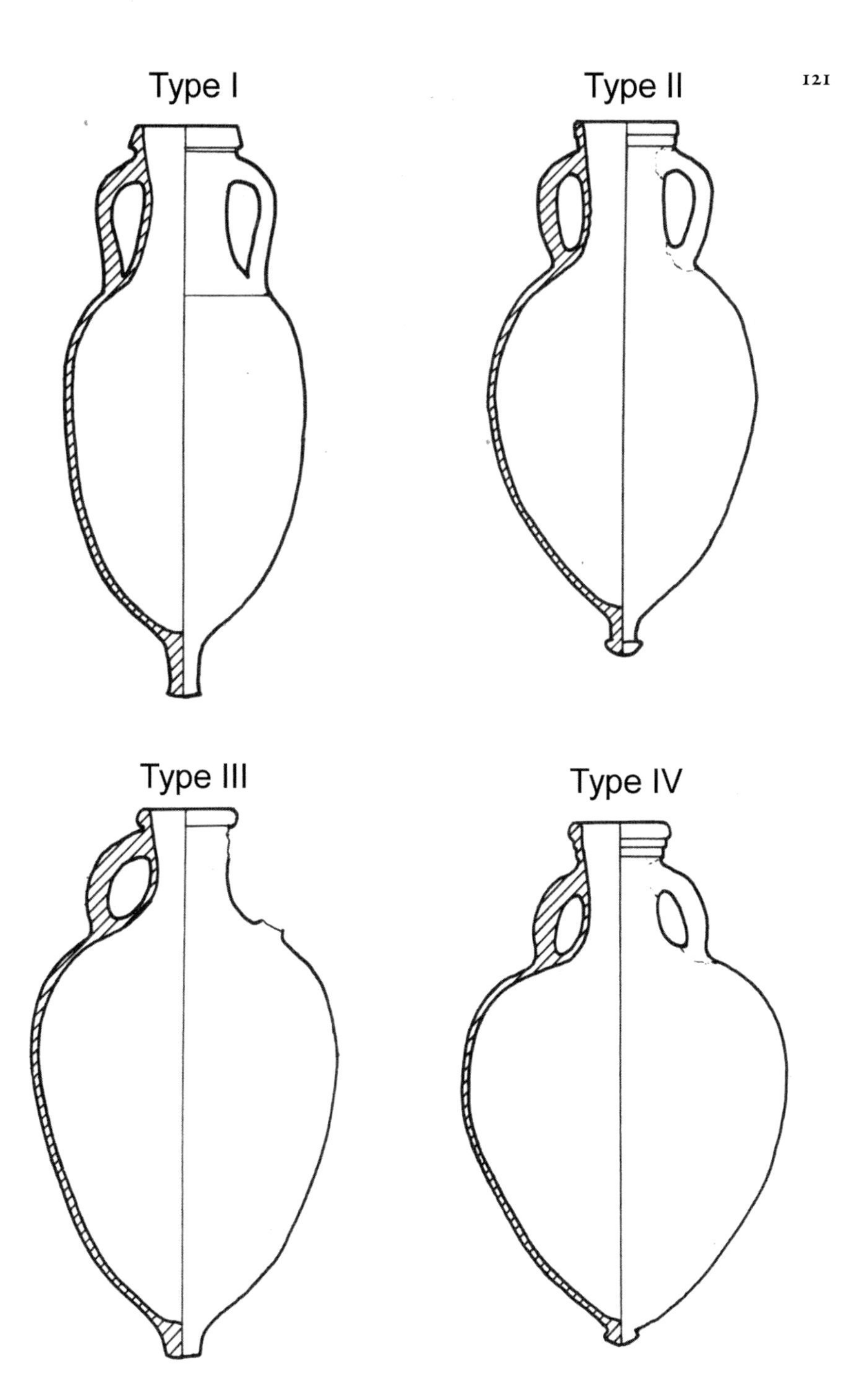
Type I
Type II
Type III
Type IV

122

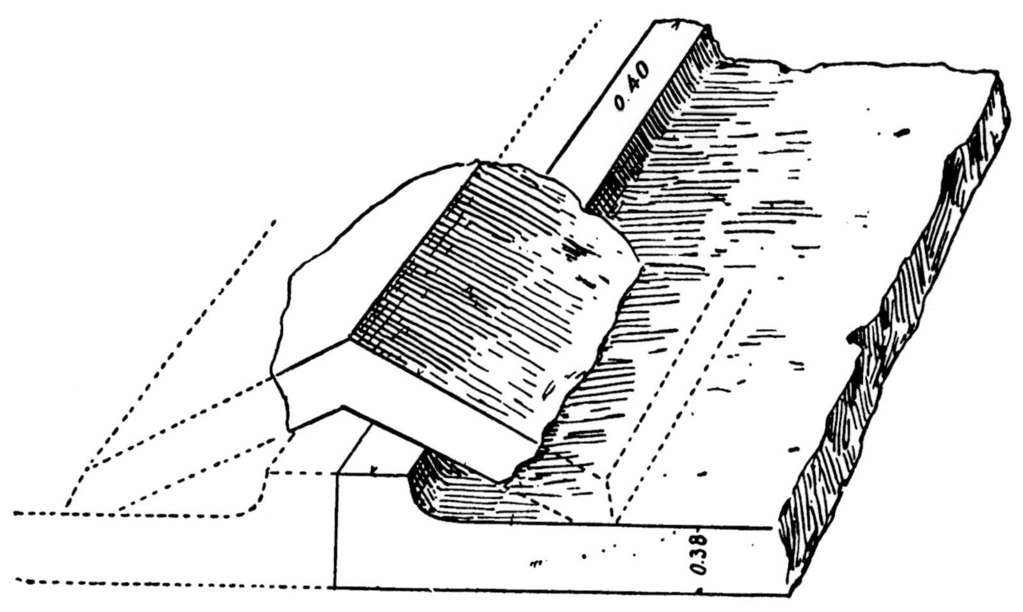

difficult, since surviving fragments show that the tiles were of several types and were cut to slot into one another in specific positions on the roof.

The archaeological evidence, however, shows that they were eventually replaced. The remains of at least two sets of marble tiles have been discovered in excavations: one of Parian marble was probably made when the temple was rebuilt in the fifth century; the second, of Pentelic marble, perhaps dates to a reconstruction under Augustus after damage done to the shrine by Sextus Pompey. The roof was of Corinthian type, with large flat tiles with raised edges set side by side on the rafters, and narrower tiles, triangular in section, covering the joints between them.

The sanctuary at the time of the sacrilege had been incorporated in the Roman colony of Croton, founded on the promontory in 194 BC.

(From Orsi 1911: 100 fig. 77)

P. Orsi, 'Crotone' in *NSc* Supplement 1911; R. Spadea (ed.), *I greci in occidente: Il Tesoro di Hera. Scoperte nel santuario di Hera Lacinia a Capo Colonna di Crotone* (Milan, 1996); Spadea, in *Atti del XLIV Convegno di Studi sulla Magna Grecia* (Taranto, 2005) 517–34.

123. The Lucanian settlement at Cività di Tricarico was probably destroyed in the Hannibalic War and rebuilt in the second century BC within the area of the former acropolis. The new buildings included a house of Romano-Campanian type with narrow entrance (*fauces*) at **a**, bedrooms (*cubicula*) at **b**, wings (*alae*) where clients could be marshalled at **c**, ceremonial bedroom (*tablinum*) of the master of the house at **d**, dining-room (*triclinium*) at **e**, and *atrium* with shallow pool (*impluvium*) for collecting rainwater off the inward sloping roof at **f**. In front of the building several shops **g** opened onto a public space, perhaps a forum. This was closed on the west side by a small temple which was also built on a contemporary Romano-Campanian plan, with central cella **h** flanked by two side *alae* **i** and broad *pronaos* **j** standing on a high plinth approached by a flight of steps **k** on the same axis as the cella.

The settlement was destroyed early in the first century BC, probably in the Social War.

M.G. Canosa, in Salvatore (ed.) *Basilicata* 111–23; O. De Cazanove, in Lo Cascio and Storchi Marino (eds.) *Modalità insediative* 170–202.

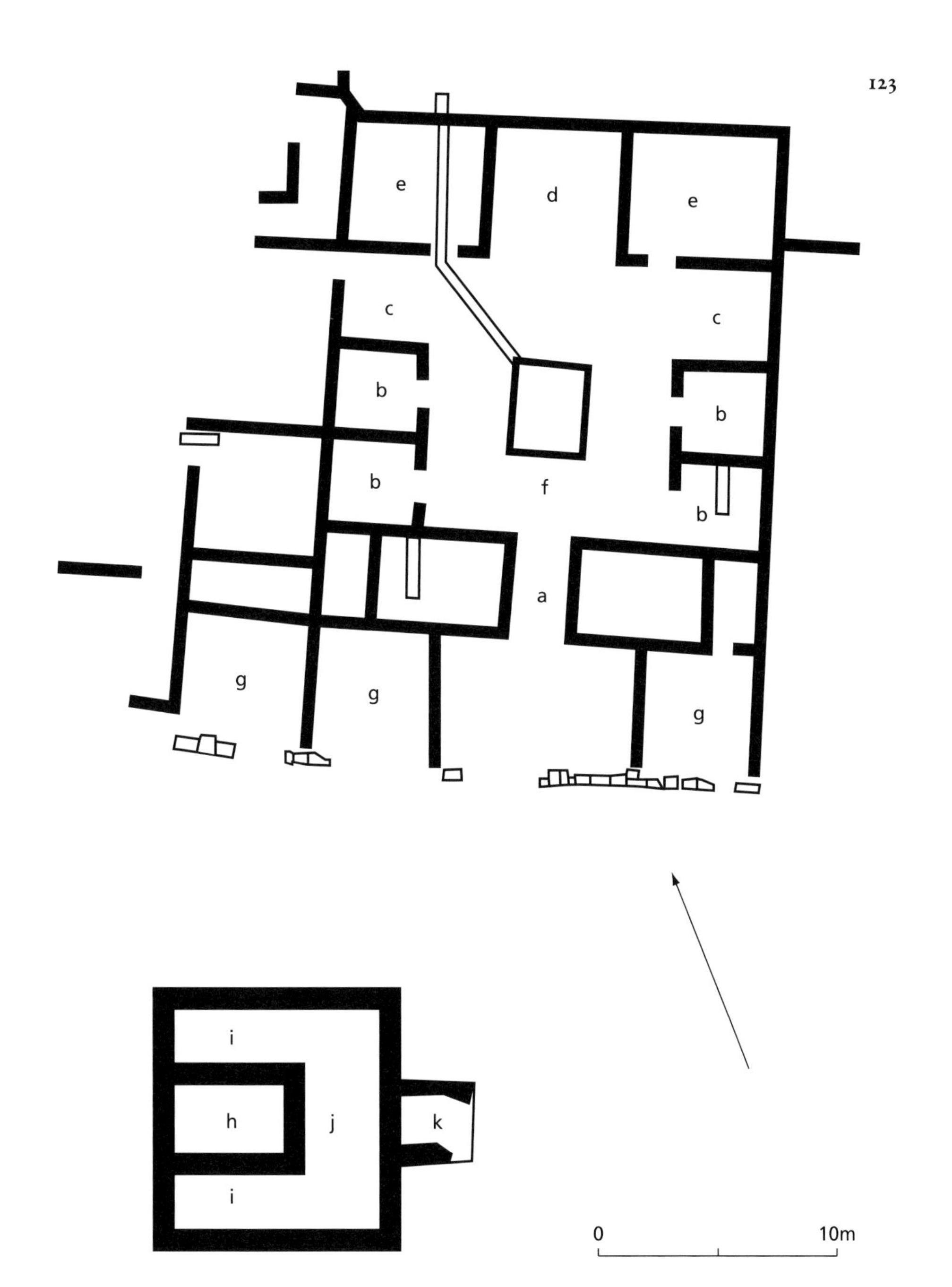

e
d
e
c
c
b
b
b
f
b
a
g
g
g
i
h
j
k
i
0
10m

7. SICILY *c.* 300 BC – 133 BC

R. J. A. WILSON

Sicily during much of the third century BC was in a state of flux. Tension between the Carthaginian possessions in the western third of the island and the Greek city-states of the remainder had been endemic for centuries, but in the aftermath of the murder of Agathocles of Syracuse in 289, and the subsequent seizure of Messina by his former Campanian mercenaries the Mamertines, a new set of military problems arose, which ultimately prompted Rome to intervene in Sicily on their behalf. This was the catalyst for the outbreak of the First Punic War between Rome and Carthage (264–241 BC). Shortly before this, probably in 270 BC, Hieron II had seized power in Syracuse, and although he briefly made an alliance with Carthage at the start of the war, he quickly changed sides and concluded a peace treaty with Rome. His subsequent unswerving loyalty to Rome, both during and after the war, meant that not only did his extensive kingdom escape the fighting and destruction in which much of western and central Sicily was embroiled, but also that peace, prosperity and political autonomy were maintained for his kingdom, with Rome's blessing, down to his death at the age of 92 in 215. During his reign Syracuse and his kingdom in eastern Sicily flourished as never before, with substantial and ambitious new building programmes at Syracuse (**124**), Morgantina (**128**, **129**) and elsewhere. The arts prospered, with goldsmiths (**126**) and silversmiths (**133**) creating works of exceptional skill; and in Archimedes Syracuse produced one of the most brilliant scientists and engineers of antiquity. Houses began to have mosaic pavements laid in the new *tessera* technique (**131**), and unconventional developments in vaulting techniques (**132**) and tomb design (**134**), as well as new Sicilian variants of both the Corinthian (**127**) and the Ionic (**154b**) capital, all point to the reign of Hieron II being one of exceptional artistic and intellectual fervour.

The Carthaginian *epikrateia* in western Sicily (**135–44**) focused on its two key strongholds of Panormus (Palermo: **135**) and Lilybaeum (Marsala: **136**), but its eastern boundaries fluctuated as places changed sides: one example is Monte Adranone, originally a Hellenized hill-top centre, and later a Carthaginian fort with barracks (**141**) and Punic temples (**142**) until its destruction in the First Punic War. The Punic ship wrecked off Marsala (**144**) may be a further witness to the hostilities of that time. Even after the incorporation of western Sicily into the Roman sphere of influence after 241 BC, aspects of the Phoenicio-Punic heritage lived on: the cult of Astarte–Venus on Mount Eryx (**143**), complete with temple prostitution, remained popular during the Roman Republic, while at Soluntum on the north coast, temples of Punic type (**139**) were still being built in the second century BC.

The political and military uncertainties around the time of the First Punic War are reflected also in the remarkable series of bronze decrees from the cities of Entella and Nakone in western Sicily (**148**), while other places, such as Lipari (**145**), have provided vivid archaeological evidence of the destruction wrought during the war. Cities took time to recover, and also to adjust to the new demands of Roman hegemony; but the establishment of the *pax Romana*, which allowed settled conditions throughout the island for the first time in its history, and the stimulus to agriculture provided by the taxation system (the *lex Hieronica*) and by the potential of selling surplus grain overseas, led to remarkable economic prosperity for many of the Sicilian cities during the second century BC. It is witnessed by the substantial rebuilding programmes of civic centres, theatres and other public buildings at places like Soluntum (**150–1**), Segesta (**149**) and Ietas (**152–3**), as well as by the erection of sumptuous private residences too (**154**). Grain continued to be the mainstay of this economic well-being, and the source of Sicily's political importance to Rome, but wine (**146**) and probably olive oil (**147**) also had important contributions to make to the agricultural economy. Yet despite being politically under the control of Rome as her first overseas *provincia*, Sicily remained during the second century BC (and for long afterwards) essentially a Greek island at heart: there are few Latin inscriptions, and only occasional signs of Roman architectural influence in the form of Italian-style temples with lofty podia – and even these were constructed with time-honoured Greek-style building methods (155).

GENERAL BIBLIOGRAPHY

M. I. Finley, *Ancient Sicily* (2nd edn, London, 1979) 109–36; G. Pugliese Carratelli (ed.), *Sikanie: Storia e civiltà della Sicilia greca* (Milan, 1985) 277–358 and 577–631; T. Fischer-Hansen (ed.), *Ancient Sicily* (Acta Hyperborea 6, Copenhagen, 1995); C. Smith and J. Serrati (eds.), *Sicily from Aeneas to Augustus* (Edinburgh, 2000) 109–60; M. Caccamo Caltabiano, L. Campagna and A. Pinzone (eds.), *Nuove prospettive della ricerca sulla Sicilia del III sec. a.C: Archeologia, numismatica, storia* (Pelorias 11, Messina, 2004); M. Osanna and M. Torelli (eds.), *Sicilia ellenistica, consuetudo italica: Alle origini dell'architettura ellenistica d'Occidente* (Rome and Pisa, 2006); E. Zambon, *Tradition and Innovation: Sicily between Hellenism and Rome* (Historia Einzelschriften 205, Stuttgart, 2008); L. Campagna, in F. Colivicchi (ed.), *Local Cultures of South Italy and Sicily in the Late Republican Period: Between Hellenism and Rome* (*JRA* Supplement 83, Portsmouth, R.I., 2011) 161–84; R. J. A. Wilson, in A. J. N.W. Prag and J. Quinn (eds.), *The Hellenistic West* (Cambridge, 2013). Syracuse: C. Lehmler, *Syrakus unter Agathokles und Hieron II: Die Verbindung von Kultur und Macht in einer hellenistischen Metropole* (Frankfurt-am-Main, 2005). First Punic War: H. H. Scullard, *CAH* VII.II² 537–54. Coins: M. Caccamo Caltabiano, B. Carroccio and E. Oteri, *Siracusa ellenistica: Le monete 'regali' di Ierone II, della sua famiglia e dei Siracusani* (Pelorias 2, Messina, 1997).

SYRACUSE: THE KINGDOM OF HIERON II (*c.* 270–215 BC)

124. Few monuments of Hieronian Syracuse survive, and of these by far the most substantial is the theatre, at 138 m in diameter the largest theatre in the Greek West. It was built on a hillside (a) in the north-west outskirts of Syracuse, in the Neapolis ('New city') district (which itself represents an expansion of the city by Hieron II), and faces south towards the Great Harbour, seen here in the background. The seating is well preserved because most of it was carved out of the natural rock; only the upper tiers were built in cut stone, now completely robbed. Little survives of the scene building: trying to distinguish different building phases from the myriad slots and post-holes in that area is far from easy, and their scholarly

124a

124b

interpretation has met with little unanimity. We do know, however, that the Hieronian scene building was decorated with figures of caryatids and probably satyrs in the *telamon* pose (cf. **152**), of which some parts survive. Valiant but unconvincing attempts have also been made to hypothesize the form of the archaic and classical theatres assumed to have been built on the same site before the Hieronian building, but the likelihood is that the ambitious Hieronian theatre, larger than its predecessors, will have removed them completely in the course of excavating a larger auditorium out of the hillside. What is certain is that the visible *koilon* (Latin *cavea*) is the work of Hieron II in or after 238 BC, because the lowest horizontal gangway (*diazoma*) is inscribed at intervals around it: the surviving names are Zeus Olympios, Hieron and his queen, Philistis (**b**: ΒΑΣΙΛΙΣΣΑΣ ΦΙΛΙΣΤΙΔΟΣ, in the genitive; only her name, not her title, is visible in the photograph), and Queen Nereis, Hieron's daughter-in-law, whom his son Gelon did not marry until 238 BC. Architecturally, Hieron's theatre is important because its seating follows a semicircular or D-shaped plan, common in the West, as opposed to the two-thirds of a circle normal in Greece and Asia Minor. Although not the earliest with such a plan (Metaponto's in southern Italy of *c.* 300 BC has that distinction), the Syracusan theatre was influential in dictating the form of later, smaller Sicilian theatres, and it was ultimately this D-shaped theatre plan, rather than the traditional theatre of ancient Greece, which was adopted in Italy and later throughout the Roman world.

(Photos **a**, **b** R. J. A. Wilson)

R. Ling (ed.), *CAH Plates* VII.1^{2} 80 no. 98; L. Bernabò Brea, *Palladio* 17 (1967) 97–154; L. Polacco and C. Anti, *Il teatro antico di Siracusa* (Rimini, 1981); Lehmler *Syrakus unter Agathokles und Hieron II* 122–35 and 172–6. Model for the Roman theatre: L. Polacco, *Numismatica e antichità classiche* 6 (1977) 107–17; F. Sear, *Roman Theatres: An Architectural Study* (Oxford, 2006) 48–50. Caryatid: G. E. Rizzo, *Il teatro greco di Siracusa* (Milan and Rome, 1923) 97–101; E. Langlotz and M. Hirmer, *The Art of Magna Graecia* (London, 1965) 301 no. 156. Metaponto: D. Mertens and A. De Siena, *Bollettino d'Arte* 67.116 (1982) 1–60.

125. The theatre at Syracuse was the focal point of a considerable building-programme undertaken by King Hieron II in the north-west quarter, which included a massive altar, 200 m long, in honour of Zeus Eleutherios – the largest anywhere in the Greek world (**a**); a Π-shaped stoa round the back of the theatre itself, of which part of the foundations is seen in **b**; and a further Π-shaped stoa on a higher level above this terrace, arranged on the

125a

125b

axis of the theatre and enclosing a vast open piazza. Here there was an already existing archaic temple with two tombs let into it in the fifth century BC, presumably indicating a hero cult; a second temple built to one side is Hieronian. Further away, another huge Hieronian stoa has been identified in the Achradina district, near the modern stadium, and an unusual circular monument, also apparently Hieronian, has been uncovered west of Piazza Adda. Considerable attention was also paid by the king to supplying the city with adequate water supplies, which were used not only for practical needs but also for conspicuous display. Slightly off centre in the terrace behind the theatre is a nymphaeum, an arched opening (visible in the centre of **b**), below which is a basin. Into it water cascades before being channelled off down the hillside and towards the city. The water was delivered by a rock-cut aqueduct, known as the Ninfeo, which brought (and still brings) water from a spring on Epipolae 1.39 km away. The aqueduct is underground throughout its length, and there are inspection manholes at intervals along it; extraordinarily, there is also a second horizontal tunnel cut in the rock immediately above the water channel itself. The purpose of this additional feature, virtually unique to Syracuse, is puzzling (a service channel to relieve direct rock pressure from above on the water channel?); it is one of three rock-cut aqueducts at Syracuse, presumably all contemporary, which share the same distinctive feature. One, the Tremilia, only 815 m long but at one point 19 m below the surface (among the deepest of all known ancient aqueducts), heads not for the city but straight for the southern precipice of Epipolae. This has given rise to speculation that the aqueduct may have driven a water-powered mill located below the cliff edge. If true, this would be a precocious example (the earliest water-mill anywhere) of ancient water-driven technological innovation – yet one wholly in keeping with the fertile creativity of Hieronian Syracuse.

(Photos R. J. A. Wilson)

Nymphaeum: Polacco (ed.), *Il teatro antico di Siracusa: Pars altera* (Padua, 1990) 41–6. Stoa above theatre: G. Voza, *Kokalos* 39–40 (1993–4) 1288–91. Altar: L. Karlsson, *Opuscula Romana* 21 (1996) 83–7; C. Parisi Presicce, in Caccamo Caltabiano, Campagna and Pinzone (eds.) *Nuove prospettive* 213–28; Lehmler *Syrakus unter Agathokles und Hieron II* 135–45. Achradina stoa: R. J. A. Wilson, *Archaeological Reports for 1995–96* (London, 1996) 67. Circular monument: G. Voza, *Nel segno dell'antico: Archeologia nel territorio di Siracusa* (Palermo, 1999) 106 fig. 83. Aqueducts: F. S. Cavallari and A. Holm, *Topografia archeologica di Siracusa* (Palermo, 1883) 95–142; R. J. A. Wilson, in G. C. M. Jansen (ed.), *Cura aquarum in Sicilia* (Leiden, 2000) 12–15.

126. These barley ears, made entirely of gold, were found in a tomb at Syracuse in 1900. Because the archaeological context is now lost, the precise date is uncertain, and the object cannot therefore be certainly linked with the age of Hieron II; but since Syracuse at that time was home to outstanding gold- and silversmiths, a Hieronian date is not impossible. Very little third-century BC gold- or silverware survives from Hieronian Syracuse, apart from a small amount of jewellery (but see **133**). The ears of barley are remarkable for their superlatively naturalistic rendering and their high technical skill, but the function of this piece is uncertain. However, the discovery of a similar example in the hands of a woman buried in the Great Bliznitsa on the Taman peninsula on the Black Sea raises the possibility that the ears of barley served as an attribute of a priestess of Demeter (presumably the occupant of the Syracuse tomb), and that it was carried by her in religious processions and the like as a symbol of her office. Whatever its precise date and purpose, the Syracuse barley ears both symbolize the economic prosperity of ancient Sicily, based above all on grain, and also provide testimony to the outstanding skill of a high-quality Syracusan goldsmith in the early Hellenistic period.

(Private collection, United States of America. Height 30 cm)

P. Wolters, *Festschrift James Loeb* (Munich, 1930) 111; D. von Bothmer, *Ancient Art in American Private Collections* (Cambridge, Mass., 1954) no. 310, pl. LXXXVII; H. Hoffmann and P. F. Davidson, *Greek Gold: Jewellery from the Age of Alexander* (Mainz-am-Rhein, 1965) no. 137; H. Hoffmann, *The Norbert Schimmel Collection* (Mainz-am-Rhein, 1974) no. 74; A. W. Johnston, *The Emergence of Greece* (Oxford, 1976) 117; N. Yalouris *et al.*, *The Search for Alexander: An Exhibition* (Boston, 1980) 135–6 no. 65, with full bibliography. Great Bliznitsa: A. Peredolskaja, *Attische Tonfiguren aus einem südrussischen Grab* (Olten, 1964) 22 and pl. 16.4. Hieronian jewellery: G. Libertini, *Il regio museo archeologico di Siracusa* (Rome, 1929) 48 nos. 32943–5. Cf. also Polybius V.80 for Syracusan silver cauldrons and *hydriae* dedicated at Rhodes; Vitruvius, IX.*Praef.* 9–10, for Archimedes and the story of a gold crown made by a Syracusan goldsmith.

127. Example of a terracotta Corinthian capital, from Tindari (ancient Tyndaris), 45 km west of Messina, probably second half of the second century BC. Late Hellenistic Corinthian capitals in Sicily tend to follow rules of their own which distinguish them from their counterparts in mainland Greece and Asia Minor. Sicilian examples generally have rather taller proportions; the central flower (missing here) tends to be heavier and clumsier; the *helices* (here replaced by leaves) on either side of the flower usually have smooth, rounded stems and spring not from lower parts of the volutes (as is customary in 'classic' Corinthian)

127

but independently; and there are no *cauliculi* – the sheaves, topped by an acanthus leaf, out of which volutes normally emerge. In addition, the leaves attached to the back of the volutes are generally much more prominent than they are in mainstream Hellenistic Corinthian; and the acanthus leaves themselves, which occupy the lower half of the capital, often display a great deal of fussy detail, and are spiky and pointed. Overall, therefore, they have a different appearance from that of their more sophisticated counterparts in mainland Greece at this time. In the course of the second century BC, this Sicilian version of Corinthian spread beyond the shores of Sicily to the Italian peninsula and to north Africa, and although there are regional variations, in essence the standard Italian Republican Corinthian capital, seen in places such as Pompeii where second-century BC buildings are still standing (for example, in the Basilica and the House of the Fawn), is closely based on this variant invented in Sicily in the course of the third century BC. Chronological uncertainties (the absence of closely dated examples) make it difficult to say exactly when and where this variant Sicilian Corinthian type first developed, but in view of what we know about Syracuse's leading role in artistic creativity during the third century BC, it would not be surprising if that city played a major part in the creation and dissemination of the new capital type. For a Sicilian variety also of the Ionic capital, see **154b**.

(Photo R. J. A. Wilson. Tindari, Antiquarium)

H. Lauter-Bufe, *Die Gesichichte des sikeliotisch-korinthischen Kapitells: Der sogenannte italisch-republikanische Typus* (Mainz-am-Rhein, 1987) 17–21, no. 27, with Taf. 9–10; H. Lauter, *Die Architektur des Hellenismus* (Darmstadt, 1986), with Taf. 35a; R. J. A. Wilson, in M. Henig (ed.), *Architecture and Architectural Sculpture in the Roman Empire* (Oxford, 1990) 72–3, with figs. 5.7 and 5.8; U. Spigo (ed.), *Tindari: L'area archeologica e l'antiquarium* (Milazzo, 2005) 47 fig. 6; L. Campagna, in G.M. Bacci and M.C. Martinelli (eds.), *Studi classici in onore di Luigi Bernabò Brea* (Palermo, 2003) 149–68.

128. In the absence of a great deal surviving of the Hieronian period at Syracuse, our best glimpse of a town of this period can be gleaned from the American excavations since 1955 at Serra Orlando, a site in east central Sicily which lay just within the confines of Hieron's kingdom. It is almost certainly to be identified as the ancient Morgantina. Situated on a 3-km-long ridge with extensive springs and fine views, the site had been occupied from the later Neolithic onwards, and had become a considerable village by the time of the Iron Age in the seventh and early sixth centuries BC. Little is known of the town which subsequently developed in the course of the later sixth, fifth and fourth centuries, but it was progressively Hellenized during this period through contact with Greek colonies on and near the east coast, particularly Lentini and Catania. It reached its heyday in the third century BC, especially during the reign of Hieron II of Syracuse, who fortified the town and embellished it with a number of fine public buildings, especially in the agora. The latter occupied a narrow valley between two hills, sloping downwards from north to south. The northern part was closed off by substantial stoas on the north, west and east (1, 2 and 3 on **a**), with a small public fountain at the angle between two of them (4); the town's council chamber (*bouleuterion*) lies just outside the agora to the north-west (5). The difference in level between the two halves of the agora was marked by a grandiose, monumental staircase, with fourteen steps on three different alignments; it may also have served as the town's *ekklesiasterion* (6). The southern part of the agora is framed by the theatre to the west (7), with seats occupying a semicircle in imitation of Syracuse's (see **124**), and by a large granary to the east (8; see **129**); a smaller granary (9) and a sanctuary of Demeter and Persephone (10) occupy the central area here. The photo (**b**) is taken from the eastern hill, looking over the southern part of the agora towards the theatre.

(**a** After B. Tsakirgis, in Fischer-Hansen (ed.) *Ancient Sicily* 124 fig. 1; **b** photo R. J. A. Wilson)

R. Ling (ed.), *CAH Plates* VII.1[2] 79–80, no. 97; B. Tsakirgis, in Fischer-Hansen (ed.) *Ancient Sicily* 123–47; M. Bell, in G. Nenci and G. Vallet (eds.), *Bibliografia topografica della colonizzazione greca in Italia e nelle isole tirreniche*, vol. XVIII (Pisa, 2010) 724–51; *Morgantina Studies* I–V (Princeton, 1981–96) and in press; preliminary reports in *AJA* 61 (1957) 151–9; 62 (1958) 155–64; 63 (1959) 167–73; 64 (1960) 125–35; 65 (1961) 277–81; 66 (1962) 135–43; 67 (1963) 163–71; 68 (1964) 137–47; 71 (1967) 245–50; 74 (1970) 359–83; 78 (1974) 361–84; and 92 (1988) 313–42. Fountain: M. Bell, *Quaderni dell'Istituto di Archeologia della Università di Messina* 2 (1986–7) 111–24. Theatre: K. Mitens, *Teatri greci e teatri ispirati all'architettura greca in Sicilia e nell'Italia meridionale c. 350–50 a.C.* (Rome, 1988) 105–8; A. Sposito (ed.), *Morgantina: Il teatro ellenistico, Storia e restauri* (Rome, 2011) (who, however, suggests that the theatre in its present form is as early as *c.* 300 BC. If so, it would be one of the very first anywhere with a semicircular auditorium; a Hieronian date seems more likely).

129. A visitor to Morgantina, entering the town from the south, would first have seen two impressive granaries flanking the way on either side, leaving him or her in no doubt about both the productivity of the surrounding countryside in its yields of wheat and barley, and the source of the wealth which enabled the creation of impressive public monuments (**128**) and rich private houses (**130–1**) in third-century BC Morgantina. Their location close to a gate in the walled circuit provided ready accessibility from the fields outside. The west granary (9 on **128a**) was at least 33 m long and 7.5 m wide. Its eastern counterpart, a portion

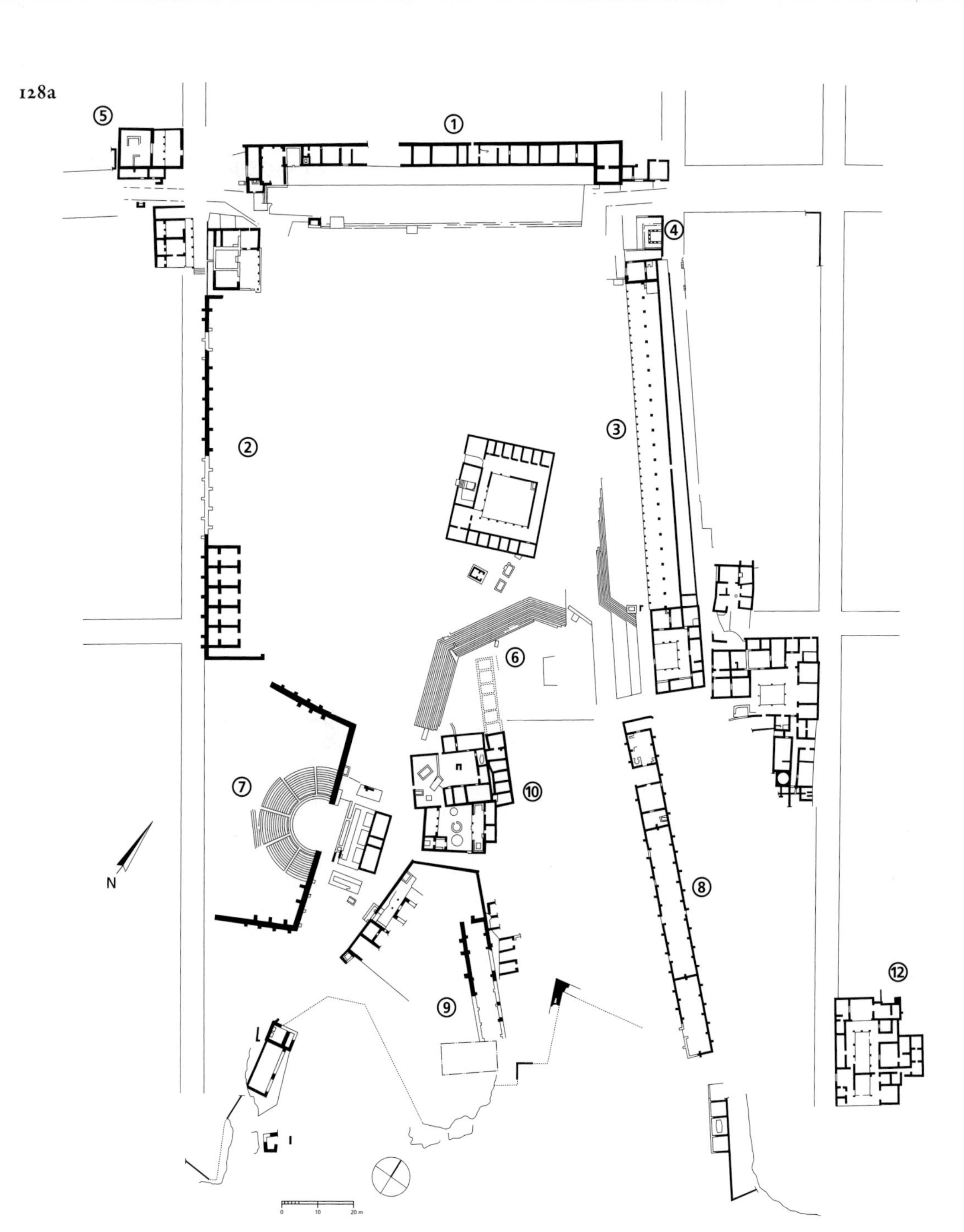

of which is seen here, was a massive 92.85 m long and a little wider (7.6 m); there are several internal subdivisions. The latter was certainly of Hieronian date, but its companion may be pre-Hieronian, since a Syracusan coin of *c.* 310/290 BC was found in the floor packing, suggesting that it may have been built and in use in the earlier part of the third century BC. However, a chronology resting on a single coin may not be reliable, and it is more likely that the granaries should be seen as a pair (they are built on the same, parallel axis), and that both are contemporary and of Hieronian date. Both buildings were given weatherproof stucco rendering on the outside. Both also were provided with buttresses,

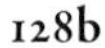

128b

129

some internal and some external, to strengthen the walls, because of the strain placed on them by loose grain in bins resting against them: this was a practice which became standard in granaries (especially military granaries) during the Roman Empire, but Morgantina's are the earliest that we know of to have employed this feature. Livy remarks on the fine appearance of the royal granaries on Ortygia at Syracuse (XXIV.21.11–12), and the Morgantina buildings, especially the huge eastern granary, must also have been striking: Deussen indeed has speculated that the latter was a gift to the city by Hieron himself. It was Hieron who introduced the *lex Hieronica*, the regulation by which all cities in his kingdom paid a one-tenth tithe on their grain produce, widely regarded as a fair and efficient taxation system (adopted also by the Roman administration in Sicily). The Morgantina granaries are testimony both to the grain-producing potential of the *ager Murgentinus* and to the appropriate organizational arrangements made for storing it in a strong, safe and dry place.

(Photo R. J. A. Wilson)

E. Sjöqvist, *AJA* 64 (1960) 130–1; M. Bell, *AJA* 92 (1988) 321–4; P. W. Deussen, in AA. VV., *Le ravitaillement en blé de Rome et des centres urbains des débuts de la République jusqu'au haut Empire* (Naples and Rome, 1994) 231–5; Lehmler *Syrakus unter Agathokles und Hieron II* 176–7; M. Bell, in A. J. N. W. Prag (ed.), *Rhetoric, Law and Taxation in Cicero's Verrines* (*Bulletin of the Institute of Classical Studies* Supplement 97, London, 2007) 124. For a Hieronian date for the western granary, see now Bell, in J. Duboulez and S. Pittia (eds.), *La Sicile de Cicéron: Lectures des Verrines* (Besançon, 2007) 187.

130. A typical well-to-do residence of the third century BC at Morgantina (The House of the Ganymede), with rooms arranged around all four sides of a peristyled walkway, itself enclosing a central courtyard or garden. Several houses of this type, some of them destroyed in the Roman attack of 211 BC, have been excavated at Morgantina and make it clear that by then the peristyle house was established in Sicily as the standard residence of the well-to-do (see also **154**). The remains of a staircase indicate that the house had at least a partial second storey, and there was a bathroom on the ground floor. Two cisterns stored rain water, one under the peristyle court, the other under an adjacent room. The columns of the peristyle are not of stone but consist of great circular slabs of terracotta with a central hole, an eccentricity presumably due to local production; they were liberally covered with stucco on the outside in imitation of marble. The peristyle as an architectural type was probably borrowed from mainland Greece, where it occurs in public buildings (such as the Pompeion at the Dipylon Gate in Athens) as early as the late fifth century BC. It was then adopted in the palaces of the Macedonian kings in the third quarter of the fourth century BC, and subsequently by other grand private houses at Pella and elsewhere by *c.* 300 BC. Stone peristyles also appear in some of the houses of Punic north Africa in the first half of the third century BC (e.g. Kerkouane: see **172**), possibly

130

through the intermediary influence of Sicily. The House of the Ganymede has three rooms with mosaic pavements (see **131**) opening onto the peristyle walkway; the latter is paved (as were two other rooms) with another fashionable floor-covering common in Sicilian Hellenistic houses for the less important chambers, that of *opus signinum* (pink mortar with a strong component of crushed brick); but in the latter case the origins for this floor-type lie in late fourth-century BC Carthage, and its use in Sicily therefore represents a borrowing from north Africa rather than the other way round.

(Photo R. J. A. Wilson)

Sjöqvist, *AJA* 64 (1960) 131–3; *opus signinum* in this house: B. Tsakirgis, *AJA* 94 (1990) 428–9. Athens, Pompeion: W. Hoepfner, *Das Pompeion und seine Nachfolgerbauten* (Berlin, 1976); other early peristyles: Hoepfner, in Hoepfner and G. Brands (eds.), *Basileia: Die Paläste der hellenistischen Könige* (Mainz-am-Rhein, 1996) 1–43; E. Walter-Karydi, in Hoepfner and Brands (eds.), *Basileia* 56–61. On the development of the Greek house in Sicily: E. De Miro, in ΦΙΛΙΑΣ ΧΑΡΙΝ: *Miscellanea di studi classici in onore di Eugenio Manni*, vol. II (Rome, 1980) 709–37; De Miro, in F. D'Andria and K. Mannino (eds.), *Ricerche sulla casa in Magna Grecia e in Sicilia* (Galatina, 1996) 17–40; H. P. Isler and D. Käch (eds.), *Wohnbauforschung in Zentral- und Westsizilien/Sicilia occidentale e centro-meridionale: Ricerche archeologiche nell'abitato. Akten–Atti* (Zurich, 1997); M. Wolf, *Die Häuser von Solunt und die hellenistische Wohnarchitektur* (Deutsches Archäologisches Institut Rom, Sonderschriften 14, Mainz-am-Rhein, 2003) esp. 79–110; and especially, in the context of Morgantina, B. Tsakirgis, in D. B. Counts and A. S. Tuck (eds.), *Koine: Mediterranean Studies in Honor of R. Ross Holloway* (Oxford and Oakville, 2009) 109–21.

131. Mosaic pavement in a house (**130**) at Morgantina, unfortunately badly damaged, which depicts the shepherd Ganymede being seized

131

by Zeus in the form of an eagle and borne up to Olympus to serve as his cup-bearer; the whole composition is set against a dark-blue background. Part of the face of Ganymede survives, as well as his legs; of the eagle only its right wing, the tip of the left and the tail feathers have been preserved. The figured panel has a border of meander pattern seen in perspective; the rest of the floor is composed of plain white *tesserae*. At the time of its discovery, the Ganymede mosaic was dated to *c*. 260/50 BC and so counted as among the earliest mosaics then known in the new *tessera* technique, in which artificially cut cube-shaped pieces of stone replaced the rounded river pebbles of earlier usage. Claims were even advanced that Sicily under King Hieron might have invented the *tessera* technique (his luxury barge, the *Syracosia*, which also had mosaic decoration, has been used as supporting evidence), and that it only later spread to Ptolemaic Egypt (and in particular Alexandria), with which Hieron enjoyed close ties.

The early date of the Morgantina Ganymede has, however, now been questioned, and a date after the middle of the third century, and probably in its third quarter, seems more likely; but it must be earlier than 211 BC, since the house in which the floor was found, although reoccupied until the mid second century BC, was no longer at that date an elite single residence. The colours used in the mosaic are varied: apart from black and white, red, yellow, green, blue, brown and grey are used, often in more than one shade. In addition to regular *tesserae*, stones cut to the required shape are present in some parts (such as in Ganymede's eyes), and very thin strips are sometimes used, for example in the eagle's wings. Another mosaic in the same house, a square of meander pattern and an adjacent fillet surrounded by an ivy-scroll border, shows a wider variety of techniques: there regularly cut *tesserae*, less regular *tesserae* and irregular chips of stone are found in the same pavement. This suggests that the Morgantina floors represent an experimental phase in the transition to fully fledged *tessera* mosaics, a process which had occurred by the beginning of the second century; similar experiments were taking place during the third century BC in several other places in the Mediterranean, and especially at Alexandria. Nevertheless, the Ganymede mosaic remains important as one of the earliest closely datable mosaics in the *tessera* technique anywhere in the Mediterranean world. No doubt there were many more in Hieronian Syracuse, but these have been entirely lost.

(Photo Morgantina Excavations, courtesy M. Bell)

K. Phillips, *Art Bulletin* 42 (1960) 243–62; D. von Boeselager, *Antike Mosaiken in Sizilien* (Rome, 1983) 397–400; B. Tsakirgis, *AJA* 93 (1989) 395–416, esp. 399–400; K. M. D. Dunbabin, *Mosaics of the Greek and Roman World* (Cambridge, 1999) 21–2; and now, more fully, M. Bell, in G. F. La Torre and M. Torelli (eds.), *Pittura ellenistica in Italia e in Sicilia: Linguaggi e tradizioni: Atti del Convegno di Studi (Messina, 24–5 settembre 2009)* (Rome, 2011) 105–23.

132. Excavation in the 1970s at Morgantina, to the west of the main archaeological zone at the centre of the city (**128**), uncovered a domed circular room just under 6 m in diameter in what is clearly a small bath-building; resumed excavation on this complex in 2003–10 has completed its plan and revealed further vaulted rooms and evidence for a semicircular metal water tank built into the masonry wall of a bath – the earliest known example of what Vitruvius called *testudines alveorum* ('the tortoises of the pools'). On coin evidence, the bath structure belongs to the middle of the third century BC. As the zone was completely abandoned after the Roman seizure of the town in 211 BC, the life of the building falls wholly within the third century BC. The precociously early examples of barrel vaults and the dome in the circular room were made not of concrete (which had not yet been invented), but of hollow interlocking tubular tiles, which are clearly visible here among the fallen debris. Each tile is cylindrical and hollow, and has a nozzle at one end to enable each to fit snugly into its neighbour; the rest of the tube is cylindrical and smooth. Each is about 68 cm long. The vaults were constructed by fastening tubes together with quick-setting lime until the roof was covered; both the inside and outside of the tubes were subsequently plastered (see photograph, left centre), so that the tubes themselves were invisible once the dome or vault was complete. This is the earliest example of a novel form of roofing that was later to be widely employed, using rather smaller tubes (normally 12 to 20 cm long), in north Africa from the later second century AD, and thereafter quite widely in the central Mediterranean world. Other circular rooms are known in bath-buildings in Hieron's kingdom, one at Syracuse excavated in the 1930s where vaulting tubes were also found, and another at Megara Hyblaea, where the roofing method is unclear. More recently, a large circular building of uncertain function has been excavated in the agora at Acrae, west of Syracuse. How it was roofed is

132

also not clear, but there was a basic framework of solid brick ribs, of which the bases are *in situ* on one side. These buildings represent exciting experiments in a new approach to interior design, both in their integration of circular halls into buildings which hitherto had had exclusively square and rectangular rooms, and in the roofing challenges that such circular rooms posed. As such, this Sicilian architectural innovation foreshadows, by more than two centuries, Roman developments in the design of interior space and the introduction of the concrete dome.

(Morgantina Excavations, courtesy M. Bell)

Morgantina: H.L. Allen, *AJA* 78 (1974) 376–9; new excavations: S. Lucore, in C. Kosso and A. Scott (eds.), *The Nature and Function of Water, Baths, Bathing and Hygiene from Antiquity through the Renaissance* (Technology and Change in History 11, Leiden and Boston, 2009) 43–59. *Testudo*: Vitruvius V.10.1; S. Lucore, *American Excavations at Morgantina: Newsletter of the Friends of Morgantina, May 2011* (Charlottesville, VA, 2011) 4–5. Syracuse: G. Cultrera, *NSc* (1938), 286. Megara Hyblaea: G. Vallet, F. Villard and P. Auberson, *Megara Hyblaea 3: Guide des fouilles* (Rome, 1983) 56. Acrae: unpublished. Circular rooms in Sicilian bath-buildings: M. Bürge, in S. Buzzi *et al.* (eds.), *Zona archeologica: Festschrift für Hans Peter Isler zum 60. Geburtstag* (Bonn, 2001) 57–66. Vaulting tubes in general: R. J. A. Wilson, *JRA* 5 (1992) 97–129; S. Storz, *Tonröhren im antiken Gewölbebau* (Mainz-am-Rhein, 1994).

133. This outstanding hoard of six gilt-silver objects was acquired by the Metropolitan Museum of New York in 1981–2 but returned to Morgantina in 2009. It consists (**a**) of two buckets with feet in the form of theatrical masks; four bowls, three of which have appliqué leaf decoration in the centre of their interiors; a *phiale* libation plate with star-burst decoration and customary central *omphalos*; a small *pyxis* with relief decoration on the lid featuring Demeter with cornucopia and the child Ploutos on her knee; a miniature altar with garlands in relief (supported by *bucrania*) decorating the side; a deep drinking-cup (*skyphos*) with projecting horizontal handles folded back on themselves, as on other known examples from Sicily (for example, a silver *kylix* from Paternò now in Berlin); a ladle; a small jug; a pair of horns; and a superb disc, probably from the lid of another, larger *pyxis*. This last (**b**) features the monster Scylla, with upper torso in human female form, entwined with a snake, while triple canine foreparts (*protomai*) and serpent tails emerge from the acanthus leaf which envelops her below the waist. Depicted hurling a rock at an unseen passing

133a

ship, she rises in arrogant triumph over a tempestuous sea from which a dolphin leaps. Almost all the raised relief work, except for her upper body, arms and face, is gilded, and many of the details on the rest of the items in the hoard are likewise treated. The *pyxis* lid is paralleled by a similar one, also of gilt silver, now in Basle (**c**); it depicts Achilles with the Amazon queen, Penthesileia. The Basle lid is dated to *c.* 220 BC by coins of Hieron II which were found inside it. Its provenance is unknown, but presumably it came from Syracuse or from some other place in Hieron's kingdom. The Morgantina hoard was uncovered illicitly in 1981, and the actual find-spot of the treasure, within a town-house, was identified by professional excavation in 1997. Inscriptions in dotted letters on the miniature altar and the small *pyxis* indicate that the hoard was 'sacred to the gods' and presumably therefore belonged to a sanctuary; two further graffiti 'from the war' (together with accompanying numismatic evidence which escaped the looters) has led to speculation that the silver treasure was brought from Syracuse on the fall of that city to the Romans in 212 BC (rather than from a sanctuary at Morgantina). Whatever its original home, the silverware was buried in the house in 211 BC, doubtless during the Roman siege of Morgantina prior to its capture that year, and was never recovered. The Morgantina hoard and the

133b

Basle lid between them give us a precious glimpse of the superlatively high level of craftsmanship that silversmiths at Syracuse reached during the reign of Hieron II.

(**a** and **b** Formerly Metropolitan Museum of Art P32295; now Aidone Museum; photos Metropolitan Museum of Art, New York; **c** Antikenmuseum Basel und Sammlung Ludwig BS608. Photo C. Niggli)

Morgantina: D. von Bothmer, *Bulletin of the Metropolitan Museum of Art* (Summer 1984) 54–60 nos. 92–106; J. R. Mertens, *The Metropolitan Museum of Art: Greece and Rome* (New York, 1987) 80–1; A. L. Slayman, *Archaeology* 51.3 (May–June 1998) 40–1; P. G. Guzzo, *Metropolitan Museum Journal* 38 (2003) 45–94. Provenance: M. Bell, in P. Pelagatti and P. G. Guzzo (eds.), *Antichità senza provenienza II: Atti del Colloquio Internazionale 17–18 ottobre 1997* (= Supplemento to *Bollettino d'Arte* 101–2, Rome, 2000) 31–41. Basle: *Führer durch das Antikenmuseum Basel* (Basle, 1966) 42; *Enciclopedia dell'Arte Antica, Supplemento* (Rome, 1970) 606 fig. 604. Paternò (*c.* 300 BC?): D. E. Strong, *Greek and Roman Gold and Silver Plate* (London, 1966) 94 with pl. 24B.

134. On the coast 32 km south of Syracuse lies the small ancient town of Helorus (modern Eloro), which had been founded as an outpost of Syracuse before the end of the eighth century BC. Little is known of Helorus during the reign of Hieron II (an elaborate stoa belongs to the second century BC rather than to the third), but 1.6 km outside the town to the north-west is the extraordinary survival of an unusual tomb dating to the second half of the third century BC. The site is marked by a striking column, known locally as La Pizzuta; built entirely of unmortared blocks, it is 3.8 m wide at the base and still 10.5 m high, and stands on a four-step stylobate. It is astonishing (and inexplicable) how and why it escaped the stone-robbing to

133c

which such conspicuous and easily dismantlable monuments of antiquity have normally fallen prey in the intervening 2,200 years. It was long falsely interpreted as a victory monument erected by the Syracusans after their battle with the surviving Athenians at the Assinaros river in 413 BC (even though the Assinaros lies nearly 5 km to the north); but that notion was overthrown in 1899, when excavation showed that La Pizzuta overlay a subterranean burial chamber. The latter was approached from ground level by a staircase, at the bottom of which was a heavy stone door with an iron handle. The main contents of the tomb had been robbed, but remains of two human skeletons and other more fragmentary bones were found, as well as a little pottery and some small amphorae; a coin of Hieron II was held in the hand of one of the deceased. The grave chamber, the walls of which were stuccoed in red and white, had three funerary couches and a stool cut out of the living rock. La Pizzuta was presumably a family tomb built by a rich and prominent Heloran, at least one of whose family died in the second half of the third century BC. The columnar tomb-marker, without parallel on this huge scale in the entire Hellenistic world, is another indication of the architectural and artistic creativity that marked the reign of Hieron II.

(Photo R. J. A. Wilson)

P. Orsi, *Mon. Ant.* 47 (1966), 264–79. Stoa: Lauter *Die Architektur des Hellenismus* 96–7 with Abb. 16b.

THE CARTHAGINIAN *EPIKRATEIA* IN WESTERN SICILY

135. The choice of Panormus ('all harbour') by Phoenician settlers towards the beginning of the seventh century BC was inspired. Situated at the head of a fine harbour in the centre of the broad sweep of the Gulf of Palermo, the site lay on a low plateau, roughly the shape of an elongated rectangle, below which the land sloped away to stream beds to the north and south. It was therefore easily defensible; and a deep indent of the coast, now mostly silted up, meant that a superb sheltered anchorage was available right under the shadow of its walls on the east side – an asset noted by Procopius (*BG* I.5.13) in the sixth century AD. The site is framed by mountains, most notably the majestic mass of Monte Pellegrino (ancient Heirkte) to the north (centre left), while immediately to the south-west (foreground) lies an extensive strip of very fertile and well-watered land, which 'is called a garden because it is full of cultivated trees' (Athenaeus XII.542A), and which the Arabs were later to dub 'The golden basin' (Conca d'Oro). Little topographical detail

135

of the urban layout is known of this Phoenician and then Carthaginian stronghold, which fell to the Romans in 254 BC; but extensive areas of the ancient necropolis to the west of the walled circuit have been investigated in advance of modern building and have yielded a wealth of finds, especially between the sixth and third centuries BC. Some stretches of the defences have also been identified. Under the Norman Palazzo Reale, for example, excavation in the 1980s revealed a 33-m section of the walls still standing up to 2.6 m high, including one of the city's gateways flanked by projecting rectangular towers, and a small round-headed postern as well. These date to the late fifth century BC and are built in perfectly squared and neatly laid blocks in imitation of Greek contemporary practice. In the early third century BC, however, the postern was blocked and the gateway narrowed, and strengthening walls in inferior-quality masonry were built on the outer face of the classical defences – no doubt in preparation for the coming showdown with Rome.

(Photos **a** C. A. di Stefano **b** R. J. A. Wilson)
C. A. Di Stefano (ed.), *Palermo punica* (Palermo, 1998).

136a

136b

136. With the destruction of Motya in 397 BC and its subsequent almost total abandonment, Carthage evidently felt the need to have a strategic base in south-west Sicily, and around the middle of the fourth century BC a new town was founded at Capo Boeo, Sicily's westernmost extremity; it was known as Lilybaion to the Greeks, Lilybaeum to the Romans (modern Marsala). The western part of the town, nearest to Capo Boeo (**a**), still lies in open ground and is partly known through excavation and, more recently, geophysics; but the structures revealed both here and elsewhere belong largely to the Roman imperial period, and little is therefore known about the town's settlement morphology between the fourth and the first centuries BC. The original orthogonal street layout is, however, partly visible in the modern town (to the right in **a**), and sections of powerful defences up to 7 m wide with projecting rectangular towers (cf. those of Carthage: **168**) have been located; they date to the fourth century BC. On the land side these walls were further strengthened by an enormous defensive ditch, up to 28 m wide, remarked upon by both Polybius (I.42.7) and Diodorus (XXIV.1.1); it contributed to Lilybaion's reputation as an impregnable stronghold. The principal harbour, now mainly silted up, lay to the north. Most of our knowledge about Punic Marsala, however, comes from its necropolis, of which substantial tracts have been uncovered during modern building works on the north side of the ancient town. The section shown here (**b**), in Via Struppa, excavated in 1984, contained rock-cut tombs for inhumation burials, either *a fossa* (a simple deep trench) or *a pozzo* (in which one or two hypogeic burial chambers open off the foot of a vertical shaft); they date mainly to the fourth and third centuries BC. In the course of the third century BC cremation at Marsala became more popular, with urns containing the ashes of the deceased either set in the rock or buried simply in the earth. They are sometimes marked on the surface by small stepped monuments (*epitymbia*), belonging mainly to the second and first centuries BC.

(Photos R. J. A. Wilson)

C. A. Di Stefano (ed.), *Lilibeo: Testimonianze archeologiche dal IV sec. a.C. al V sec. d.C.* (Marsala, 1984); Di Stefano, *Lilibeo punica* (Marsala, 1993); R. Giglio, in M. G. Griffo Alabiso (ed.), *Marsala* (Marsala, 1997) 63–87; B. Bechtold, *La necropoli di Lilybaeum* (Palermo and Rome, 1999).

137. Found at Marsala in 1882, this example is the finest Punic stele from Sicily, crisply incised in the local white limestone. Both the iconography and the text of the inscription are closely matched by stelai in north Africa. In the shallow pediment at the top are symbols of the sun and crescent moon. Below are three betyls (aniconic objects of religious devotion) side by side, such triplism being frequent in Punic religion (cf. **159b**). In the register below, an incense burner (*thymiaterion* in Greek) is shown in the centre, while to the right a priest approaches with hands upraised. To the left is the so-called 'symbol of Tanit', the all-powerful principal goddess of the Carthaginian pantheon (cf. **159a**, **182**). The neo-Punic inscription below reads:

To lord Baal Hammon; (this stele) was dedicated by Hanno, son of Adonibaal, son of Gerashtart, son of Adonibaal, because (the lord) has listened to Hanno's voice (and) blessed him.

It was probably erected (on grounds of style and of the characters of the neo-Punic script) in the third century BC. Both text and iconography, by analogy with examples at Carthage and elsewhere, indicate that the stele probably stood in Lilybaeum's *tophet*, but this has yet to be confirmed by other discoveries at and near the stele's find-spot, in the Timpone di S. Antonio locality on the south side of the town.

(Palermo, Museo Archeologico Regionale inv. 11258. Height 0.4 m; width 0.21 m)

M. G. Guzzo Amadasi, *Le iscrizioni fenicie e puniche delle colonie in Occidente* (Studi Semitici 28, Rome, 1967) 57–8, Sicilia 5; G. Garbini, *Kokalos* 13 (1967) 66–7; A. M. Bisi, *Oriens Antiquus* 7 (1968) 99; Bisi, *Karthago* 14 (1968) 227–34, at 228–9; Di Stefano (ed.) *Lilibeo* 70–1 no. 51; M. L. Uberti, in AA. VV., *Da Mozia a Marsala: Una crocevia della civiltà mediterranea* (Marsala, 1990) 109; Di Stefano *Lilibeo punica* 39. Location of *tophet*: E. Caruso, *Terze giornate internazionali di studi sull'area elima: Atti* (Pisa and Gibellina, 2000) 234–40. Carthage comparanda: A. M. Bisi, *Oriens Antiquus* 5 (1966) 232–7.

138. The Phoenicians settled three major cities in western Sicily: Motya, Panormus (**135**) and Soloeis (S. Flavia, on the coast 17 km east of Palermo). The original urban settlement in the eighth century BC, referred to by Thucydides (VI.2.6) as Soloeis, is now known to have lain on the coast around the bay, taking advantage of a sheltered anchorage, but lacking a naturally good harbour. Little is known about it (it is now largely obscured by modern houses and dense orange groves), but kilns and tombs belonging to the archaic and classical periods (sixth–fifth centuries BC) have been identified. The original Soloeis on the sea was abandoned in the second half of the fourth century BC and replaced by a new town perched on the hillside above. Usually known by its Roman name of Soluntum (Italian Solunto), the new town flourished, and its excavated ruins, which largely belong to the second and first centuries BC, constitute an excellent example of a Sicilian Hellenistic hill-town (see **150**). By then it had largely lost any distinctive Punic character, and its theatre and public buildings are indistinguishable from those of Hellenistic towns elsewhere in Sicily outside the Carthaginian sphere of influence. However, the Punic cubit of measurement was still used for some buildings at Soluntum in the second century BC; three houses have the characteristic Punic style of cistern, elongated with parallel sides and rounded ends; and some dwellings maintain the desire for privacy in the Punic manner, blocking off a view into the heart of the house from the street by introducing dog-legs and U-turns – a feature characteristic of Punic houses in north Africa. More strikingly Punic in character, however, are two sanctuary areas at Soluntum. One is discussed below (**139**); the other is an open-air sanctuary on Soluntо's main north–south street, illustrated here. In the centre is an altar platform from which three upright slabs rise, a distinctive form found occasionally in the Phoenician homeland and also, significantly, at Selinus in south-west Sicily. The altar table inclines slightly towards a small basin, no doubt for catching the sacrificial blood. It may represent a survival from the original town of the late fourth century BC, but nothing else of such an early date is visible at Soluntum today, and it more probably dates

137

138

to *c.* 200 BC or a little later. If so, the precinct then may have been larger; at any rate the existing surrounding wall contains a reused inscription not earlier than 76/75 BC, and so the wall it contains cannot be earlier than this. On the other hand, the rising ground does not allow space for the shrine that might be expected to accompany such an altar; so the site remains somewhat enigmatic. The deity honoured is unknown.

(Photo R. J. A. Wilson)

V. Tusa, in AA. VV., Mozia, vol. II (Rome, 1966) 143–53; M. L. Famà, *Sicilia Archeologica* 12.42 (1980) 7–42, at 8–16 and 33–7; R. J. A. Wilson, *Sicily under the Roman Empire* (Warminster, 1990) 285–6; A. Cutroni Tusa, A. Italia, D. Lima and V. Tusa, *Solunto* (Itinerari XV, Rome, 1994) 66–8. Inscription (honouring Sex. Peducaeus as *propraetor*): unpublished.

139. Just above the agora at Soluntum is another religious precinct, partly uncovered in the early nineteenth century and further explored in the 1960s: the plan here combines these two separate but complementary excavations. The precinct contained several shrines, probably five in all, each consisting of an elongated main chamber and a rear area where the cult statue was displayed. Four of the shrines are arranged in pairs, side by side with a central party wall; they do not, however, communicate with each other. One of these shrines (A) contained **140**; marble fragments of another statue or statues were found in the adjacent chamber (B). Another pair of *sacella* (D and E) contained respectively a statue of Mercury, now lost, and, remarkably, a sixth-century-BC seated goddess, now headless, which is housed at the Museo Archeologico Regionale in Palermo. The latter must have been a venerated cult statue brought from archaic Soloeis. Between the two pairs of shrines lay another similar structure (C), but with a single cell at the back; this too was surely a shrine. The date is controversial. Its most recent excavator, Vincenzo Tusa, thought that it went back to the foundation of the city in the late fourth century BC, and there may well be a sanctuary of that date below the visible remains; but there is nothing else standing at Soluntum today which is indisputably earlier than *c.* 200 BC, and this complex is probably therefore a rare example of a late-Punic, multi-deity religious precinct, perhaps of around 150 BC (cf. **140**).

The temple-type, with a long, narrow approach to a 'holy of holies' at the far end, is ultimately based on the Phoenician-built temple of Solomon in Jerusalem, reconstructable from precise Biblical

139

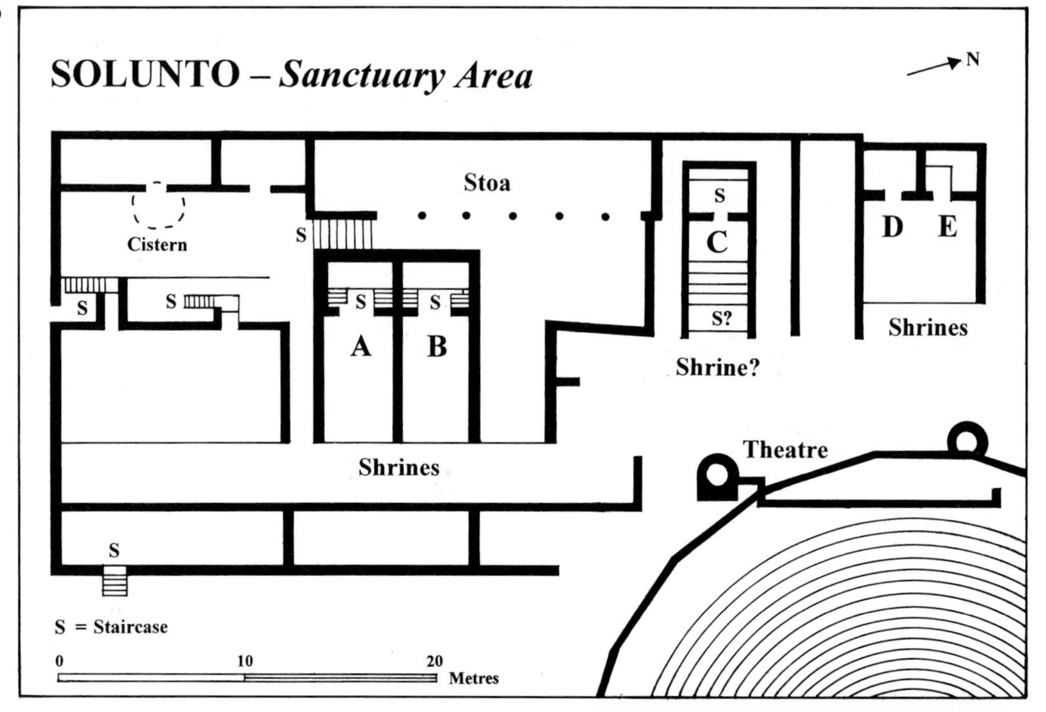

140

description; in the West, the closest parallel is the shrine excavated at Sidi Bou Said in Tunisia in 1917.

(R. J. A. Wilson)

D. Lo Faso Pietrasanta Duca di Serradifalco, *Cenni su gli avanzi dell'antica Solunto* (Palermo, 1831) 11–14; di Serradifalco, *Le antichità della Sicilia*, vol. v (Palermo, 1842) 64–6; V. Tusa, *Palladio* 16 (1967) 155–63; A. Wiegand, *MDAIR* 98 (1991) 121–30, at 125–6; Cutroni Tusa, Italia, Lima and Tusa *Solunto* 81–4; Wilson, in A. Spanò Giamellaro (ed.), *Atti del v Congresso Internazionale di studi fenici e punici: Marsala 2000* (Palermo, 2005) 914–17. For a very different reading of this temple, linking it closely with the adjacent theatre (with which, however, it is not axially aligned), and interpreting the pair of buildings as a 'temple-theatre' complex of the type known in late Republican Italy, see C. Albanese, in Osanna and Torelli (eds.) *Sicilia ellenistica, consuetudo italica* 177–92. Jerusalem: I *Kings* 6–7; M. H. Fantar, *Kerkouane*, vol. III (Tunis, 1986) 137 fig. 16. Sidi Bou Said: Fantar *Kerkouane*, vol. III 35–7 and 123 fig. 3.

140. For all the non-Greek appearance of the layout of the sanctuary at Soluntum in **139**, the well-preserved cult statue of Zeus which came from one of the shrines (A in **139**) is essentially a piece of provincial Hellenistic Greek sculpture owing nothing to the Punic tradition; such heavy dependence on the Greek heritage is characteristic of much 'Punic' art, even in north Africa (see **161**, **165**). Its identity as Zeus seems likely (although the absence of surviving attributes makes certainty impossible); it has also been interpreted, however, as Hades and as Baal Hammon. The statue, which was found in the nineteenth century, is the product of a vigorous style of local sculpture dictated in part by the poor quality of the available stone; it would have been liberally covered with stucco and no doubt highly painted. The god is shown seated with his left hand upraised, holding a sceptre (or possibly a thunderbolt); the right hand has been wrongly restored and was originally lower and outstretched. The feet rest on a footstool decorated with sphinxes and a central spiky acanthus leaf in the tradition of Sicilian Corinthian capitals (see **127**), surmounted by a palmette. The throne supports displayed at either side probably do not belong. Whether the sculptor who created it came from Soluntum itself or from a nearby larger centre such as Palermo is unknown, because little large-scale sculpture, and none as complete as this piece, has survived elsewhere from Hellenistic western Sicily, and the absence of comparanda makes conclusions difficult. A second-century BC date is likely, probably *c.* 150 BC; an attempt to date it after 46 BC on the evidence of an alleged appearance of Venus Genetrix on one of the throne supports does not convince. This impressive piece, which is over life size, not only provides an indication of the sort of rugged but far from incompetent work that a Sicilian school of sculptors was capable of producing at this time, but also that there was money to spare in a small Sicilian town such as Soluntum to pay for an ambitious commission of this kind.

(Palermo, Museo Archeologico Regionale. Height, excluding footstool, 1.65 m)

W. von Sydow, *MDAIR* 86 (1979) 229–30 with earlier literature; N. Bonacasa, in Pugliese Carratelli (ed.) *Sikanie* 296, pl. 327–30. Hades: S. Ferri, *Le Arti* 4 (1942) 255; W. Hornbostel, *Serapis* (Leiden, 1973) 350 note 2. Baal Hammon: Tusa *Palladio* 16 (1967) 159; Tusa, in S. Buzzi *et al.*, (eds.) *Zona archeologica* 433–8. Date after 46 BC: C. C. Vermeule, in M. L. Gualandi, L. Masei and S. Settis (eds.), *Aparchai: Nuove ricerche e studi sulla Magna Grecia e la Sicilia antica in onore di Paolo Enrico Arias* (Pisa, 1982) 637; cf. Wilson, *Sicily under the Roman Empire* 354–5 with note 77.

141. Monte Adranone is a stupendous hill top, 920 m high, in south-west Sicily, dominating the Belice valley to the west and looking towards the coastal plain on the south. First inhabited by indigenous settlers from the later Iron Age, it came under the influence of Greek Selinus when that colony was founded on the coast in the last quarter of the seventh century BC. Its ancient name was Adranon, still preserved in the modern appellation, and quite distinct from the ancient city of the same name on the slopes of Etna in eastern Sicily (modern Adrano), with which it has sometimes

141

been confused. The extent of Greek influence is most clearly attested in its necropolis, with individual burials of the sixth and fifth centuries BC laid in tombs made of large blocks of local sandstone with cover slabs of the same material, much as at Greek Selinus; plentiful grave goods with superb-quality imports of Attic black- and red-figure pottery attest to its wealth. But this was frontier country between the respective Carthaginian and Greek spheres of influence in western Sicily, and when Selinus fell into the hands of the Carthaginians at the end of the fifth century BC, Monte Adranone became a natural fortress and look-out post for them at the eastern limit of their Sicilian territories. Most of the structures uncovered on Monte Adranone belong to this Punic period, including the powerful stone defences, between 2 m and 2.8 m wide, guarding the more vulnerable western approach to the hill-top site; they are pierced by three narrow gateways (one of them later blocked) and have projecting rectangular towers at intervals along the circuit. Within is a variety of structures, including modest dwellings, store-buildings, rain-water cisterns and two temples (142). Just inside the south gate are the remains of a substantial courtyard building (57.5 m × 38.5 m) with about thirty rooms ranged on all four sides of a central court. One room contains an olive press, clearly a secondary addition. Interpreted by the excavator as a farm, the building seems too imposing for such a function, and an alternative view, that this was the barracks of the Carthaginian garrison, is entirely plausible. Adranon was besieged and captured by the Romans during the First Punic War (Diodorus XXIII.4.2, where it is described as a *kome*, a 'village'), and vivid destruction levels were found on the site. There was little subsequent occupation, although the finding of an early silver denarius, which should not be before *c.* 211 BC, hints at ephemeral later activity, perhaps during a short-lived Roman reoccupation at the time of the Second Punic War.

(Photo R. J. A. Wilson)

E. De Miro, *Kokalos* 13 (1967) 180–5; G. Fiorentini, *Kokalos* 18–19 (1972–3) 241–4; 22–3 (1976–7) 451–5; Fiorentini, *Monte Adranone* (Itinerari 16, Rome, 1995); Fiorentini, *Monte Adranone: Mostra archeologica* (Palermo, 1998). Barrack interpretation: M. Torelli and F. Coarelli, *Sicilia* (Guide archeologiche Laterza, Rome and Bari, 1984) 105.

142. At the highest possible level area of rock at Monte Adranone, in an 'acropolis' zone defined by its own inner defences and entrance, is a rectangular building measuring 31 m × 10 m. This was originally a simple tripartite building, consisting of a central part open to the sky flanked by small rectangular rooms, that to the north-west (in the background of this photograph) being divided

142

into two. The three parts of the building were not inter-communicating but were entered individually through doorways in the south-west wall. Architectural features found fallen in the south-east chamber (in the centre of the photograph) suggest a certain level of architectural embellishment, in the Doric order. Later other rooms were added, including a further partitioned chamber on the north-west, and a portico along the south-west façade (to the left in the photograph). In the centre of the open area are two square bases, with stucco traces on top suggesting a possible pillar-like superstructure, giving rise to speculation that 'betyls' (conical-shaped features) stood here, traditional objects of veneration in Phoenician religion. A small circular area around each stone base is paved, and numerous animal teeth were found here, along with ash and other signs of burning. This was interpreted as having a ritual function, and the building therefore as a rare example of a Punic temple. Perhaps the two partitioned rooms on the north-west held cult images, since they bear some superficial resemblance to the *sacella*, also subdivided, at Soluntum (**139**), although the latter are larger and more elongated. Dating evidence is so far unpublished; the temple is assumed to belong to the first half of the third century BC. A water cistern, perhaps to aid ritual ablutions, lies immediately adjacent to the south-west (top left in the photograph). Lower down the hill, a second simpler sanctuary has been identified (21 m × 8 m), with another open court and a single room alongside. The court also has two betyl bases, not axially placed but closer to one wall. A great quantity of animal bones, as well as over 200 Sikel-Punic coins, was found among the burnt debris, again interpreted as evidence for ritual activity. There is no evidence for terracotta votives of any kind, and so the identity of the divinities venerated is unknown; the location of the temple in the photograph, at the highest available terrace on Monte Adranone, would be appropriate to the sky-god Baal. There are no precise parallels for this form of temple in the western Punic world, but the absence is not surprising in view of the paucity of excavated examples.

(Photo R. J. A. Wilson)

G. Fiorentini, in ΦΙΛΙΑΣ ΧΑΡΙΝ: *Miscellanea di studi classici in onore di Eugenio Manni*, vol. III (Rome, 1980) 907–15; Fiorentini, in M. Barra Bagnasco and M. Clara Conti (eds.), *Studi di archeologia classica dedicati a Giorgio Gullini per i quarant'anni di insegnamento* (Alessandria, 1999) 67–78; and bibliography to **141**.

143. The temple of Astarte–Aphrodite–Venus on Monte Erice in western Sicily, the ancient Eryx, was largely swept away by the builders of the Norman

143

castle (seen here) in the twelfth century. The cult of Astarte was presumably established on this hill by the Phoenicians soon after they had settled at nearby Motya: the temple prostitution, which remained a feature of the cult down into Roman times, is undoubtedly of Phoenician origin, as with Phoenicio-Punic cults of Astarte–Aphrodite elsewhere in the Mediterranean world (such as Palaipaphos in Cyprus, or Sicca Veneria in Tunisia). Indeed, links with the latter were especially close: the sacred doves of the goddess at Eryx were held to have migrated to Sicca Veneria each year, returning after a nine-day interval, and festivals marked this *anagoge* and *katagoge*. Erice is a stunning mountain top 751 m high, prominently visible in what is otherwise predominantly flat terrain; it was a natural focus for religious cult. An alternative version of its origins, promoted at the time of the Roman Republic (and again under Augustus), saw it as a foundation by the Elymians, the indigenous peoples of western Sicily. This version, however, was probably invented for propaganda purposes, since the Elymians were claimed by some writers as descendants of refugees from Troy, and Aeneas, also a Trojan, is made to put in to Eryx on his way to Italy (Virgil, *Aen.* V.759f.). The cult comes into sharper focus after 241 BC, when it was already under the administrative control of Segesta (strengthening no doubt the Elymian credentials of Eryx, since Segesta was an Elymian foundation). The cult of Venus Erycina now became an official Roman one, and later it was to be established in Rome itself: an *aedes* in her honour on the Capitoline Hill was vowed by Q. Fabius Maximus after the defeat at Lake Trasimene (217 BC), following consultation of the Sibylline books (Livy XXII.9.10; X.10; XXIII.30.13–14; XXXI.9); and another temple of Venus Erycina, outside the Porta Collina, was dedicated in 181 BC by L. Porcius Licinius as *duumvir* (Livy LX.34.4). There were sanctuaries, too, of Venus Erycina in Syracuse, southern Italy, Sardinia, Greece and Africa. The Eryx sanctuary was guarded by a 200-strong body of slaves, the *Venerii*; 17 Sicilian towns were charged a tax to pay for them and to raise revenues for the sanctuary (Diodorus IV.83.4–7). The cult enjoyed great popularity during the Republic (Diodorus IV.84.4).

(Photo R. J. A. Wilson)

Nenci and Vallet (eds.) *Bibliografia topografica* vol. VII 349–78. Temple: *NSc* (1935) 294–328. Diffusion: B. Lietz, *La dea di Erice e la sua diffusione nel Mediterraneo* (Pisa, 2012).

144. The well-preserved remains of a ship, probably of the second half of the third century BC, were excavated between 1971 and 1974 off the north-west tip of Isola Grande, about 11 km north of Marsala (Lilybaeum). It was built of pine planking with oak tenons and frames of oak or maplewood; the keel was sheathed in lead. About 200 letters or words in Phoenicio-Punic script were found to have been painted on the wood during construction, giving instructions to carpenters on such matters as where to put nails and how the floors were to be placed in relation to the keel. There is

144

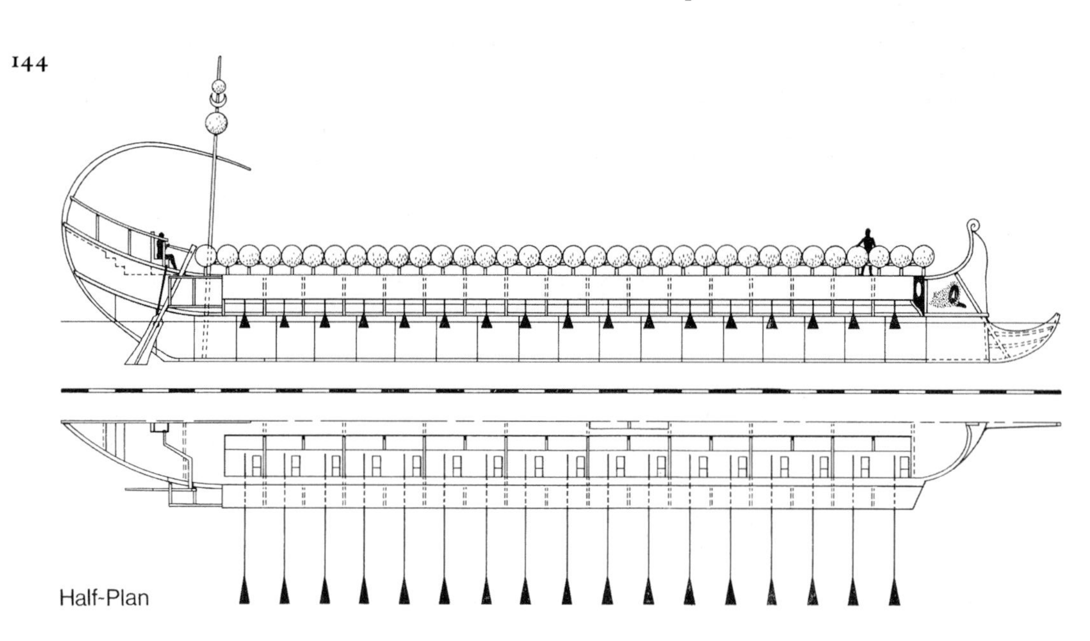

no doubt, therefore, that this is a Punic ship, made in all likelihood either in Carthage or in one of the Carthaginian-controlled ports of western Sicily. It carried no cargo, and the finds, apart from considerable quantities of stone ballast (for stability), were presumably therefore used by the ship's crew. They include cylindrical Punic amphorae and Greco-Italic wine amphorae, both compatible with a north African or Sicilian origin for the ship, and a small assemblage of table and plain pottery, believed to be largely of Italian type. Other indications of food provision for the crew were suggested by the animal bones found on board, which included ox, sheep/goat, fallow deer, pig and horse, as well as a small dog (the master's pet or the ship's mascot?); a single human skeleton presumably represents a victim when the ship went down. Sampling sent for radiocarbon testing indicated a date of 235±65 BC, and it was therefore suggested by the excavator that the ship, along with another identified 70 m to the south, also with at least one Punic carpenter's letter, were among the 50 Carthaginian warships known to have been sunk off the Aegates Islands (which lie immediately west of Isola Grande) in 241 BC, at the conclusion of the First Punic War. However, the excavated vessel was less than 5 m wide and a little over 30 m long (with an estimated displacement weight of 120 tonnes); if a military galley (as reconstructed here), she would have been a small one, with only a single bank of rowers. Both the absence of a ram and the presence of lead sheeting on the exterior of the hull and of ballast within, however, point rather to a mercantile function for the ship, notwithstanding the absence of cargo. Perhaps this was not a warship as such but a merchant vessel commandeered to join the Carthaginian fleet, possibly as a supply vessel, which then got caught up in the events of 241 BC. Certainly the 27° angle from the horizontal in which the ship was found suggests that the ship was travelling at speed when disaster struck, perhaps fleeing from the site of the battle. The latter is now known to have taken place north-west of Levanzo, 24 km away, in an area where ten ship's rams of bronze, from both Roman and Punic ships, have so far (2007–12) been discovered.

(Marsala, Museo Archeologico 'Baglio Anselmi')

H. Frost *et al.*, *Lilybaeum (Marsala): The Punic ship. Final excavation report* (*NSc* Supplemento al vol. 30 (1976), Rome, 1981); Frost, *Archéologia* 170 (1982) 42–50, at 46–7 (reconstruction); A. J. Parker, *Ancient Shipwrecks of the Mediterranean and the Roman Provinces* (British Archaeological Reports International Series 580 Oxford, 1992) 262–4 no. 661. Second ship: Parker *Ancient Shipwrecks* 264 no. 662; Frost *et al. Lilybaeum* 265–70. Battle site: M. L. Famà (ed.), *Antiche testimonianze di pace e guerra dal mare di Trapani* (Trapani, 2007); S. Tusa, *Archeologia e storia nei mari di Sicilia* (Udine, 2010) 219–28; S. Tusa and J. Royal, *JRA* 25 (2012) 7–48.

CITIES IN SICILY: SETTLEMENT, SOCIETY AND ECONOMY

145. The volcanic island of Lipari, in the Aeolian archipelago between the Italian mainland and Sicily (but only 37 km from the latter), was settled by Cnidians from Asia Minor *c.* 580 BC, one of the last Greek colonies in Sicily (**a** shows its acropolis). An important source of pumice and alum, Lipari was also of strategic naval importance because of its position, and its capture by Rome in the First Punic War was therefore a key objective; indeed, Carthaginian withdrawal from the whole of the Aeolian Isles was a specific stipulation of the peace treaty between Carthage and Rome at the close of that war in 241 BC (Polybius I.63.3). The town had resisted siege in 258 BC, when the consul Atilius Calatinus attacked it (Polybius I.24.13), but it fell to more determined Roman efforts in 252/1 BC (Polybius I.39.13). Excavations along the Greek walls of the fourth century BC on the west side of the town have found dramatic evidence of this second Roman attack. Stone blocks, in part ripped by the defenders from the walls themselves, seemed to have been hurled down on the attackers; nine catapult balls up to 21 cm in diameter, all but one in non-local stone (and so perhaps Roman projectiles), were found, as well as smaller, rounded beach pebbles that were probably also used as missiles, a huge quantity of iron arrow tips up to 12 cm long, and lead slingshot. A hoard of 320 bronze coins was associated with the debris, mostly Liparan issues (the obverse showing a male bearded god, the reverse a trident and the legend ΛΙΠΑΡΑΙΩΝ), but significantly with an admixture of Carthaginian issues as well. Together with two other contemporary hoards, one on the acropolis and another in a rubbish fill, which also show very similar compositions, the coins provide witness of commercial links with Carthage leading up to the First Punic War, clearly stimulated by Carthage's recognition of the island's strategic importance in any future showdown with Rome. **b** shows some of the material found in these destruction layers of 252/1 BC as presented in museum display.

145a

145b

(**b** Museo Archeologico Regionale Eoliano 'Luigi Bernabò Brea'; both photos R. J. A. Wilson)

L. Bernabò Brea and M. Cavalier, *Meligunìs Lipára*, vol. IX pt II (Palermo, 1998) 182–3 and 191–2, with Tav. CCXX–CCXXIII.

146. One of the mainstays of the Sicilian economy during the Roman Republic (and earlier) was wine, probably the second most important agricultural commodity which the island produced after grain. Archaeological evidence for the wine trade is, however, scanty, not least because the study of Sicilian amphorae at this period is still in its infancy. The type of amphora known as Greco-Italic, introduced in the later fourth century BC, was certainly produced at a number of Sicilian centres and continued in circulation down into the second century BC, when it was replaced by the Dressel 1 container. The latter, first introduced in Campania and central Italy, rapidly caught on as the wine container *par excellence* and was imitated in a number of different wine-producing areas; future research is likely to identify Sicilian versions of it. One place which very probably produced wine amphorae in the third and second centuries BC is Naxos in eastern Sicily. The site of the Greek colony had been largely abandoned since the end of the fifth century BC, soon to be replaced as a town by Tauromenion (Taormina) perched on the rock above; but a roadside village on the coast, inheriting the name of the classical city although on a slightly different site, developed in the Hellenistic period and continued into Roman times. That the area was important for its grapes, grown on the fertile volcanic soil on the slopes of Mount Etna, is clear from the sixth century BC onwards, when the silver coins struck by Naxos feature the head of Dionysus, a Silenus figure and bunches of grapes. In the third/second centuries BC a version of the Greco-Italic amphora, of which a profile of the neck and handles is shown in **a**, was stamped ΝΑΞΙΟΣ. I take this to be a reference to Naxian wine production (*sc. oinos*), rather than the

146a

146c

146b

name of the private individual who produced the wine (which has also been suggested); either way it is likely to have been made in or near Naxos. The stamps occur largely in eastern Sicily, with many in Syracuse, and others from Acrae, Capo Passero and Naxos itself; but it is also known at Marsala in western Sicily and at Licata in central southern Sicily, and its export is attested to northern Italy and to the Greek Peloponnese. Other Sicilian vintages which are named in the Latin sources of the early empire must have been establishing their reputations in the late Republic, and Cato (*De agri cultura* 6.4) specifically mentioned a *vinum Murgentium*. Another indication of the importance of wine production is the frequency with which bunches of grapes appear on the Late Hellenistic city coinages (in the third/second centuries BC) of Calacte, Catania, Halaesa, Hybla, Enna, Termini Imerese and Agrigento. The first of these, an issue of Calacte (the ancient town underlying modern Caronia, near the north coast), is shown here (**b–c**): the obverse shows a head of Dionysus crowned with an ivy wreath, while the reverse (**c**) depicts a bunch of grapes with the legend ΚΑΛΑΚΤΙΝΩΝ.

(**a** Marsala, Museo Archeologico 'Baglio Anselmi'; diameter of neck 15.3 cm; stamp 5 cm × 1.3 cm.; **b–c** London, British Museum Calacte 3)

Wine in Republican Sicily: A. Tchernia, *Le vin de l'Italie romaine* (Rome, 1986) 49–53; Wilson, *Sicily under the Roman Empire* 22–3 with 354, note 70. The stamp Naxios: Wilson, in G. Nenci (ed.), *Sicilia epigrafica: Atti del Convegno di Erice (15–18 ottobre 1998)* (Pisa, 2000) 531–56, at 532–3 and 586–7; B. Garozzo, in *Guerra e pace in Sicilia a nel Mediterraneo antico (VIII–III sec. a.C.)* (Atti delle quinte giornate internazionali di studi sull'area elima e la Sicilia occidentale nel contesto mediterraneo, Erice, 12–15 ottobre 2003, Pisa, 2006) 729; contrast F. Cordano, in I. Berlingò *et al.* (eds.), *Damarato: Studi di antichità classica offerti a Paola Pelagatti* (Pisa, 2000) 270–3. Naxos stamp at Marsala: A. Brugnone, *Kokalos* 32 (1986) 111 no. 18. Calacte coins: *BMC* Sicily, Calacte 3–4; E. Gabrici, *La monetazione del bronzo nella Sicilia antica* (Palermo, 1927) 121 nos. 7–10; R. Calciati, *Corpus Nummorum Siculorum: La monetazioe di bronzo*, vol. 1 (Milan, 1983) 129–30. Other coins with grapes: *BMC* Sicily, Catana 57, Alaisa 4, Agrigentum 146, Enna 5, Thermae Himeraeae 5, Hybla 1, Aluntium 87.

147. In addition to wine and grain, the olive was another mainstay of the Sicilian economy – and primarily the production of olive oil, in demand for lighting, cooking and for use in the gymnasium and the baths, but also olives for consuming as food: the fourth-century BC Sicilian poet Archestratos, who wrote a work on gastronomy, recommended 'wrinkled and over-ripe' olives (Athenaeus II.56c), and Varro (*de Ling. Lat.* VII.86) mentions another Sicilian speciality, a dish of preserved olives (*epityrum*) served after cheese. The Triocala area near Caltabellotta west of Agrigento was reported by Diodorus (XXXVI.7.3) to be 'wonderfully planted with vines, olive trees and all kinds of fruit' in the second century BC, and olive trees feature in the rental lists of public land at Halaesa. At Tauromenium (Taormina) an inscription of the first half of the second century BC indicates the annual need of over 1,000 gallons of oil for the town's gymnasium. The importance of the olive is further suggested by the choice of olive wreaths or branches as motifs on the Late Hellenistic coinages of Haluntium and Tyndaris. How far olives and especially olive oil became an export commodity during the Hellenistic period, however, is unclear: no undisputed examples of Sicilian-made oil amphorae (as distinct from containers believed to have carried wine: see **146a**) have yet been identified. Certainly, Sicilian oil had been exported to Africa in the fifth century BC: Diodorus, writing of Agrigento in the year of its sack by Carthage (406 BC), says specifically 'The greater part of their territory was planted with olive trees, from which they gathered an abundant harvest and sold

147

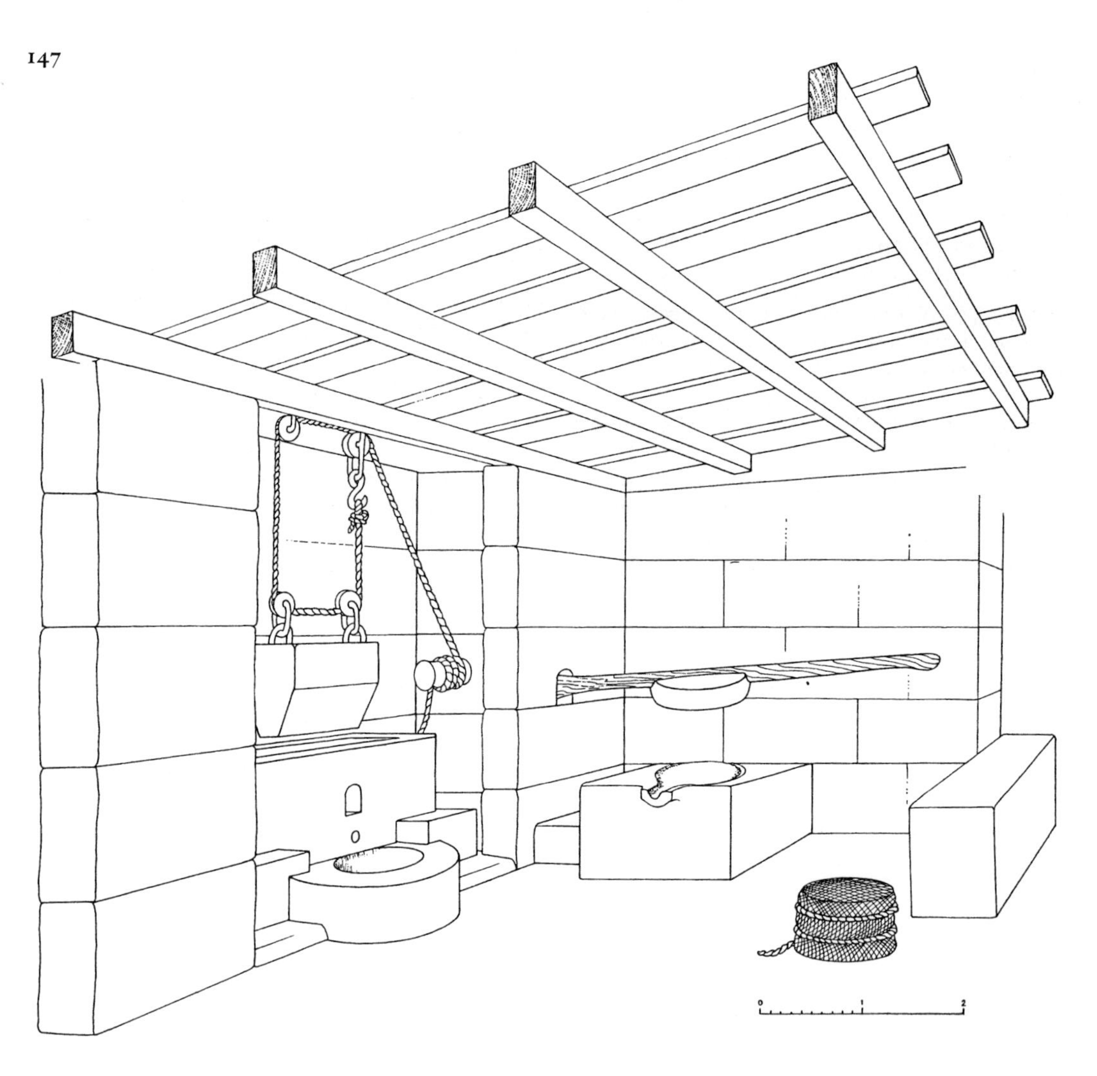

to Carthage; for Libya [i.e. Africa] at that time was not yet planted with trees' (XIII.81.4–5). A neat archaeological illustration of oil production at Agrigento, albeit small-scale, is provided by the olive-processing plant excavated on the Rupe Atenea there, and shown here in an artist's reconstruction. To the left was a basin in which the olive pulp was first prepared, and any oil extracted during this process poured through the hole in the base to an underfloor cistern, the circular opening of which is visible. To the right is the stone press base, on which the container with the olive pulp (made of rush and rope, seen here on the floor) was placed; a horizontal wooden beam anchored in the wall provided the downward pressure on the container. The liquid issuing from the press (a mixture of oil and water) was then doubtless transferred to the cistern to allow the oil and water to separate out: water, with a heavier specific gravity, sinks in time to the bottom, allowing the oil to be skimmed off. The olive press was built in the second half of the fourth century BC. Other archaeological evidence for olive-processing in Sicily at this period includes the press inside a third-century BC courtyard building at Monte Adranone (see **141**), and another on the acropolis at Selinus, which must predate the abandonment of that city *c.* 250 BC.

Halaesa: *IG* XIV, 352; Taormina: ibid. 422; coins: *BMC* Sicily, Aluntium 8, Tyndaris 14. Agrigento olive press: J. A. De Waele, *NSc* (1980) 417–25.

148. An extraordinary cache of bronze tablets inscribed with the texts of official decrees was found in western Sicily by unknown metal-detectorists in the 1970s and smuggled out of Italy onto the international antiquities market. Two emerged later, of which one, shown here, has made its way to the safety of Palermo Museum; the others, by contrast, are in private custody and are accessible only through photographs. The one illustrated here is the Ninth Decree (and last) in the series, but the Seventh has now been shown to be a modern forgery. Of the remaining eight, it is clear from the texts themselves that seven are decrees of the ancient city of Entella (Rocca d'Entella), in the Belice valley in central western Sicily, and were probably found there; one, however, was a decree of the so far unidentified city of Nakone, but whether this was found elsewhere or with the others at Entella is unclear. All were intended for display in a public place as a way of promulgating their contents: the Nakone decree's text states that it was put up in the porch (*pronaos*) of the temple of Zeus Olympios there, while four of the Entella tablets were displayed in the city's *bouleuterion*, and the remaining three were set up in the temple of Hestia. All are dated, either by reference to the holder of the chief priesthood (the *hieronymos*) or to those who held the archonship for the year in question (here Artemidoros son of Eielos, and Gnaios son of Oppios), but there are no clues to an absolute dating in the texts, and scholars have ranged in their suggestions for the chronology of the tablets between the end of the fourth and the end of the third centuries BC. Mention, however, in the Fourth Decree of the activities of a man who was surely a Roman official, Tiberius Claudius of Antium (Anzio), seems inconceivable before the First Punic War, and the mention of a Mamertine, Minatos Corvios, in another (the Fifth) as being among the people of Petra must surely post-date the Mamertine capture of Messina in 285 BC; if so, the Geloioi of the Second Decree are likely to refer to the inhabitants of Phintas (Licata), built to replace the old Gela further east after the latter's destruction in 282 BC. In all likelihood the tablets refer to the unsettled times of the First Punic War, probably between 254 BC and its end in 241 BC, after which this part of Sicily fell within Rome's sphere of influence (formal recognition of it as a *provincia*, however, came later: *CAH* VII.II^2 570–2). The explicit mention of synoecism in four of the Decrees, and its implied existence in the Ninth Decree, are also in keeping with the atmosphere of political and military upheaval at the time of the First Punic War. The Ninth Decree, shown here, dated on the first day of the month of Panamos and set up in the *bouleuterion*, records the decision of both the council and the citizen assembly of Entella to grant to the people of Segesta 'for all time' good will (*eunoia*) and reciprocal citizen rights (*isopoliteia*), in return for help given by the Segestans, which had included working for the release and safe return home of captured Entellans.

(Palermo, Museo Archeologico Regionale 'A. Salinas' ID 13687. Height 20.7 cm; width, 14 cm at base)

B. Lavagnini, in V. Giustolisi, *Nakone ed Entella alla luce degli decreti recentemente apparsi e di un nuovo decreto inedito* (Palermo, 1985) 16–31; G. Nenci, *Annali della Scuola Normale Superiore di Pisa* ser. 3 17 (1987) 19–28; *SEG* XXXV, 999. On the Entella decrees in general, see C. Ampolo (ed.), *Da un'antica città di Sicilia: I decreti di Entella e Nakone* (Pisa, 2001), with comprehensive bibliography.

149. Segesta, 30 km north-west of Entella, is another example of an indigenous hill-top town of

148

the interior of western Sicily, gradually Hellenized from the early sixth century BC through contacts with the Greek colony of Selinus to the south, and also through wider Mediterranean links: its famous unfinished fifth-century BC Doric temple, situated on a hill outside the town to the west, is an outstanding witness of the impact of Greek culture. The other well-preserved monument at Segesta is the theatre, set on the side of Monte Barbaro with stunning views to the north. This has been traditionally taken to be a building of the fourth century BC, but recent excavation has provided clear evidence, on the basis of both architectural detail and of archaeological stratigraphy, that the theatre visible today belongs to the second century BC, although an early Hellenistic predecessor of *c.* 300 BC is still conjectured to lie beneath. The strictly semicircular plan of the present building, if ultimately derived from the Hieronian theatre at Syracuse (**124**), likewise points to a date not before the late third century BC at the earliest; and the Pan figures decorating the scene building are probably also not pre-Hieronian. The stage building was two-storey, with the use of Doric columns below and Ionic above, as at Solunto (**151**). Other elements of the Late Hellenistic town have emerged in recent years through patient excavation below early medieval structures: they include the agora, set on a flat terrace south-west of the theatre, and flanked on its east side by a magnificent, two-storey, Π-shaped stoa; a fragmentary *bouleuterion* of the late second century BC immediately to its north; and the remains of some houses. Segesta shows, therefore, as do Solunto and Monte Iato, that the inland towns of western Sicily were flourishing during the second century BC: urban regeneration was under way in the form of extensive rebuilding programmes, no doubt as a direct result of the establishment of the *pax Romana* and the stimulus of greater agricultural productivity which existed under the new regime.

(Photo R. J. A. Wilson)

R. Camerata Scovazzo (ed.), *Segesta 1: La carta archeologica* (Palermo, 1996); Camerata Scovazzo, in AA. VV., *Seconde giornate internazionali di studi sull'area elima: Atti* (Pisa and Gibellina, 1997) 205–26. Theatre: P. Marconi, *NSc* (1929) 295–318; A. von Gerkan, *Festschrift für Andreas Rumpf* (Krefeld, 1952) 82–92; Mitens *Teatri greci* 109–12; F. D'Andrea, in AA. VV. *Seconde giornate* 429–50; L. Campagna, in AA. VV. *Seconde giornate* 227–49; A. Wiegand, *Das Theater von Solunt: Ein besonderer Skenentyp des Späthellenismus auf Sizilien* (Deutsches Archäologisches Institut Rom, Sonderschriften 12, Mainz-am-Rhein, 1997) 44–7; A. De Bernardi, in AA. VV. *Terze giornate* 369–87 (who, however, believes that the Pan figures go back to the fourth-century BC theatre). *Bouleuterion*: M. De Cesare and M. C. Parra, in AA. VV. *Terze giornate*

273–86; M.C. Parra, in Osanna and Torelli (eds.) *Sicilia ellenistica, consuetudo italica* 109–12. Agora and stoa: C. Ampolo *et al.*, *Annali della Scuola Normale Superiore di Pisa* ser. 5 (2010) 2/2 Supplemento, 3–49; Ampolo (ed.), *Agorai di Sicilia, agorai d'Occidente* (Pisa, in press).

150. Soluntum, situated on the north coast of Sicily 16 km east of Palermo, is an excellent example of a Sicilian Hellenistic hill town, perched on a ledge on the side of Monte Catalfano with a dramatic vista of the bay of S. Flavia and of the coastline as far as Termini Imerese (Thermae Himeraeae) and beyond. The original urban settlement (see **138**) lay on the coast around the bay. Before the end of the fourth century BC it was abandoned, and a more inconvenient but militarily more secure site on the hillside above was chosen instead. Much of the heart of the city was uncovered in excavations during the nineteenth century and then more especially in the 1950s and 1960s. Despite the hilly terrain, a strict orthogonal grid was imposed (many 'roads' incorporating stepped sections were clearly for pedestrians only), and towards the end of the main north-west–south-east *decumanus* lay the agora, with two-storey stoa to one side, and a large public cistern beyond. On the terrace above the agora was the theatre (**151**) and, beside it, a small *bouleuterion*. A courtyard building beside the theatre might have served as a gymnasium; a gymnasiarch is attested on a first-century BC inscription. Most of these buildings in their visible form belong to the second century BC, when Soluntum, along with many other Hellenistic towns in Sicily, seems to have been fundamentally re-shaped; but a small public bath-house elsewhere in the town, inserted into a pre-existing building, may be as late as the first century AD. Many houses are known, the larger ones conforming to the standard peristyle house of the Greek Hellenistic tradition; a lingering concession to Punic ideas in a handful of the houses has been referred to above (see **138**). The town went into decline during the first century AD and was abandoned by the end of the second century or early in the third.

(Photo R. J. A. Wilson)

A. Adriani *et al.*, *Odeon ed altri monumenti archeologici* (Palermo, 1971); Cutroni Tusa, Italia, Lima and Tusa *Solunto* with other earlier bibliography. Theatre: see **151**. Houses: Wolf *Die Häuser von Solunt.*

151. The theatre at Solunto is situated immediately above the agora, looking out eastwards over the gulf of Termini Imerese. The same debate about the chronology of the Segesta theatre (**149**) has applied equally to that at Solunto. It was excavated in the 1950s by Vincenzo Tusa, who dated it to the late

150

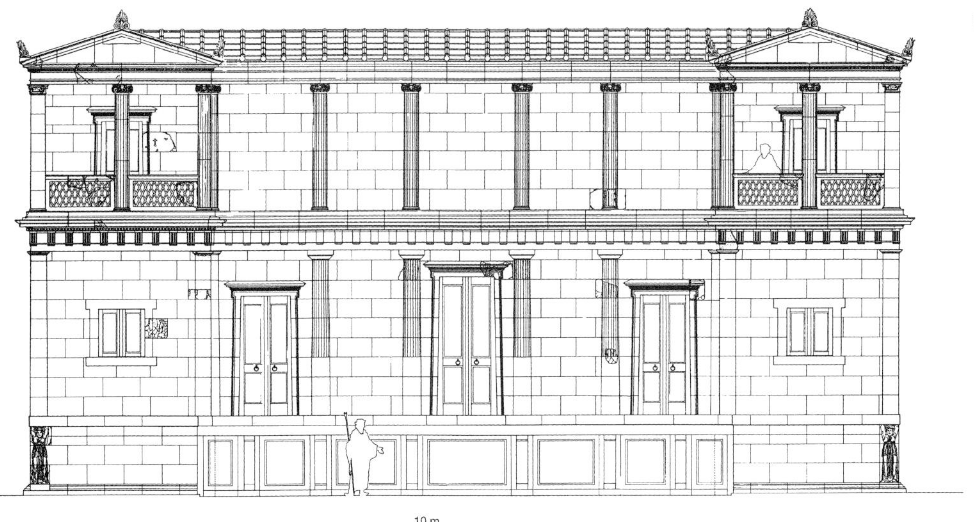

fourth century BC (with some later modifications), soon after the founding of Soloeis/Soluntum on its new hillside site. There clearly was a simple theatre of that date on the site, and fragments of it have been identified; but the building in the form that we see today almost certainly belongs to the second century BC, like that of Segesta. This has emerged particularly from a study of the architectural ornament of the surviving remains of the *skene* (Latin *scaenae frons*), seen here in one possible reconstruction. The plan of the stage building is very similar to those of Segesta (**149**) and Monte Iato (**152**): a raised stage in front of the standard two-storey back wall is flanked on either side by short projecting wings (*paraskenia*), which embrace the stage on either side. There were the customary three doorways (probably of the tall Macedonian type widespread in Hellenistic theatres) in the centre of the rear wall. The screen wall was decorated with engaged half-columns, Doric in the lower storey, Ionic above. The upper storey of the wings has balustraded screens across the front and freestanding columns: actors could appear here as and when the action demanded. On the extremities of the wings at ground level (if their placement here is correct) is a pair of caryatids, decorative sculpture of a type matched in the Hieronian theatre at Syracuse (**124**) and at Monte Iato (**152**), although there on a much more substantial scale.

(After Wiegand *Das Theater von Solunt*, Beilage 20)

Wiegand *Das Theater von Solunt*; dating: ibid. 52–5. Earlier studies: V. Tusa and L. Natoli, in A. Adriani *et al. Odeon ed altri monumenti* 85–92 and 105–12; Mitens *Teatri greci* 113–15; C. Courtois, *Le bâtiment de scène des théâtres d'Italie et de Sicile* (Providence, R.I. and Louvain-la-Neuve, 1989) 274.

152. Monte Iato, the ancient Ietas, which lies 30 km south-west of Palermo, is situated on a lofty hill top (852 m high) with stunning views in all directions (**154a**). From the middle of the sixth century BC onwards, the indigenous settlement here was progressively influenced by Greek culture from Selinus to the south, most obviously in the form of a small Greek temple of *c.* 550/30 BC; Greeks may already have been living on the hilltop by then. Not surprisingly, therefore, Ietas, by the Hellenistic period, like so many of the indigenous hill-towns of inland Sicily, had become thoroughly Hellenized. One clear manifestation of such acculturation is provided by its theatre. The scene building was decorated with at least four substantial pieces of sculpture executed in the local limestone, each composed of three superimposed blocks and standing 2 m high. Two show maenads (of which **152** is one), each wearing a *peplos* and ivy wreath, and two depict satyrs: such companions of Dionysus are entirely appropriate in a theatre, where drama was under the patronage of that god. They are shown in *telamon* pose, with their arms raised to head level as though supporting the architectural member above; precisely where, however, the statues stood in the stage building is not clear, since they had been subsequently dismantled for use as building-blocks in walling of the early medieval period which badly damaged substantial parts

152

of the theatre (Ietas was not finally destroyed and abandoned until 1246). The Monte Iato figures have been dated on stylistic grounds to the original theatre on the site in the late fourth century BC, which would make this the earliest known theatre in the Greek world to have had large-scale sculptural adornment; more probably, the Monte Iato building took its inspiration from the Hieronian theatre at Syracuse (**124**), which is also known to have had female figures in *telamon* pose adorning it. The archaistic mannerism of the central 'swallow's tail' fold in the maenad's drapery also suits a date after the mid third century BC rather than earlier. That the Syracuse theatre provided the prototype is further suggested by a terracotta maenad and satyr from a second-century BC house at Centuripe (once part of Hieron's kingdom) in eastern Sicily, which are iconographically identical to the statues at Monte Iato. The latter probably date from a substantial reshaping of the theatre which took place not long after 200 BC.

(San Cipirello (PA), Museo Civico inv. S11; limestone. Height 1.99 m)

C. Isler Kerenyi, in H. Bloesch and H.P. Isler (eds.), *Studia Ietina*, vol. 1 (Zurich, 1976) 30–48; G. Pugliese Carratelli (ed.), *The Western Greeks: Classical Civilization in the Western Mediterranean* (London, 1996) 748 no. 376. Monte Iato theatre: H. P. Isler, *Monte Iato* (Guida archeologica, 2nd edn. Palermo, 2000) 46–62; Isler, in *Sicilia Archeologica* 33.98 (2000) 201–20. Centuripe maenad and satyr: Pugliese Carratelli (ed.) *Sikanie* pl. 389–92. Chronology: R.J.A. Wilson, in Henig (ed.) *Architecture and Architectural Sculpture* 69–71; Wiegand *Das Theater von Solunt* 48–51; F. D'Andria, in P. Minà (ed.), *Urbanistica e architettura nella Sicilia greca* (Palermo, 2005) 184; Sear *Roman Theatres* 48–9; L. Campagna, in Osanna and Torelli (eds.) *Sicilia ellenistica, consuetudo italica* 20–1.

153. Immediately adjacent to the theatre at Monte Iato (1), the Swiss excavations of the past forty years have excavated several buildings of the agora of this hill-top town. The buildings at the north-east corner and on the east side have yet (2012) to be fully uncovered; but while some buildings on the south side go back to the fourth century BC, the main layout of the north and west sides of the agora was constructed in two separate phases during the second century BC. Next to the theatre's stage building lay a small council chamber (*bouleuterion*: 2), and an adjacent hall with central peristyle which has been tentatively interpreted as a *prytaneion*. To its south, on the other side of some small offices, was the north stoa, some 56 m long. All this part of the complex was built *c.* 150 BC. The north stoa has

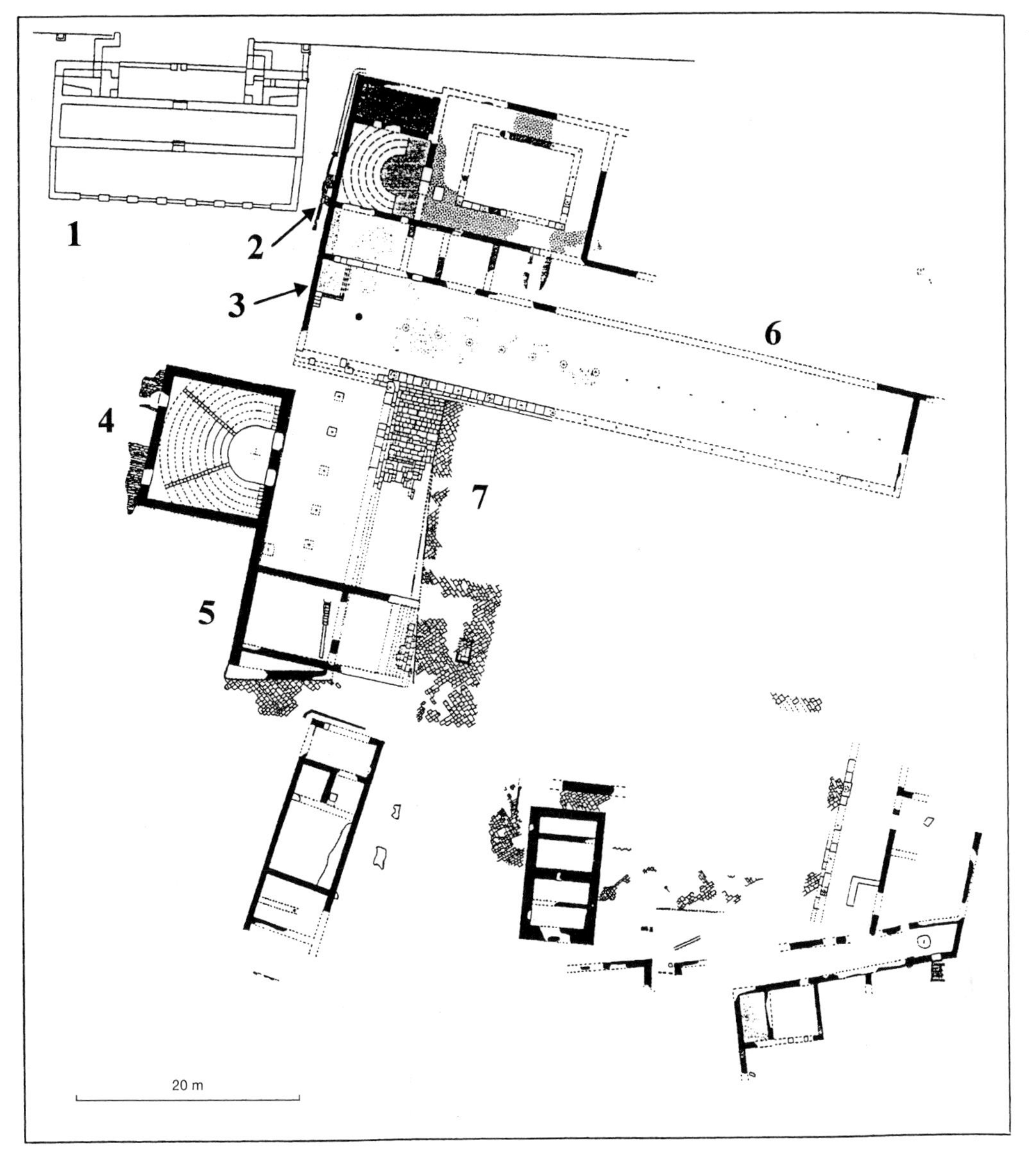

a platform (tribunal) at its north-west corner (3), probably to accommodate the presiding magistrate who sat here during court hearings. The use of stoai in Hellenistic and early imperial Sicily to fulfil the same function as the Roman basilica is suggested also by the discovery of an inscription referring to a '*basilica*' in a stoa on the agora at Halaesa, another hill-town 95 km to the east. Intriguingly, in a fresh building initiative on the west side of the agora *c.* 130 BC, a second, larger *bouleuterion* (4) was built, clearly to replace the original one: it formed part of a single building unit which included a new west stoa (7) and a temple (5). The building of the new council chamber implies an expansion in the number of members of the *boule*, perhaps brought about by an increase in the town's population. It has been further suggested that an influx of new settlers may have been a consequence of the changes which followed the settlement of Sicily by Publius Rupilius after the slave wars of 135–132 BC, and the discovery here of roof tiles stamped with the letters P I R has been seen as possible evidence for his official involvement in the rebuilding programme in the town centre at this time; but this interpretation seems improbable. The small temple (5) at the south end of the west stoa is one of the first in Sicily to be built in the Roman style with raised podium, frontal aspect and approach staircase.

H.-S. Daehn, *Studia Ietina III: Die Gebaüde an der Westseite der Agora von Iaitas* (Zurich, 1991); Isler *Monte Iato* 31–44; Isler, in *Seconde giornate* 1020–2; Isler, in *Terze giornate* 715–17. Most recent work on agora: C. Reusser *et al.*, *Antike Kunst* 54 (2011) 72–82; 55 (2012) 113–18.

154. This two-storey house (**a**) at Monte Iato (Ietas) is one of the largest and most elaborate known in Hellenistic Sicily. Built around a central peristyle, there are 25 rooms on the ground floor alone, which occupies 828 m^2; if the upper storey extended over the same area, the total number of rooms may have approached 50. Four of the ground-floor rooms are, however, shops, including a probable *fullonica*. That the house had two storeys is clear not only from the collapsed debris from above, found in the ground-floor rooms during excavation, but also from the remains of the peristyle, which had two superimposed rows of columns, the lower in the Doric order, the upper Ionic. There were two rain-water cisterns, one under the central court, the other under an adjacent room. Some floors were paved in good-quality *opus signinum* (see **130**) and, in at least two cases, with mosaic (both very fragmentary, since they had collapsed from the first floor; one has a rosette design). There is even a small bath-suite on the ground floor, an unusual feature in Sicilian Hellenistic houses (**130** also has one). The period of construction of the house has been dated to *c.* 300 BC by its excavator, and the direct influence of Macedonian palatial architecture has been claimed. Certainly the archaeological evidence indicates that there was a dwelling on this site at the end of the fourth century BC; but it seems more likely that the house as we see it today is substantially later, having been totally rebuilt, probably in the first half of the second century BC (*c.* 180?); to it were added a dozen rooms on the west side, including the bath-suite, at some later stage. The house collapsed, possibly during an earthquake, around the middle of the first century AD, and was not rebuilt. Although superimposed use of the orders occurs in Macedonian tomb façades in the later fourth century BC, no examples so early are known in the West; the earliest examples of *opus signinum*, from Carthage, also date to the late fourth century, so again its occurrence at Monte Iato, if the house is really *c.* 300 BC, would be a precociously early use of this floor technique, which is not generally reckoned to have reached Sicily until some time in the third century BC; and the style of architectural ornament also suggests a

154a

154b

date in the second century BC rather than earlier. In particular, the use of the Sicilian Ionic capital (**b**), with volutes on all four corners rather than on just two faces as on the classic Ionic capital, and with a pair of palmettes placed at a 45° angle next to the volutes, is an original Sicilian architectural development which may well, like the distinctively Sicilian version of the Corinthian capital (see **127**), have been the product of the artistic originality that was a hallmark of the Syracuse of King Hieron II in the second half of the third century BC. The Monte Iato house can therefore be taken as a token of the wealth and sophistication of a member of the town's elite during the Roman Republican period, when agricultural production in Ietas' *territorium* is likely to have been flourishing, and when there were considerable profits to be made for those owning extensive landed estates.

(**a** Photo R. J. A. Wilson; **b** H. P. Isler, University of Zurich)

K. Dalcher, *Studia Ietina VI: Das Peristylhaus I* (Zurich, 1994); Isler, *Monte Iato* 66–85. Macedonian influence?: Isler, in Hoepfner and Brands (eds.) *Basileia* 252–7. Pavements: H.P. Isler, in R.M. Carra Bonacasa and F. Guidobaldi (eds.), *Atti del IV Colloquio dell'Associazione Italiana per lo Studio e la Conservazione del Mosaico* (Ravenna, 1997) 19–32, with discussion of dating on 1027–8. Architectural ornament: W. von Sydow, *MDAIR* 91 (1984) 245, 313–14 and 350 no. 20; L. Campagna, in La Torre and Torelli (eds.) *Pittura ellenistica in Italia e in Sicilia* 193–210 (where the moulded stucco cornices of this house are dated to no earlier than 200 BC). Other discussions of the chronology of the house (all supporting a second-century BC date): L. Campagna, in La Torre and Torelli (eds.) *Pittura ellenistica in Italia e in Sicilia* 189–93; Campagna, in Colivicchi (ed.) *Local Cultures of South Italy and Sicily* 164–5; E. C. Portale, *Seia* n.s. 6–7 (2001–2) 64–75; Portale, *Archeologia Classica* 57 (2006) 80–1. Sicilian Ionic: A. Villa, *I capitelli di Solunto* (Rome, 1988) esp. 26–35; Wilson, in Henig (ed.) *Architecture and Architectural Sculpture* 72–3 with fig. 5.9 (distribution map) on 74; also 75–6 and note 24 on 87 (the Monte Iato house).

155. The main agora of Akragas (Roman Agrigentum; modern Agrigento) has not been precisely located, but the *ekklesiasterion* (seen here in the foreground) and the *bouleuterion* have been, in the San Nicola district, where the modern archaeological museum lies: the agora surely awaits discovery on the flat ground immediately adjacent to the east. Another open space lined by stoai near the south gate has been identified as a second or lower agora, on the basis of Livy's statement (XXVI.40.8–9) that troops entering from that gate marched into the market place: this has led some scholars, I think erroneously, into thinking that the agora must lie near the south gate. Livy implies in fact that the forum lies *in media urbis*, which is what the San Nicola district is. The *ekklesiasterion*, an area for citizen assemblies, consisted of nineteen rows of seats partly rock-cut (those

155

visible here) describing three-quarters of a circle; it had a diameter of *c.* 48 m. It is estimated to have held a maximum of 3,000 people. It was built in the years around 300 BC and is approximately contemporary with the earliest phase of the *bouleuterion* (which lies 50 m to the north, on the other side of the museum). By the later second century BC, if not before, it had fallen into disuse, and the seats were covered by an open paved piazza with an *exedra* seat (lower right). The temple (background), known traditionally as the 'Oratory of Phalaris', was built in the years around 100 BC, with a square altar in front of it (foreground, left). The deity worshipped is unknown and does not survive on a fragmentary inscription found during excavations, and thought by most to have belonged to the temple. One of very few monumental Latin inscriptions in Sicily of Republican date, it refers to the name of the dedicator, surely an Italian immigrant. Both the frontal aspect of the temple (it was tetrastyle and prostyle) and its lofty podium represent a borrowing from the language of Roman temple architecture, but the construction technique, in large, carefully squared blocks of local tufa laid without mortar, and the absence of any mortared rubble in building the podium, are wholly within the Greek tradition of temple-building. The hybrid order, with Ionic columns supporting a Doric frieze, displays characteristic Sicilian irreverence at this period for the standard architectural rules. The building may, therefore, be the work of a Sicilian architect working for a Roman patron.

(Photo R. J. A. Wilson)

Temple: P. Marconi, *Agrigento: Topografia ed arte* (Florence, 1929) 123–4; Wilson, in Henig (ed.) *Architecture and Architectural Sculpture* 75 and 87 note 22 (cf. also 83–4 on Doric/Ionic admixture); E. De Miro and G. Fiorentini, *VI. Agrigento romana: Gli edifici pubblici civili* (Pisa and Rome, 2011) 29–40. Gymnasium: De Miro and Fiorerntini *Agrigento* 71–95; G. Fiorentini, *Sicilia Antiqua* 6 (2009) 71–109. *Ekklesiasterion*: E. De Miro, *Palladio* 17 (1967) 164–8. *Bouleuterion*: De Miro, *Quaderni dell'Istituto di Archeologia della Università di Messina,* 1 (1985–6) 7–12.

8. CARTHAGE AND HER NEIGHBOURS

R. J. A. WILSON

The main part of this chapter (156–78) deals with the material culture of Rome's great rival, Carthage. Founded, according to tradition, in the late ninth century BC by the Phoenicians, Carthage enjoyed rapid expansion, and in time grew to dominate the whole of the African littoral from the Straits of Gibraltar to Tripolitania, as well as controlling parts of Sicily, Sardinia and Spain. This dominance led inevitably to a showdown with the Mediterranean's other super-power, Rome, ending in Carthage's utter destruction at the hands of her enemy in 146 BC (178). Despite her enormous wealth and her commercial and military successes, Carthage never developed a highly distinctive art of its own, and instead borrowed freely both Greek and Egyptian elements in style and iconography (161–3, 165). The outcome was an amalgam rather than a truly original material culture, although some items, especially the apotropaic terracotta masks (160), the charming miniature glass pendents (164) and the curious copper-alloy hatchet-razors (166) are distinctively Carthaginian. So too is the worship of their own version of an all-powerful mother goddess, Tanit, with her own special sign (173), seen in innumerable examples of stelai (159, 182) dedicated to her and to her consort, Baal Hammon. Their demand for appeasement in the form of child-sacrifice in open-air sanctuaries, *tophet*s (158), is an aspect of Carthaginian ritual which even Rome found repugnant.

Little is known of Carthage's urban layout (156, 157), apart from some well-preserved houses (174–5), but both her powerful and enormously long defences (168) and the second-century artificial harbours (176) bear impressive witness to the city's wealth and organizational capabilities. For a clearer picture of urban life, the small town of Kerkouane (170–71) on the Cape Bon peninsula, never re-settled by the Romans, gives a unique insight into many aspects of Punic culture – especially its domestic architecture, which demonstrates a fondness for privacy as well as for ablutions in the shape of ubiquitous hip-baths (172). The latter are lined with a special waterproof type of mortar mixed with crushed brick (*opus signinum*), also used for floors (173); this material seems to have been an invention of the Carthaginian world towards the end of the fourth century BC and was later to be widely adopted by the Romans.

Carthaginian culture and language also had a far-reaching impact on the indigenous peoples of north Africa outside the areas under Carthaginian control (179–87). Collectively known as the Numidians, and comprising various major subgroupings such as the Massyli and the Masaesyli, they occupied much of the area north of the Sahara in present-day Algeria and southern Tunisia (see map in *CAH* VIII^2 144). The Numidians come into sharper focus from the later third century BC onwards, when they enter the pages of Roman history under such kings as Syphax (*c.* 213–202 BC) and Massinissa (203–148 BC) (179), who seem to have encouraged settled agriculture and urban nuclei rather than nomadism, and who adopted Punic (182) rather than Libyan (180) as the language of court. Little is known archaeologically of these Numidian settlements, but the impressive and distinctive hill-top temples at Chemtou and Kbor Klib (183–4), and the great stone-built mausolea at Le Medracen, Siga, Dougga (185–7) and elsewhere, demonstrate the ambition of some of their building-projects, and display an eclectic cultural mix of Greek, Carthaginian and Egyptian elements.

GENERAL BIBLIOGRAPHY

Carthage: H. H. Scullard, *CAH* VII.II^2 486–569; W. V. Harris, *CAH* VIII^2 142–62; S. Lancel, *Carthage: A History* (Oxford, 1995); *Hannibal ad portas: Macht und Reichtum Karthagos* (Stuttgart, 2004). Numidians: H. G. Horn and C. B. Rüger (eds.), *Die Numider* (Cologne and Bonn, 1979); G. Sennequier and C. Colonna (eds.), *L'Algérie au temps des royaumes numides* (Paris, 2003). Well-illustrated general accounts: H. Slim and N. Fauqué, *La Tunisie antique: De*

Hannibal à Saint Augustin (Paris, 2001); S. Lancel, *L'Algérie antique* (Paris, 2003).

CARTHAGINIANS IN NORTH AFRICA, SIXTH TO SECOND CENTURIES BC

156. Carthage, Qart Hadasht or 'New Town' (*Karchedon* to the Greeks, *Carthago* to the Romans), was founded by the Phoenician city of Tyre. According to tradition (Timaeus, fr. 60), this took place in 814/13 BC, but until recently nothing earlier than the middle of the eighth century BC had been discovered at Carthage, suggesting that the traditional foundation date was too early. Now radiocarbon dating of several cattle bones from an early deposit consistently to *c.* 800 BC, if confirmed by further work, may indicate that the traditional foundation date might be right after all. The site chosen was at the tip of a peninsula protected by what is now Lake Tunis to the south and by a wide bay (now another lake) to the north; silting has considerably changed the coastal morphology since antiquity. There was a fertile plain to the west, and a natural harbour must also have been present, although its location has so far escaped detection. The twin harbours, one rectangular, the other circular, which dominate the topography on the southern side of the ancient city today, are not earlier than the first half of the second century BC (**176**). An earlier artificial channel in the same area, 2 m deep and not more than 20 m wide, which had silted up in the fourth century, may have been navigable and connected to port installations, but more probably the original harbour lay a little further south-west, as an indentation (now silted up) on Lake Tunis. Close to this was the *tophet* (**158**), which was already in use in the second half of the eighth century BC. The main nucleus of the city lay further north, on the flattish ground at the foot of a range of small hills. The latter were used for the numerous necropolises which ringed the town on the north and north-east sides, some of which are here indicated by name (**a**). The cemetery closest to the urban area, on the Byrsa, was eventually covered by housing at the end of the third century BC, when Carthage expanded northwards at its moment of greatest prosperity and size prior to the catastrophe of 146 BC (**175**). Few other details are known of the layout of the Punic town, apart from the remains of houses. The agora is believed to lie close to the sea, but has not been located; what may be part of a temple of the fifth century BC has been found by German excavators (**178**) just inland from the coast; a small shrine to Tanit nearby is also known. The possible course of the defences of the final phase, dating to the first half of the second century BC, is indicated here (**b**: 1–6). It enclosed a much bigger area than the inhabited city: known as the Megara, the land outside the city but within the walls 'was cultivated with vegetables and had plenty of ripe produce' (Appian, *Libyca* 117). The defences seem to have cut off the entire tip of the peninsula, so forming the longest walled circuit (34 km) of any city in the classical or Hellenistic world (**168**).

Strabo XVII.3.14; Appian, *Libyca* 95–6; H. H. Scullard, *CAH* VII.II² 499–502; J. G. Pedley (ed.), *New Light on Ancient Carthage* (Ann Arbor, 1980); W. Huss, *Geschichte der Karthager* (Munich, 1985); H. Hurst, in B. Cunliffe (ed.), *Origins: The Roots of European Civilization* (London, 1987) 135–47; A. Ennabli (ed.), *Pour sauver Carthage* (Paris and Tunis, 1992); Lancel *Carthage*; A. Ennabli, *Carthage retrouvée* (Tunis, 1995); M. H. Fantar, *Carthage: Approche d'une civilisation*, vol. 1 (Tunis, 1993) 109–63; Fantar, *Carthage: The Punic City* (Tunis, 1998). Cemeteries: H. Benichou-Safar, *Les tombes puniques de Carthage* (Paris, 1982). The Megara: M. Sznycer, in *Histoire et archéologie de l'Afrique du Nord* (IIIᵉ Colloque International, Paris, 1986) 119–31. Early cattle bones of *c.* 800 BC: R. Docter, H. G. Niemeyer, F. Chelbi and B. M. Telmini, *Antwerpse Vereniging voor Romeinse Archeologie Bulletin* 5 (2004) 62; H.-G. Niemeyer, in Niemeyer, R. F. Docter and K. Schmidt (eds.), *Karthago: Die Ergebnisse der Hamburger Grabung unter dem Cardo Maximus* (Mainz, 2007) 869.

157. Dominating the site of Carthage today is the hill still called by its ancient name, the Byrsa. This photograph shows the view from it south-eastwards, looking over the site of the Punic city towards the second-century BC harbours (see also **176a**, with the Byrsa hill crowned by its nineteenth-century church in the background). In the distance is the Bay of Tunis and the twin peaks of Djebel Bou Kornein, where an open-air sanctuary to Baal and his Roman equivalent, Saturn, is known. The Byrsa hill lay at the northern limits of the Punic town and was crowned by a temple of Eshmun, the Carthaginian equivalent of Asclepios: this was 'the most famous, and the richest, of all [Carthaginian] temples', a sanctuary approached by a grand stairway of sixty steps (Appian, *Libyca* 130; cf. Strabo XVII.3.14). The senate of Carthage sometimes met there in the second century BC (Livy XLII.24.3), and in 146 BC, during the Roman siege, it was a last desperate place of refuge. Nothing can be known of it archaeologically, however, because later Roman re-managing of the Byrsa sliced off the top of the hill (and with it the ruins of the Eshmun

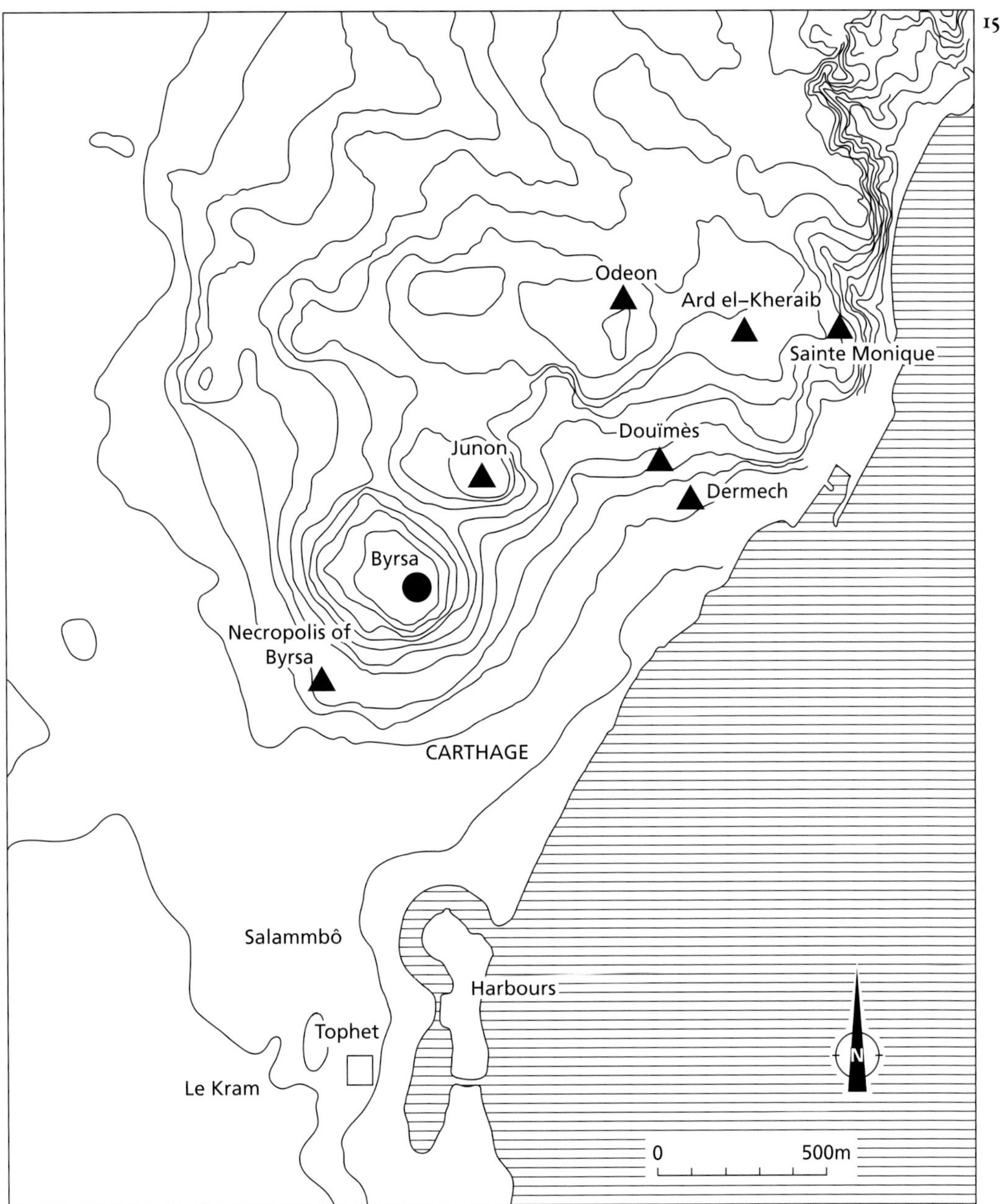

temple) as part of wholesale levelling works to create a magnificent forum complex (see **175**). The etymology of the name Byrsa is uncertain but is presumably semitic; the attempt to derive it from the Greek *bursa*, an 'ox-hide', is probably the work of later myth-builders. It gave rise to the story, entirely fictional, that Carthage's founder, Queen Dido-Elissa, on being offered as much ground as an ox-skin could cover, cut up one such skin into the smallest of strips, joined them together, and so reserved for the new settlement an area estimated by one ancient commentator (Servius, on Virgil, *Aen.* I.367–8) to have a circumference of 22 stades (*c.* 4 km).

156b

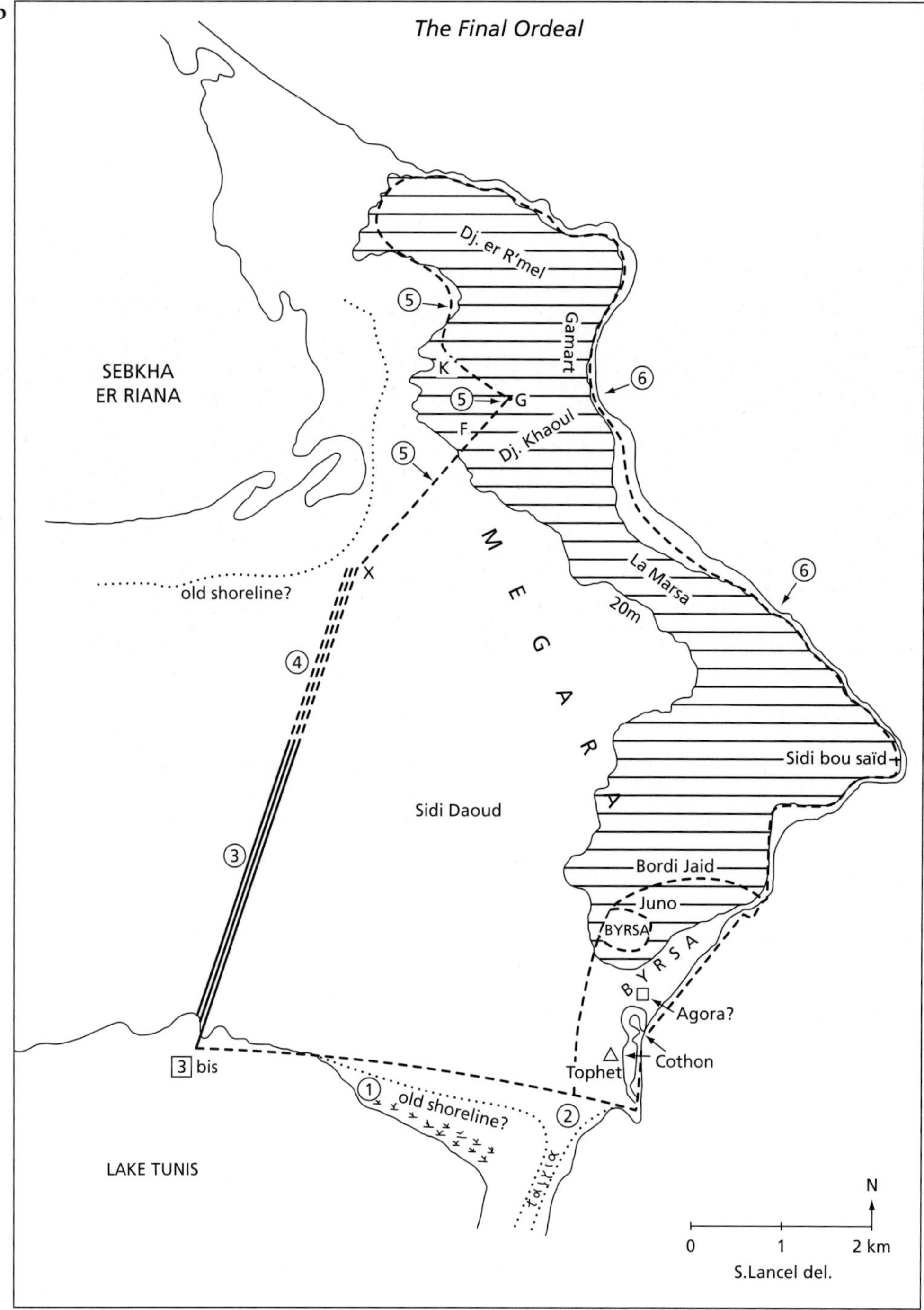

The Final Ordeal
SEBKHA
ER RIANA
Dj. er R'mel
Gamart
Dj. Khaoul
K
G
F
X
5
6
4
3
1
2
3 bis
old shoreline?
M E G A R A
La Marsa
20m
Sidi bou saïd
Sidi Daoud
Bordi Jaid
Juno
BYRSA
B Y R S A
Agora?
Cothon
Tophet
old shoreline?
LAKE TUNIS
N
0
1
2 km
S.Lancel del.

(Photo R. J. A Wilson)

Eshmun temple: Fantar *Carthage* vol. I 146–7. Etymology: W. Huss, *Klio* 64 (1982) 403–6; 65 (1983) 319.

158. The most important deities of the Carthaginian pantheon were the all-powerful god Baal and his companion, Tanit. Worship of them was in the form of human and animal sacrifices which took place in sacred open-air precincts known as *tophets*. This is a semitic word which does not occur in inscriptions but is used in the Old Testament to refer to a sanctuary at Jerusalem, where child-sacrifice also took place (*Jeremiah* 7:31–2; II *Kings* 23:10). The *tophet* at Carthage, discovered in 1921 on the southern outskirts of the ancient city (the Salammbô quarter), was a vast, walled precinct covering at least 6,000 m^2. Excavations have taken place on various occasions, most recently in the 1970s; the photograph shows one in progress in the 1930s. Pottery urns containing partially cremated bones were placed in the soil and their position indicated on the surface by a stone marker. In the sixth and fifth centuries BC this took the form of a block (*cippus*) carved with a 'throne' containing an oval or bottle-shaped betyl (see **159**), but from the fourth century BC a taller and slimmer stele became the norm. One stele of this type appears to show a priest with an infant cradled in his arm, presumably about to be sacrificed (*CAH* VII.II[2] 516 Figure 58). Sacrifices were continuous from the later eighth century BC down to the destruction of the city in 146 BC, and it has been estimated that approximately 100 were made each year, making a total of some 60,000 dedications in all; about 20,000 urns have been recovered so far. The 1970s excavations, which provided the first statistical data from the site, showed that the substitution of an animal (normally a sheep or goat) for a human infant was already practised from the seventh century BC but that the proportion varied over time: nearly one-third of seventh- and sixth-century urns contained animal rather than human cremations, whereas in the fourth century BC that figure dropped to one-tenth. Another change is that whereas down to the sixth century BC the human bones were those of new-born babies, a majority of sacrifices in the fourth century were of infants between the ages of 1 and 3, and one-third of the urns at this time contained the remains of two or even three children. The reasons for these changes and indeed for the need to have child-sacrifice at all are hard to explain. DNA research may in the future be able to demonstrate whether all the children are male, in which case Carthaginian practice presumably reflected the Biblical command to sacrifice the male first-born (*Exodus* 22:29; the *tophet* in Jerusalem, however, was for daughters as well as

158

sons), and whether or not two or more children in the same urn come from the same family. Some have seen the rite as a form of birth control, but that does not explain the sacrifice of toddlers. Moscati has suggested that the classical sources were peddling vicious propaganda, and that the children had already died from natural causes before being cremated. 'Sacrifice', however, demanded suffering and hardship (in this case of the parents) for it to work with the deity, and this element is removed if the *tophet* is to be viewed as little more than a gigantic child cemetery. In any case, forensic analysis of twenty infants from the *tophet* at Motya in Sicily has found no evidence of disease.

(DAI Rome neg. 57–163)

G.-C. Lapeyre and A. Pellegrin, *Carthage punique (814–146 avant J.-C.)* (Paris, 1942) pl. II. On the *tophet* in general: L. E. Stager, in Pedley (ed.) *New Light on Ancient Carthage* 1–11; Stager, in H. G. Niemeyer (ed.), *Phönizier im Westen* (Mainz-am-Rhein, 1982) 155–66; Stager, in Ennabli (ed.) *Pour sauver Carthage* 73–5; S. Brown, *Late Carthaginian Child-Sacrifice and Sacrificial Monuments in their Mediterranean Context* (Sheffield, 1991); S. Moscati, *Gli adoratori di Moloch: Indagine su un celebre rito cartaginese* (Milan, 1991); S. Moscati and S. Ribichini, *Il sacrificio dei bambini: Un aggiornamento* (Rome, 1991); H. Hurst, *JRA* 7 (1994) 325–8; Lancel *Carthage* 227–56; M. F. Aubet, *The Phoenicians and the West: Politics, Colonies and Trade* (2nd edn, Cambridge, 2001) 248–56; *Hannibal ad portas* 247–61.

159. The individual stelai which come from *tophet*s, both at Carthage and elsewhere, have much to tell us about Carthaginian religion, and especially its devotion to the principal deities, Tanit and Baal. Whereas Baal was familiar from the Phoenician homelands, Tanit was not, and she took over from Astarte as the principal female deity after the introduction of her cult in the fifth century BC (see **161**). Baal was a god of the remote hill regions, especially of mountain tops, but also of the fertile plains, and he was also a god of the sky – in other words, a universal god; Tanit (TNT in Punic, Thanneth or Thinith in Greek) was principally a goddess of the sky, and so provider of that precious commodity, rain. Over 7,000 stelai in honour of Tanit and Baal (usually named in that order on inscriptions) have been found in the *tophet* of Salammbô at Carthage, giving an idea of the popularity of worship of these supreme Carthaginian deities in the period down to 146 BC. **a** shows the limestone stele which can be seen in **158** in its original position in the *tophet*; it belongs to the third or early second century BC. In a central rectangular recessed panel is depicted the so-called Tanit symbol, a solid triangle surmounted by a horizontal bar and a circular disc representing the sun, with a crescent moon above (cf. also **173**). The presence of the sun and moon is here a reminder that Tanit is a universal goddess, queen of the heavens as well as mistress of life on earth. The Punic script

159a

159b

reads: 'To the Lady, to Tanit, face of Baal, and to the Lord, to Baal Hammon; vowed by Bodmilqart, son of Hanno, son of Milkyaton, son of Bery, son of Ty.' **b** comes from Hadrumetum (Sousse) and lacks an inscription. The upper part of the stele, which is damaged, is divided by flat bands into four sectors. In the upper pair is a sun and crescent moon on the left, and the 'Tanit symbol' on the right. Below is a pair of triple betyls (*baetuloi*), standing on an altar with concave sides and horizontal moulding. The betyl, an aniconic simple stone of various shapes, was a symbolic representation of the divinity. It is a widespread feature of Phoenicio-Punic religion in all areas of its influence, except for the Iberian peninsula, and can occur singly, in pairs or in triplicate, as here. For further examples of *tophet* stelai, see **182**.

(**a** Carthage, Musée de Carthage. Height 59 cm; width 33.5 cm; thickness 16 cm; **b** Paris, Musée du Louvre AO 5183. Height 44 cm; width 23 cm; thickness 10 cm)

a *Corpus Inscriptionum Semiticarum* I.3, no. 5507; *Carthage: L'histoire, sa trace et son écho* (Paris, 1995) 109; R. J. A. Wilson, in T. Phillips (ed.), *Africa: The Art of a Continent* (London, 1995) 557–8 no. 7.15; *Hannibal ad portas* 260 no. 8.

b A. Cacan de Bissy and J. Petit (eds.), *De Carthage à Kairouan* (Paris, 1983) 42 no. 17; M. Seefried-Brouillet (ed.), *From Hannibal to Saint Augustine* (Atlanta, 1994) 56–7 no. 43. Comparable and also from Sousse: *Hannibal ad portas* 46 nos. 1 and 261 no. 13. On stelai in general, see M. Hours-Miedan, *Cahiers de Byrsa* 1 (1951) 15–160; M. L. Uberti, in E. Lipinski (ed.), *Dictionnaire de la civilisation phénicienne et punique* (Turnhout, 1992) 424–5 with bibliography; C. Mendleson, *Catalogue of Punic Stelae in the British Museum* (British Museum Occasional Paper 98, London, 2003).

160. Terracotta masks are first found in Phoenicia in the eleventh and tenth centuries BC, but they are more characteristic of Phoenician settlement overseas, in Sicily, Sardinia and especially north Africa. Most western examples come from tombs (these three all come from Carthage), where they clearly had an apotropaic function, to ward off evil spirits from inhabiting the tomb; the suggestion that they represent a specific deity, such as the demon Humbaba of Mesopotamian origin, seems less likely. Some masks are life size and may have been worn by worshippers in religious processions (hence the cut-out eyes, to allow visibility), but most are smaller than life size and, in view of their prevalence in tombs, may have been made expressly for the grave. The three shown in **160** are good general representative examples of their type. The left-hand image, with unusual negroid features, is one of the earliest to come from the Carthage necropolises. Dating to *c.* 600 BC it possesses a large, flat nose, protruding ears, almond-shaped eyes pointing downwards towards the nose, and a mouth with only one side turned up, giving the face an awkward leer. The cheeks are marked by a sharp horizontal carination (as also on the middle image), and there are three raised button-like knobs, made up of concentric circles, on the central axis of the head between its crown and the eyebrows; the middle one is surmounted by a crescent. The provision of such decorative detail is characteristic of these masks: it may, on the later examples, have been driven by a *horror vacui*, a desire to leave no surface of the face unadorned (cf. middle and right-hand images). The other two masks were made about a century later (*c.* 500 BC). The grinning face of the middle image is typical, the effect of depicting the mouth with turned-up corners; the eyes are crescent-shaped, the nose is raised and the teeth are also shown. The mask is decorated by horizontal

160

lines on the cheeks and by a rectangular scored panel with three crosses from the bridge of the nose to the crown. The right-hand image is more unusual in showing a bearded man with a small, unsmiling mouth and prominent staring eyes (which are solid, not hollow). The hair and beard are indicated by a series of impressed open circles, in the case of the beard sometimes overlapping with each other. There is a suspension hole at the top of the head. These distinctive terracotta objects, along with the glass amulets (**164**), are among the most strikingly original products of Carthaginian craftsmen.

(Tunis, Musée du Bardo. Image left: height 21 cm; width 15.5 cm; thickness 11 cm; image centre: height 16 cm; width 13 cm; thickness 10 cm; image right: height 20 cm; width 14.5 cm; thickness 8.5 cm)

Left: P. Gauckler, *Nécropoles puniques de Carthage* (Paris, 1915) pl. CXCVIII; C. G. Picard, *Karthago* 13 (1965–6) 9–55, at 11–12, pl. I.1; M. Yacoub, *Le Musée du Bardo (Départements antiques)* (Tunis, 1993) fig. 18a; A. Ciasca, in S. Moscati (ed.), *The Phoenicians* (Milan, 1988) 356–9 and no. 231; Lancel *Carthage* 61 fig. 37; *Carthage: L'histoire* 45. **Centre:** *Carthage: L'histoire* 45; Picard, *Karthago* 13 14–15 with pl. II.9. **Right:** Picard, *Karthago* 13 19–20 no. 23 with pl. V.19; Picard *Carthage* (1964) 67, pl. 24; S. Moscati, *The World of the Phoenicians* (London, 1973) pl. 24; Lancel *Carthage* 62, fig. 38; *Carthage: L'histoire* 37. For all three, see Wilson, in Phillips (ed.) *Africa* 553 nos. 7.9a–9c.

161. This terracotta statuette of a standing female figure from a Carthage necropolis, probably made around 500/470 BC, provides an illustration of the eclecticism of much of Punic artistic production. The figure wears a diadem (*stephane*), and the hint of a smile, the long tresses of hair arranged in three braids on each shoulder and the cylinder-like treatment of the lower half of the body all recall Greek Ionian models of the late archaic period. Yet the pose, with the figure clasping a *tympanon* (tambourine) in front of her, is not Greek; rather, it is paralleled in numerous representations from the eastern Mediterranean of the oriental goddess of fertility, Astarte. Unusually, considerable remains of the original painted decoration on this terracotta survive: there is a band of alternating blue and red triangles decorating her chest, and a vertical stripe of rosettes set on a red ground adorning the lower part of her *himation*; rosettes, too, decorate the *stephane*, and there is 'rouge' (red circles) on her cheeks. The feet are bare. Despite its similarity to the eastern iconography of Astarte, however, this statuette may rather be intended to represent Tanit, the principal all-powerful goddess of the Carthaginians. A seventh-century BC dedication to

161

'Tanit Astarte', from Sarepta in Phoenicia, suggests that originally the two divinities may have been identical, but worship of Tanit is rare in the East, while in north Africa, although dedications to both are found, it is above all Tanit who predominates, especially after her cult gained increasing momentum from the fifth century BC onwards.

(Carthage, Musée de Carthage. Height 33 cm)

Catalogue du Musée Alaoui, Supplément II (Paris, 1921) pl. XVIII.2, no. 339; J. Ferron, *Antiquités Africaines* 3 (1969) 11–33, at 11 with fig. 1.2; Cacan de Bissy and Petit (eds.) *De Carthage à Kairouan* 51 no. 31; Ennabli *Carthage retrouvée* 51; Lancel, *Carthage* 67 with fig. 42a. Comparable example: *30 ans au service du patrimoine* (Tunis, 1986) 62–3 no. II.10 (also Carthage). Sarepta inscription: J. B. Pritchard, *Recovering Sarepta, a Phoenician City* (Princeton, 1978) 104–8. On Astarte in north Africa: C. Bonnet, *Astarté: Dossier documentaire et perspectives historiques* (Rome, 1996) 97–108; on Tanit: F. O. Hvidberg-Hansen, *La déesse TNT: Une étude sur la religion canaanéo-punique* (Copenhagen, 1979, 2 vols.).

162

162. Terracotta bust of a bearded male figure with untidy wavy hair, wearing a high headdress decorated with plumes (?) on his head. It was found 500 m west of the *tophet* area at Carthage in a small Late Hellenistic shrine (the 'Carton chapel', named after its excavator), probably built in the first half of the second century BC; the bust is assumed to be contemporary with it. The terracotta almost certainly portrays a god, and Baal Hammon is the most probable candidate, but the fact that certainty is not absolutely assured about its identity is a reminder of how few unambiguous depictions we have of the members of the Punic pantheon: generally, Carthaginians preferred symbolic rather than anthropomorphic representations of their gods before the Roman period. In fact, identification of the bust as that of Baal Hammon rests mainly on its similarity to an undoubted depiction of that god, seated, also in terracotta, from the mid first-century AD sanctuary of Bir Bou Rekba (Thinissut) near Hammamet; he too has a plumed headdress. Baal means 'master' or 'lord' in semitic, but the origin of the epithet Hammon, found in Phoenician religion as early as the ninth century (in an inscription from Kilamuwa, modern Zincirli), is still disputed. The root appears to mean 'burning', appropriate in view of his association with the rite of immolation by fire (see **158**); but it has also been interpreted as meaning 'protector', as 'lord of the perfume altar' (referring to the burning of incense), as 'baldaquin' (and, by extension, 'small temple'), or as derived from the Amanus Mountains on the border of Syria with Cilicia, at the eastern foot of which Kilamuwa happens to lie. In other words, no consensus about the precise significance of the name Hammon has yet been reached among scholars.

(Carthage, Musée de Carthage. Height 31.8 cm; width 18.4 cm; depth 16.5 cm)

L. Carton, *Sanctuaire punique découvert à Carthage* (Paris, 1929) 15–16 no. 28 with pl. IV fig. 8 (middle); Cacan de Bissy and Petit (eds.) *De Carthage à Kairouan* 45 no. 23; Lancel *Carthage* 345 fig. 218 left; *Carthage: L'histoire* 29. Bir Bou Rekba statue: *Carthage: L'histoire* 105; A. Merlin, *Le sanctuaire de Baal et de Tanit près de Siagu* (Paris, 1910) 17 with pl. II.2. Baal Hammon: P. Xella, *Ba'al Hammon: Recherches sur l'identité et l'histoire d'un dieu phénicopunique* (Rome, 1991) esp. 229–34.

163. This tiny gold pendent, found in a necropolis at Kerkouane, represents a standing goddess with a lion's head; in both hands she holds an ivy leaf, one with its glass inlay still present. She wears a long-sleeved robe, the lower part of which is covered by the wings of a bird. On her head is a solar disc with the divine snake (*uraeus*). The pendent is hollow and was clearly designed to take an amulet; the ivy leaves, a borrowing from Greek Dionysiac imagery, are probably meant here to have an apotropaic sig-

163

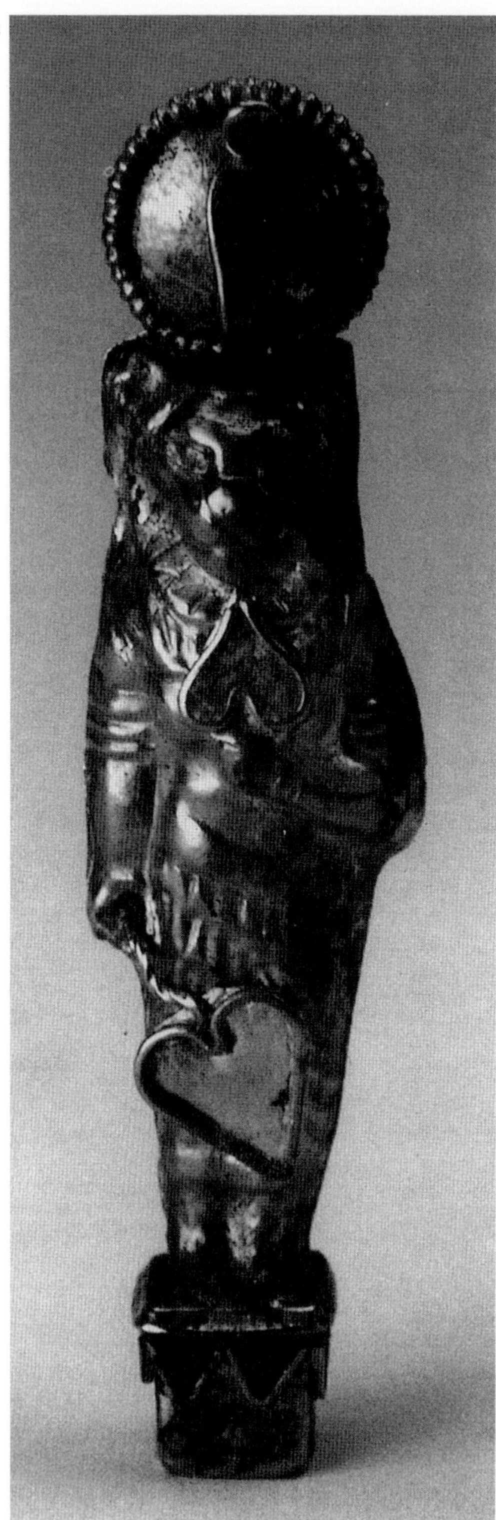

nificance as a symbol of prosperity, as they were later to have in Roman times. Both the lion's head (rather than that of a lioness) and the solar disc link this goddess closely with the Egyptian goddess Sekhmet. But the amulet is not Egyptian; rather it was produced by a Punic workshop in north Africa, where this goddess seems to have taken on a distinctive identity of her own. The feature of the bird's wings dress is found also on sarcophagi of the elite (cf. **165b**), and the same image recurs in a series of striking terracotta images from the sanctuary of Tanit at Bir Bou Rekba, near Hammamet. Here the image of the lion-head goddess is closely matched with that featured on a Roman denarius issued in 42 BC, where the same lion-head goddess appears, holding a Tanit symbol, and labelled as the *g(enius) t(errae) A(fricae)*. By at least the first century BC, therefore, the Sekhmet-like figure had come to stand for the goddess Tanit and, more generally, as a personification of Africa as a whole. The date of the Kerkouane amulet cannot be established with precision, but it is certainly no later than the mid-third century BC.

(Tunis, Musée du Bardo inv. 2840. Height 4.1 cm; width 1 cm; thickness 0.6 to 0.8 cm)

A. Ben Abed Ben Khader and D. Soren (eds.), *Carthage: A Mosaic of Ancient Tunisia* (New York and London, 1987) 146 no. 9. For much simpler gold amulets with lion head alone, cf. B. Quillard, *Karthago* 16 (1970–1) 10–14, 21–5. Bir Bou Rekba: Merlin *Le sanctuaire de Baal et de Tanit* 7 and 44–7 with pl. III.1. Denarius: *RRC* no. 460/4.

164. These two miniature heads were found in 1898 in the Sainte Monique necropolis, the furthest away from Carthage of the major necropolises which ringed the city on its north side (see **156a**), by the priest who pioneered systematic excavation there, Father Alfred-Louis Delattre (1850–1932). Both represent bearded males and are made of striking core-formed polychrome glass. That on the left has a face and nose in brilliant yellow, with blue eyebrows, a white mouth, and eyes outlined in blue with blue irises on a white ground; but the circlets of the blue beard and hair have fallen off, as has the suspension hole. That on the right is in superb condition, with similar markings to its companion head, but with white face and yellow mouth. They belong to a series of glass heads made in both Phoenician and Punic centres in the eastern and central Mediterranean from the sixth to the third centuries BC; but production at Carthage moved up an artistic gear in the later fourth century and at the beginning of the

third, when these examples, among the most striking of their kind, were produced. The suspension holes indicate that they were intended as pendents, and examples have been found strung in groups together with beads to serve as necklaces, but they have also been found individually in tombs, where they clearly had an apotropaic value: their dilated, staring eyes were designed to ward off evil spirits in the grave. The vast majority depict male heads (female heads are much rarer), and there are also examples of ram's heads, doves, dogs and chickens. It is not clear whether the male and female heads have religious connotations as representations of deities; it has been suggested that the bearded male is Baal Hammon, the younger male faces Eshmun or Melqart, and the female head Tanit, but this is not certain. Not surprisingly, these masterpieces of the Carthaginian glass-maker's craft sometimes travelled far outside the area of Punic influence: a pair, for example, has been found in a La Tène Iron Age grave of *c.* 350 BC at Saint-Sulpice near Lausanne in Switzerland, and they have even been found as far afield as the Black Sea.

(Carthage, Musée de Carthage; **a** height 6 cm; width 3.9 cm; thickness 3 cm; **b** height 6.5 cm; width 4.3 cm; thickness 3 cm)

A.-L. Delattre, *CRAI* (1898) 214; P. Berger, *Musée Lavigerie de Saint-Louis de Carthage* vol. 1 (Tunis, 1900) 252–3 with pl. XXXV.8–9; Cacan de Bissy and Petit (eds.) *De Carthage à Kairouan* 61–2 nos. 54 and 57; Ennabli *Carthage retrouvée* 60–1; *Carthage: L'histoire* 87. Glass amulets in general and some other examples: M. Seefried, *Les pendentifs en verre sur noyau des pays de la Méditerranée antique* (Rome and Paris, 1982), with interpretation as deities on 59–62; Ben Abed Ben Khader and Soren (eds.) *Carthage* 144–5 no. 8; Moscati (ed.), *The Phoenicians* 480–2; Seefried-Brouillet (ed.) *From Hannibal to Saint Augustine* 45–6 nos. 15–16; Lancel *Carthage* 217–18. Examples in Lausanne: G. Kaenel and P. Crotti (eds.), *Celtes et romains en pays de Vaud* (Lausanne, 1992) 24 fig. 13.

165. Father Delattre was responsible for other astonishing discoveries at Sainte Monique. The wealth of this necropolis is above all demonstrated by the numerous substantial sarcophagi discovered there, some of limestone, but over a dozen of white marble. Four of these were exceptional in bearing full-length relief sculptures, two of male figures, and two female. They are depicted lying on their backs on each sarcophagus' lid, which itself was carved in the form of a pitched roof – a feature obscured by the sculptured figures except at either end. The pair shown here are in the Musée de Carthage in Carthage. The male figure (**a**), who wears a beard, is dressed in a long robe and holds his right hand up to shoulder level with the palm outwards; his left hand grasps a small container

165a

with a lid. The female figure (**b**) wears a veil on her head surmounted by a small Egyptianizing falcon, and has her hair arranged with two groups of ringlets (mostly obscured in the veil) falling down to her shoulders on either side of her head. Her tunic is tautly pulled over her breasts; her limbs are draped with giant bird's wings on which subtantial remains of blue paint survive (red and traces of gilding were also reported at the time of excavation); and she holds another small container in her left hand (very similar to that carried by the male figure), as well as a dove in her right hand. Of the pair from the same necropolis now in the Louvre in Paris, the male figure is almost the same as the one still in Carthage; the female figure, by contrast, is that of a conventionally dressed woman in a mourning pose, with left arm across her waist, and her right arm drawing up a veil around her head. The chronology of these elaborate sarcophagi is not absolutely certain, but they were probably made in the later fourth century BC or in the first half of the third. Much smaller examples for cremation burials (ossuaries) with identical male figures on the lids are also known. Interpretation is difficult. Some have seen the figures as representing the deceased, but neither the garb nor the gestures of the figures support this. The pair shown here are often called the 'priest' and 'priestess', and the motif of the upraised hand can be interpreted, as on the hatchet-razors (**166**) and on some funerary and votive stelai, as one of adoration in the presence of an unseen deity; but it is difficult to believe that the female figure here depicts a priestess, since the bird's wings elsewhere are paralleled only on undoubted representations of a goddess – as in the little gold pendent from Kerkouane (**163**), and on a terracotta statue of Roman date from Bir Bou Rekba. Both probably depict Tanit, and the same may therefore also be the correct interpretation of **165b**; if so, the male figure (**165a** and its counterpart in Paris?) may also have been intended as a deity (Baal Hammon?), in which case the upraised hand is in benediction rather than adoration. The milieu that produced the sarcophagi is also problematical. There is an identical male sarcophagus lid from Tarquinia, which has led some to think of manufacture by Etruscans; but the whole notion of anthropoid sarcophagus lids is first Egyptian and then Phoenician in origin, and both their iconography and style suggest rather that they were created in a Punic workshop in Carthage, possibly by Greek-trained sculptors. Certainly the use of imported white marble, presumably from Greece itself in the absence of suitable north African

165b

material being available at this time, would also suggest Greek expertise and collaboration at the disposal of a Punic workshop.

(Both Carthage, Musée de Carthage; white marble; **a** length 1.93 m; width 0.72 m; height 0.65 m; **b**: length 1.97 m; height 0.76 m; width 0.68 m)

A.-L. Delattre, *CRAI* (1903) 23–33; Delattre, *Les grands sarcophages anthropoïdes du Musée Lavigerie à Carthage* (Paris, n.d., *c.* 1904); A. Héron de Villefosse, *Monuments Piot* 12 (1905) 79–111; G. and C. Charles-Picard, *Daily Life in Carthage* (London, 1961) 158–61; G. Picard, *Carthage* (London, 1964) pl. 62–3; G. C. and C. Picard, *The Life and Death of Carthage* (London, 1968) 162–5 (arguing that they were produced by Sicilian craftsmen in Carthage); Benichou-Safar *Les tombes puniques* 128–35 with fig. 71; Cacan de Bissy and Petit (eds.) *De Carthage à Kairouan* 46–7 no. 25; Moscati (ed.) *The Phoenicians* 293–5, 297 and 613 nos. 172–3; Lipinski (ed.), *Dictionnaire* 391 fig. 283; Lancel *Carthage* 325–30 with figs. 194–6; Ennabli *Carthage retrouvée* 71; *Carthage: L'histoire* 101; *Hannibal ad portas* 284–5 no. 61. Ossuaries: J. Ferron, in Lipinski (ed.) *Dictionnaire* 335–7; Benichou-Safar *Les tombes puniques* 241–3. Bir Bou Rekba: see bibiography for **163**. Etruscan sarcophagus from Tarquinia: J. Carcopino, *MemPontAcc* ser. 3 1 (1921) 109–17; J. Ferron, *Latomus* 25 (1966) 704–7.

166. Copper alloy 'hatchet-razors' of the type shown here are very frequent finds in tombs at Carthage, Kerkouane and elsewhere in the later fourth and third centuries BC. Basically rectangular in shape, each razor has one curved end, the blade (here damaged), while the other end is invariably shaped in the form of a stylized swan's neck and head; occasionally the latter's eyes are inlaid with glass (blue pupils on a white ground) for extra decorative detail. A suspension hole is attached to the central plate of the razor, which is decorated on both sides with engraved scenes. The hatching at the top of each represents the swan's wings. One side shows a woman wearing a long cloak and a veil, with arms outstretched before her; the other depicts a figure in long Egyptian-style robe and domed hairstyle, with the right arm stretched forward and upraised. Both gestures suggest adoration in front of a (imagined) deity. Both figures have a palm branch in front of them and a crescent moon (symbol of Baal as sky-god) near the head. The first of these figures shows imitation of Greek Hellenistic models; the other is inspired by Egyptian sources. Such a mixture of Greek and Egyptian models is common on these hatchet-razors and reflects the eclecticism of Punic visual culture as a whole; but there is no reason, despite the high technical skill of the best razors, to think that they were the work of Greek

166a

166b

artists resident in Carthage, as has sometimes been claimed. Common subject matter included divinities (Melqart, Horus, Hermes, Heracles), animals (boar, bull, griffin, lion, dolphin) and plants (palm trees, lotus, palmettes, rosettes). Without parallels in Phoenicia, they are a peculiarity of Carthaginian origin (they are also found in Sardinia and Spain, where local production imitated imported examples). They are invariably found in tombs, both in male and female graves, usually near the head of the deceased; they were clearly not designed to be used in life. It is assumed that they had symbolic use in connection with rituals for the dead: Punic inscriptions on a couple of examples from Carthage refer to the purificatory depilation of the deceased.

(Paris, Musée du Louvre inv. AO 3489. Length 15 cm; width 5 cm)

A.-L. Delattre, *Cosmos* 44 (1901) col. 55b–56a with figs. 60–1; E. Acquaro, *I rasoi punici* (Rome, 1971) 47–8 no. 55 with fig. 24.1 and pl. X.1; Picard *Karthago* 13 (1965–6) 67–8 no. 27 fig. 59; Seefried Brouillet (ed.) *From Hannibal to Saint Augustine* no. 60. For hatchet-razors in general: Picard *Karthago* 13, 55–88; Moscati (ed.) *The Phoenicians* 111 and 428–35 (and 635–6 nos. 305–11); S. M. Cecchini, in Lipinski (ed.) *Dictionnaire* 371–2; Lancel *Carthage* 207, 338–9. Comparanda: Cacan de Bissy and Petit (eds.) *De Carthage à Kairouan* 78 nos. 100–2; *30 ans au service du patrimoine* (Tunis, 1986), 85 no. II.44; Ben Abed Ben Khader and Soren (eds.) *Carthage* 160–2 no. 26; *Carthage: L'histoire* 47. Greek artists?: J. Vercoutter, *Les objets égyptiens et égyptisants du mobilier funéraire carthaginois* (Paris, 1945) 306–7; cf. C. Picard, *Antiquités Africaines* 14 (1979) 108.

167. In the village of Ksour Essaf, 12 km southwest of Mahdia in what is now eastern Tunisia, a Punic chamber tomb with three separate cells was discovered in 1909. One of them contained four large ovoid jars against one wall and an excellently preserved sarcophagus made of cedar wood (1.8 m long) standing against the back wall. The sarcophagus contained an inhumation burial of a man lying on his back. In a niche above the sarcophagus was a lamp and the splendid gilded bronze cuirass shown here. The breastplate (right) is decorated with circular discs in the upper part (over the chest), and a helmeted head of Athena/Minerva below; there is an indentation along the upper edge (decorated with a string of acorns in relief), to accommodate the lower part of the neck. Other decorative elements include acanthus scrolls, a lotus flower, Ionic colonnettes and a pair of tiny

167

bull's heads. The decoration of the back protector is almost identical, but has a row of circles (miniature *paterae*?) along the upper edge, four Ionic colonnettes rather than two, and rosettes adorning the twin circular discs. The two plates were linked by chains and intermediate rectangular pieces at the waist and over the shoulder: these were decorated with palmettes and further circular discs. There is no doubting that this loose-fitting breastplate (the type is known as a *kardiophylax*, 'heart-protector') is of south Italian Greek workmanship: the overall shape with the triple protrusions along each side is paralleled on Samnite and Apulian armour in Karlsruhe, London, Naples, Malibu and elsewhere, and an almost identical breastplate to the Ksour Essaf example, with very similar decoration (including the Minerva heads), was found at Ruvo in Apulia; it is now in Naples. Most seem to have been made during the later fifth and the whole of the fourth centuries BC, although the highly decorated ones may be a little later. Perhaps, therefore, the Ksour Essaf set of armour was purchased, or more probably seized (perhaps it was stripped from the body of a slain opponent), by a Carthaginian soldier in Hannibal's army during his Italian campaign at the end of the third century BC; alternatively, the deceased may have served as a mercenary in Italy at a rather earlier date. It was taken back home, and later proudly buried with the warrior as a trophy of his military service in a foreign land.

(Tunis, Musée du Bardo; each plate is 84 cm long and 68 cm wide)

A. Merlin, *Monuments Piot* 17 (1909) 125–37; P. Connolly, in J. Swaddling (ed.), *Italian Iron Age Artefacts in the British Museum* (London, 1986) 117–25, at 117–18 with fig. 6a; Moscati (ed.) *The Phoenicians* 68–9 and 635 no. 302; *Carthage: L'histoire* 147, 149; Ennabli *Carthage retrouvée* 91. Ruvo parallel: G. Fiorelli, *Catalogo del Museo Nazionale di Napoli: Armi antichi* (Naples, 1869) 3 no. 19; Malibu: inv. no. 96.AC.232.A–B. Other examples: *Studi sull' Italia dei Sanniti* (Rome and Milan, 2000) 58 and 65 fig. 11 (pot from Caudium showing horseman wearing one); 172 and 182 fig. 23 (Apulia?).

168. The earliest settlement at Carthage in the eighth to sixth centuries BC was not, on present evidence, defended by a walled circuit; but in the second half of the fifth century BC, as Carthage's reputation as an ambitious and aggressive Mediterranean city-state grew, she equipped herself with powerful defences. Little of them has been found, so their full course is unknown, but they seem to have left the *tophet* and the harbour zone outside the defended area. German excavations in the so-called 'Magon quarter' (**174**), on the sea about 1 km north-east of the *tophet*, have revealed a short stretch of these fifth-century defences, together with a gateway flanked by rectangular towers (**a**). With its lower courses built of massive stone blocks for stability (one block alone has a weight of over 13,000 kg), the wall was 10 cubits (5.2 m) thick and was rendered in white stucco on its exterior face. In the second century BC, the gate here, which was set back from the shoreline (the wall taking a short deviation inland at this point), was eliminated and demolished, and a fresh stretch of wall was built in a straight line at the water's edge (**b**). The distinction shown in the models between towers with open-top crenellations in the fifth-century walls (**a**), and roofed and enclosed towers on the second-century (**b**) defences, is pure hypothesis, not supported by any archaeological evidence. Much more is known about the second-century defences, thanks to Roman sources which described them in the context of the events of the Roman attacks on Carthage in 149/6 BC. While following the line of and reusing the fifth-century defences along the coast, they embraced the harbour area and *tophet* to the south and then on the west cut across the isthmus from Lake Tunis to the south up to the coast near Gammarth in the north (see **156b**). The total circuit would then be about 32 km, which corresponds well with Livy's figure of 34 km (23 Roman miles: *Per* 51) – longer even than the Greek walls of Syracuse of 402/397 BC, the longest in the Greek world (27 km). Appian (*Libyca* 95) says that the Carthage wall was 30 cubits (about 15 m) high and had towers at intervals of every 60 m. He also talks of a 'triple wall' (*triplon teichos*), but archaeological discoveries in the 1940s along the line of the west defences, the weakest sector (across the isthmus), showed that this should read 'triple line of defences', the three elements being a ditch 20 m wide, a timber stockade on a clay bank and the wall itself; only the wall, however, was thought necessary on the south and for the seaward defences to the east. The length, complexity and strength of these defences (no wonder Rome took four years to take the city) attest to Carthage's determination as a super-power to make herself impregnable, and also to the considerable technical expertise, manpower and money required to build and maintain defences on this gigantic scale.

(DAI Rome 76.306, 319)

H.H. Scullard, *CAH* VII.1[2] 499–500; Fantar *Carthage* vol. I 119–22; Lancel *Carthage* 136–9, 152–4, 189–90 and 415–19. Walls in the Magon quarter: F. Rakob, in

168a

168b

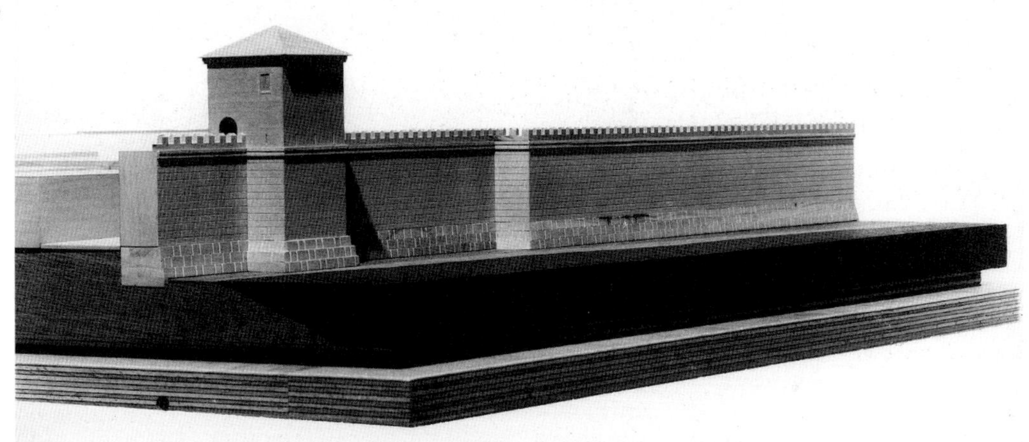

Ennabli (ed.) *Pour sauver Carthage* 32–3; Rakob (ed.), *Karthago*, vol. I (Mainz-am-Rhein, 1991) 165–71.

169. Nearly all of our knowledge of Punic buildings and urban layout comes from archaeology; epigraphic reference to construction does not seem to have been part of the Carthaginian way of doing things. A very rare exception is this inscription, probably of the late third or early second century BC. The text is damaged and not all scholars agree as to the precise translation of what remains, but it certainly records the opening of a street leading to an open piazza called New Gate Square, presumably close to the city walls, and it also gives us the names of the presiding chief magistrates (*suffetes)* of Carthage, Safat and Adonibal, who held office in the year of construction. It names the men who worked on the project as Abdmelqart (chief overseer?) and 'Bodmelqart, son of Baalhanno, son of Bodmelqart', the road construction engineer. Rather remarkably, these are followed by a listing of the trades of others who had a hand in the project, clearly not normal building labourers but a motley crew who turned up (or were compelled?) to provide the workforce: 'tradesmen, porters, packers [?] from the part of the town on the plain, the weighers of small change [?] and those who have neither [...] and those who do, the gold-smelters, the craftsmen who make vessels [?], those employed in working the furnaces, and the makers of sandals [?]'. The impression is given of rather ad hoc arrangements in the building industry, which apparently lacked a pool of skilled labour to call on. Perhaps the road went through an artisan and manufacturing district of Carthage, and it was precisely these tradesmen who had most to gain from the resulting improvement to the city's infrastructure. The laying-out of a new street and the distinction made between 'the part of the town on the plain' from the higher parts around the Byrsa hill indicate that the building expansion, which greatly enlarged the city towards the end of the third century BC (see **174**, **175**), was already under way. The predominance of personal names which incorporate reference to one of the gods of the Carthaginian pantheon (here Baal, Melqart) is typical of Punic nomenclature.

(Carthage, Musée de Carthage; black limestone. Length 25 cm; height 11 cm; thickness 5 cm)

A. Mahjoubi and M. H. Fantar, *RendAccLinc* ser. 8, 21, fasc. 7–12 (1966) 201–10; A. Dupont-Sommer, *CRAI* (1968) 116–33; Cacan de Bissy and Petit (eds.) *De Carthage à Kairouan* 30 no. 1; J. Ferron, *Le Muséon* 98 (1985) 45–78;

Ferron, *Africa* 9 (1985) 23–49; *30 ans au service du patrimoine* (Tunis, 1986) 56 no. II.1; Moscati (ed.) *The Phoenicians* 129; Lancel *Carthage* 142–4; M. Sznycer, *Semitica* 51 (2001) 31–55.

170. The small Punic town of Kerkouane (it covers about 8 ha within the defences) is unique in north Africa in being the only extensively excavated Punic settlement which was not overlain by a Roman successor. It lies on a bluff next to the sea at the eastern end of the Cape Bon peninsula, but apparently lacks a decent harbour; erosion, however, which has clearly claimed part of the town, may have significantly altered the ancient topography. Its origins go back to the sixth century BC, when it was still an indigenous (Numidian) village, but it soon came under Carthaginian influence. A direct consequence of this was its destruction *c.* 310 BC, almost certainly by Agathocles of Syracuse during a bold pre-emptive strike on Africa during his long struggle against Carthage. It was destroyed again in the middle of the third century BC, probably *c.* 253 BC by M. Atilius Regulus during the First Punic War, and was not thereafter resettled. The great majority of the excavated remains belong, therefore, to this last phase of the town's existence, between the rebuilding at the end of the fourth century and its definitive destruction sixty years later. The street-grid is somewhat irregular, dominated here by a wide curving street; the strictly orthogonal planning so popular with the Greeks has been eschewed in favour of a more relaxed urban development (contrast **175**). A couple of small open spaces and a temple (**171**) have been found, but no other certain public building. Most instructive are the remains of many houses (**172**); in addition, pottery production at the site is attested by kilns and workshops. The town was protected by defences of two periods, an inner wall with defensive towers, probably pre-dating the late fourth-century BC destruction, and an outer, parallel wall completed on the eve of the First Punic War. Two large and some smaller necropolises, with many shaft graves and a handful of chamber tombs, all of the sixth/third centuries BC, are known nearby.

(Photo R. J. A. Wilson)

Definitive excavation report: M. H. Fantar, *Kerkouane* (3 vols., Tunis, 1984–6). Shorter syntheses: Fantar, *Kerkouane: Une cité punique au Cap-Bon* (Tunis, 1987); Fantar, *Kerkouane: A Punic Town in the Berber Region of Tamezrat* (Tunis, 1998; rev. edn 2007).

171. The most enigmatic, and at the same time significant, structure uncovered at Kerkouane is the building interpreted, surely correctly, as a temple. It is the largest sanctuary of semitic type in the western Mediterranean; only one other complete example of pre-Roman date is known in north Africa, at Carthage, and that is very small. The touch of architectural pretension, in the form of a pair of projecting piers flanking the entrance, mark the building out as something special. A vestibule on the right with benches is of uncertain function (its interpretation as a 'banqueting room' is probably fanciful). Beyond was a spacious open courtyard with a square base (an altar?) in front of a pair of contiguous podia,

170

171

each 2.8 m square, the more southerly a later addition. This was either where the images of the divinities worshipped here originally stood, or they were offering tables for votives. Rooms at the rear of the sanctuary are again of uncertain purpose, either for feasting or to serve as the residential quarters of the priest. A new dimension to this sanctuary has been added by the excavation in 2001 of the foundations

of a square 'chapel', to the left of the entrance into the precinct; it is 7 Punic cubits square (3.15 m^2). Perhaps forming a freestanding *aedicula* with four columns on each side (fragments of Egyptian-style cornices belonging to it were located), it enclosed a central base 3 cubits square (1.35 m^2), the emplacement for an altar or betyl. Another, larger square base lies beyond. The plan of the temple as a whole, with a large open-air courtyard, and rooms opening off it at the same level, is characteristic of semitic sanctuaries, and both features were later enshrined in the 'Romano-African' temple, a type widespread in the African provinces during the Roman Empire. The divinity worshipped is unknown, but fragments of terracotta statues and statuettes appear to show both a female divinity and also a male bearded god wearing a cap. Perhaps this was another Baal–Tanit sanctuary, but this is not certain. The original arrangements of the sanctuary were, however, later altered, and a fresh wall defining a new room was built up against the primary podium; at the same time, rooms in the north range were converted into a pottery workshop, including clay dumps and a kiln. Since this industrial activity is incompatible with the sacred function of the original building, the presumption must be that religious worship was suspended here before the final abandonment of Kerkouane *c.* 253 BC.

(Photo R. J. A. Wilson)

Fantar, *Kerkouane* vol. III 147–221; Fantar, *Kerkouane: Une cité punique* 161–81; Fantar, *Kerkouane: A Punic Town* 54–63 and 73. Origin of Romano-African temples: A. Altherr-Charon, *Antiquité Classique* 46 (1977) 389–440; P. Pensabene, *Africa Romana* 7 (1990) 251–93.

172a

172. Kerkouane is particularly rich in examples of Punic domestic architecture. Houses tend to have a narrow entrance from the street leading to a central light-well, off which other rooms open (cf. **175**). The entrance from the street was generally placed off-centre, thus denying a view of the heart of the house from the street and enhancing the occupants' privacy. Just one or two houses at Kerkouane have the extra element of a peristyle at the centre of the house (one is visible in the background of **a**), but this, a borrowing from the Greek Hellenistic world, was a comparatively fresh innovation in Greece and Magna Graecia in the first half of the third century BC, so it is unsurprising to find it occurring rarely at Kerkouane, since the town had already been abandoned by the mid third century BC. Many of the houses had a second storey, as is clear from the lower parts of a stone staircase in many of them; some have a well-head in the central courtyard. Common too is the presence of a hip-bath (in the foreground of **a**), another borrowing from the Greek world; but whereas Greek examples tend to be manufactured items of terracotta, the Kerkouane hip-baths are made of walling liberally covered with *opus signinum* (see **173**). Sometimes these baths are accompanied by elaborate drains and soak-aways to take away the used water (**b**, with well-head in front of the hip-bath); occasionally the bottom of the bath has the extra refinement of black and white tesselated decoration, perhaps secondary repairs to the original *opus signinum*. Kitchens are rarely identifiable except in larger and richer houses, when built ovens are occasionally present. The upper parts of these houses probably had mud-brick superstructures (cf. **175**). The absence of roof tiles makes it very probable that the roofs were flat, since (as modern Tunisian domestic architecture ubiquitously demonstrates) a pitched roof is unnecessary in a land where rainfall is infrequent.

(Photos R. J. A. Wilson)

Fantar, *Kerkouane* vol. II; Fantar, *Kerkouane: Une cité punique* 93–158; Fantar, *Kerkouane: A Punic Town* 40–53. Privacy aspect of Punic houses: R. Daniels, *Oxford Journal of Archaeology* 14 (1995) 79–95 (Volubilis).

172b

173

173. In addition to being employed in the construction of hip-baths, the material known as *opus signinum* was widely used at Kerkouane for flooring in private houses. *Opus signinum* (so-called from the town of Signia in Italy which was renowned for its brick-making) is mortar mixed with crushed fragments of brick and tile, giving it a distinctive red appearance. The example here at Kerkouane has the additional adornment of individual *tesserae* of white stone placed at regular intervals throughout the matrix of the floor to enliven it. Also decorative is the device in front of the threshold to another room: it is a 'symbol of Tanit' (cf. **159**), one of three in *opus signinum* at Kerkouane, which is probably used here as a general all-purpose apotropaic symbol rather than as a specific reference to the cult of Tanit. Simpler, well-dated versions of *opus signinum* are certainly known in Carthage in the fourth century BC, and a rudimentary version appears to go as far back as the fifth century BC; so it seems certain that *opus signinum* was essentially a Punic invention. It is also very possible that this is the type of floor (with the addition of pieces of inlaid yellow marble at intervals) that Cato described in disparaging terms as *pavimenta punica*, as though their Carthaginian origin was widely acknowledged in the Roman world; but this has been disputed. What is certain is that *opus signinum* was in widespread use in Sicily by the first half of the third century BC, as the houses of Morgantina in particular attest (see **130**), and later spread to Italy, where it was common in the second and first centuries BC. Its use continued in north Africa, Sicily and Sardinia down into the first century AD. In its fine-ground versions *opus signinum* quickly got a reputation for being watertight (cf. **172**), and it was later to be used throughout the Roman world for such practical purposes as the lining of cisterns.

(Photo R. J. A. Wilson)

Fantar, *Studi Magrebini* I (1966) 57–65; Fantar, *Kerkouane* vol. I 493–514. Origin of the term *opus signinum*:

RE 2A (1923) 2359–60; Pliny, *NH* XXXV.46.165. Early use of *opus signinum*: K. M. D. Dunbabin, *AJA* 83 (1979) 265–77; Dunbabin in P. Johnson, R. Ling and D. J. Simth (eds.), *Fifth International Colloquium on Ancient Mosaics* vol. 1 (Portsmouth, R. I., 1994) 32–9; in Africa: Dunbabin, *Mosaics of the Greek and Roman World* (Cambridge, 1999) 101–3 with references; F. Rakob, in Rakob (ed.), *Karthago* vol. 1 220–5. *'Pavimenta punica'*: M. Gaggiotti, *Africa Romana* 5 (1988) 215–21; *contra* P. Bruneau, *MEFRA* 94 (1982) 639–55.

174. By contrast with Kerkouane, the remains of Punic Carthage are deeply buried beneath later Roman and Byzantine overlay, and are usually glimpsed only in small trenches, touching but rarely exposing completely the pre-Roman levels. However, in German excavations next to the sea on the south-east side of Carthage (an area dubbed by them the Magon quarter, after the late sixth-century BC aristocratic general, Mago: Justin XVIII.19), a clearer vision of some grand residences dating to the last period of Punic Carthage (late third century BC–146 BC) has been obtained. The line of the fifth-century city wall was altered here at the very beginning of the second century BC, eliminating a major sea gate, and a strip of ground along the shore was reclaimed (**168**). The area was then occupied by a number of spacious peristyle houses with central colonnaded courtyards, of the type rare at Kerkouane (where in any case the courts are tiny in comparison: **172a**). The photograph here shows the layout of one such courtyard (marked out in modern materials). The circular opening on the far side gave access to a rainwater storage cistern, of characteristic elongated shape, which lies under the courtyard. One house in this quarter here covers as much as 1,500 m^2; all have remains of stuccoed decoration, and most have fragmentary remains of *opus signinum* floors (see **173**) and also simple, irregularly laid tessellated pavements. The latter are generally composed of red *tesserae* (made from brick) with or without interspersed white *tesserae*. Some attempted limited polychrome with three or more coloured stones, but fully developed patterns covering the whole floor, whether geometric or figured, are unknown. The houses in this quarter, clearly one of the most fashionable in Carthage (helped by its seaside location), had at least two storeys. Surrounding streets, here as elsewhere in pre-Roman Carthage, were gravelled, not paved, and lack drainage facilities and sewers.

(Photo R. J. A. Wilson)

F. Rakob, *MDAIR* 91 (1984) 5–12; G. Stanzl in Rakob (ed.), *Karthago* vol. 1 8–49; F. Wiblé, in ibid. 93–111, 133; O. Teschauer, in ibid. 135–89.

174

175

175. Exceptional conditions have preserved for us on the Byrsa hill at Carthage an extensive quarter of Punic housing contemporary (*c.* 200–146 BC) with that discovered in the Magon quarter (**174**), but one considerably lower down the social scale. In Roman times the Byrsa became the centre of the developed Roman city and the site of a vast forum, basilica and temple complex – showpiece architecture which was only completed in the mid second century AD. To create the necessary piazza, gigantic earth-moving efforts were required: the summit of the Byrsa hill was sliced off (removing in the process any surviving traces of the temple of Eshmun, one of Carthage's most hallowed pre-Roman sanctuaries: see **157**). The earth and rubble were then dumped on the lower slopes of the hill to provide the artificial terracing, contained where necessary within new revetment walls. Huge Roman concrete piers, to support heavy structures above and to lessen the chances of subsidence, can be seen in the background of the photograph. The earth fill, now removed, has ensured the remarkably fine preservation of Punic houses (foreground). The area had been used as a necropolis in the archaic period, followed by a loose-knit artisan quarter for metalworkers in the fourth and third centuries BC. It was only, however, formally incorporated within the city in the last phase prior to 146 BC, when pre-Roman Carthage reached its greatest extent: these houses were therefore built on the very northern fringes of the Punic city. The 'Hannibal' quarter (as it was named by its French excavators) has a strictly orthogonal urban grid (in contrast to Kerkouane: **170**) and spacious streets of beaten earth, 6–7 m wide; the frequency of staircases along them indicates that they were not intended for wheeled traffic. The *insula* of houses at the centre of the photograph measures 31 m × by 15.65 m, the equivalent of 60 × 30 Punic cubits; it contained three houses 10 cubits wide and in length occupying the full 30-cubit width of the *insula*, together with pairs of smaller houses at either end of the *insula*, making seven dwellings in all. The apparently cramped living conditions would have been alleviated by at least one upper storey, and probably more (although Appian's reference to six-storey houses near the 'acropolis' in the storming of Carthage in 146 BC is probably exaggerated: *Libyca* 128). Stairwells are suspected, but staircases must all have been of timber (again in contrast to Kerkouane: **172**). Dividing walls between the properties are of rubble construction separated at intervals by stone orthostats, a building technique, known to modern scholarship as *opus Africanum*

(a term for which there is no ancient authority), which later continued in ubiquitous use in Roman north Africa. Interior partition walls in each house, however, were often of mud brick or *pisé* construction, all liberally rendered with white stucco. The house in the centre of the photograph ('House 4') has a long narrow entrance corridor from the street at the left, which leads off-centre (as at Kerkouane: see **172**) to a central light-well. The other rooms of the house open off it, including the main reception/living-room to the left of it. The house's Punic cistern, of the usual narrow round-ended form (cf. **174**), lies beneath it, with access to its water from the square opening in the light-well. This and other houses in this quarter give a vivid insight into living conditions at Carthage in the final years of the city up to the devastating sack of 146 BC.

(Photo R. J. A. Wilson)

S. Lancel *et al.*, *Byrsa* vol. I (Rome, 1979) and *Byrsa* vol. II (Rome, 1982); Lancel *et al.* in Pedley (ed.) *New Light on Ancient Carthage* 13–27; Lancel and J.-P. Morel, in Ennabli (ed.) *Pour sauver Carthage* 43–68; Lancel *Carthage* 156–72; J.-P. Morel, *Vie et mort dans la Carthage punique d'après les fouilles de Byrsa* (*VII*[e]*–VII*[e] *siècles av. J.-C.*) (Tunis, 2000).

176. On the south side of Carthage the remarkable pair of artificial harbours still form a striking element in the local topography. The description in Appian (*Libyca* 96), based on the eye-witness account of Polybius, makes it clear that the outer, rectangular harbour was the commercial port and that the inner circular one (**a**, with the Byrsa hill in the background) was the military harbour; but it was only thanks to British excavations in the 1970s that any details of the latter were revealed. The very creation of the harbours themselves represented an enormous undertaking: each required the excavation of about 125,000 cubic metres of soil. On the circular island in the military harbour was a series of gently inclining ramps, with wooden cross-pieces embedded transversely in stonework to form the slipways down which ships could be launched; 30 vessels in all could have been housed there, in ship-sheds mostly 5.5 m wide and up to 45 m long (**b**). More ramps were discovered on the harbour's outer bank on the north side, and if these are projected to fill the whole of the exterior edge of the circular harbour, there was room for the berthing of a further 140 ships (**c**). This count of 170 warships, an impressive indication of Punic naval strength, does not quite reach the number of 220 given to us by Appian, but the latter's total may, of course, have been inflated. To reach the sea, ships from the inner circular harbour had to pass through the linking

176a

176b

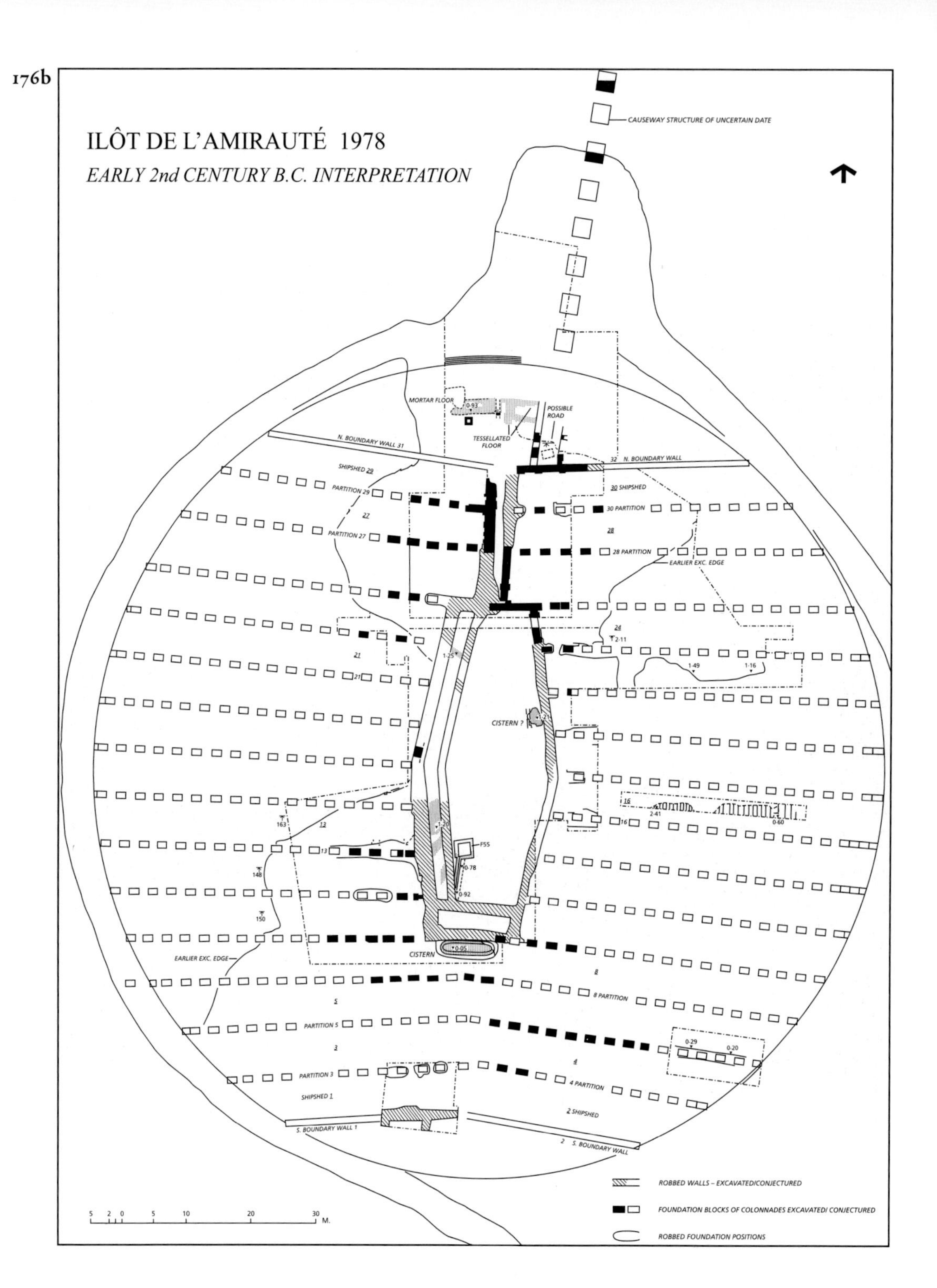
ILÔT DE L'AMIRAUTÉ 1978
EARLY 2nd CENTURY B.C. INTERPRETATION
CAUSEWAY STRUCTURE OF UNCERTAIN DATE
MORTAR FLOOR
POSSIBLE ROAD
TESSELLATED FLOOR
N. BOUNDARY WALL 31
32 N. BOUNDARY WALL
SHIPSHED 29
PARTITION 29
30 SHIPSHED
30 PARTITION
PARTITION 27
28 PARTITION
EARLIER EXC. EDGE
CISTERN ?
F55
CISTERN
EARLIER EXC. EDGE
8 PARTITION
PARTITION 5
PARTITION 3
4 PARTITION
SHIPSHED 1
2 SHIPSHED
S. BOUNDARY WALL 1
2 S. BOUNDARY WALL
ROBBED WALLS – EXCAVATED/CONJECTURED
FOUNDATION BLOCKS OF COLONNADES EXCAVATED/ CONJECTURED
ROBBED FOUNDATION POSITIONS
5 2 0 5 10 20 30 M.

176c

176d

channel into the rectangular merchant harbour to the south, and thence via a further channel to the open sea. The last, according to Appian, was 70 feet wide and closed when necessary with iron chains. Appian also says that two Ionic columns stood at the entrance to each shipshed, and this detail has been included in the model suggesting their original appearance (**d**). The structure at the centre of the island is presumably the site of the naval headquarters mentioned by Appian, where the admiral in control of operations had a vantage point, and where the trumpet giving the signal for warship movements was sounded; certainly the manoeuvrability of so many ships in such a confined space needed considerable navigational and organizational skills. The date of the harbours on archaeological evidence is not before *c.* 200 BC, but construction around then is unlikely in view of the peace treaty signed with Rome after the defeat of Zama in 202 BC, which stipulated that the maximum size of the Carthaginian fleet should be ten triremes (Polybius XV.18; Livy ref. XXX.37.2). It seems probable, therefore, that these harbours were built around the middle of the second century BC as part of the Carthaginian war effort for the conflict with Rome in 149–6 BC; if so, the period of active use of the inner harbour in its original function as a military dockyard is likely to have been very short.

(**a** R. J. A. Wilson; **b** after Hurst 1979; **c** the late Peter Connolly; **d** Henry Hurst)

H. Hurst, *Antiquaries Journal* 59 (1979) 19–49; Hurst, in Ennabli (ed.) *Pour sauver Carthage* 81–5; H. H. Scullard, *CAH* VII.II[2] 500; Fantar, *Carthage* I 123–30; Lancel, *Carthage* 172–82.

177. Carthage herself was comparatively late to strike coinage. Under Greek influence the Phoenician settlements of western Sicily, which were under Carthaginian control, were already striking silver coins in the fifth century BC; even the early fourth-century BC silver coins bearing the legend QRTHDST, a so-called 'Siculo-Punic' issue, were undoubtedly made in Sicily rather than in north Africa (*pace CAH* VII.II[2] 507), but whether the legend refers to Carthage or rather to a major city in western Sicily such as Lilybaeum is disputed. In Carthage, however, the earliest coins were not struck until the middle of the fourth century BC, and issues in gold, electrum and bronze were thereafter produced in a weight which corresponds to a Phoenician rather than a Greek standard. The coin dies chosen, however, were derived from earlier Siculo-Punic models – on the obverse, the female head facing left, based on the Arethusa of Syracusan Greek coinage (now no doubt re-interpreted in a Punic context as an image of Tanit), and on the reverse a horse, either standing or as a *protome*, with or without accompanying palm tree. Silver coinage did not commence until the early third century, presumably with easier Carthaginian access to Spanish silver. The example shown here, with a star above the horse, is a silver double shekel issued during the First Punic War (after 255 BC and before 241). A particularly careful gold issue of about the middle of the third century BC has been interpreted as being struck to pay Greek mercenaries in the employ of the Spartan Xanthippus, the pro-Carthaginian buccaneer who inflicted a crushing defeat on Regulus' army in Africa in 256/5 BC during the First Punic War (Polybius I.32–4); but the chronology of the coin issue is not certain. In the last half-century before the sack of Carthage in 146 BC, Carthaginian coinage was in decline: the artistic standard fell away, and the metal content was debased, presumably to divert resources to the war effort against Rome.

(British Museum, Department of Coins and Medals, RPK p. 216.1.I)

CAH VII.II[2] 507–8 with figs. 57a–b; G. K. Jenkins and R. B. Lewis, *Carthaginian Gold and Electrum Coins* (London, 1963); P. Marchetti, *Histoire économique et monétaire de la deuxième guerre punique* (Brussels, 1978); M. H. Crawford, *Coinage and Money under the Roman Republic: Italy and the Mediterranean Economy* (London, 1985) 133–6;

177

178 

E. Acquaro, in Moscati (ed.) *The Phoenicians* 464–73; H. R. Baldus, in *Hannibal ad portas* 294–313. Arethusa as Tanit: Baldus, *Chiron* 18 (1988) 1–14. Gold issue connected with Xanthippus?: Baldus *Chiron* 18 (1988) 171–9. Siculo-Punic coinage: G. K. Jenkins, *Revue Suisse de Numismatique* 50 (1971) 25–78; 53 (1974) 23–41; 56 (1977) 5–65; 57 (1978) 5–68; J. R. W. Prag, *Bollettino di Archeologia* 1 (2010) Volume Speciale A/A2/2, 1–10.

178. In an excavation at Carthage in Rue Ibn Chabaat, in the heart of the Punic city close to the Magon quarter (**174**), a complex stratigraphy was revealed, extending from the eighth century BC to Byzantine times. In the fifth century BC, part of the site was occupied by a well-built ashlar structure interpreted as a temple, although only small fragments of its walling could be uncovered. The attempted reconstruction of the sanctuary's plan, therefore, as a cella flanked by aisles and preceded by a columnar vestibule (a Doric capital is among the finds), is based more on comparanda from Phoenicia than on the actual structure discovered at Carthage, although the remains of another, very small, temple, apparently to Tanit, were found only 100 m to the north-west in 1991. Similarly conjectural is the deity worshipped in the Rue Ibn Chabaat sanctuary: Appian (*Libyca* 127; Valerius Maximus I.1.18) mentions a temple of Apollo as being next to the agora, which may have been situated in this general area. The identity of Apollo in the Punic pantheon is itself problematical (he is also named in the treaty of 215 BC, the Greek translation of which is provided by Polybius VII.9.2), but Apollo is traditionally linked with the semitic god Resheph. Resheph is, however, only very rarely attested at Carthage, although one inscription refers to a 'servant at the temple of Resheph'. Nevertheless, the sanctity of this zone in Punic times seems confirmed by the discovery of numerous votive terracottas and ritual vessels. The most astonishing find, however, was that of 4,762 clay seals, a selection of which is shown here. The seals would have been of unbaked clay but were fired to terracotta in the sack of Carthage in 146 BC, when this part of the city was engulfed in flames. The seals were fastened to individual papyrus rolls, belonging to an extensive archive appropriate in a temple setting: the papyri had completely perished in the fire, but the impressions of the fabric of the papyrus were preserved on the rear side of each seal. The seals fall into a number of distinct categories: those that display the cartouches of Egyptian Pharaohs; those that are Egyptianizing, in that they depict Egyptian subjects such as Isis, Horus, Bes, a sphinx, even a sistrum; those that are genuinely Punic, such as the 'sign of Tanit' (cf. **159a** and **173**); and those that are derived from Greek gemstones or coin images. Many of the seals bear the name of the Pharaoh Tuthmosis III (1483–1450 BC), in the form of sixth-century BC copies of the original seal-stone; but one Pharaoh of the Fifteenth Dynasty, Mayebre (1663 BC–?), is represented (thirty times) by an original Egyptian seal of the seventeenth century BC. One can only speculate how this seal-stone survived in circulation for so long, presumably handed down from generation to generation (in a priesthood?), and perhaps revered for its magical properties. The Greek images derive mostly from gemstones of the sixth/fourth centuries BC (with a few Hellenistic examples), some of them with Punic owner-names: this suggests that Greek gem-cutters sometimes worked for Carthaginian patrons on commission. This remarkable hoard of seals not only graphically documents the destruction of Carthage in 146 BC, it also neatly exemplifies the dependence of Carthage on the two major foreign influences which pervade all levels of Punic visual culture, those of Greece and Egypt.

(Photo: the late F. Rakob)

F. Rakob, in Rakob (ed.), *Karthago,* vol. II (Mainz-am-Rhein, 1997) 1–9; D. Berges, ibid. 10–214; T. Redissi, in Rakob (ed.), *Karthago,* vol. III (Mainz-am-Rhein, 1999) 4–92; D. Berges, *MDAIR* 109 (2002) 177–223; *Hannibal ad portas* 241–4. Resheph inscription: *Corpus Inscriptionum Semiticarum I.1* no. 251. Temple of Tanit: Niemeyer, in Niemeyer, Docter and Schmidt (eds.) *Karthago* 217–33 (fourth century BC).

NUMIDIANS

179. Coinage was initially struck by the Numidian kings from the reign of Syphax (*c.* 213–202 BC) down to the fall of Carthage in 146 BC, and the influence of Carthage, in its metrology, in its use of Punic in the coin legends and in the popularity of the reverse image of a horse (directly borrowed

179a  

obverse reverse

179b  

obverse reverse

179c  

obverse reverse

from Punic coinage: **177**), shows its debt to the Punic numismatic tradition. The obverse invariably shows the portrait of the issuing king, generally bearded (only Vermina, Syphax's son (ruled 202–192), is shown as clean-shaven), and they often wear the royal diadem in affectation of Hellenistic Greek monarchs. Illustrated here is the first bronze coinage of Syphax, showing the king with pointed beard and hair combed back straight from the forehead; his head is bare (**a**, obverse). By contrast his more Hellenized later coinage shows his hair short and curly, and the beard neat; he also wears a diadem (**b**, obverse). The reverse die on both coins shows a rider (presumably the king) on a galloping horse, with cloak flying out behind (**a** and **b**, reverses). Both coins bear the same legend, SPQ HMMLKT, '(with) Syphax ruling', written in Punic script (see **180**). Massinissa's portrait similarly displays a mass of curly hair, with the king wearing either a laurel wreath or a diadem (**c**, obverse). He has a straight, slightly pointed nose, and a jutting, bearded chin. The reverse die depicts a horse in front of a sceptre, symbol of royal power (**c**, reverse). Strangely, Syphax's and Massinissa's coinage, although plentiful, was only issued in bronze, suggesting that the purpose of coining for propaganda or dynastic purposes (which would demand silver or gold issues) was lost on them.

(Copenhagen, National Museum: Royal Collection of Coins and Medals)

G. K. Jenkins, *Sylloge Nummorum Graecorum. Denmark. North Africa: Syrtica–Mauretania* (Copenhagen, 1969) nos. 490–1 and 493; J. Mazard, *Corpus Nummorum Numidiae Mauretaniaeque* (Paris, 1955) 18–21 and 30–43; J. M. C. Toynbee, *Roman Historical Portraits* (London, 1978) 89–90; H. R. Baldus, in Horn and Rüger (eds.) *Die Numider* 188–94, 644–9; Crawford *Coinage and Money* 140–1; J. Alexandropoulos, *Les monnaies de l'Afrique antique (400 av. J.-C.–40 ap. J.-C.)* (2nd edn, Toulouse, 2007) 141–71 and 393–9; D. Guérin, in Sennequier and Colonna (eds.) *L'Algérie au temps des royaumes numides* 101–2, 132–4; C. Sintès and Y. Rebahi (eds.), *Algérie antique: Catalogue de l'exposition 26 avril au 17 août, Musée de l'Arles et la Provence antiques* (Arles, 2003) nos. 4–15.

180. Although Punic was the language affected at court by Numidian kings such as Massinissa, and was used for coin legends (**179**) and for dedications in Punicized sanctuaries within the Numidian kingdom (such as at Constantine: **182**), the everyday language of the Numidians was Libyan. The language has not been fully decoded, but the existence of bilingual texts, such as the Dougga mausoleum inscription (**187b**), as well as recognizable toponymns and personal names, allows for its partial interpretation. The alphabet, which consisted only of consonants, is ultimately derived from the semitic alphabet; the shapes of the letters are predominantly geometric. The majority of the inscriptions which survive (over 1,300) are funerary and date to the third and second centuries BC, but there are certainly some that date to the fourth century BC. The oldest texts of all, however, have been ascribed to the sixth or even the seventh century BC, although secure chronological indicators are scarce. In any event, the claim that the Libyan alphabet was invented by Massinissa, made by some ancient sources, is false, although he might have standardized one version of it. The language was normally written from bottom to top, but many texts came to be inscribed from right to left under the influence of Punic. While most densely found in the Numidian heartlands of Algeria and western Tunisia, Libyan inscriptions have also been discovered in northern Morocco and in modern-day Libya. Although clearly deriving from a common origin, there are a number of different alphabets and letter forms, but these display no clear geographical or chronological pattern, and earlier attempts to divide Libyan into a 'western' and an 'eastern' variety are no longer tenable. Remarkably, a version of the letters is apparently used by the Tuareg today, who call it *tifinagh* ('the signs'), although in our ignorance of the ancient language caution is necessary before the former can be claimed as the latter's direct descendant. The example shown here, a gravestone, was found in 1874 at Bordj Hellal (the ancient Thunusida), between Chemtou and Bulla Regia, and has three lines of vertical letters, read from bottom to top (where it is damaged). A partial translation in Punic in the central recessed panel reads: 'For Yagouakani, son of Kanardat, son of Masylan, have these stones been erected.' The

reference to 'stones' in the plural remained a puzzle until the discovery in the early 1980s of another stele with identical Libyan letters which clearly records the same, presumably important, man. The latter stele, now in Chemtou museum, would have stood when complete an imposing 3.6 m high, as did no doubt also its twin. Such a double memorial to the deceased is unique in Libyan epigraphy. Also unique is its use of writing in two different directions: as is known from a third fragment, published in 1997, the first line read horizontally from left to right, and the rest read vertically from bottom to top as usual. The former practice occurs on only a handful of Libyan inscriptions and is clearly due to the influence of Latin; a date in the first century BC is likely.

(Paris, Musée du Louvre AO 5144. Height 1.57 m)

General: J.-B. Chabot, *Recueil des inscriptions libyques* (Paris, 1940–1); G. Camps, *BAC* n.s. 10–11B (1974–5) 143–66; O. Rössler, in Horn and Rüger (eds.) *Die Numider* 89–97; L. Galand, *Antiquités Africaines* 25 (1989) 69–81; M. Brett and E. Fentress, *The Berbers* (Oxford, 1996) 37–41; M. O'Connor, in P. T. Daniels and W. Bright (eds.), *The World's Writing Systems* (Oxford, 1996) 112–16 and 119; J. N. Adams, *Bilingualism and the Latin Language* (Cambridge, 2003) 245–7. Distribution: M. Ghaki, *BAC* n.s. 17B (1981) 183–6; K. Kitouni-Daho, *Carte des inscriptions libyques* (Aix-en-Provence, 1982). Morocco: L. Galand, J. Février and G. Vajda, *Inscriptions antiques du Maroc*, vol. 1 (Paris, 1966) 1–78. Bordj Hellal stelai: Chabot *Recueil* no. 72; Sznycer, *Semitica* 27 (1977) 47–57; Seefried Brouillet (ed.) *From Hannibal to Saint Augustine* no. 60; M. Ghaki, *Africa* 9 (1985) 7–11; Ghaki, *MDAIR* 104 (1997) 387–91.

181. The site of the ancient Numidian capital and later Roman city of Cirta, the modern Constantine (so called after the Roman emperor of that name who rebuilt it in the fourth century AD), is seen here from the north-west. The city occupies a formidable rocky plateau defended by sheer drops on the north side and on the west, and on the east by the deep gorge of the river Rhummel (the ancient Ampsagus). The beginning of the latter is marked by the dip in the skyline just to the left of centre in the photograph. The spectacular gorge, which is narrow as well as deep, measures up to 125 m in depth at its maximum extent. Cirta's stunning natural position, and its easy defensibility (the main approach was via a single spur on the south-west side of the city), made it a favourite with the Numidian kings. Syphax, whose kingdom stretched as far west as the Moroccan border, named this his eastern capital (Siga was his western seat: **185**), but when Massinissa gained control of this sector of eastern Numidia, it became the hub of his vast Numidian

181

kingdom. This was centred on eastern Algeria and western Tunisia, but Massinissa exercised control from the Moroccan border all the way into Tripolitania. Strategically, Cirta is well positioned to control the surrounding area of the so-called Great Plains, the agricultural yields of which no doubt supplied Massinissa with much of his vast wealth: at his death in 148 BC he was reputed to have left each of his 44 children 875 ha of land.

(Photo R. J. A. Wilson)

S. Gsell, *Atlas archéologique de l'Algérie* (Algiers and Paris, 1911) 17 no. 126; A. Berthier, *La Numidie: Rome et la Maghreb* (Paris, 1981) 159–77; *Encyclopédie berbère,* vol. XIII (Aix-en-Provence, 1994) 1964–77 (Cirta); K. Kitouni-Daho, in Sennequier and Colonna (eds.) *L'Algérie au temps des royaumes numides* 95–6.

182. Very little survives of the Numidian phase of Cirta's past, except for *disiecta membra* in the city's museum, and a small quarter of housing of the third/second century BC, together with the remains of an oil press, which has been excavated on the left bank of the Rhummel on the slopes of Sidi M'Cid. The Punic style of these houses lends support to literary sources which stress the increasing Punicization of the Numidian court under Massinissa, and a further witness of this phenomenon is the extramural sanctuary at El-Hofra, 1 km south of the city centre. Here in 1875 and again in 1950 enormous numbers of votive stelai were found, over 800 in all, erected in honour of Baal and Tanit (but the emphasis in the inscriptions here, by contrast with the *tophet* at Carthage (**159**), is on Baal). Nearly 300 bore inscriptions, all in Punic apart from 17 in Greek and 3 in Latin; there are none in Libyan script. This, the most westerly of all known Baal–Tanit sanctuaries, was established in the late third century BC and was at its zenith in the second century – largely coinciding with the reigns of Massinissa and his son Micipsa. They provide an eloquent demonstration of Numidian Punicization: the stelai are provincial versions of the kind commonplace at Carthage and elsewhere in the Punic sphere (cf. **159**). Of the two examples selected here, **a** shows the familiar symbol of Tanit, here holding a *caduceus*, with a dolphin depicted below; the dedicator was Arisham son of Shamarbaal. **b** adds a votive hand, as well as the crescent moon and sun disc above; the dedicator was Hannibal son of Baalhanno. In view of the overwhelming predominance of the Punic script and of Punic names in these stelai (although some Numidian names are certainly also present), it might seem more likely that these are the dedications of an immigrant community at Cirta rather than cosmopolitan Numidians thoroughly embracing Punic culture, religion and even nomenclature; on the other hand, the extent to which the latter phenomenon occurred is not to be underestimated. It is striking that no inscriptions in the Libyan script have been found anywhere in Cirta.

(Paris, Musée du Louvre. **a** inv. AO 1013; height 56 cm; width 9.5 cm; thickness 7.5 cm; **b** inv. AO 5308; height 50 cm; width 17 cm; thickness 8.5 cm)

A. Berthier and R. Charlier, *Le sanctuaire punique d'El Hofra à Constantine* (Paris, 1952 and 1955); E. Künzl, in Horn and Rüger *Die Numider* 117–18; F. Bertrandy and M. Sznycer, *Les stèles puniques de Constantine* (Paris, 1987) nos. 2 and 125; Lancel *L'Algérie antique* 54–6. Sidi M' Cid: A. Berthier, *Antiquités Africaines* 16 (1980) 13–26.

183. Chemtou, situated in the fertile Bagradas valley in what is now north-west Tunisia, was famed in antiquity as the source of a fine yellow marble (*marmor Numidicum*: Pliny *NH* V.2), which was widely used from Augustan times onwards in prestige imperial building projects. Before 46 BC, however, Chemtou lay outside the Roman province, some 19 km west of one of the Numidian royal capitals, Bulla Regia. Its ancient name, Simitthu, is Numidian rather than Roman in origin. The quarries at Chemtou were first exploited by the Numidian kings in the second century BC, and the marble certainly reached as far west as Cirta (**181**), over 160 km away, where a stele and a couple of Corinthian capitals (which were never carved in this material in Roman times) attest to its use by the Numidians. But by far the most striking Numidian monument carved in the yellow marble is located at Chemtou itself, crowning the easternmost of the three hills which dominate the site, with stunning views in all directions. **a**, looking eastwards down the Bagradas valley, gives a hint of this, and also shows a detail of the monument's south foundations with the use of dovetail clamps, originally lead-filled; the wall to the left is part of a modern simulation of the monument's mass, and the structures to the right are Roman. Careful study of the building's foundations and the fallen remains of its architectural and sculptural adornment allows for the reconstruction of a monument 12.15 m long and 5.64 m wide, once standing nearly 10 m high (**b** shows a model suggesting its original appearance). The ornament is an eclectic mix of Egyptian, Hellenistic Greek and Numidian elements. Situated on a three-step stylobate, the monument is two-storeyed. The lower

182a

182b

183a

storey has a central doorway in one of the long sides crowned by a sun-disc and *uraeus*, symbol of Egyptian royal power. The doorway is flanked by pilasters crowned by florid Corinthianizing capitals; there are further pilasters at the corners. The upper parts of the walls of this storey are decorated with, alternately, Numidian shields and breastplates (with a Medusa head and Athena's aegis among emblems on the shields). A garland frieze runs above. The upper storey is decorated with engaged Doric columns surmounted by a Doric frieze. It has been dated on the basis of architectural style and pottery fragments to the second half of the second century BC. Its original function as a Numidian temple seems assured, although (since only foundations survive) reconstruction is problematic: in particular it is not known if the 'doorway' framed only a niche, as Rakob suggested, or whether it led to an inner chamber or indeed to an upper floor. A suggestion that the monument was erected in honour of Massinissa (who died in 148 BC) by his son and successor Micipsa is perhaps less likely than the alternative interpretation, that it was intended as a temple to Baal-Hammon, the Punic god also worshipped by the Numidians (cf. **182**), especially (although not of course conclusively) in view of

183b

its later (Roman) use as a temple of Saturn. The building is an eloquent indicator of the wealth and sophistication of Numidian royal society in the second century BC, and of its openness to the influence of Hellenistic Greece and Egypt for its architectural detail; but the overall form of the monument is distinctively Numidian.

(**a** Photo R. J. A .Wilson; **b** DAI Rome 79.1740)

F. Rakob, in Horn and Rüger (eds.) *Die Numider* 120–9, 464–9; Rakob, in P. Gros (ed.), *Architecture et société de l'archaïsme à la fin del la république romaine* (Paris and Rome, 1983) 325–47, at 327–9; Rakob (ed.), *Simitthus*, vol. II (Mainz-am-Rhein, 1994) 1–38. Constantine stele and one of the capitals of yellow marble: Horn and Rüger *Die Numider* 470 and 564.

184. The only monument in pre-Roman north Africa which provides a reasonably close parallel in form and function to **183** is another two-storey rectangular structure at Kbor Klib, in the central Tunisian uplands. It lies 25 km north-east of Mactar, in a prominent position with views in all directions (both it and **183** were clearly designed to be seen from afar). An elongated monument, 45.4 m long and 8.9 m wide (and perhaps once 10 or 11 m high), built of large limestone blocks, it is divided into three parts by openings in one of the long sides, in which staircases were inserted giving access either to an upper floor, or to a chamber or chambers (shrines?) located within the monument (**a**). The base of a much smaller rectangular structure, probably an altar, lies immediately adjacent to the west, aligned with the central axis of the main monument. Kbor Klib also, like **183**, had shield and body-armour decoration in relief along the sides of the monument; a bust of Artemis decorates at least one of the shields. Reconstruction of the upper storey is more problematical (the number of surviving blocks is far fewer than at Chemtou), but Ionic freestanding columns, possibly the full length of the building, formed part of it (**b** shows one conjectural restoration). Slender dating evidence, based on the style of the architectural detail, suggests a date in the middle or second half of the second century BC for Kbor Klib; certainly it cannot be as late as the mid first century BC, so that earlier conjecture that it was a Roman victory monument erected by Julius Caesar after 46 BC can be discounted. An alternative theory, that it was a victory monument built to commemorate the battle of Zama (202 BC) by Massinissa, who had assisted in the Roman defeat of Hannibal, also seems improbable. Quite apart from problems of dating (if the monument has been correctly ascribed to *c.* 150/100 BC), the battle of Zama in 202 BC took place near Zama Regia, almost certainly to be identified with Sakiet Sidi Youssef,

184a

far away on the Tunisio-Algerian border 32 km west of Le Kef. The modern village of Jama, which lies 20 km to the north-east of Kbor Klib, and where excavations have been proceeding since 1999, is therefore likely to be Zama M[inor], referred to on an inscription (*CIL* VIII 16442). Once again the absence of parallels (except at Chemtou) makes interpretation of Kbor Klib uncertain, but the most likely explanation, especially in view of its prominent position, is that it is another Numidian temple in honour of the god of the sky, together with accompanying altar. The attempt by Saumagne and more recently by Ferchiou to see it as a grave monument, with hypothetical burial chambers at the upper level (now lost), reached by the staircases, fails to convince.

(Photo **a** R. J. A. Wilson; **b** after Ferchiou 1991)

A. Lézine, *Architecture punique: Recueil de documents* (Paris, n.d., *c.* 1959) 113–14; Lézine, *Carthage Utique: Études d'architecture et d'urbanisme* (Paris, 1968) 183–5; Rakob, in Horn and Rüger (eds.) *Die Numider* 120–9; Rakob, in Gros (ed.) *Architecture et société* 328–9; Rakob *Simitthus* II 31–6. Tomb interpretation: C. Saumagne, *Revue Tunisienne* (1941) 250–1; N. Ferchiou, *Quaderni di archeologia della Libia* 14 (1991) 45–97; E. Polito, *Antiquités Africaines* 35 (1999) 64–5. Victory monument of Julius Caesar: G. C. Picard, *Les trophées romains* (Paris, 1957) 208–16. Victory monument to commemorate Zama: D. Ross, *Kbor Klib and the Battle of Zama* (Oxford, 2005).

185. The western capital of one of the sub-groups of the Numidian peoples, the Masaesyli, was situated at Siga, a town 4 km inland from the coast on the river Tafna (the ancient Siga); this lies in what is now western Algeria, 64 km from the Moroccan border. Little is known of the Numidian settlement itself, and not much more about its Roman successor, yet on a hill 221 m high, south-east of the town but on the other side of the river, stand the remains of a remarkable Numidian mausoleum with stupendous views in all directions. This has an unusual plan, basically triangular in shape but with concave sides 7.2 m long, and stands on a three-step stylobate. It is made up of large blocks mortared together, an unusual feature of Numidian architecture in north Africa (where blocks are normally placed without mortar, with or without the help of iron or lead cramps: cf. **183a**). Today the monument stands only some 3.5 m high (**a**), but remains of the fallen superstructure allow for the reconstruction of a tower tomb about 30 m high, with false doors of tall Macedonian type in each side of the first storey, and a pyramid roof above (**b**). Some roughly hewn relief decoration, including human faces, also survives, but which part of the monument these figures adorned is unknown. The tomb chambers beneath are reached by a series of underground barrel-vaulted passageways, approached from outside the monument. Pottery and stylistic evidence suggest a date *c.* 200 BC, so it might have been built by Syphax, whose western capital Siga was (he was defeated by Massinissa in 203 and died in captivity in Italy), or else by his son Vermina (king between 201 and 191 BC) or one of his descendants. Whereas the barrel vaulting of stone and the false doors suggest the clear influence of the Macedonian tombs at Vergina and elsewhere, the tower tomb-type probably reached the Numidians via the world of Punic funerary architecture. The closest parallels for mausolea of triangular shape with concave sides are to be found at Sabratha in Libya, a Phoenician foundation subsequently under Carthaginian control. There two are known: of one only the foundations survive, but the better-preserved example ('Mausoleum B') was much more elaborately decorated than the mausoleum at Siga, and it is also somewhat later (second century BC). Another triangular Punic example, smaller and less well preserved, is known on the island of Jerba.

(**a** R. J. A. Wilson; **b** DAI Rom 79.710)

F. Rakob, in Horn and Rüger (eds.) *Die Numider* 149–57 and 456–61; Lancel *L'Algérie antique* 41–4; J.-P. Laporte, in Sennequier and Colonna (eds.) *L'Algérie au temps des royaumes numides* 88–91. Sabratha: A. Di Vita, *MDAIR* 83 (1976) 273–85. Jerba (Henchir Bourgou): J. Weriemmi-Akkari, *Reppal* 1 (1985) 189–96.

185a

185b

186. The Numidian mausoleum known as Le Medracen lies in what is now a wild and desolate setting in the foothills of the Aurès mountains, 35 km north-east of Batna in central northern Algeria. Unlike other Numidian royal mausolea which are situated on lofty hilltops, this one lies towards the rear of a wide valley, set against a backdrop of hills (**a**). Although it formed part of a cemetery of lesser tombs, the settlement where the people who were buried here actually lived is still unknown. Le Medracen is an impressive circular tomb 59 m in diameter, built of sandstone blocks (**b**). Its exterior façade is decorated with sixty Doric engaged columns, surmounted by an overhanging curved *cavetto* (cornice) of Egyptian origin (**c**); three false doors do something to break the monotony of the perimeter wall. There is a stepped pyramid roof, the mausoleum's total height being 18.5 m. The entrance to the tomb chamber is via steps leading underground just outside the monument on the east, and then along a straight internal corridor 17 m long giving access to the burial chamber at the heart of the tomb. Remarkably, seventeen logs of cedar were still in place in the roof of this corridor in 1970; a radio-carbon dating of samples suggested a date

186a

186b

in the third century BC, making this the earliest in the series of grandiose north African mausolea of pre-Roman date. The excellent workmanship of the whole and its size and decoration suggest a royal patron. The name of Gaia (who died in 206 BC), father of Massinissa, has been proposed, but we do not really know if he was buried here: there must have been other third-century royal Numidian

186c

kings or princes who did not make it to the pages of history. The circular form is interesting: some have seen it as a monumentalization of the modest circular tombs or *bazinas* which are common in pre-Roman Numidia; but it is not impossible that the builder of Le Medracen was taking his lead from none other than the tomb of Alexander the Great in Alexandria (about which curiously little is known). Be that as it may, the circular form was imitated in the early first century BC by a second great circular Numidian mausoleum, the 'Tomb of the Christian Woman' near Tipasa, and later still by the tomb built in 28 BC by the founder of another royal dynasty, the emperor Augustus in Rome.

(Photos R. J. A. Wilson)

G. Camps, *CRAI* (1973) 470–516; Rakob, in Horn and Rüger (eds.) *Die Numider* 132–8; Rakob, in Gros (ed.) *Architecture et société* 329–32; J. Fedak, *Monumental Tombs of the Hellenistic Age* (Toronto, 1990) 137–8; Sennequier and Colonna (eds.) *L'Algérie au temps des royaumes numides* 109–12; Lancel *L'Algérie antique* 53–4 (but with an earlier chronology, *c.* 300 BC). 'Tomb of the Christian Woman': Rakob, in Horn and Rüger (eds.) *Die Numider* 138–42; Lancel *L'Algerie antique* 67–9. Circular shape of Alexander's tomb?: H. Thiersch, *JDAI* 25 (1910) 55–97; F. Coarelli and Y. Thébert, *MEFRA* 100 (1988) 761–818.

187. Dougga (the ancient Thugga) was in origin a Numidian settlement in what is now north central Tunisia. Little is known of its pre-Roman phase, but a few stretches of its defences, the irregular street-grid enshrined in the Roman town plan and a Numidian mausoleum of the first half of the second century BC all bear witness to this period of Dougga's past. The mausoleum is a tower tomb, 21 m high (**a**), of more slender dimensions and more elegant proportions than the earlier one at Siga (**185**). The 9-m square base, set over the tomb chamber, is decorated with Phoenicio-Cypriot ('Aeolic') corner pilasters, repeated also at the corners of the third storey. Above the base rises a square second storey, enlivened with engaged Ionic columns and surmounted by a curving, overhanging *cavetto* (cornice), an Egyptianizing feature not unlike that at Le Medracen (**186b**). At the base of the uppermost storey are relief panels depicting chariots; the top is crowned by a small pyramid. Sculptural decoration in the round included horsemen at the four corners on the base of the top storey, and sirens or sphinxes at the corners of the pyramid. A small sitting lion is at the summit. The monument was substantially intact until 1842, when the British consul in Tunis demolished it to extract the bilingual inscription (**b**), now in the British Museum – a shameful act of colonial 'archaeology'. The surviving inscription, in both Punic (on the left in **b**) and in Numidian (Libyan) script (see **180**), is one of a pair (the other was already illegible in the nineteenth century). The lost text probably gave the name of the deceased buried in the tomb; this one appears to list the men responsible for its construction, starting with Ateban, son of Iepmatath, son of Palu, and continuing with Abdarish son of Abdashtart, Zimer (Ateban's son) and Managai son of Warsakan. Carpenters and ironworkers who worked on the project are also listed. The names are all Numidian except for Abdarish, who is clearly Punic: perhaps he was the principal architect called in to build the tomb. If so, the Dougga mausoleum gives us a rare glimpse of Carthaginian Hellenistic funerary architecture (itself heavily influenced, no doubt, by developments in the contemporary Greek world), which with a few exceptions (see **185**) is largely lost to us; but a two-storey Punic mausoleum at Henchir Djaouf near Zaghouan, also with Aeolic pilaster capitals, provides a smaller, if less sumptuously decorated, parallel from a Punic context. The Dougga mausoleum also furnishes us with a further illustration of the penetration

187a

187b

of Punic culture and the Punic language into the orbit of the Numidian aristocracy.

(**a** Photo R. J. A. Wilson; **b** courtesy of the Trustees of the British Museum)

C. Poinssot and J. W. Salomonson, *CRAI* (1959) 141–9; C. Poinssot, *Les ruines de Dougga* (Tunis, 1958) 58–61; Rakob, in Horn and Rüger (eds.) *Die Numider* 156–8; *Hannibal ad portas* 66 nos. 1–2 (where it is seen, I think wrongly, as a commemoration of Massinissa *c.* 150 BC). Inscription: J.-G. Février, *Karthago* 10 (1959–60) 51–7; J. Ferron, *Africa* 3–4 (1969–70) 83–109; G. Camps, *Encyclopédie berbère*, vol. VII (Aix-en-Provence, 1989) 1008–11 (Ateban). For the older, alternative view, that the tomb is that of Ateban, an otherwise unknown Numidian prince (improbable, not least because his son is one of the named builders), see Chabot *Recueil* no. 1; Horn and Rüger (eds.) *Die Numider* 576–7. Henchir Djaouf: C. Poinssot and J. W. Salomonson, *Oudheidkundige Mededelingen* 44 (1963) 57–81.

9. IBERIA

S. J. KEAY

During their expulsion of the Carthaginians from south and east Iberia (218–205 BC), the Romans came into contact with a range of unfamiliar peoples. They referred to them collectively as the Iberians, or as individual peoples. For archaeologists, the term 'Iberian' is usually equated with a range of shared cultural characteristics, such as a preference for proto-urban settlement or specific artistic styles, even though there are marked regional differences between them. The material culture of the Iberian peoples was a distinctive and original blend of later Bronze and Iron Age regional traditions. Orientalizing influences of the Phoenicians and Greeks were important early stimuli, manifested most clearly in the spectacular stone sculptures from south-eastern Spain, but they also exercised a longer-term influence upon the development of different scripts, architecture, defensive technology, and the form and decoration of ceramics. Carthaginian influence is harder to detect owing to the short duration of its colonial presence in Iberia (237–206 BC) and because it is difficult to distinguish in the archaeological record. By contrast, the peoples of central Iberia, such as those described by Greek and Latin writers as 'Celtiberians', were heirs to different traditions. They exhibited strong continuity from the preceding Bronze Age in terms of their patterns of settlement, religious practices and artistic traditions. However, this was tempered with elements of 'Celtic' culture derived from temperate Europe and indirect Mediterranean influence, often through the medium of other native peoples. This is reflected in aspects of their distinctive settlement patterns, art, social structure, metalwork, language and script.

In many ways, the spread of Roman power in Iberia between the late third and late second centuries BC was largely conditioned by some of these cultural differences and the contrasting landscapes in which the peoples lived. Detailed analyses of the historical evidence reveal that Roman commanders in the field used a range of military and diplomatic techniques to subject these peoples to Roman control. Abundant historical sources make it clear that this resulted in an uneven process of conquest that culminated, but did not end, in particularly intense phases of conflict conventionally referred to as the Lusitanian (155–139 BC) and Celtiberian (155–133 BC) Wars. Rome's experiences during this period were highly influential in helping her to define her attitudes to provincial peoples in the West at an early stage of imperial expansion. Insofar as there was any military strategy at all, it was short-term and largely a response to local circumstances coupled with the perceived importance to governors of success in the provincial arena to their political career at Rome. In 197 BC, Iberia was divided into the two *provinciae* of Hispania Citerior and Hispania Ulterior. Initially these were loosely defined areas of primarily military authority, within which subject populations were administered largely through the agency of native elites. Exploitation of the Hispaniae began in the earlier second century BC onwards. In Citerior, the re-working of the Carthaginian silver mines of the south-east was begun, taxes began to be collected on a more regular basis and locally minted silver coins were issued, all prior to the later second century BC. In Ulterior, however, the mines of the Sierra Morena were not exploited by Rome until the later second century BC, and locally minted silver coins were absent. Agricultural exploitation seems to have largely continued pre-Roman practice, since Roman-style farms do not appear in much of eastern Citerior until the first century BC, while in Ulterior they are essentially a feature of the early imperial landscape. Exploitation of Iberia's resources, therefore, does not seem to have been systematic until the end of the Republican era. Historical and archaeological evidence for the large-scale settlement of Italians and Roman citizens prior to the late second and early first centuries BC is hard to substantiate. Outside the key centres of Roman power at Tarraco (Tarragona), Carthago Nova (Cartagena) and Corduba (Córdoba), Roman foundations were rare. Some, like Italica (205 BC) and Carteia (171 BC) consisted of mixed Italic and indigenous populations settled within or close to existing centres of strategic importance, while the material culture of the inhabitants of Valentia (138 BC) suggests that a proportion of them at least were Italic settlers. At the same time, some native settlements were abandoned or lost importance, although many others throughout both provinces continued to be occupied well into the first century BC and beyond.

Apart from rare fortifications, Roman influence in the form of stone-cut and mosaic inscriptions, building types (primarily houses), coins issued locally and minted at Rome, foodstuffs (principally wine), eating habits (as reflected in black-gloss and thin-walled ceramics) and funerary sculpture only starts to become visible in Iberia from the later second century BC onwards; furthermore, they are adopted piecemeal by individuals and communities rather than forming part of a cultural package. This situation means that it is difficult to chart Roman or Italic influence in any meaningful way prior to this time, apart from the presence of occasional fortified sites. Nevertheless, recent research is beginning to show that when it starts to appear it is most prevalent amongst communities in the lower Ebro valley and some areas of the Mediterranean coast of Hispania Citerior. One imagines that the centres of Roman power at Tarraco, Carthago Nova and Emporion were key centres of influence in this, although some of the rare Roman foundations would also have played their part, particularly Valentia (Valencia), where recent work has revealed very clear evidence of Italic material culture and burial practices. Evidence for Roman cultural influence in Hispania Ulterior is considerably rarer, where Corduba (Córdoba) seems to have had less of an impact in this sense. Those members of local elites who did adopt these cultural traits absorbed them into the indigenous cultural mainstreams in the context of social reproduction, bringing about a form of Iberian and Roman cultural bricolage. However, the wholesale cultural transformation of native communities was a long and gradual process that did not really begin until the later first century BC onwards and continued through much of the first century AD.

GENERAL BIBLIOGRAPHY

Our understanding of the period covered by this volume has greatly improved in recent years as a result of much new archaeological work. Excavations have begun at last to clarify the character and chronology of Phoenician and Greek sites, with the notable exception of Gadir itself. Prehistorians have made significant progress in characterizing the social structure of pre-Roman peoples and of their material culture (ceramics and metalwork etc.), which has shed new light on the possible meanings of descriptions passed to us by the classical sources. This has been particularly significant amongst the peoples of central Iberia. Rescue excavation within such modern towns as Tarragona, Cartagena, Córdoba, Valentia and Huesca have done much to clarify uncertainties surrounding the layout and material culture of Rome's earliest towns in Iberia. With the exception of coins, and to some extent sculpture, rather less work has been done on the material culture of their inhabitants. Rural populations are less well understood, being less 'visible' to archaeological surveys for a variety of reasons.

L. Abad Casal (ed.), *De Iberia in Hispaniam: La adaptación de las sociedades ibéricas a los modelos romanos* (Soria, 2003).

L. Abad Casal, S. Keay and S. Ramallo Asensio (eds.), *Early Roman Towns in Hispania Tarraconensis* (*JRA* Supplement 62, Portsmouth, R. I., 2006).

M. Almagro Gorbea and G. Ruiz Zapatero (eds.), *Palaeoetnología de la Península ibérica. Complutum 2–3* (Madrid, 1993) 469–99.

C. Aranegui (ed.), *Los Iberos: Príncipes de occidente* (Actas del Congreso Internacional (Barcelona, 1998).

M.E. Aubet, *The Phoenicians and the West: Politics, Colonies and Trade* (2nd edn, Cambridge, 2001).

F. Beltrán Lloris, 'Writing, language and society: Iberians, Celts and Romans in north-eastern Spain in the second and first centuries BC', *BICS* 43 (1999) 131–51.

F. Burillo Mozota, *Los celtíberos: Etnias y estados* (Barcelona, 1998).

A. Burnett, 'Latin on coins of the western Empire' in A. Cooley (ed.), *Becoming Roman, Writing Latin: Literacy and Epigraphy in the Roman West* (*JRA* Supplement, 48, Portsmouth R.I., 2002) 34–40.

P. Cabrera Bonet and C. Sánchez Fernández (eds.), *Els grecs a Ibèria: Seguint les passes d'Hèracles* (Barcelona, 2002).

C. Domergue, *Les mines de la péninsule ibérique dans l'antiquité romaine* (Paris, 1990).

M. P. García-Bellido and L. Callegarin (eds.), *Los Cartagineses y la monetización del mediterráneo occidental (Anejos de Archivo Español de Arqueología* XXII, Madrid, 2000).

J. L. Jiménez Salvador and A. Ribera Lacomba (eds.), *Valencia y las primeras ciudades romanas de Hispania* (Valencia, 2002).

S. Keay, *Roman Spain* (London, 1988).

'Recent archaeological work in Roman Iberia (1990–2002)', *Journal of Roman Studies* 93 (2003) 146–211.

A. Nünnerich-Asmus, *Heiligtümer und Romanisierung auf der Iberischen Halbinsel: Überlegungen zu Religion und Kultureller Identität* (Mainz, 1999).

J. Richardson, *Hispaniae: Spain and the Development of Roman Imperialism 218–82 BC* (Cambridge, 1986).

188. Map of Iberia during the Roman conquest.

(Keay *Roman Spain* 26)
Courtesy of Chris Unwin.

189. Plan of the Phoenician colony at Toscanos (Málaga). This small site was founded around the beginning of the eighth and abandoned at around the early sixth century BC. It supported a population of about 1,000 individuals and comprised small houses set in a grid of narrow streets running south-west to north-east. The absence of evidence for public buildings and a hinterland suggests that it did not have an urban function and that it was essentially a trading centre. A similar picture can be inferred from the neighbouring sites of Chorreras and Morro de Mezquitilla. Light industrial activity of a later date has been found on the nearby hills of Alarcón and Peñón to the west. The Phoenicians were a major cultural influence in southern Iberia. Their earliest colony, which was established at Gadir (Cádiz) near to the mouth of the Guadalete on the Atlantic coast in the ninth century BC, was the westernmost point of Phoenician expansion. Further colonies were set up along the Mediterranean coast at Malaka (Málaga), Sexi (Almuñécar) and Abdera (Adra) and lesser sites. The focus of their interest was the key natural resources of the region, particularly metals, needed by the Phoenician city-states of the Levant. Their influence in southern Spain and Portugal can be measured in terms of the distribution of Phoenician-style ceramics and other kinds of material culture on indigenous sites, as well as the sanctuaries closely modelled on complexes in Phoenicia that have been discovered at Coria del Río and El Carambolo, near Seville.

(M. E. Aubet Semmler, *Tiro y las colonias fenicias de occidente* (Barcelona, 1987))

H. G. Niemayer, *Madrider Mitteilungen* 3 (1964) 38–44; H. G. Niemayer, in B. Cunliffe and S. Keay (eds.), *Social Complexity and the Development of Towns in Iberia from the Copper Age to the Second Century AD* (Proceedings of the British Academy 86, Oxford, 1995) 67–88; J. L. Escacena Carrasco and R. Izquierdo de Montes, in D. Ruiz Mata and S. Celestino Pérez (eds.), *Arquitectura oriental y oriemtalizante en la Península Ibérica* (Centro de Estudios del Próximo Oriente. Lenguas y Culturas del Antiguo Oriente Próximo 4, Madrid, 2001) 123–57.

190. Sculpture of an armed Iberian warrior standing by the side of his horse. These sculptures form part of a group of over 1,400 pieces discovered at the site of Cerrillo Blanco (Porcuna, Jaén) between 1975 and 1979. This was the site of one of the cemeteries of ancient Ipolka (Porcuna), one of the key Iberian settlements of upper Andalucía. The group is the most spectacular example of a tradition of orientalizing sculpture which adorned the tombs of regional elites in southern Iberia between the sixth and fourth centuries BC: another major group has been recently discovered at El Pajarillo (Huelma, Jaén). Research suggests that the sculptures date to the first half of the fifth century BC and that they derived from a range of monuments, including tombs and a 'Warrior Monument'. It has been suggested that the piece illustrated here represents an actual event, immortalizing one of the regional conflicts that took place within the proto-state system of southern Iberia. Most of the sculptures seem to be inspired by themes from the Greek after-life. They are thus symptomatic of the ways in which Greek cultural symbols were adopted in an alien cultural context by native elites, contributing towards their social and political dominance in the region.

(Photo P. Witte PLF 3007)

J. A. González Navarrete, *Escultura Ibérica de Cerrillo Blanco* (Jaén, 1987); I. Negueruela Martínez, *Los monumentos escultoricos ibéricos del Cerrillo de Porcuna (Jaén)* (Madrid, 1990); M. Molinos, *El santuario heroico de 'El Pajarillo' Huelma (Jaén)* (Jaén, 1998).

191. Iberian settlement at the Plaza de Armas de Puente Tablas (Jaén). Urban development was well established in southern Spain prior to the arrival of Rome. The Plaza de Armas settlement was first discovered in 1971 and is located on a steep-sided plateau a considerable distance to the south of the river Guadalquivir in upper Andalucía. The earliest activity at the site dates to the ninth century BC, although the main periods of occupation date to between the seventh and third centuries BC. Its most prominent features are the wall and square bastions which completely surround the site and which were built from stone footings and mud brick. During the sixth and fifth centuries BC the settlement was regularly planned, with intersecting streets, small single-family houses with two storeys and a building identified as a possible aristocratic residence. No public buildings have yet been located. The site was eventually abandoned

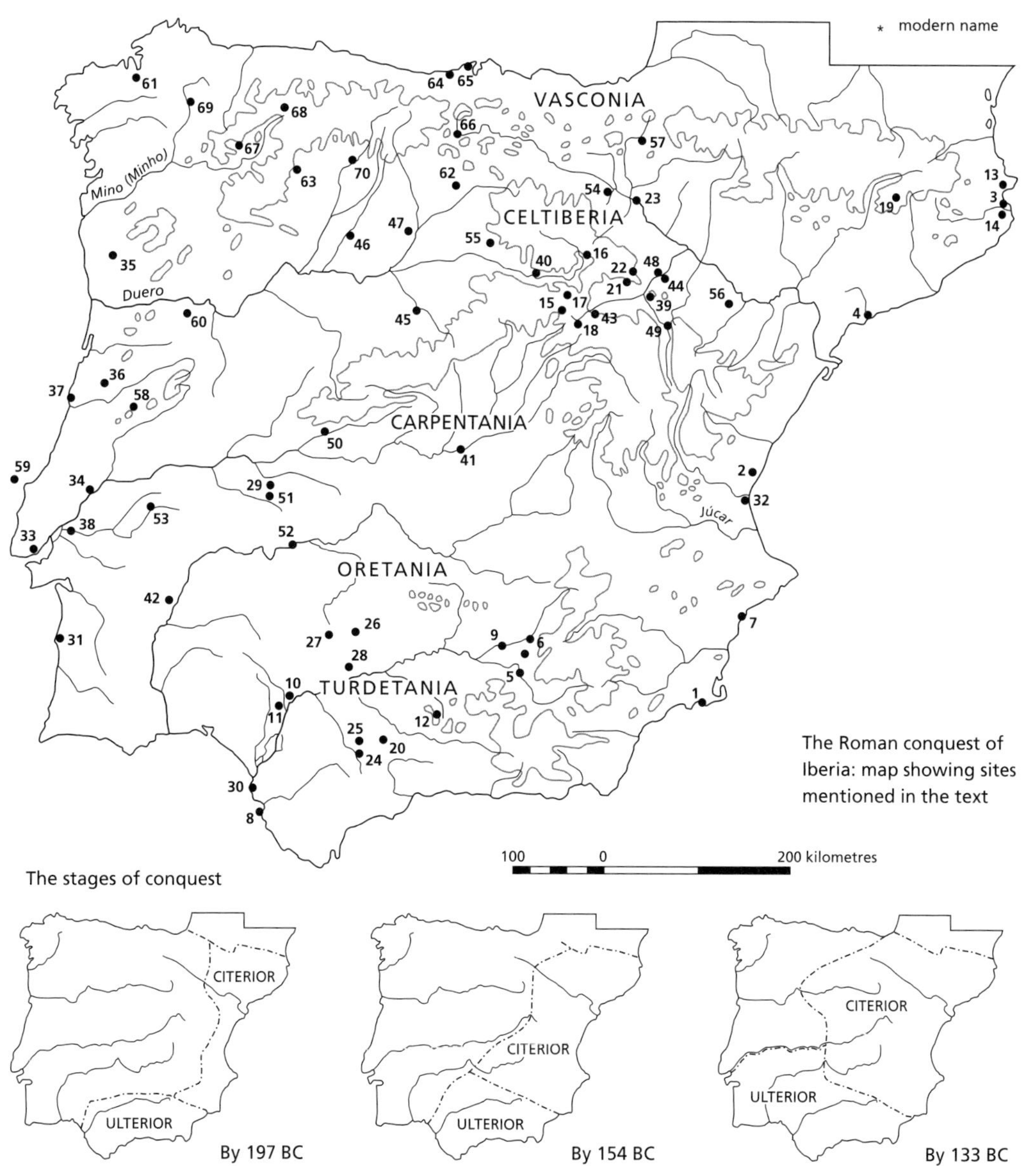

The Roman conquest of Iberia: map showing sites mentioned in the text

189

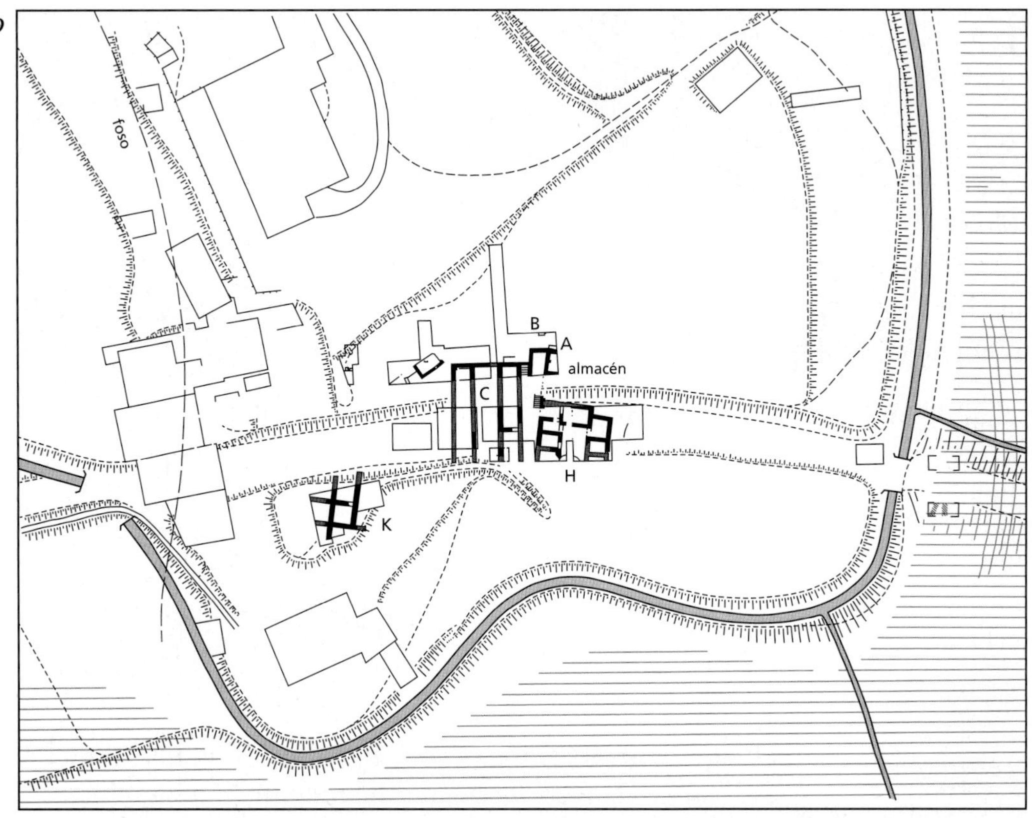

during the third century BC. In general, little is known about the layout and internal development of Iberian centres. However, this site, together with Tejada la Vieja (Huelva), provide us with clues as to the layout and development of much larger regional centres, such as Carmo (Carmona), Kastulo (Castulo) and Ipolka (Porcuna), where the record is less clear.

(Photo A. Ruiz Rodríguez and Manuel Molinos)

A. Ruiz and M. Molinos, in *Anuario Arqueológico de Andalucía III: Actividades Sistemáticas* (Seville, 1986); A. Ruiz, in Cunliffe and Keay (eds.) *Social Complexity* 89–108.

192. View southwards over the defences of the Greek colony of Emporion (Empúries) in north-east Spain. The earliest settlement was established on the site of a small Bronze Age community in the sixth century BC by a group of Phokaian Greeks from Massalia (Marseilles). It was located on an offshore island, known to archaeologists as the *palaiapolis* and identified with present-day Sant Martí d'Empúries; a new settlement, referred to today as the *neapolis*, was established on the mainland shortly afterwards, in the fifth century BC. The Greek phases of the *neapolis* are difficult to trace, owing to their being largely buried beneath structures of Roman Republican and early Imperial date. However, recent excavations at the southern end of the town have revealed a sequence of substantial defences dating to between the fifth and second centuries BC. The enclosed area was subdivided into small building lots by a fairly regular street grid. The character of the Greek houses is known only from those that survived in adapted form into the Roman period. A small agora with stoa and open area provided the political and commercial focus of the community at the centre of the town. At its south-west corner was a small sanctuary to Asklepios, which was first established in the fourth century BC. Cemeteries have been located to the south (Bonjoan, Granada and Parking cemeteries) and west (Marti and Muralla Norte cemeteries) of the town. During the fifth and fourth centuries BC Emporion became a hub of trade between Massalia and the Iberian communities of eastern Spain, the lower Ebro valley and the emerging Iberian archaic states of south-east Spain. Abundant Attic black-

and red-figure pottery is the clearest evidence of this. This trade was a key factor in the development of the Iberian peoples of eastern Iberia prior to Rome.

(Photo Museu d'Arqueologia de Catalunya – Empúries)

J. Puig y Cadafalch, in *Anuari de l'Institut d'Estudis Catalans* II (Barcelona, 1908) 150–94; E. Sanmartí i Grego, in *La Magna Grecia e il lontano Occidente: Atti del XXIX Convegno di Studi sulla Magna Grecia* (Naples, 1990) 389–410; E. Sanmartí Grego, P. Castanyer i Masoliver and J. Tremoleda i Trilla, in W. Trillmich and P. Zanker (eds.), *Stadtbild und Ideologie: Die Monumentalisierung hispanischer Städte zwischen Republik und Kaiserzeit* (Munich, 1990) 117–44; X. Aquilué, *Intervencions arqueològiques a Sant Martí d'Empúries (1994–1996): De l'assentament precolonial a l'Empúries actual* (Monografies emporitanes 9, Girona, 1990); P. Rouillard, *Les grecs et la Péninsule Ibérique du VIIe au IVe siècle avant Jésus-Christ* (Paris, 1991); X. Aquilué, P. Castanyer, I. Masoliver, M. Santos and J. Tremoleda i Trilla, in Abad Casal, Keay and Ramallo Asensio (eds.), *Early Roman Towns* 19–31.

193. Plan of the Iberian settlement at the Puig de Sant Andreu (Ullastret, Girona). It is located in rich agricultural lands close to the Greek colony of Emporion (Empúries) and was founded in the course of the sixth century BC. It was located on a triangular-shaped hill which at its highest point was some 30 m above the surrounding plain. Steep scarps afforded adequate defence on the eastern side, while the west, south and north were fortified with substantial walls, bastions, towers and gates at the beginning of the fourth century BC. The street plan conformed to the topography of the hillside, while there were two temples at its highest point, a small open area identified as an agora, and a large number of small houses with cisterns. An area of grain storage pits was identified at the northern end of the site. The Puig de Sant Andreu provides us with one of the most complete plans of an Iberian settlement in eastern Spain. However, its scale and the abundant evidence for Greek influence from nearby Emporion make it an exceptional one. There is little doubt that it played a key role as a middle-man in trade between Emporion and the communities of north-east Spain.

191

192

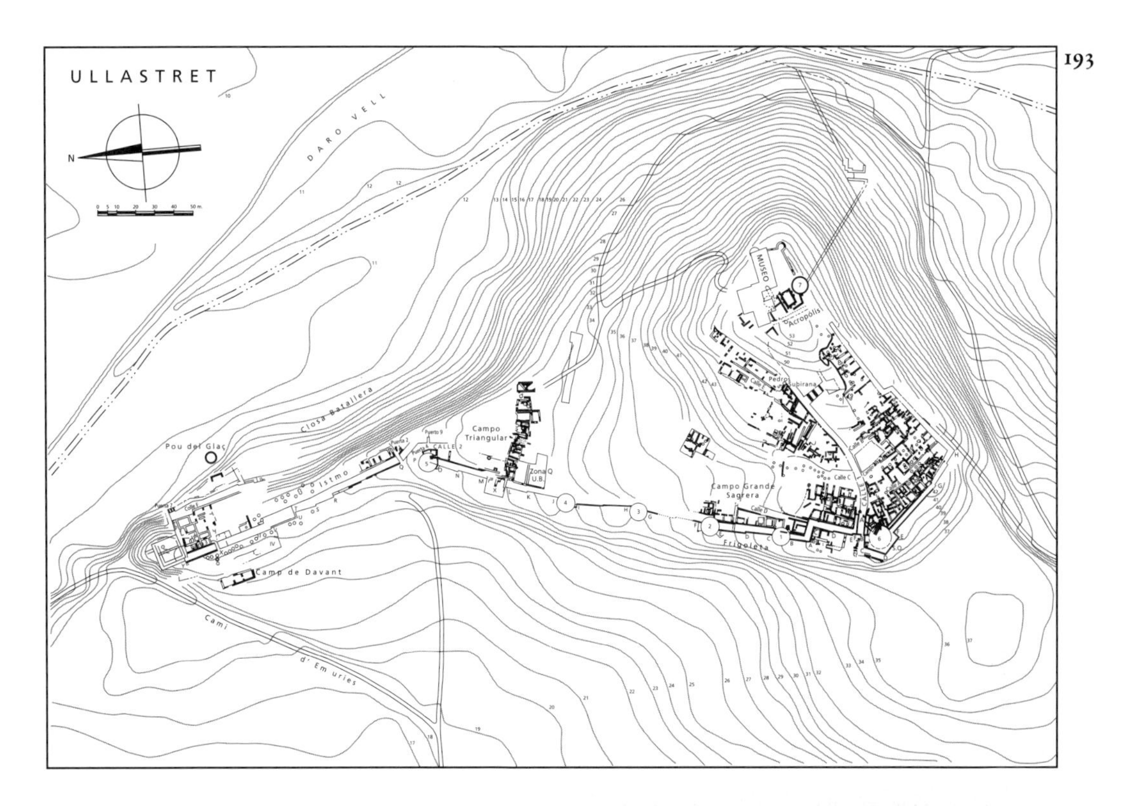

(M. A. Martín Ortega, *Ullastret: Guía de las excavaciones y su museo* (Girona, 1977) (fig. opposite p. 8))

M. Oliva Prat, in *Anales del Instituto de Estudios Gerundenses* VII (Girona, 1953) 294ff.; Ortega, *Ullastret*

194. The Puerta de Sevilla at the western edge of ancient Carmo (Carmona, Seville). It has been suggested that the core of this gate dates to the eighth century BC, and that the tower in the foreground, with its characteristic ashlar masonry, was originally built as a bastion at an early stage of the Carthaginian occupation of southern Spain. This lends support to the view that control of Carmo was pivotal to Carthage's dominance of the lower Guadalquivir valley up to and during the Second Punic War. The gateway at the left of the picture was later modified under Augustus and again during the Muslim domination of southern Spain. Carmo was located at the eastern edge of the Alcores, a rocky bluff which lies to the east of ancient Hispalis (Seville). It visually dominates much of the lower Guadalquivir valley and is visible from contemporary settlements up to 70 km away. The exotic imported pottery and ivory finds from excavations at one of its cemeteries at the Cruz del Negro illustrate its importance as a centre of trade between the native Tartessian populations of the lower Guadalquivir valley and the Phoenicians of the Mediterranean and Atlantic coasts from the eighth century BC onwards. The dense sequence of Roman, Arab and later structures within the walls of Carmona means that Phoenician and Carthaginian levels lie at great depth and are, as yet, poorly understood. Recent work suggests that the Roman Republican town was not particularly extensive and hints at continued occupation through into the early imperial period.

(Photo S. Keay)

Ak-Himayari, *Kitab ar-rawd fi habar al aktar*, vol. III (Textos Medievales 10, Valencia, 1963) 195; A. Jiménez Martín, *La puerta de Sevilla en Carmona* (Sevilla, 1989); J. Beltrán Fortes, in A. Caballos Rufino (ed.), *Carmona romana: Actas del II Congreso de Historia de Carmona* 135–58 (Seville, 2001).

195. Interpretative sketches of the small Iron Age oppidum of Las Cogotas (Ávila) in central Spain. This hilltop site was first occupied in the late Bronze Age (1200–850 BC). During the later Iron Age (fifth to second centuries BC) it was a key settlement of the Vettones people and consisted of two distinct enclosures which were walled with four gates. Unlike many Graeco-Roman towns, there was no regular street-grid and the main residential occupation comprised small one-storey strip houses flanking winding paths in the upper enclosure. The lower enclosure and the land outside its walls were used by artisans for collective services, the grazing of livestock and for periodic markets. While the settlement is not urban in the Roman sense it tells us something about the social organization of the Vettones and other peoples of central Iberia prior to Rome. The classical sources speak of towns in central Iberia as if they were towns in the Graeco-Roman tradition. However, archaeological research such as this is beginning to show that central Spain was a cultural cross-roads. Settlements varied in size from the larger oppida, such as Ulaca (Ávila), to the many small fortified enclosures (*castros*) and owed much to regional Bronze Age social traditions, with admixtures of 'Celtic', Iberian and, eventually, Roman influence.

(After Ruiz Zapatero and Álvarez Sanchis 1995: fig. 11)

J. Cabré, *Excavaciones en Las Cogotas: Cardenosa (Ávila). I: El Castro (Junta Superior de Excavaciones y Antigüedades* 110, Madrid, 1930); G. Ruiz Zapatero and J. Álvarez Sanchis, in Cunliffe and Keay (eds.) *Social Complexity* 209–35 and fig. 11.

196. Stone sculpture of a verraco from El Tiembolo (Ávila). Verracos are stone sculptures of bulls which have been found standing in isolation in the Castilian countryside, but are usually sited quite close to native oppida. These have long been interpreted as examples of Iron Age native art with possible religious connotations. Recently, however, analyses of these in their landscape context have suggested that they may have symbolized the richness of a given area and the organizing ability of its society. They may also have defined the control exercised by individual communities over certain

195

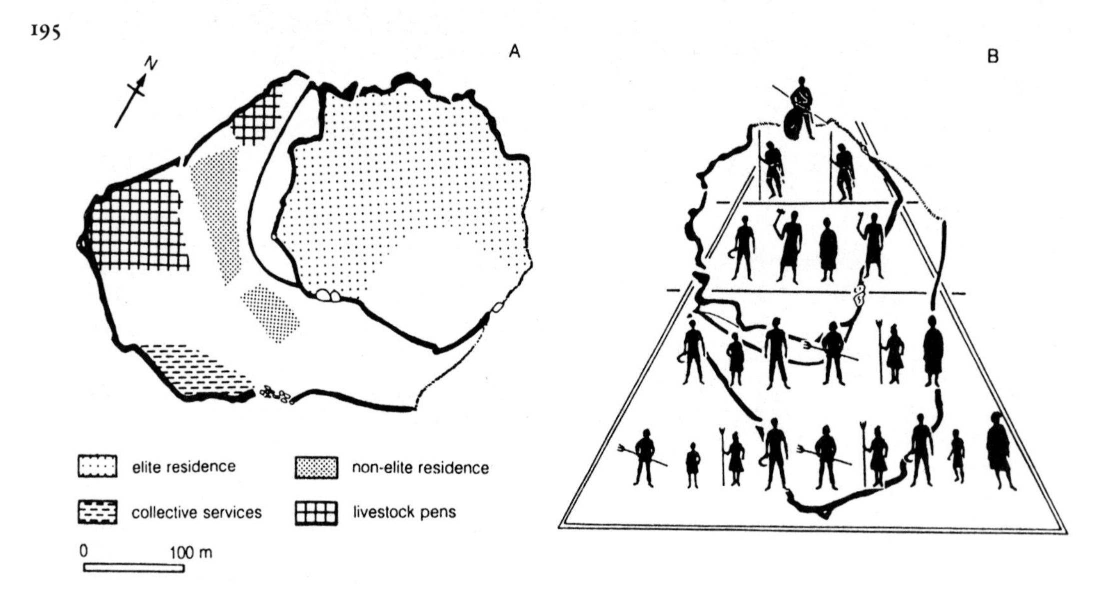

196

key resources, since they were sited on good-quality soils close to lands suitable for grazing. Access to these would have been a key element in the economy of regional oppida, such as Las Cogotas (Ávila), Ulaca (Ávila) and Mesas de Miranda (Ávila). This much can be deducted intuitively from the historical sources, but the verracos may point to ways in which this control was manifested on the ground.

(Photo P. Witte R107–92–10)

G. López Monteagudo, *Esculturas zoomorfas celtas de la Peninsula Ibérica* (Madrid, 1989); J. Álvarez-Sanchis, *Trabajos de Prehistoria* 47 (1993) 201–33; J. Álvarez-Sanchis, *Los señores del ganado: Arqueología de los pueblos prerromanos en el occidente de Iberia* (Madrid, 2003).

197. Aerial view of Arse-Saguntum (El Castell, Sagunto). This was sited at the mouth of the river Palancia on the Mediterranean seaboard, dominating the line of the main coastal road, the 'Via Heraklea'. Most of the structures visible in the foreground of the photograph are of Roman and later date. The site of the Iberian centre lay on the western sector of the hill of El Castell, which can

197

be seen in the upper right hand of the photograph. Little is known about the nature of the Iberian settlement, apart from traces of its defensive wall, an adjacent cemetery, a sanctuary on the eastern sector of El Castell (foreground of the photograph) and a seaport at La Grau Vell a few kilometres to the south-east. Iberian Arse-Saguntum was a major centre of the Edetani, and played a crucial role in the trade of Attic black- and red-figure pottery between the Greek colonies of Massalia (Marseilles) and Emporion (Empúries) and the Iberian communities of the south-east. A lead letter of the fifth century BC from Emporion speaks of a merchant (Basped) trading with Saigantha (Saguntum). The distribution of coins issued by Arse-Saguntum up the Palancia valley suggest that it was also a key point of contact for trade between the Mediterranean and central Iberia. By the time of the Second Punic War, Saguntum had become a major political centre with its own senate (Livy XXI.14) and, as is well known, played a pivotal role in the conflict between Rome and Carthage. The layout of the Republican town is poorly known. However, available evidence suggests that it was established in the eastern sector of El Castell (in the foreground of the photograph) and the hillside below, leading in time to the abandonment of the earlier Iberian settlement. Known buildings include a temple and forum (see **204**), an *artemision* (Pliny *NH* III.16.216), a temple to Venus (Pliny *NH* III.97.6–8) and a small temple near the sea (Polybius III.97.6–8). The seaport at the Grau Vell was an important focus of trade with Italy throughout the Republican period.

(Photo Paisajes Espanoles inv. 553173)

P. Rouillard, *Investigaciones sobre la muralla ibérica de Sagunto (Valencia)* (Trabajos Varios del SIP 62. Valencia, 1979); C. Aranegui Gascó, *Sagunto: Oppidum, emporio y municipio romano* (Barcelona, 2004) 32–57; C. Aranegui Gascó, in Abad Casal, Keay and Ramallo Asensio (eds.) *Early Roman Towns* 63–74.

198. Plan of a possible early Roman military establishment (*praesidium*) at Emporion (Empúries). Recent excavations on the hill overlooking the Greek colony have revealed structures which have been identified as a *praesidium* of the first half of the second century BC. Its precise layout is unclear, owing to its demolition and replacement by the Roman town of Emporion in the first century BC (see **203**). It took the form of a rectangular area enclosed by cyclopean walls, within which were four cisterns lined with *opus signinum* (each 1.3 m wide × 11.5 m long); nothing is known about any possible military accommodation. Outside the walls were a number of possibly contemporary grain-storage pits. The most likely historical context for this structure would have been the re-establishment of peace by Cato in north-east Citerior after the revolts of 197–195 BC, during which Emporion played a key

198

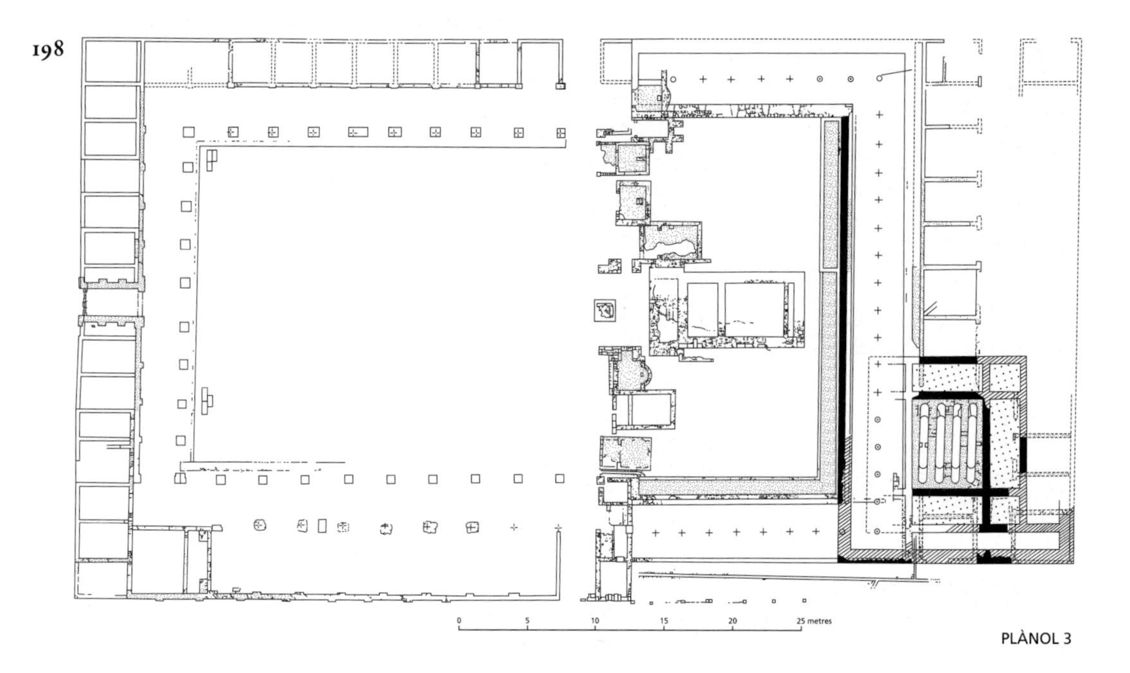

role as a Roman strategic centre. The paucity of archaeological evidence for Roman military sites in Republican Citerior, particularly for the period of Rome's struggle with Carthage, makes this an especially important site (see also **199**).

(X. Aquilué, R. Mar, J. M. Nolla, J. Ruiz de Arbulo and E. Sanmartí, *El Forum Romà d'Empúries* (Barcelona, 1983) 36, Plànol 3).

199. The Torre de Minerva and Roman fortifications at Tarraco (Tarragona). A large hill overlooking the Iberian coastal settlement at Tarragona was fortified by Rome towards the end of the third and the beginning of the second centuries BC. These 6-m high fortifications still enclose three sides of the hill which is now covered by the medieval town of Tarragona. Its footings were built from large cyclopean masonry blocks, while the wall itself was cut from large ashlar blocks, pierced by small gateways, and provided with at least three Hellenistic-style masonry towers. The Torre de Minerva (**b**) is the most complete surviving example of these. It is well known for its catapult emplacement and a small bas-relief (**a**) of the goddess Minerva with shield and spear – generally understood to be the earliest surviving Roman sculpture from the Iberian peninsula. There is also an inscription in archaic Latin cut into one of the ashlar blocks in the tower, which reads 'M. Vibio Menvra' and which can be translated as 'From M. Vibius for Minerva'. This is one of the best-known early Roman military sites in Iberia (see also **198**). In the later second century BC the walls were extended down to the Iberian centre near the sea, forging both sites into a single Roman urban unit for the first time. Tarraco was a major strategic centre for the pacification of north-east Spain by Rome, as well as for the co-ordination of military campaigns in Celtiberia between the later third and later second centuries BC.

199b

199a

(Photos P. Witte **a** R22–74–9N; **b** R22–74–10N)

N. Lamboglia, in *Miscelanea Arqueológica I: 25 aniversario de los cursos de Ampurias 1947–1971* (Barcelona, 1974) 397ff.; T. Hauschild, *Butlletí Arqueològic* 6–7 (1977) 11–38; G. Alföldy, *ZPE* 43 (1981) 1–12; X. Aquilué, X. Dupré, J. Massó and J. Ruiz de Arbulo, *Revista d'Arqueologia de Ponent* 1 (1991) 271–98; J. Ruiz de Arbulo, in Abad Casal, Keay and Ramallo Asensio (eds.) *Early Roman Towns* 33–43.

200. Plan showing the location of known archaeological sites within the early Roman town of Italica (Santiponce), to the north-west of Seville. Appian (*Iber.* 38) records that Italica was established by Scipio Africanus in 206 BC after the battle of Ilipa Magna (Alcalá del Río). This was not a colonial foundation and initially was probably little more than a community of wounded veterans who were added to a pre-existing native Iberian (Turdetanian) settlement. Little is known about the layout of this

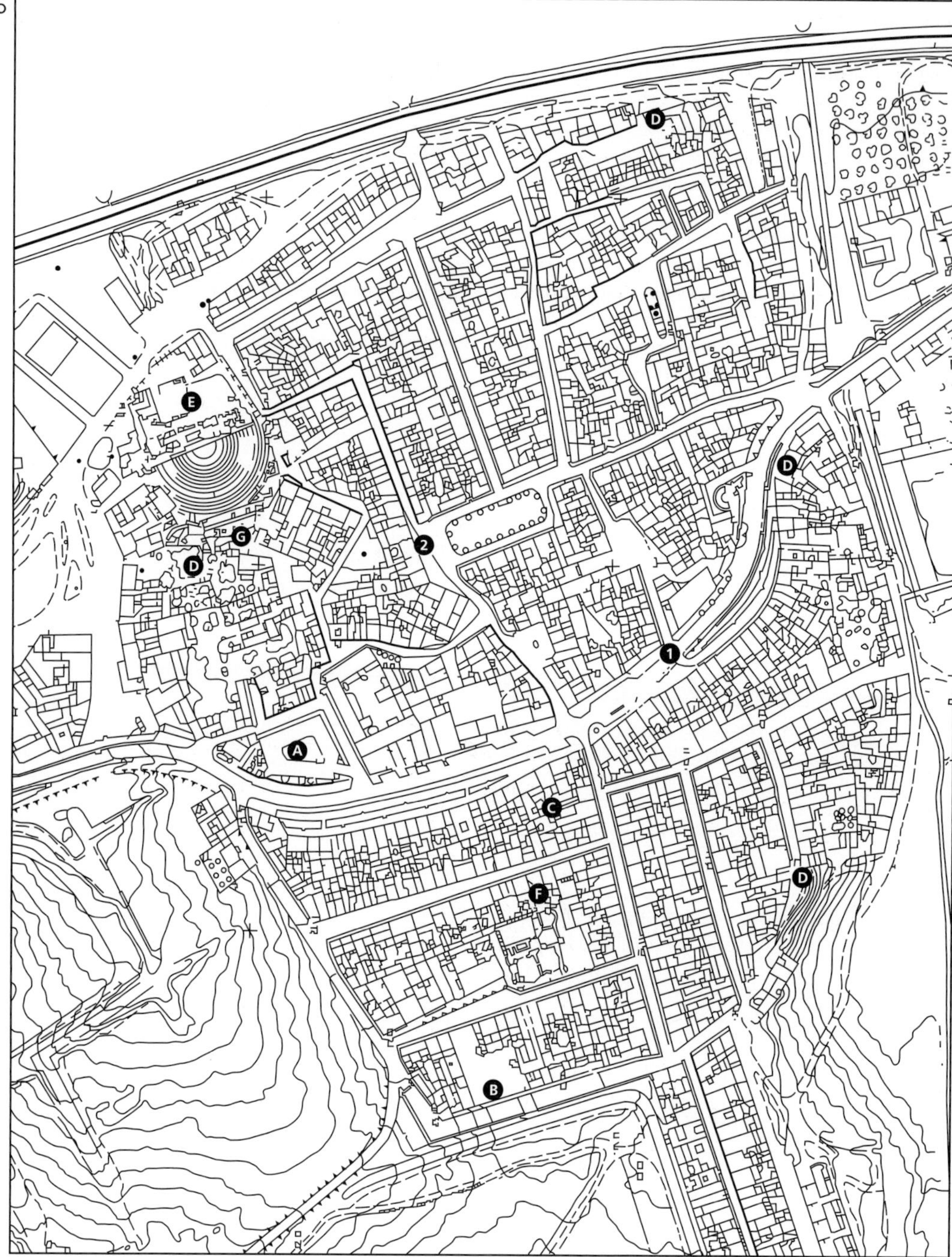

Fig. 2. Plan of Santiponce showing the location of sites referred to in the text:

Modern features

1. Avenida de Extremadura • 2. Plaza de la Constitición

Sites

A. Pajar de Atillo • B. Possible 'capitolium • C. Trahius mosaic at Avenida de Extremadura n°56
• D. Sections of town wall at different locations E. Theatre and adjacent portico
• F. Baths of 'Trajan' • G. Casa de La Venus

key early Roman town, since much evidence was obliterated during the building of Santiponce in the early seventeenth century. In view of this, recent suggestions that it was an early Italic-style town centred upon a *capitolium* are difficult to sustain. However, while there is evidence for the existence of occasional exotic monuments, such as the trophies from Zakynthos presented to the community by L. Aemilius Paullus in the mid second century BC, the material culture was predominately native in character. However, the strategic importance of Italica's position will have ensured that it played a significant role during the wars against Viriathus towards the middle of the second century BC. It was also a key focus in the movement of copper, lead, silver and iron ores from the Aznalcóllar mines and others in the Sierra Morena to the river Guadalquivir. Italica is only mentioned occasionally by historical sources in the course of the second century BC. However, it played an increasingly important regional role from the earlier first century BC onwards and received major boosts to its urban development under Augustus, and especially Hadrian.

(S. Keay, in León Alonso and Caballos Rufino 1997: fig. 2)

A. García y Bellido, *Colonia Aelia Augusta Italica* (Madrid, 1960); S. Keay, in P. León Alonso and A. Caballos Rufino (eds.), *Italica MMCC* (Seville, 1997) 21–47; Caballos Rufino, *Itálica y los italicenses* (Seville, 1994); Caballos Rufino, J. M. Fatuarte and J. M. Rodríguez Hidalgo, *Itálica arqueológica* (Seville, 1999) 21–5.

201. Plan of the Roman siege-works at Numantia (modern Numancia). This was an important centre

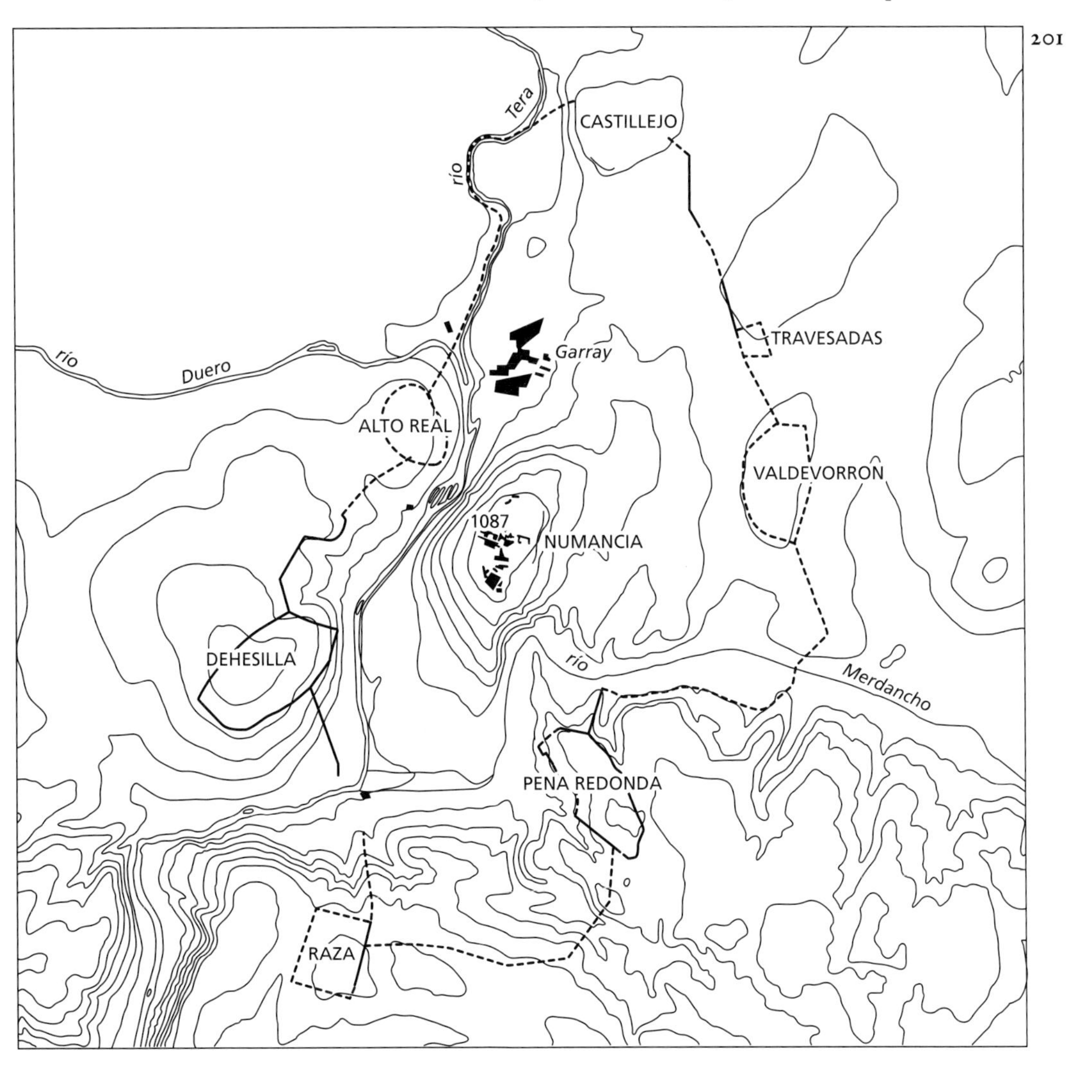

of the Arevaci, a Celtiberian people, who played a key role in the Celtiberian Wars against Rome (155–133 BC). It is located on a low hill near modern Garray (near Soria) in the Duero valley in central Iberia. It was first occupied during the Bronze Age and had been walled and subdivided into a number of intersecting streets by the fourth century BC; the cemetery lay a short distance to the north. After being the focus of a number of conflicts and skirmishes in the earlier second century BC, it witnessed the final denouement of the Celtiberian Wars in 133 BC. Scipio Aemilianus isolated Numantia from neighbouring communities and constructed an elaborate siege-works. These were described by Appian (*Iber.* 92), elements of whose account were borne out by archaeological excavations undertaken by Adolf Schulten at the beginning of the twentieth century. The town and its immediate hinterland were enclosed by a stone circumvallation 9 km in length (2.5 m by 3 m wide) which was interspersed by watchtowers and eight forts. After a blockade lasting eight months Numantia's 4,000 inhabitants finally capitulated, and many were sold as slaves. The Roman siege-works around Numantia are the best source of evidence for Roman military tactics during the Republican period.

(W. Trillmich, T. Hauschild, M. Blech, H.G. Niemeyer, A. Nünnerich-Asmus, and A. and U. Kreilinger, *Hispania Antiqua: Die Denkmäler der Römerzeit* (Mainz, 1993) abb. 35b)

A. Schulten, *Numantia: Die Ergebnisse der Ausgrabungen 1905–1912 I: Die Keltiberer und ihre Kriege mit Rom* (Munich, 1914); A. Jimeno, *AEA* 75 (2002) 159–76.

202. Plan of the Roman camps at Renieblas (Soria). One of the best-known camps in the vicinity of Numantia are those at Renieblas. They were located a short distance to the east of Scipio Aemilianus' siege-works of 133 BC. Schulten's excavations at the site revealed at least four superimposed camps. Camps I and II were related to the campaigns of the early to mid second century BC;

202

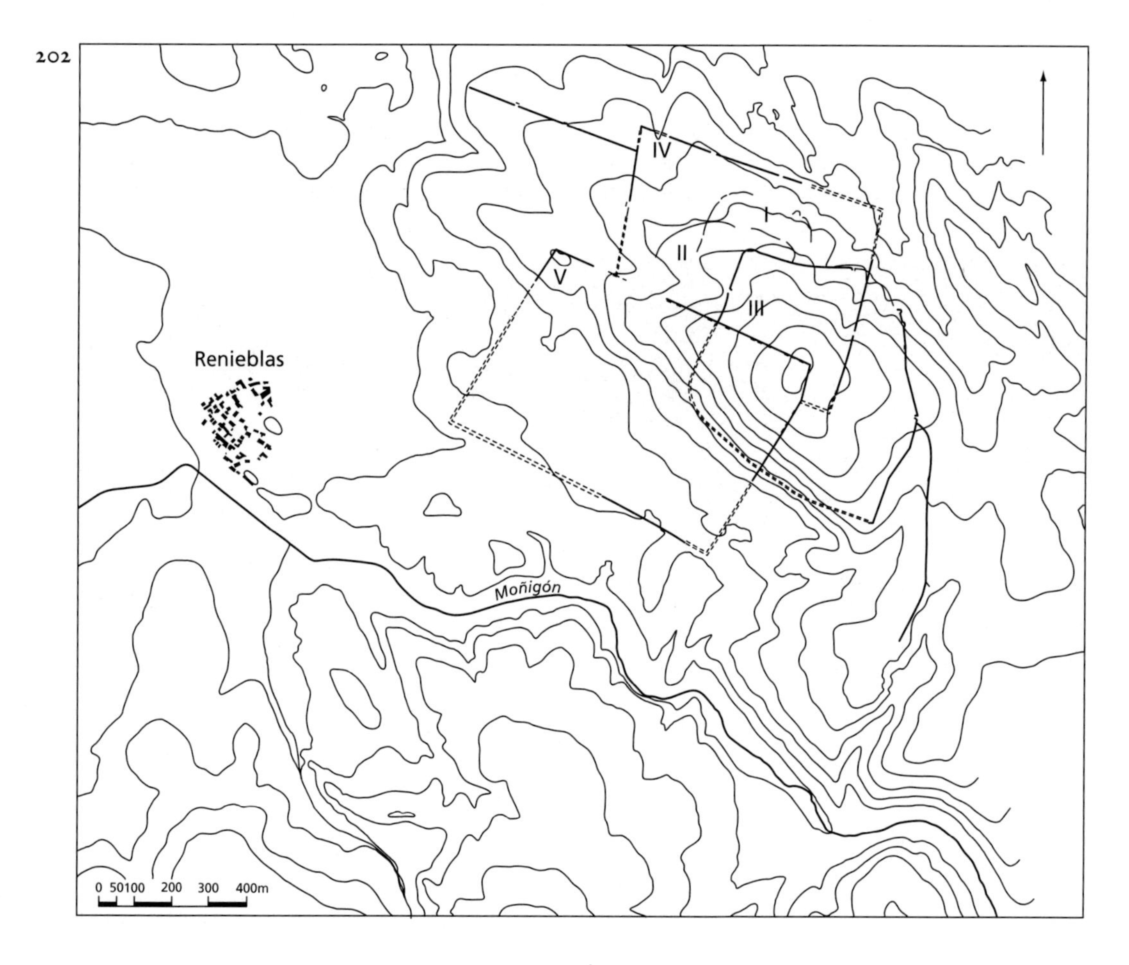

Camp III was associated with Nobilior's campaign of 153–152 BC; Camps IV and V are understood to have been established in 75/4 BC during the Sertorian Wars. These camps are particularly important since they were used on a number of different occasions and have the potential to shed light on the organization of the Roman army in the field at different times during the second and first centuries BC. They also allow Polybius' description of the organization of the Roman army during the second century BC (Polybius VI) to be checked against the archaeological evidence. The layout of Camp III (45Ha) bears out elements of his descriptions, being irregular, with groupings of barrack blocks and a small annexe for allied troops on the south-east. By contrast, Camp V was essentially rectangular in shape. However, none of the plans are complete, and one should be cautious about reading too much detail into them.

(Trillmich, Hauschild, Blech, Niemeyer, Nünnerich-Asmus, and A. and U. Kreilinger *Hispania Antiqua* abb. 35a)
Schulten *Numantia*; Jimeno *AEA* 75 (2002) 159–76.

203. Aerial photograph of the early Roman town at Emporion (Empúries). It was originally thought to have been founded de novo on a low plateau overlooking the Greek colony around 100 BC after the demolition of an earlier military establishment (*praesidium*) (see, **198**). Recent work, however, suggests that it may have been established in the course of the first century BC. The town occupied the greater part of an elongated rectangular enclosure (22.5 ha) defined by a substantial wall with cyclopean base and concrete wall. Most is known about the southern sector of the town. Broad roads with drains subdivided the enclosed space into regular *insula* blocks (35 m × 70 m). A forum complex dominated the centre of the town. At its northern end stood the *capitolium* on a tall podium within a *temenos* defined by a cryptoporticus and overlying portico; the space to the south was given over to the forum, with a row of tabernae running along its southern side. A suite of public baths of first-century BC date was built immediately to the north-east of the forum. Little is as yet known about the northern sector of the town, although geophysical survey confirms the continuation of the street-grid detected further south and the existence of densely packed residential occupation. Likewise little is known about other public buildings or the layout of residential buildings within the town: those visible in the photograph (Casas Romanas 1 and 2) date to the later Republican and early imperial periods. Despite suggestions that this town may have been a *colonia*, nothing is known of the historical circumstances surrounding its

203

foundation. However, its juxtaposition with the Greek town and a possible native settlement to its south suggest that it was the focus of a unique multi-cultural community.

(Photo Museu d'Arqueologia de Catalunya – Empúries)

Aquilué, Mar, Nolla, Ruiz de Arbulo and Sanmartí, *El Forum Romà d'Empúries P. Gros, L'architecture romaine I: Les monuments publics* (Paris, 1996) 151–5; X. Aquilué, P. Castanyer i Masoliver, M. Santos and J. Tremoleda i Trilla, *Empúries* 52 (2000) 261–79; X. Aquilué, P. Castanyer i Masoliver, M. Santos and J. Tremoleda i Trilla, in Abad Casal, Keay and Ramallo Asensio (eds.) *Early Roman Towns* 19–31.

204. Photograph of the Republican temple at Saguntum (Sagunto). At some time around the beginning of the second century BC a Roman-style religious complex was built at the site of the Plaza de Armas on the eastern edge of the hill of El Castell, on the site of the extramural Iberian sanctuary (see **197**). It comprised three cellae, a *pronaos* and *antae*; immediately to the west of this was a small *sacellum* in which were discovered bronze figurines of Heracles Dexioumenos and Liber Pater. The temple lay at the head an elongated public square (60 m long), from which derived some sculpted reliefs of individuals in military dress, and at the end of which was a building consisting of a central vaulted structure with adjacent vaulted cisterns. The presence of this complex on the site of the Iberian sanctuary provides evidence for the reconstruction of Saguntum by Rome at some point after its sack by Hannibal in 219 BC (Livy XXI.14) and subsequent liberation from Carthaginian control in 212 BC. It has been suggested that there was an important symbolic value in founding the new religious focus of Saguntum on the site of the earlier Iberian sanctuary.

(Photo S. Keay)

C. Aranegui, *Cuadernos de Arquitectura Romana I: Templos Romanos de Hispania* (1992) 67–82; Gros *L'architecture romaine* I: 151–2; C. Aranegui, *Sagunto: Oppidum, emporio y municipio romano* (Barcelona, 2004); Aranegui Gascó, in Abad Casal, Keay and Ramallo Asensio (eds.) *Early Roman Towns* 63–74.

205. Mosaic inscription to Atargatis from Carthago Nova (Cartagena). A small shrine and adjacent ritual bath dedicated to Atargatis (= Dea Syria), one of the most important Syrian deities, was recently discovered on the hill of El Molinete, traditionally identified as Hasdrubal's *arx*. It was part of a sanctuary in which there was also a large *temenos* and italic-style temple of late second-century BC date, possibly dedicated to

204

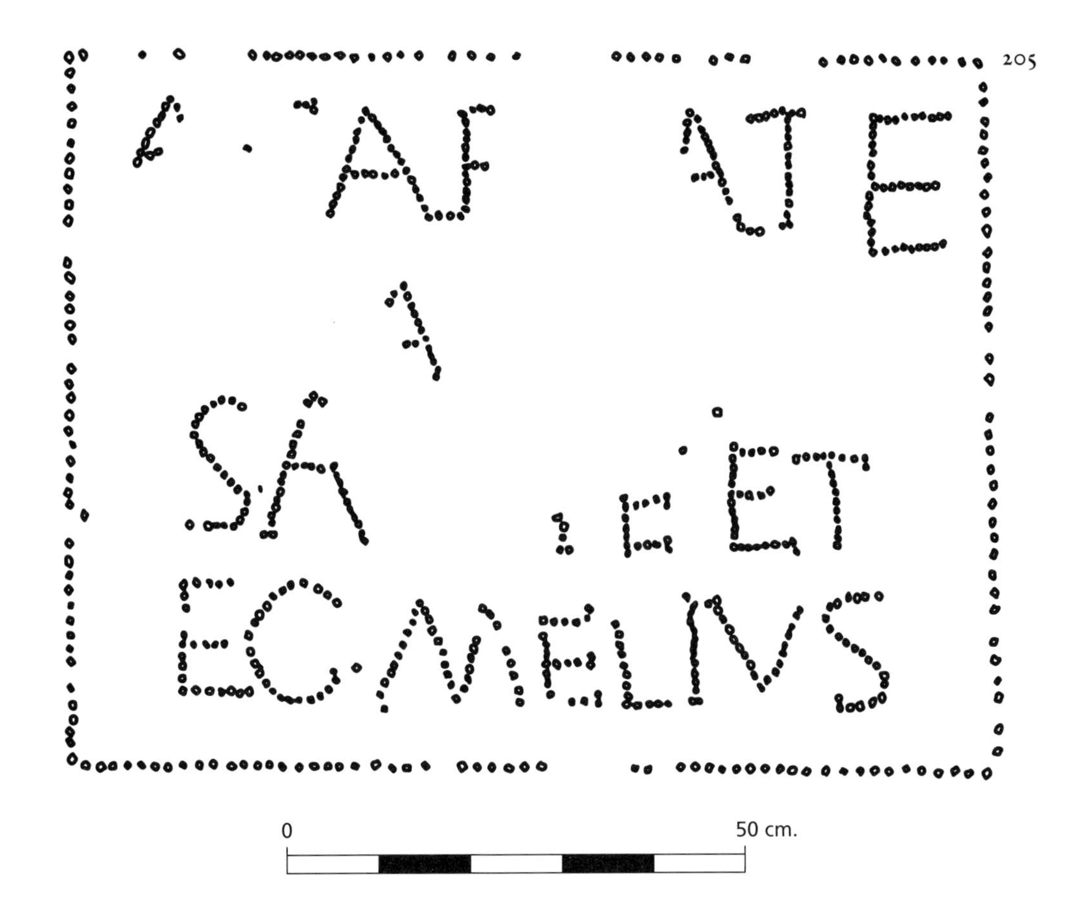

Asklepios (Eshmun). Further inscriptions from the site mention Isis and Serapis. Carthago Nova was established by Hamilcar Barca in 229/8 BC and, following its capture by Rome in 209 BC, retained key elements of its Punic culture until well into the Republican period. The discovery of the Atargatis mosaic lends credence to reports in classical sources that Punic sanctuaries to Eshmun (Asklepios), Baal Hammon (Cronos) and Chusor (Hephaistos) continued to play an important role in the town during the Roman period. Nevertheless, the existence of a *collegio* at the town in the later second century BC points to the presence of increasing numbers of Italians and Romans. Their impact can be measured by the presence of *opus signinum* floors at the town and the dedication of a rural shrine by Marcus Aquinius Andro to Iovi Stator at the Cabezo Gallufo, a short distance to the south-east of Carthago Nova.

(S. Ramallo Asensio, *Los mosaicos romanos de Carthago Nova (Hispania Citerior)* (Murcia, 1985) 45–6 fig. 7)

S. Ramallo Asensio and E. Ruiz Valdes, *Archivo Español de Arqueologia* 67 (1994) 79–102; J. M. Abascal and S. Ramallo Asensio, *La ciudad de Carthago Nova III (1): La documentación epigraphica* (Murcia, 1997) nr. 205; S. Ramallo Asensio, in Abad Casal, Keay and Ramallo Asensio (eds.) *Early Roman Towns* 91–104.

206. Lead ingot from Carthago Nova (Cartagena) in the Museo Municipal de Cartagena. The stamps on ingots such as this often bear the names of Roman citizen businessmen based at the town during the late second and early first centuries BC, such as Cnaeus Atellius, Publius Nona Nucerinus, Lucius Planius and Publius Roscius. The wealth of Carthago Nova lay in its role as a centre for the export of silver mined in south-east Iberia, the principal source of silver for Roman coinage from about the middle of the second century BC onwards. The Cartagena–Mazarrón region in the immediate neighbourhood of the town was very rich in argentiferous galena: Polybius states that 40,000 workers produced 25,000 drachmae a day for the Roman state within a 70 km radius of the town (Strabo III.147–8). Carthago Nova would also have benefited from its proximity

206

to the mouth of the river Segura, and the movement of silver mined in the Sierra Morena to the north of Castulo (Linares) to the Mediterranean from the later second century BC onwards. Lead was an important by-product of the silver production process. Ingots from the Cartagena–Mazarrón mines are attested at the mines themselves, the harbour of Carthago Nova and at wreck sites around the western Mediterranean. Silver production at Carthago Nova seems to have ceased by the end of the first century BC.

(Photo S. Keay)

C. Domergue *AEA* 39 (1966) 41–72; Domergue, *Catalogue des mines et des fonderies antiques de la péninsule ibérique*, vol. II (Madrid, 1987).

207. Plan of Sector A of the Roman Republican mining settlement at Valderrepisa (Fuencaliente, Ciudad Real). This site lies in the Sierra Morena mountains to the north of the river Guadalquivir. It covered 4ha and was established as a regularly planned centre with a piped water system in one phase at some time between the mid second and mid first centuries BC. Houses were constructed from stone footings with mud-brick walls and tiled roofs. In sector A they were used for residence, storage and the washing of metals: in sectors B and C they were employed for the dumping of slag, lead and kiln debris. The Sierra Morena to the north of Castulo (Linares), in which the site lies, was one of the richest mining areas of Republican Hispania. It is also an area where archaeological work at such mines as those at La Loba (Córdoba), Cerro del Plomo (Jaén), El Centenillo (Jaén) and the Mina Diógenes (Ciudad Real) has shed light upon the living conditions of miners and related personnel. Valderrepisa was the centre of a wide catchment area of mines, and its processed metals were transported by donkey across the Sierra Morena down to Isturgi (Andújar) and onwards to the hub of Castulo. They would have been subsequently transported either north-eastwards to Carthago Nova (Cartagena) and onwards to Rome, or down the river Guadalquivir to Hispalis (Seville) and eventually Gades (Gadir).

(C. García Bueno and C. Fernández Ochoa, *Mélanges de la Casa de Velázquez* 29 (1993) 25–50 and fig. 1.)

208. Coins issued by native mints in Hispania Citerior: (**ai–ii**) a denarius of Arekorata–Areikoratikos (Agreda, Soria), (**bi–ii**) an *as* of Konterbia Karbika–Segobriga (Fosos de Bayona, Cuenca), (**ci–ii**) a denarius from Iltirta (Lleida) and (**d**) an *as* from Kese (Tarragona). The obverse and reverse types are fairly standardized, although the latter records the name of the issuing authority in Iberian or Celtiberian script. They were loosely

207

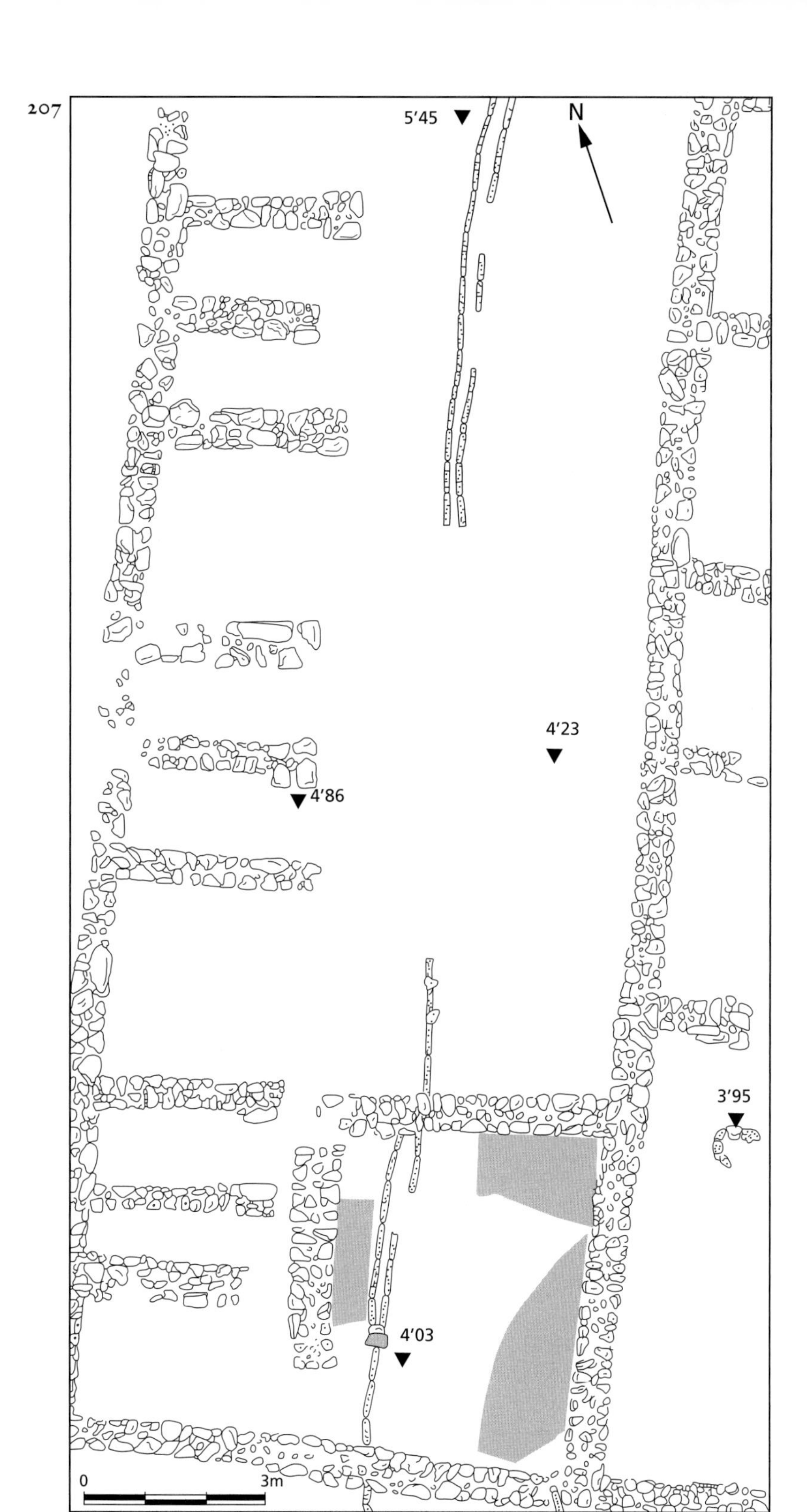

208a

208b

based on the weight system of contemporary Roman coinage. Prior to the arrival of Rome, the issue and use of coins in northern Iberia were largely restricted to the Greek colonies of Rhode (Roses) and Emporion (Empúries) and a handful of major Iberian centres. The date and rationale behind the subsequent introduction of coin issues by Iberian and Celtiberian communities in Hispania Citerior are open to dispute. Some scholars suggest that they appeared towards the end of the third and beginning of the second centuries BC, as native responses to the new military and economic realities of the province. Others have interpreted them as an obligation imposed on subject communities by Rome so that they could pay for the upkeep of Roman armies in the field from about the middle of the second century BC onwards.

(British Museum: **a** 72:18; **b** 72: 23; **c** 72:8; **d** SNG 541)

A. Vives, *La moneda hispánica* (Madrid, 1926); L. Villaronga, *Corpus nummum hispaniae ante Augusti aetatem* (Madrid, 1994); M. Crawford, *Coinage and Money under the Roman Republic: Italy and the Mediterranean Economy* (London, 1985) 84–102; F. Beltrán Lloris, in M. Campo (ed.), *La moneda en la societat ibèrica II: Curs d'història monetària d'Hispania 26–27 de novembre de 1998* (Barcelona, 1998) 101–17.

208c

208d

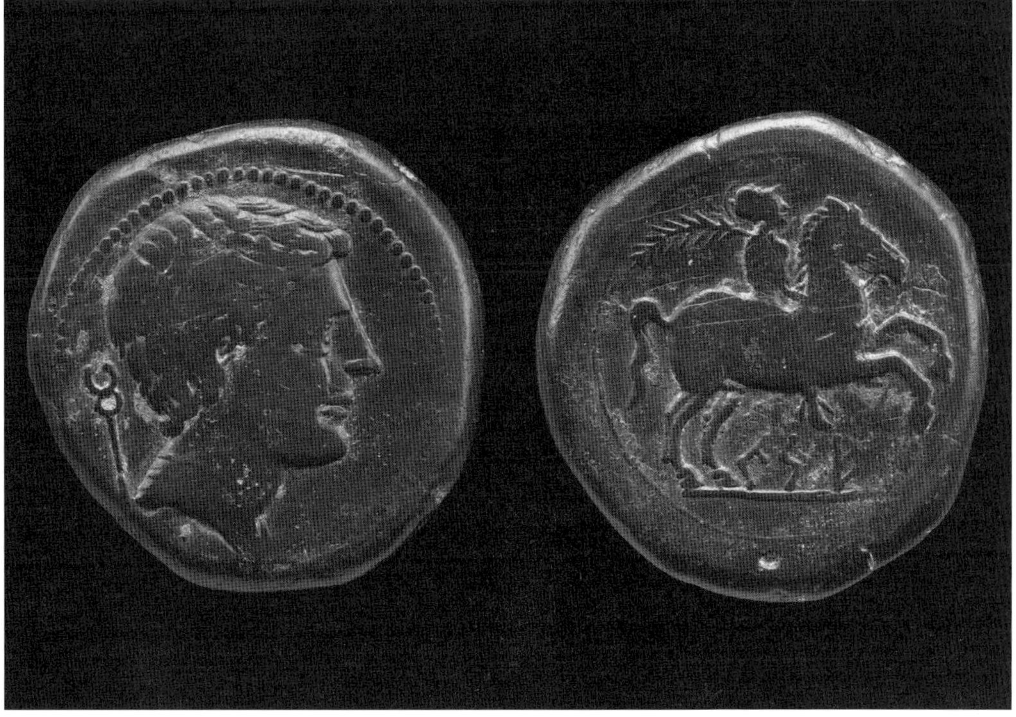

209. Bronze *asses* issued by the native mints of (**ai–ii**) Kastilo–Kastulo (Linares), (**bi–ii**) Obulco–Ibolka (Porcuna), (**ci–ii**) Carmo (Carmona) and (**di–ii**) Gadir (Cádiz) in Hispania Ulterior. The earliest coins introduced to southern Iberia were those issued at Gadir, and the 'Hispano-Carthaginian' issues minted during the Carthaginian occupation of the region from 237 BC. The majority of coinages, however, do not make their appearance at most communities until the later second century BC. They were thus later than those issued in Hispania Citerior and differed from them in the fact that they were all of bronze, even though the region was rich in silver resources. The southern Iberian coinage seems to have shared two prevailing weight standards: Carthaginian

and Roman. The established urban tradition in the region ensured that, unlike northern Iberia, there was substantial variation in the symbols chosen for the obverse and reverse types of the coins. It is especially marked in the reverse legends, as with those illustrated here. Recent analysis suggests that there is a geographical coherence to these differences, with Latin issues predominating in western Ulterior, a mixture of Iberian and Latin in the centre, south Iberian to the east, and Lybio-Phoenician and Phoenician to the south. There is still no consensus about the function of this coinage. Issues varied greatly in volume, regularity and areas of circulation, and it is likely that they represented native responses to growing monetary needs following the increased presence of regular Roman coinage from the later second century BC onwards.

(British Museum: **a** 613:52; **b** 613:45; **c** 613:43; **d** 613:61)

Vives, *La moneda hispánica*; Villaronga, *Corpus nummum hispaniae*; F. Chaves Tristán, in S. Keay (ed.), *The Archaeology of Early Roman Baetica* (*J R A Supplement*, 29 Portsmouth, R. I., 1998), 147–70.

210. Plan and mosaic of the Casa 1.1 Likinete at the Celtiberian settlement at Caridad de Caminreal

(Teruel) in the Ebro valley. This medium-sized (12.5 ha) site was occupied between the second and earlier first centuries BC. Excavations revealed that it was subdivided into regular *insula*-style blocks and that one of these was partly occupied by a large (91.5 m^2) square house laid out in the italic tradition. It comprised a range of rooms arranged around the four sides of a central peristyle, most of which had mud-brick walls, mortar and clay floors and one *opus signinum* floor with mosaic decoration. Despite the obvious Italic parallels for this house, it clearly had a native owner. The *opus signinum* floor of the *tablinum* (dining-hall) was decorated with a *tessera* inscription in Iberian which records that it was the work of an individual with the Celtiberian name of Likenete, who was a native of Usekerte, a town to be identified with Osicerda (Alcañiz). This site needs to be understood in the context of the gradual appearance of Italic-style houses, temples and architectural decoration of such native settlements as Contrebia Belaisca (Botorrita) and Azaila (Teruel), the appearance of apparently new Roman settlements such as La Cabañeta (Burgo de Ebro) and the use

210

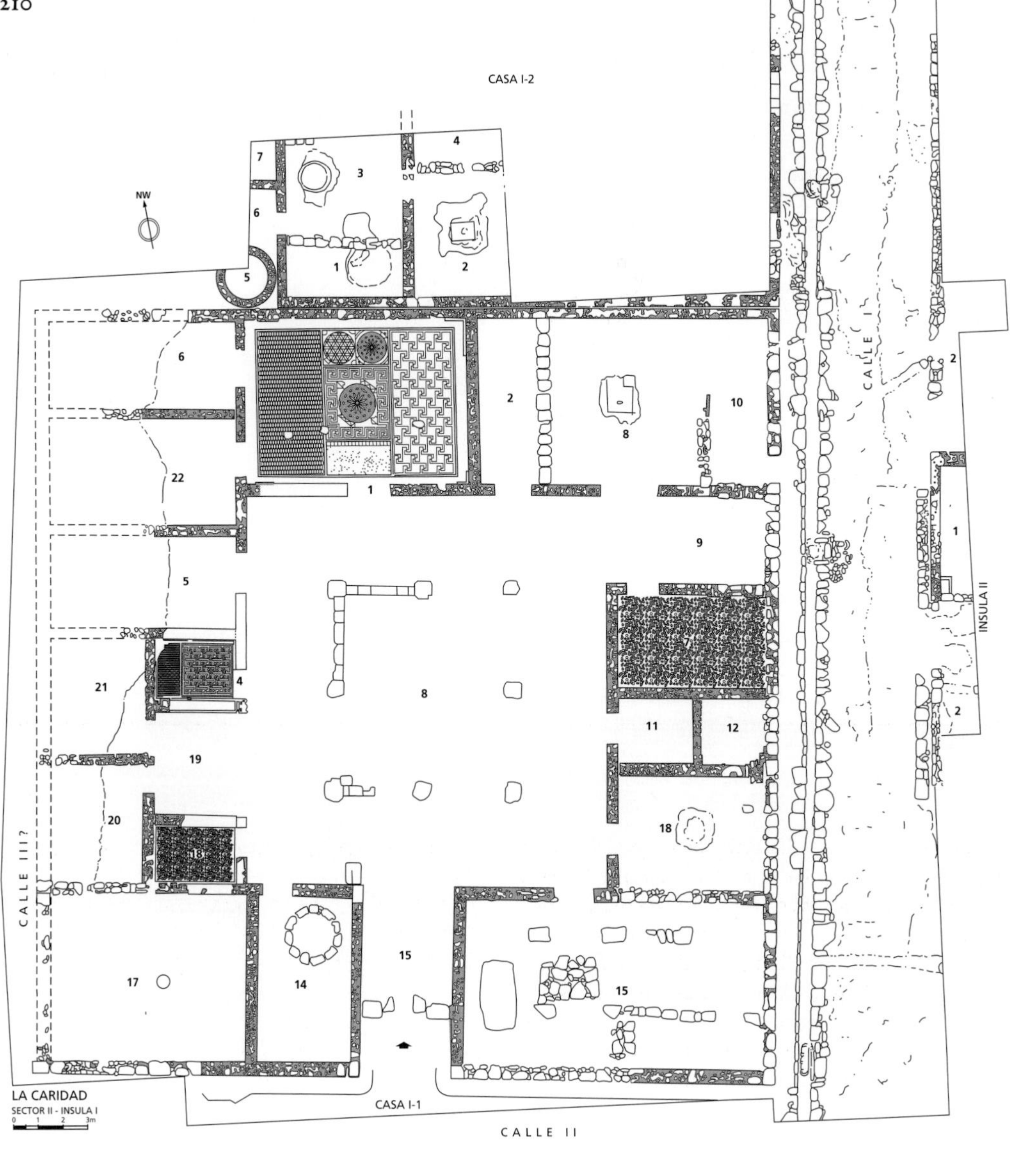

of Roman law for local disputes, as recorded by the *tabula contrebiensis*. Together, they epitomize the way in which the Ebro valley began to play a key role in the transmission of Roman cultural influence to Celtiberia from Tarraco, Emporion and other centres in coastal Iberia from the later second and earlier first centuries BC onwards.

(J. D. Vicente Redón, M. P. Punter Gómez, C. Escriche Jaime and A. I. Herce San Miguel, in Beltrán Lloris 1991: fig.7)

J. D. Vicente Redón, M. P. Punter Gómez, C. Escriche Jaime and A.I. Herce San Miguel, in M. Beltrán Lloris (ed.), *La casa hispanorromana* (Zaragoza, 1991) 81–129; J. De Hoz, in F. Beltrán Lloris (ed.), *Roma y el nacimiento de la cultura epigraphica en occidente* (Zaragoza, 1995) 57–84 esp. 73–4; P. Sillières, in M. Navarro Caballero and S. Demougin (eds.), *Élites hispaniques: Ausonius Publications, Études 6* (Bordeaux, 2001) 173–83.

211. Plan (**a**) of the Iberian sanctuary at the Cerro de la Ermita at La Encarnación de Caravaca

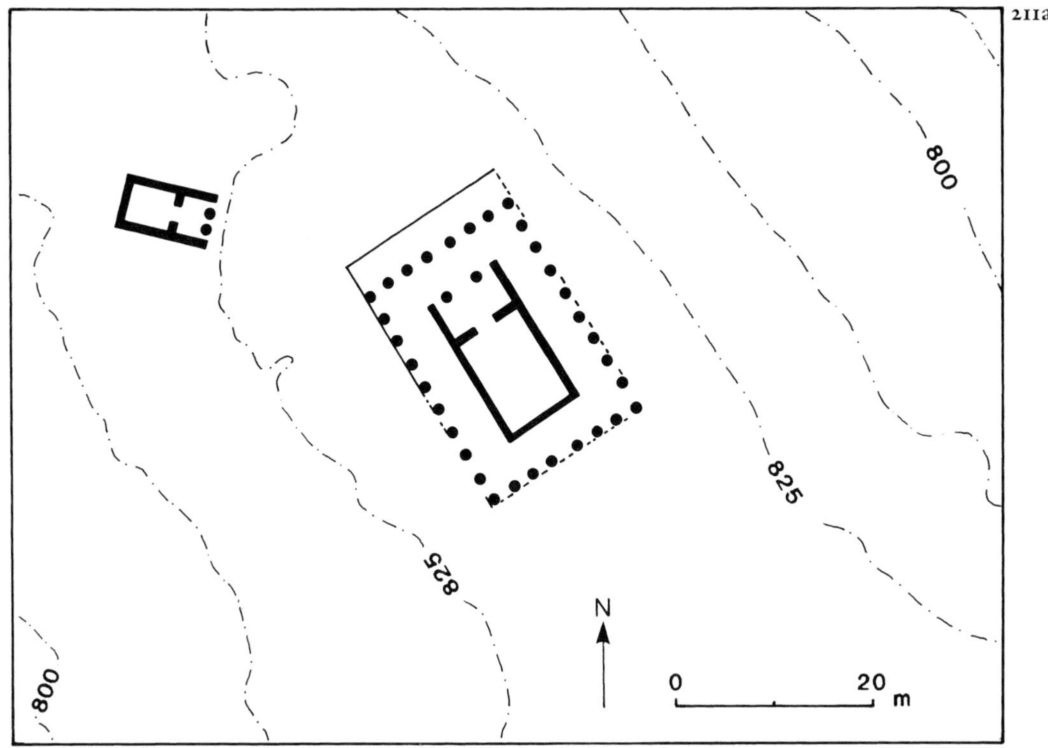

(Murcia). Detail (**b**) of a terracotta from the same site. In the course of the second century BC two Italic-style temples were built at this site, which is close to the native settlements of Los Villares and Villaricos, and 80 km from the sea. The earliest structure, Temple A, was oriented north-east/south-west and consisted of a small *cella* (6 m × 5.1 m) *in antis* with two columns and ionic capitals. The later Temple B was located at the highest point of the site and on a north-south orientation. It was also larger (27.25 m × 17.3 m), peripteral and octostyle with attic bases and ionic capitals. The closest parallel for this building is to be found in the eastern Mediterranean, echoing the Eastern influence evident in cults practised at Carthago Nova (Cartagena). Their roofs and pediments were adorned with terracotta antefixes and plaques decorated with floral motifs, which have central Italian parallels of the second century BC. This sanctuary is important in showing the extent to which local elites were prepared to transform the ritual space of an important regional sanctuary. How far it represents a displacement of native religious practice by Roman ritual is an open question.

(S. Ramallo Asensio, *Archivo Español de Arqueología* 66 (1993))

S. Ramallo, *Cuadernos de Arquitectura Romana 1: Templos Romanos de Hispania* (1992) 39–65; Ramallo, *Archivo Español de Arqueología* 66 (1993) 71–98.

212. Male head (**a**) and togate torso (**b**) from the Iberian sanctuary at the Cerro de los Santos (Albacete). **a** dates to the third century BC, while **b** dates to the second or first century BC. These and many other sculptures from this site make it one of the best-known native sanctuaries in the Iberian peninsula. During the last two centuries BC it underwent a major transformation with the construction of an Italic-style temple similar to that of Temple A at La Encarnación de Caravaca (Murcia). This was *in antis* and decorated with ionic capitals. Votive offerings at the site included a large number of stone sculptures, including masculine heads, standing female statues and togate statues similar to **b**, which may represent local elites. One of these bears the Latin inscription 'L. Lic(i)ni'. This presumably refers to the name of the person fulfilling a vow implicit

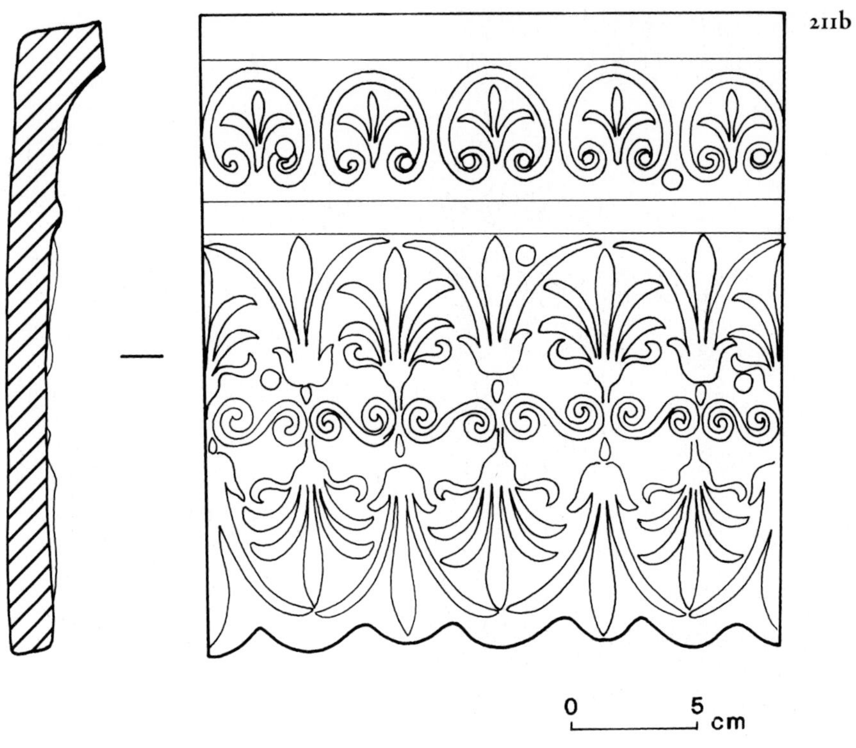
211b
0
5 cm

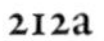

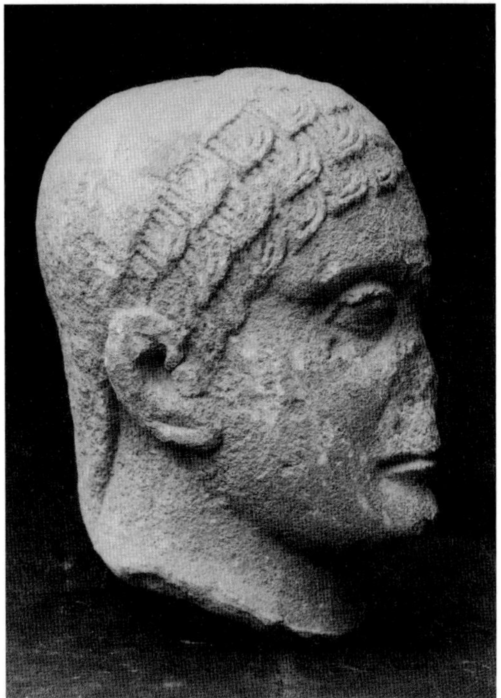

212a

212b

in the raising of the statue. It is probable that the Cerro de los Santos was a major pan-Iberian sanctuary and as such would have acted as the focus of regional peoples throughout the later Iberian and early Roman periods. It was located close to the great north–south coastal route, the Via Heraklea.

(Photos Archivo Mas)

P. Paris, *Essai sur l'art et l'industrie de l'Espagne primitive* (Paris, 1904); E. Ruano Ruiz, *Cuadernos de Prehistoria y Arqueología* 15 (1988) 253–73; M. L. Sánchez Gómez, *El santuario de El Cerro de los Santos (Montealegre del Castillo, Albacete) (Nuevas aportaciones arqueológicas,* Albacete, 2005) 61–92.

10. GAUL

GREG WOOLF

The territories that would eventually form the Roman province of Gallia Transalpina (later Narbonensis) had no geographical, ethnic, cultural or historical unity before the last century BC. Ecologically they consisted of a series of interconnecting littoral plains between the Pyrenees and the Alps, together with the quite different environments with which they had been linked since prehistory. To seaward a series of lagoons prolonged the coastal landscapes of north-east Spain and then gave way to the delta of the Rhône, the marshes of the present-day Carmague and lastly through the Étang-de-Berre to the more rugged coastline of Liguria. Inland, the littoral connected to small plains surrounded in the west by *garrigues* (areas of low brush characteristic of arid Mediterranean environments) and then to the broad lower valley of the Rhône with its fertile alluvial soils. West of the Rhône, in present-day Languedoc, the *garrigues* fed back into the foothills of the Cevennes, the southern ramparts of the Massif Central. East of the Rhône, the rich landscapes of Provence and the barren plain of the Crau rose, via the Var to the *avant-pays* of the Alps. The diverse ecological resources of these landscapes and the relatively easy communications between them had promoted localized exchanges of goods, technologies and people since at least the Bronze Age. Further inland, the Gallic Isthmus gave access via the valley of the Aude to the basin of the Garonne and to the Atlantic, while the Rhône gave access to Burgundy and beyond. But in much of the region connections along the coast to Catalonia in the west and to Liguria in the east were more important.

From Ullastret in Spain to Ensérune, the small hill-forts known locally as oppida (not to be confused with the larger and generally later sites given the same name in northern Europe) were apparently occupied by related peoples writing the Iberian script and using ceramics often termed Iberic. Some groups speaking Celtic languages occupied territory further inland: the Volcae Arecomisci in what is now the plain of Nîmes, and the Vocontii and Allobroges of the middle Rhône were the most important. Many consider them to have been relatively recent arrivals in the period of migrations that also brought Celtic-speaking peoples into central Europe. All these peoples shared broadly similar technology by the third century BC. All produced hard, thin-walled ceramics, much of it made on the wheel; all had long ago mastered iron-working; and many were using writing, employing either Iberian script west of the Rhône or a version of the Greek alphabet further east. All the local settlements were built in an architecture based on dry-stone walling. The scale and complexity of these settlements varied enormously, those along the coastal plains of Languedoc being on the whole larger and more complex – with elaborate entrances, towers, citadels and religious structures – while those, like Nages, surrounding the plain of Nîmes and the inland settlements of the Var being generally smaller. Most were fortified, and dispersed settlement was apparently rare. Those closest to Marseilles adopted some new architectural and apparently also agricultural techniques. It is generally considered that the spread of arboriculture in the region reflected transfers of technology from visitors and colonists.

None of these peoples developed the navigational skills to travel far overseas, but many participated in long-distance exchange with various visitors. Best attested are the Greeks, especially following the foundation of Marseilles by refugees from Phocaea around 600 BC. Greek cities and trading posts stretched from Agde to Nice. But there were certainly other visitors too. Etruscan wine amphorae from the seventh and sixth centuries BC have been found on around 100 sites between the Hérault and the Rhône rivers. Punic amphorae are known from large numbers of sites in Languedoc from the sixth century and are present east of the Rhône, including at Marseilles. A mid sixth-century Etruscan wreck has been excavated off Antibes: alongside its cargo of Etruscan wine amphorae it carried vessels in *bucchero nero* and Etrusco-Corinthian ceramic from Cerveteri, some Greek amphorae and a Punic lamp. A lead tablet inscribed in Etruscan and Ionian Greek has been recovered from the Iberian oppidum of Pech Maho. Coastal sites such as Lattes have provided precise documentation of the changing patterns of exchange. Best studied is the appearance of a mass of wine amphorae in the region, first Massiliot appearing on a limited number of sites, then Greco-Italic and eventually the characteristic Dressel I sequences showing a close connection with central Italy. A focus of much recent research has been the attempt to decide how much the most complex settlements, such as Glanum, owed to these influences, and how the development of the wine trade influenced local societies.

Roman interest in the region was, to begin with, sporadic and came from a number of directions. A land route from Italy to Spain, known as the Herculean way, was important during the wars in Spain that began with the Second Punic War. It continued in use throughout the second century, at the end of which the Via Domitia was constructed along much of its length. It has been reasonably suggested that Romans began to operate in the western end of Languedoc as a consequence of campaigns in Spain and became involved in the area east of the Rhône quite separately as the result of wars in Liguria. The alliance with Marseilles was claimed to be ancient, but probably does not predate the Hannibalic War. A series of campaigns in the 120s BC led Roman armies up the Rhône valley into conflicts with some of the larger polities of the interior, notably the Allobroges of the middle Rhône and the Arverni, whose centre of power was close to Clermont-Ferrand. These wars, although short, combined with the Cimbric migrations to make clear that in Gaul, as in Spain, Rome could not control the littoral without controlling the other regions with which it was intimately interconnected. A colony was founded at Narbonne – the mouth of the Gallic Isthmus – in 118 BC. The province itself may not have emerged before the early 60s. By the time Caesar added Transalpina to his original province of Cisalpine Gaul, there were large-scale Roman financial interests in the south and some southern Gallic peoples were involved with Roman politics. Cicero's *pro Quinctio* mentions ranches and slave traders in the south, his *pro Fonteio* provides much-discussed evidence of taxes on the wine trade and he depended on testimony from the Allobroges to expose Catiline in 63 BC. During Caesar's campaigns of the 50s, the province provided a safe base of operations and a source of auxiliary troops, and was apparently completely peaceful. This is the same period in which the material culture, and particularly the architecture of the region, begins to resemble that of Italy. But it was colonization in the triumviral period that would really transform these landscapes and remake them in a Roman image.

GENERAL BIBLIOGRAPHY

Accounts of research until 2008 and a number of themed supplements are provided by the *Revue Archéologique de Narbonnaise* (*RAN*). For the prehistoric background, see M. Py, *Les Gaulois du Midi: De la fin de l'âge du bronze à la conquête romaine* (Paris, 1993); and M. Dietler, *Archaeologies of Colonialism: Consumption, Entanglement, and Violence in Ancient Mediterranean France* (Berkeley, 2010). G. Barruol, *Les peuples préromains du sud-est de la Gaule* (*RAN* Supplement 1, Paris, 1969) remains important on the region east of the Rhône. See now *Peuples et territoires en Gaule méditerranéen: Hommage à Guy Barruol* (*RAN* Supplement 35, Montpellier, 2003). On connections with temperate Europe, see A. Duval, J.-P. Morel and Y. Roman (eds.), *Gaule Interne et Gaule Méditerranéenne aux IIe et Ier siècles avant J.C.: Confrontations chronologiques* (*RAN* Supplement 21, Paris, 1990).

On Marseilles and its relations with its neighbours, the series *Études Massaliètes* is essential, especially M. Bats, G. Bertucchi, A. Congès and H. Treziny (eds.), *Marseille grecque et la Gaule* (*Études Massaliètes* 3, Aix-en-Provence, 1992). For a splendid overview, see the catalogue *Voyage en Massalie: 100 ans d'archéologie en Gaule du Sud*. For the Roman conquest, C. Ebel, *Transalpine Gaul: The Emergence of a Roman Province* (Leiden, 1976) and S. L. Dyson, *The Creation of the Roman Frontier* (Princeton, 1985) offer contrasting accounts. More focused on economic penetration are G. Clemente, *I romani nella Gallia meridionale (II–I sec. a.C.): Politica ed economia n'età dell'imperialismo* (Bologna, 1974) and E. Hermon, *Rome et la Gaule transalpine avant César, 125–59 av. J.-C.* (*Diáphora* 3, Naples, 1993). The reconfiguration of the landscapes of the Mediterranean following Roman colonization is largely outside the scope of this chapter but is treated in exemplary fashion by P. Leveau, P. Sillières and J.-P. Vallat, *Campagnes de la Méditerranée romaine* (Paris, 1993). A particularly useful collection of papers on this theme is A. Bouet and F. Verdin (eds.), *Territoires et paysages de l'âge du fer au Moyen Âge: Mélanges offerts à Philippe Leveau* (Bordeaux, 2005).

PREHISTORY

213. The oppidum of Les Castels à Nages is one of the best-studied examples of a characteristic settlement type of the late prehistoric Languedoc, a fortified centre on the edge of a plateau overlooking the plain, in this case the Vaunage. From the Bronze Age there had been a general demographic growth in the region, including the appearance of larger and larger settlements. But the site at Nages itself was unoccupied until the early third century BC. During the middle of that century a rampart with towers was constructed, and within it an orthogonal street plan dividing regular blocks of houses of uniform size and design. The site was expanded in stages during the second century and the older sector was replanned, again on a common plan, along with a common drainage system. Five phases of ramparts have been identified. The site remained in occupation until the turn of the millennia, when it was gradually abandoned, presumably in favour of lower-lying sites. Only in the final phases do public buildings, probably all cultic, appear. These developments are often taken as signs of an indigenous urbanism and are sometimes attributed to Greek influence, but the architecture is entirely local. It is also clear the site benefited not only from control of the agricultural land below it but also from its location on a number of routes. The economy, however, remained fundamentally local, based on arable cultivation – storage *dolia* and hand mills are among the most common artefacts found in the houses – together with stock-raising and some hunting. A large proportion of ceramic was made very locally, more than half of it without the wheel until the middle of the last century BC.

(Photo J.C.N. Coulston)

M. Py, *L'oppidum des Castels à Nages, Gard: Fouilles 1958–1974* (*Gallia* Supplement 35, Paris, 1978); M. Py, *Culture, économie et société protohistoriques dans la région nîmoise* (*Collection de l'École Française à Rome* 131, Paris, 1990); *Carte Archéologique de la Gaule* 30/3 *Le Gard* (Paris, 1999) 483–517.

214. The oppidum of Ensérune, located halfway between Béziers and Narbonne, had a history of occupation from the mid sixth century BC to the early first century AD. Built along a slender ridge nearly 1 km long and barely 100 m wide it commands spectacular views of the surrounding plains and the coastal lagoons to the south. Chosen for its defensive strength, this location also explains its abandonment around the turn of the millennia, when low-lying sites replaced many hill-forts across the Roman west. During this long occupation there are signs of a growth of population, wealth and social stratification. At Ensérune this led to extending the settlement over the western burial area in the second century. Eventually there are elements of monumental architecture, including column capitals that seem inspired by Greek style, even if they are not technically close to them. At least two large public structures were built before the end of the third century BC. Parallels are beginning to be found in a number of similar settlements. It is also clear that some of the inhabitants were relatively wealthy. There is a mass of painted Iberian ceramic, and some of the large houses had rooms with built-in storage jars, as in the example illustrated. Ensérune gives an idea of the potential complexity and wealth of some indigenous settlements prior to the Roman conquest.

(Photo R.J.A. Wilson)

J. Jannoray, *Ensérune: Contribution à l'étude des civilisations pré-romaines de la Gaule méridionale* (Paris, 1955); H. Gallet de Sancerre, *Ensérune: Les silos de la terrasse est* (*Gallia* Supplement 39, Paris, 1980).

215. Entremont. This hill-fort, today situated on a small plateau just north of Aix-en-Provence (Roman Aquae Sextiae), provides precious information on the evolution of local societies over the second century BC. At its foundation, now dated to between 190 and 170 BC, it was confined to the summit of the plateau. A massive wall augmented natural defences and enclosed a series of blocks of houses organized along an orthogonal street plan. Around the middle of the century Entremont quadrupled in size to cover 35,000 m^2. The expansion involved building new blocks of housing on the northern and eastern slopes, creating a 'Low City' to the older settlement's 'Upper City'. The second phase was accompanied by even more massive ramparts, 3 m thick, and reinforced with a line of 13 huge towers to the north. Only a part of the site has been excavated. Traces of two attacks have been found, the first identified with the Roman wars of the 120s, after which there was a sporadic reoccupation until a second attack around 100 BC.

Alongside the expansion of the settlement as a whole it has been possible to trace the emergence of new levels of social hierarchy, or at least wealth. The houses of the first period are small and simple in construction, typically 13–15 m^2 in plan. There was one sanctuary, to judge from material reused in the rebuilding. The second phase is less well known than the first – less of it has been excavated – but in some houses the rooms are larger, and the number of rooms in each increases, and in some cases upper storeys are suspected. One large hypostyle hall with a colonnade is known on which twenty or so severed heads were displayed. There are also three fragmentary stone statues of a kind completely novel in the region, all apparently warriors.

214

215

This, and the large number of Massiliot coins, suggests strong links with Marseilles, but the imported ceramic and wine amphorae show Entremont was connected to the wider west Mediterranean world and beyond, at least at second hand.

(Photo J. C. N. Coulston)

Voyage en Massalie 100–11, summarizing new research; F. Benoit, *Gallia* 26 (1968), 1–31; Benoit, *Entremont, capitale celto-ligure des Salyens de Provence* (Paris, 1969).

216. Roquepertuse. The seated statue of a warrior, displayed here in the Musée d'Archéologie Mediterranéenne in Marseilles before the 'skull portico' from the same site, is a vivid example of the new representative arts that appeared on a series of southern sites in close contact with Greek cities, especially east of the Rhône. The statuary was made of limestone, and at Roquepertuse alone traces of paint survive. Besides these dramatic examples there is also the statue of a bird. Relatively little is known of the exact organization of space of this portico monument, but comparisons can be made with that at Entremont and with survivals from several other sites east of the Rhône. All date to the last three centuries BC. The earliest examples use real skulls mounted in niches, as here and at La Cloche, but carved stone heads soon supplement and eventually replace them.

(Photo Brigitte Lescure)

Voyage en Massalie 165–71. On portico monuments, see the dossier in *Documents d'Archéologie Méridionale* 15 (1992).

216

MARSEILLES

217. The walls of Hellenistic Marseilles. The foundation of Massalia by Phocaeans either in 600 or after 545 BC fleeing the advance of the Persian Empire is well documented in Greek texts. The city's subsequent role as a Roman ally made it important in Roman history too. More recently a mass of archaeological research has been conducted on the characteristic wine amphorae produced there and widely distributed in southern Gaul, while major excavations at the site of the Marseilles Bourse (Stock Exchange) have improved our understanding of the development of the Greek city.

Its territory seems to have been very restricted for the first 300 years of the city's existence, but during the late third and early second centuries (the Hellenistic period) Massaliot exports show a growing territory east of the Rhône. Etruscan wine and ceramics were replaced by Massiliot wine and local pottery that imitated *bucchero* and Attic black-gloss wares. Massaliot wine was traded as far as Toulouse, Catalonia and Liguria, and examples have been found from Burgundy, Tuscany, Sicily and Carthage. West of the Rhône, however, Punic-style amphorae made in Catalonia – perhaps near the Greek city of Ampurias – were more important. By the middle of the third century BC, Greco-Italic wine amphorae from central and southern Italy began to replace these types, preparing the way for the enormous quantities of Italian wine imported into Gaul in the last century BC.

It is against the background of growing political power and rapidly expanding trade that the Hellenistic city should be assessed. The original archaic settlement was on the promontory of Saint Laurent, and the city expanded inland as it grew, creating an acropolis on the hill top of Les Moulins. Archaic contexts have produced a mass of Etruscan and Attic fineware, and a pair of ships in the harbour area. The excavation at the Bourse site produced traces of a late sixth-century wall, and in this sector successive fortifications replace it on much the same lines. The image shows the foundations of the archaic wall lying ahead of the much better-preserved south tower of the Hellenistic circuit, built in the second century. During the late classical and Hellenistic periods the city evidently acquired a series of monumental temples, baths and extensive port installations (described by Strabo IV.1.4). Only the latter have been investigated archaeologically, and the details of the internal organization of Marseilles are much less well understood than for the Roman and subsequent periods.

217

(Photo J. C. N. Coulston)

Marseille: Trames et paysages urbains de Gyptis au roi René (*Études Massaliètes* 7, Aix-en-Provence, 2001); *Carte Archéologique de la Gaule* 13/3 *Marseille et ses environs* (Paris, 2005); A. Hemary, A. Hesnard and H. Tréziny (eds.), *Marseille grecque: La cité phocéenne (600–49 av. J.-C.)* (Paris, 1999); G. Bertucchi, *Les amphores et le vin de Marseille, VI s. avant J.-C.—II s. après J.-C.* (*RAN* Supplement 25, Paris, 1992); F. Laubenheimer, *Le temps des amphores en Gaule: Vins, huiles et sauces* (Paris, 1990).

218. Olbia de Provence. Best known archaeologically of the series of Greek cities that stretched from Agde (Agathe) to Nice (Nikaia) via Rhoudanousia, Tauroeis/Tauroenion and Antipolis. By the end of the last century BC these were generally regarded as either Phocaean or Massiliot colonies, and were politically dominated by Marseilles. Agathe at least was occupied from the late fifth century BC. Nice, Olbia and Tauroeis were apparently founded in the Hellenistic period. But there is evidence for commercial exchanges between Greeks and local populations from the archaic period all along this coast, and in some cases at least the foundations seem to be military outposts set up on the site of much older trading bases.

The site of Olbia consists of a fortified square with sides of around 165 m, backing onto the sea. The earliest (fourth-century) phase of fortifications is massive, with walls 3.5 m thick; the later phase was more elaborate and included some towers. The interior of the settlement was planned on a Hippodamian grid. Most buildings were of brick built on stone socles and were apparently thatched. The reorganization of the site in the Roman period has removed most traces of the Hellenistic occupation, but a probable temple has been located, and the housing gives an impression of broadly uniform levels of wealth. Detailed studies of the ceramic show evidence for Greek eating practices and for some trade in ceramic with Italy, perhaps with Punic Africa and even further afield.

(Photo Michel Bats)

Voyage en Massalie 206–10; M. Bats, *Vaisselle et alimentation à Olbia de Provence (v. 350–50 av. J.C.): Modèles culturels et catégories céramiques* (*RAN* Supplement 18, Paris, 1988).

219. St Blaise is a small hill-top site of 5.5 ha on the western side of the Étang-de-Berre. Traces of occupation from the seventh century show it was at the centre of networks of commerce used by locals, Etruscans and Greeks. It may also have been associated with salt extraction. What distinguishes it from other indigenous oppida are the walls shown here, the masonry, parapets and towers of which show clear traces of architectural techniques learned from its Greek neighbours. Constructed between 175 and

218

219

145 BC on the site of an archaic rampart, and associated with Phase Vb of the site, these are the main traces of a complete reorganization of the urban plan of the settlement which included the deliberate destruction of the preceding houses. Whatever its relationship with the growing political power of Marseilles, St Blaise shows the scale of transfers of technology in the region. The site was abandoned, apparently following a siege, in the 120s BC.

(Photo R.J.A. Wilson)

Voyage en Massalie 32–6, *Carte Archéologique de la Gaule* 13/1 *L'Étang-de-Berre* (Paris, 1996) 285–305.

220. Plan of Glanum at the end of the second century BC. The site is located in a narrow valley running through the range of Les Alpilles. Extensively excavated since the mid 1940s, Glanum is now most usually interpreted as a local tribal sanctuary that in the course of the second century BC developed into something closely resembling a small Hellenized town. Unlike many late prehistoric sites – but like Nîmes – it developed into a small but prosperous Roman community, from which there remain a number of Latin inscriptions. Later Roman structures have, however, obscured the precise nature of the Hellenistic settlement.

The sanctuary may have been important to the local tribe the Salluvii. The name attested on second-century coins is Γλανικων. A later altar is dedicated GLANI ET GLANICABUS, presumably naming the deity. A later dedication to VALETUDO (Health) and the find of an oculist's tablet have suggested to many that this was a healing shrine. The material culture is broadly similar to that of other indigenous sites in the region, but the second-century coinage and the strong Greek influences on private and public architecture alike are without parallel. Among the structures are a rampart, a nymphaeum, a building resembling a *bouleuterion*, a 'Tuscan' (Italianate) temple, a peristyle-monument originally identified as a market, a monumental well approached by a flight of steps and a series of grand houses. Recent excavations have disentangled several phases of building in the case of the temple and the '*bouleuterion*' and perhaps other buildings, but the stratigraphy remains poor. Around Glanum the gorge was terraced in several places, and a series of staircases constructed. Once considered a Massiliot cult place, Glanum is now usually considered a unique site where a wealthy local aristocracy was able to appropriate elements of a new architectural idiom to create a genuinely unique centre.

(Anne Roth-Congès)

Carte Archéologique de la Gaule 13/2 *Les Alpilles et la Montagnette* (Paris, 1999) 264–73; Anne Roth-Congès, *JRA* 5 (1992) 39–55; H. Rolland, *Fouilles de Glanum (Saint-Rémy-de-Provence)* (*Gallia* Supplement 1, Paris, 1946).

ROMAN CONQUEST

221. Coinage. A large number of precious-metal coins circulated in southern Gaul and have been found on both Greek and indigenous sites. As elsewhere in Europe, coins inspired local imitations, images from the coinage of Marseilles in the east and of Ampurias and Rhode further west being among the most popular. These silver issues probably did not function as money so much as valuable and compact commodities.

In **a** we see the reverse, in **b** the obverse, of the following five coins, described left to right, top to bottom:

1 a Massaliot drachma, with the bust of Artemis on one side and on the other a lion beneath the monogram ΜΑΣΣΑ

2 the Bridiers groups of coins – named for the site of a large hoard – imitate the horseman reverse types of the Greek city of Emporiae (Ampurias) in Spain and also owe something to Spanish imitations of that coinage. (Part of the coinage of Emporiae was produced for Roman purposes during the Second Punic War and, as a result, was much copied in Spain.) They were apparently distributed mainly in the Massif Central and provided a model for much late Iron Age coinage.

3 The silver coins with the bust of a horse on the reverse are one of a series of types produced in the Rhône valley, perhaps by the tribe of the Cavares. Several origins have been suggested for the motif: the Romano-Campanian coinage of central Italy is one possibility, Punic tetradrachms are another. The legends use characters found in the local alphabets of northern Italy. The stylization of the horse's head has been connected with La Tène art. These coins illustrate once again the diversity of influences or models available in the region and the relative freedom with which local peoples could select from them when making original compositions. Like the architecture of Glanum, the statuary of Entremont, and the Iberian and Celtic inscriptions from the entire region, this relative freedom contrasts strongly with the increased stylistic conformity which followed the imposition of provincial institutions around the turn of the millennia.

220

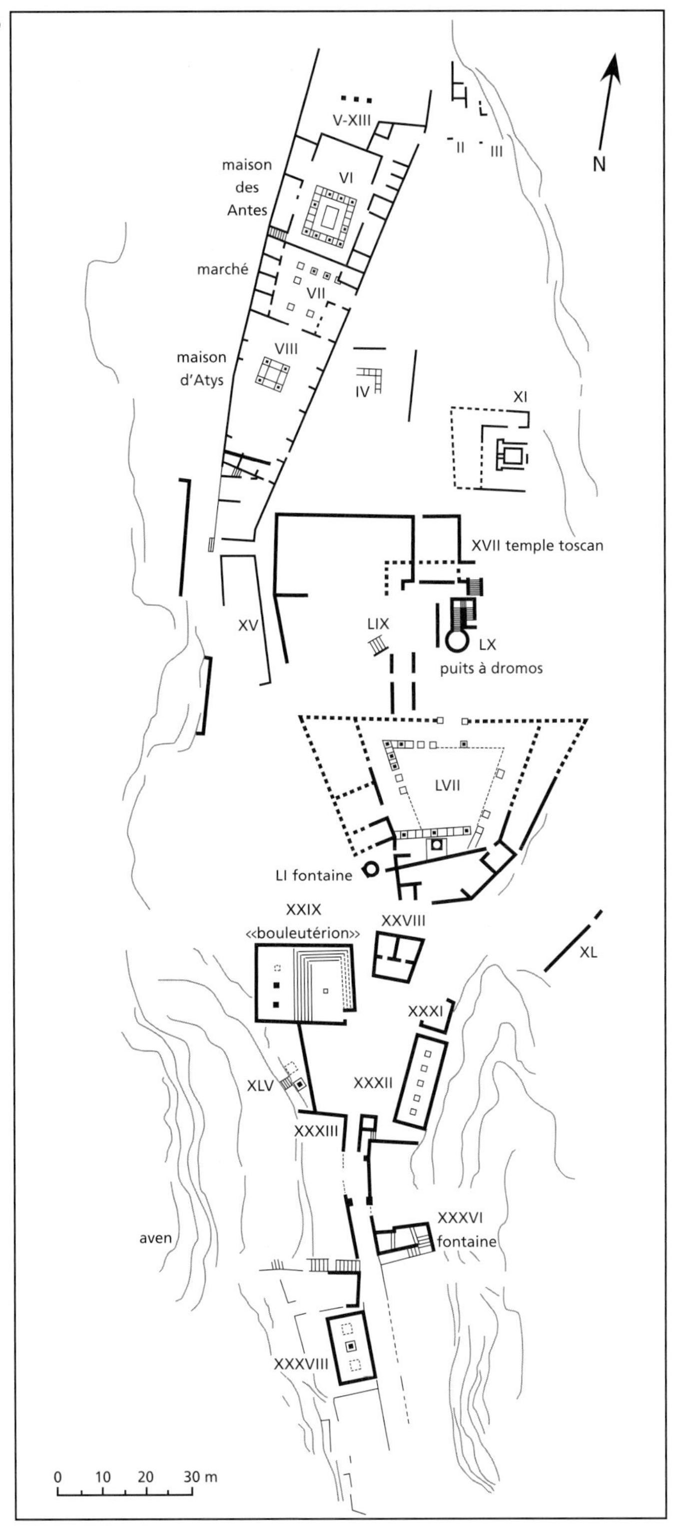

N
V-XIII
II
III
maison
des
Antes
VI
marché
VII
maison
d'Atys
VIII
IV
XI
XVII temple toscan
XV
LIX
LX
puits à dromos
LVII
LI fontaine
XXIX
<<bouleutérion>>
XXVIII
XL
XXXI
XLV
XXXII
XXXIII
XXXVI
fontaine
aven
XXXVIII
0 10 20 30 m

221a

4 Monnaies à la croix. Based ultimately on the coinage of Rhoda in Spain, coins of this type, characterized by a reverse divided into four sections each containing a different image, were made and circulated in a broad zone north of the Pyrenees and west of the Rhône, especially in the Gallic Isthmus around Toulouse.

5 Imitation of coinage of Rhoda. The rose design on the reverse, a symbol of the Greek city, has undergone less change than the head on the obverse which shows clearly the stylization of classical images in accordance with a different aesthetic.

(Photos British Museum neg. 338161)

M.H. Crawford, *Coinage and Money under the Roman Republic: Italy and the Mediterranean Economy* (London, 1985); D. F. Allen and D. Nash, *The Coins of the Ancient Celts* (Edinburgh, 1980); A. Deroc, *Les monnaies gauloises d'argent de la vallée du Rhône* (*Études de Numismatique Celtique* 2, Paris, 1983).

222. The Via Domitia crossing the oppidum of Ambrusson. This site was one of a series that sat just above the coastal plain, a series that also included the pre-Roman settlements at Nîmes and Nages. Their original locations probably reflect the defensive advantages of hill-top sites combined with the economic advantages of location along an ecotone from which two different environments could be exploited. Occupation and an urban layout can be traced back to the mid third century BC at Ambrusson itself.

When land communications from Spain to Italy became important, some of these sites assumed new roles as way-stations along a route that avoided the coastal lagoons. The Roman roads eventually

221b

62117

led from the Ebro through Catalonia and the Languedoc to cross the Rhône just north of Arles before dividing into a southern coastal route via Aix, Fréjus and the Ligurian coast and a northern one that climbed the Durance valley before descending into Italy via Susa and Turin. Much of the route, however, consisted of sections of existing roads between oppida suitably upgraded. The paved surface of the road here at Ambrusson, in which wheel ruts are visible, demonstrates the technological difference. The oppidum had been sited at the crossing of the river Vidourle: here an eleven-arch bridge 180 m in length was constructed to make it viable for wheeled vehicles in all weathers.

(Photo R.J.A.Wilson)

G. Castellvi, J.-P. Comps, J. Kotarba and A. Pezin, *Voies romaines du Rhône à l'Ebre: Via Domitia et Via Augusta* (Documents d'Archéologie Française 61, Paris, 1997) 24–9, 42–3, 60–8.

223. Domitianic milestone. The fact that this milestone, found in 1949 just 20 Roman miles south of Narbonne, is the oldest Latin inscription in the Gallic provinces illustrates very clearly the limited nature of Roman impact on the area before the mid first century BC. The inscription reads 'Cn. Domitius Cn. f./Ahenobarbus/ Imperator XX', that is 'Gnaeus Domitius Ahenobarbus, son of Gnaeus, General. 20 miles'. The title 'imperator' refers to his victory in 121 BC, but the milestone is clearly dated after he returned in 118 to found the colony of Narbonne at the head of the Étangs de Bages and de Sigéan. A small town located on the other side of Narbonne, halfway to Nîmes, has the name *Forum Domitii*. The term Via Domitia

222

223

refers properly to the stretch of road between the Rhône and the Pyrenees. This landscape, and the names of some Gallic Domitii, records the traces of a provincial *clientela* of the kind better known in northern Italy.

(Photo R.J.A.Wilson)

M. Gayaud, *Narbonne antique des origines à la fin du* IIIe *siècle* (*RAN* Supplement 8, Paris, 1981) 127–30; *AE* (1952) 38; (1963) 131.

11. NORTHERN ITALY

JONATHAN WILLIAMS

In the middle and late Republic, the significance of northern Italy (i.e. the region between the Apennines and the Alps) for Romans was twofold: it was the unfamiliar homeland of the feared and hated Gauls who, as was believed, had utterly destroyed the city of Rome in 387 BC; secondly, it was a fertile plain of fabulous extent and wealth: 'a plain surpassing in fertility and size all others in Europe we know of' (Polybius II.14.7). Together, these two factors explain much about the motivation behind, and the course of, the Roman conquest and colonization of the north.

What was northern Italy like before the Romans conquered it? The archaeological record suggests a mostly scattered settlement pattern. Burial rites, object types (particularly weaponry and metalwork) and decorative motifs betray close affinities with styles also current north of the Alps, conventionally called 'La Tène', after an important archaeological site in Switzerland. This has generally been understood as evidence for the credibility of the story, told by Livy and others, of the invasion and settlement of much of northern Italy by Gauls who migrated across the Alps at some point between 600 and 400 BC.

By the end of our period (133 BC), after an age of conquest which lasted about a century, from the first transapennine campaigns in the 280s to the final defeat of the Gauls in the late 190s, the landscape had undergone profound changes, particularly south of the Po. An extended period of organized large-scale development between 190 and 170, involving confiscation of lands, deforestation, drainage, colonial foundations, road-building and centuriation, transformed much of the Cispadane region along the line of the newly built Via Aemilia. The effect on the local populations was no less marked: the two principal Gallic peoples south of the Po, the Boii and Senones, seem to have vanished in the second century BC. Colonization north of the Po was more limited in extent, but the impact of the Roman conquest on the region was still considerable. There was probably large-scale unofficial migration from peninsular Italy over the Po in the second century BC, while the Via Postumia of 148, extending across the whole width of the plain from Genoa to Aquileia, laid the basis for further colonization in the first century. Ethnic developments were also less abrupt than they seem to have been south of the Po: the Insubres, Cenomani and Veneti survived as peoples into the late Republic.

Northern Italy was the first large area of non-Mediterranean Europe whose land and people were systematically conquered and redeveloped in a manner which later came to be characteristic of many areas of the Empire. As such, its history and prehistory are of particular significance for the understanding of the development of Roman imperialism.

GENERAL BIBLIOGRAPHY

Prehistory

E.A. Arslan, 'The Transpadane Celts' in Moscati *et al.* 1991: 460–70.

G. Fogolari and A.L. Prosdocimi, *I Veneti antichi* (Padua, 1988).

M.T. Grassi, *I Celti in Italia* (Milan, 1991).

R. De Marinis, 'Liguri e Celto-Liguri' in G. Pugliese Carratelli (ed.), *Italia, Omnium Terrarum Alumna* (Milan, 1988) 159–259.

V. Kruta, 'I Celti' in Pugliese Carratelli (ed.) *Italia, Omnium Terrarum Alumna*, 263–311.

A. Morandi, *Celti d'Italia: Epigrafia e lingua* (*Popoli e Civiltà dell'Italia Antica* XII.2, Rome, 2004).

S. Moscati, O.-H. Frey, V. Kruta, B. Raftery and M. Szabó (eds.), *The Celts* (Milan, 1991).

C. Peyre, *La Cisalpine Gauloise du IIIe au Ier siècle avant J.-C.* (Paris, 1979).

P. Piana Agostinetti, *Celti d'Italia: Archeologia, lingua e scrittura* (*Popoli e Civiltà dell'Italia Antica* XII.1, Rome, 2004).

L. Prosdocimi, 'The language and writing of the early Celts' in Moscati *et al.* *The Celts* 51–9.

P. Santoro (ed.), *I Galli e l'Italia: Catalogo* (Rome, 1978).

M. Schönfelder (ed.), *Kelten? Kelten! Keltische Spuren in Italien* (Mainz, 2010).

D. Vitali, 'The Celts in Italy' in Moscati *et al.* *The Celts* 220–35.
— *Tombe e necropoli galliche di Bologna e del territorio* (Bologna 1992).

Romans and Romanization

D. Allen (ed. J.P.C. Kent and M. Mays), *Catalogue of the Celtic Coins in the British Museum* II: *Silver Coins of North Italy, South and Central France, Switzerland and South Germany* (London, 1990) (= *BM*).

E.A. Arslan, 'Celti e Romani in Transpadana', *Études Celtiques* 15 (1976–8) 441–81.

A. Calbi and G. Susini (eds.), *Pro Poplo Ariminese* (Bologna, 1995).

R. Chevallier, *La romanisation de la celtique du Pô* II: *Essai d'histoire provinciale* (Rome, 1983).

A. Degrassi, *Inscriptiones Latinae Liberae Rei Publicae: Imagines* (Berlin, 1965) (= *Imagines*).

E. Gabba, 'I Romani nell'Insubria: Trasformazione, adeguamento e soppravivenza delle strutture socio-economiche galliche' in *2° Convegno Archeologico Regionale: Atti* (Como, 1986) 31–41.
—'La conquista della Gallia Cisalpina' in G. Clemente, F. Coarelli and E. Gabba (ed.), *Storia di Roma*, vol. II.1 (Rome, 1990) 69–77.

W.V. Harris, 'Roman expansion in the West' in *CAH* VIII^2 107–62.

N. Purcell, 'The creation of provincial landscape: The Roman impact on Cisalpine Gaul' in T.F.C. Blagg and M. Millett (eds.), *The Early Roman Empire in the West* (Oxford, 1990) 7–29.

EARLY INSCRIPTIONS: CELTIC AND VENETIC

224. Dedicatory inscription from Prestino (near Como: discovered 1966). *Transcription*:

uvamokozis _plialeθu_uvltiauiopos_ariuonepos_siteš _tetu

This important inscription is written from right to left in a version of the north Etruscan alphabet called Lepontic, which is also found on a number of other inscriptions and graffiti found in the area of the Lombardy lakes. It is a dedication: uvamokozis plialeθu seems to be the name of the dedicator, uvltiauiopos ariuonepos those of the dedicatees in the dative plural. Its language, also called Lepontic, has been classified as belonging to the Celtic family of languages, but the dating has been contested. Recent epigraphic evidence strongly suggests an early date, perhaps the sixth century BC, for this inscription and, hence, for the presence of Celtic languages, and of ethnic Celts, within Italy.

When the Gauls first crossed over the Alps into Italy is a hotly debated question. Literary sources offer a variety of dates ranging from about 600 BC (Livy) to shortly before the sack of Rome in 387 BC (Appian, Diodorus). Historians have turned to datable material evidence such as this text to resolve the issue.

Language affiliation is often regarded as the most secure means of identifying the ethnic origin of cultures otherwise only known archaeologically. In this case, the linguistic evidence of dated Lepontic inscriptions has been used to identify the Golasecca culture of early Iron Age Lombardy as ethnically Celtic, and to support the earlier date of *c.* 500 BC for the Gallic invasion of Italy found in Livy. But language does not necessarily determine ethnic identity. Nor can archaeological evidence be used to authenticate much later literary accounts in this manner.

224a

224b

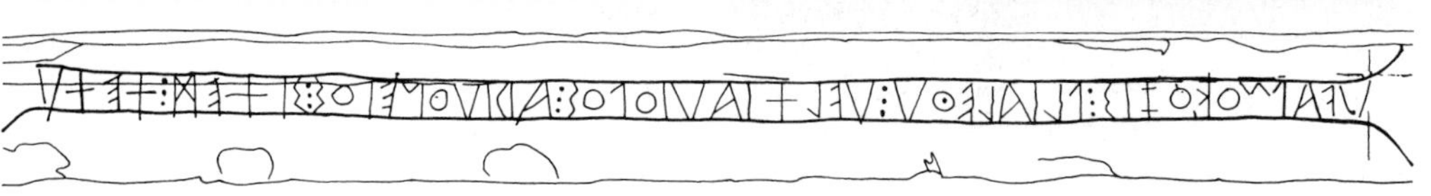

(Civico Museo Archeologico P. Giovio, Como. Length 3.75 m; height 1.5–1.9 cm; width 3.1–3.5 cm; sandstone)

M. Lejeune, *Lepontica* (Paris 1971) 96–123; A.L. Prosdocimi, in D. Vitali (ed.), *Celti ed etruschi nell'Italia centro-settentrionale dal v secolo a.C. alla romanizzazione: Atti del Colloquio Internazionale* (Bologna, 1987) 561–81; J.H.C. Williams, *Beyond the Rubicon* (Oxford, 2001) 187–94.

225. Funerary inscription from Padua (discovered *c.* 1960). *Transcription:*

[....].s.θerope.i..a[..] uχeriio.i..e.k/[up]eθari.s..e.χo

The part of the plain towards the Adriatic has always been inhabited by a people of very great antiquity. They are called the Veneti; they differ in customs and dress from the Celts only slightly, but they speak a different language. (Polybius II.17.5)

So wrote Polybius about the people of northeast Italy known as the Veneti to the Romans and the Enetoi to the Greeks. Their origins were widely canvassed as Trojan, by Cato the Elder among others, but Polybius rejected such mythical material and argued instead that they were indigenous. The Veneti appear only infrequently in the literary historical record because, for the most part, they were allies rather than opponents of the Romans, first mentioned as such in 225 BC on the occasion of the Gallic invasion (Polybius II.23.2, 24.7). Archaeology has proved more informative about the distinctive traits of Venetic material culture and language.

This funerary stele, one of a group of grave reliefs from Padua (ancient *Patavium*), points up some of the differences between Venetic culture and contemporary developments in the 'Celtic' west and south of the Po Valley in the later Iron Age (fourth and third centuries BC), in particular the use of writing and the production of figurative art. Conventionally dated to the fourth century BC, the monument shows a chariot presumably conveying the soul of the deceased to the realm of the dead. It is inscribed retrograde in the Venetic alphabet with a dedicatory formula in which the object addresses the reader: 'I (eχo) am the grave monument (?) (ekupeθaris) for [name]'. Venetic, long thought to be Illyrian in origin, now tends to be classified as an Italic language. The alphabet was adapted from Etruscan as early as the sixth century BC.

225

(Museo Archaeologico, Padua. Foto Gabinetto Fotografico Musei Civici di Padua. Height 7.8 cm; width 6.9 cm; depth 2.2–2.6 cm)

G.B. Pellegrini and A.L. Prosdocimi, *La lingua venetica*, vol. 1 (Padua 1967) 331; A.L. Prosdocimi, in *Padova Preromana* (Padua, 1976) 25–37, 302; Fogolari and Prosdocimi *I veneti antichi* 99–105, 284–6.

THE LA TÈNE STYLE IN NORTHERN ITALY AND THE CELTS

226. Gold torque from Santa Paolina di Filottrano (near Ancona). In his account of the battle of Telamon between Romans and Gauls in 225 BC, Polybius mentions the golden torques (neck-rings) and armlets worn by the Celtic warriors (Polybius II.29.8–9). The torque was among the most potent of visual symbols associated with the Gauls in the Roman imagination (cf. **233b**). Torques like this one, found at the important cemetery near Santa Paolina di Filottrano (Marche), perhaps served as a status-symbol when worn by men. This example was found in a female grave.

Several other graves in the cemetery, both male and female, contained bronze domestic vessels, implements and drinking gear – Greek pottery and Etruscan bronzes – together with helmets, swords with scabbards and spearheads made in the La Tène style also found in northern Europe and often associated with Celtic art. The pottery allows a dating to the middle of the fourth century BC, which makes this and other contemporary material from the Marche some of the earliest datable finds associated with the presence of transalpine Celts in Italy. The ancient literary sources locate a people called the Senones in this region.

The presence of La Tène-style objects, particularly torques and weaponry, in contexts together with Greek and Italian luxury goods is usually interpreted as evidence of a new invasive

226

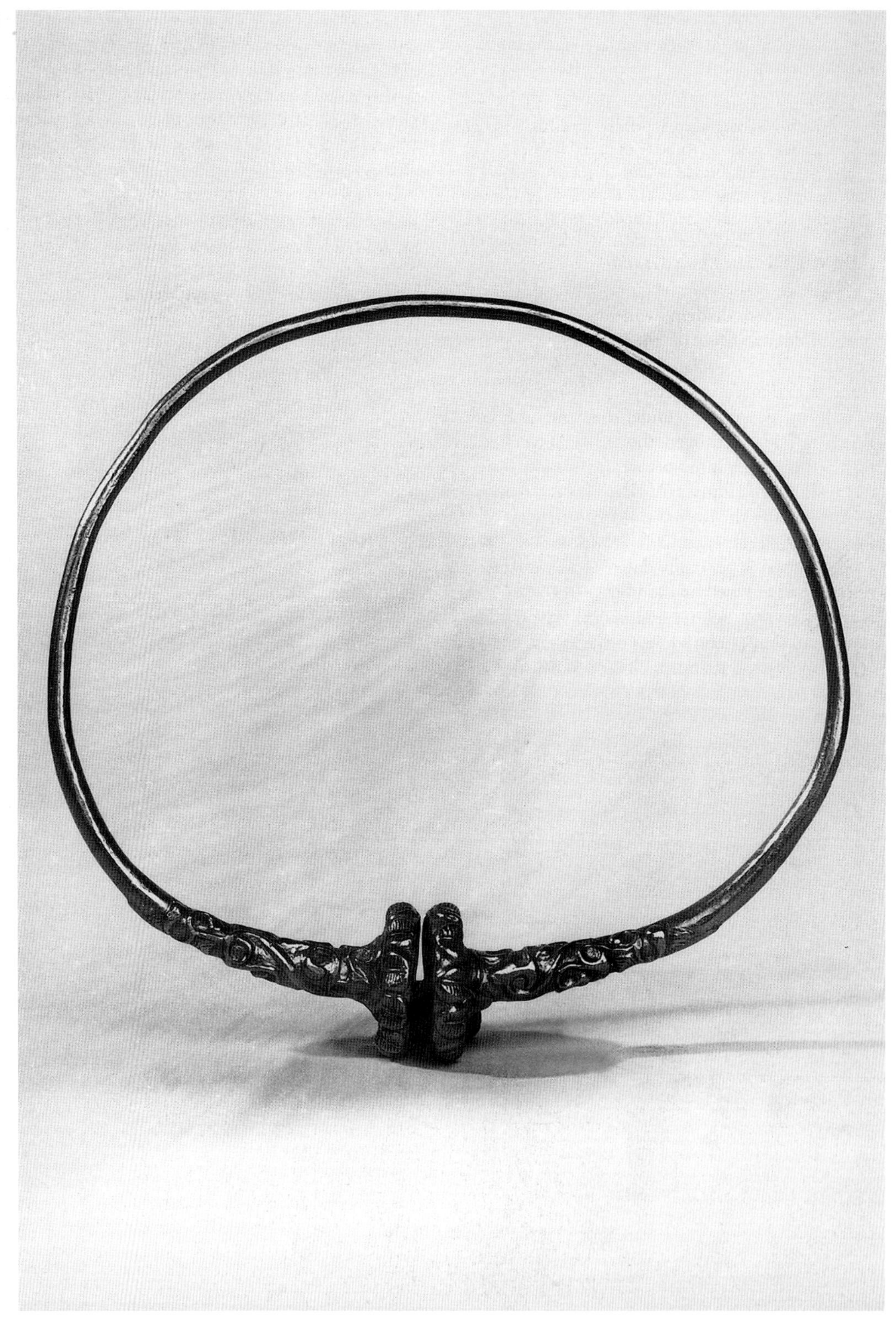

Celtic population in northern Italy, whose earliest manifestation in literary sources is the sack of Rome in 387 BC.

(Museo Archeologico Nazionale delle Marche, Ancona (3697); Archivio Fotografico, Soprintendenza Archaeologica delle Marche neg. 4191. Diameter 1.57 cm; Weight 230.5 g)

E. Baumgaertel, *Journal of the Royal Anthropological Institute* 67 (1937) 231–86 esp. 236, pl. XIX fig. 1; Kruta, in Carratelli *Italia* esp. 286–7; M. Landolfi, in D. Lollini (ed.), *Il Museo Archeologico Nazionale delle Marche* (Rome, 1989) 45–7; M. Landolfi, in Moscati *et al. The Celts* 286.

227–8. Golden diadem, wine-cups and strainer from Bologna. One of the richest graves from northern Italy associated with the Celts comes from the Benacci cemetery at Bologna (Tomb 953). Pliny records that, under the name of Felsina, Bononia had once been the main Etruscan city north of the Apennines before being conquered by the Gallic Boii (Pliny *HN* III.115). Livy mentions its surrender to the Romans, along with most of the Boii, in 196 BC (L.33.37.4).

This burial is generally dated to the early third century BC. As well as the objects shown, it contained a bronze helmet and sword, spearheads, a strigil and other luxury items of Italian (i.e. not La Tène-style) production, including gaming pieces. The appearance in northern Italy of richly accoutred inhumations containing both weapons and vessels associated with wine-consumption is a new development in the Po valley of the fourth–third centuries BC. It is clear testimony to a significant cultural change in the region, at least as regards funerary practices.

The appearance of such graves is generally associated with ancient literary accounts of the Gallic invasion of Italy of *c.* 400 BC. Some versions of the story stress the fascination exerted by the luxuries of Italy upon the northern invaders as an important motivation behind their migration (D.Hal. *AR* XIII.10–11; Plut. *Cam.* 15; Pliny *HN* XII.5). But the decisive role of mass-migrations as general explanations of observed archaeological change is debated. Even in this case, when there is literary evidence in support, the likely cultural significance, or even the historicity, of the Gallic invasion of Italy is perhaps open to question.

(Museo Civico Archeologico, Bologna (diadem = R 147; cups = 154–7; strainer = R 152). Museo Civico Archeologico, Bologna (DIA 777 & 778). Diadem: 24 cm × 10 cm; cups: height 7.5–10 cm ; strainer: length 3.38 cm)

E. Brizio, *Atti e Memorie Rom.* ser. III.5 (1887) 457–93; G. Sassatelli, in Santoro (ed.) *I Galli e l'Italia* 118–21; Vitali, in Moscati *et al. The Celts* 283–94.

227

228

229

229. Decorated iron helmet from Canosa di Puglia (Bari). In the fourth century BC a new style of war-helmet appeared in Italy, a development often associated with the Celtic invasion of the north. This example, found in a richly endowed grave near Bari in southern Italy (**97**), is comparable with similarly highly decorated examples found at Agris (Charente) and Amfreville (Eure) in France. Others, less sumptuous in appearance, have been found in Italy at Bologna and Monte Bibele (cf. **227**, **228**, **231**), and the cemeteries of the Marche associated with the Senones (cf. **226**). The influence of the helmet type was far-reaching: it was adopted by the Roman army and continued in use until the late Republic.

The decorative motifs, in bronze with red coral inlay, are characteristic of the so-called 'Waldalgesheim' style of La Tène art which arose in the mid–late fourth century BC (cf. also **226**). The style is named after a particular group of finds in the Rhineland and is generally considered to be Celtic. But there is some debate over its region and culture of origin, whether northern Europe or Italy, as indeed over the form of the helmet.

The real question is whether it is at all appropriate to classify artefact and decorative styles primarily in ethnic terms – in this context, designating La Tène objects as 'Celtic' and interpreting them as evidence of the presence of Celts. With particular reference to the Canosa helmet, attempts to explain its southerly provenance in terms of wandering Celtic mercenaries are, if not necessarily wrong, at least limiting.

230

(Antikensammlung, Staatliche Museen zu Berlin – Preussischer Kulturbesitz (L. 80); photo Ingrid Geske/bpk. Height 25 cm; max. diameter 23.3 cm)

NSc (1896), 491ff.; P. Jacobsthal *Early Celtic Art* (Oxford, 1944) 146–52 and pl. 258–60; Kruta, in Moscati *et al. The Celts* 193–213 esp. 200–1.

230. Grave-goods from Ceretolo (near Bologna). This grave assemblage, dated to the mid third century BC, was discovered in 1877. Its distinctive feature is the comparative lack of luxury Greek or Italian material that characterizes earlier graves in Emilia-Romagna and the Marche (cf. **227–8**): apart from a single bronze wine-jug (*oinochoe*), La Tène weaponry predominates: sword, iron sword-belt, spearhead, shield-boss.

The disappearance of luxury imports from Celtic-style graves south of the Po in the third century BC tends to be explained as a consequence of the Roman conquest of Italy south of the Apennines, on the grounds that the Celts were thereby deprived of the opportunity to acquire them in the course of mercenary activity in Etruria and southern Italy. The final disappearance of La Tène material throughout northern Italy in the late third–early second centuries is in turn explained by the Roman conquest of the entire region.

Both developments might alternatively be understood within the broader context of changes in funerary practice north of the Po and beyond the Alps. Like Ceretolo, the graves from the large third-century BC cemetery at Carzaghetto in the region north of the Po where the Cenomani were probably located lack luxury imports and contain mostly La Tène-style material; while the apparent trend across northern Europe in the second century BC, from Switzerland to the Hungarian plain, is anyway for burial evidence to disappear from the archaeological record.

These two kinds of explanation are characteristic of different trends in the interpretation of the European Iron Age: the one tending to look to historical events, the other examining chronological and regional patterns within the archaeology itself.

(Museo Civico Archeologico, Bologna (sword: R 271; spearhead: R 273; belt-chain: R 274 and 275); (DIA 769); sword: 6.6 cm; spearhead: 4.2 cm; belt-chain: 4.65 cm × 16.2 cm.)

D. Vitali, in Santoro (ed.) *I galli e l'Italia* 129–32; Vitali, *Tombe e necropoli* 380–90; Grassi *I celti in Italia* 95–7.

231. Monte Bibele: general view and plan of cemetery. Most of the archaeological evidence relevant to the Celts of Italy was discovered in the nineteenth century. The most important recent discovery in the field is the important cemetery and settlement site at Monte Bibele in the Apennines near Bologna. The cemetery consists of a series of graves extending downhill in rows on a west-facing slope. The chronological sequence they present clearly illustrates the major changes in funerary practice that have come to be associated with an invasive Celtic presence in northern Italy.

The earliest graves towards the top of the hill, dating to the early fourth century BC, show characteristics typical of Etruscan funerary practices. In the latter part of the century, however, La Tène weaponry begins to be deposited in tombs, together with the drinking gear familiar from other burial contexts (cf. **227–8**). The insinuation of these new customs into the cemetery without any apparent evidence for destruction or discontinuity has been taken as indicating the peaceful integration of incoming Celts into what had been an ethnically Etruscan settlement. Recent scientific analysis of human remains from the cemetery suggest that the majority of individuals buried at the site were local. A minority may have been from further afield, though it is not clear where exactly.

The related settlement site consisted of forty to fifty stone-built houses, many probably with more than one floor, while carbonized botanical and tool remains indicate that the inhabitants were engaged in agricultural activities as well as importing various foodstuffs. Perhaps unsurprisingly, this site presents a very different picture of life among the transapennine Celts from that given by Polybius, who describes them as living in unwalled villages, lacking all possessions save cattle and gold (Polybius II.17.9–11).

(Prof. Daniele Vitali, Università degli Studi di Bologna, Dipartimento di Archeologia)

231a

231b

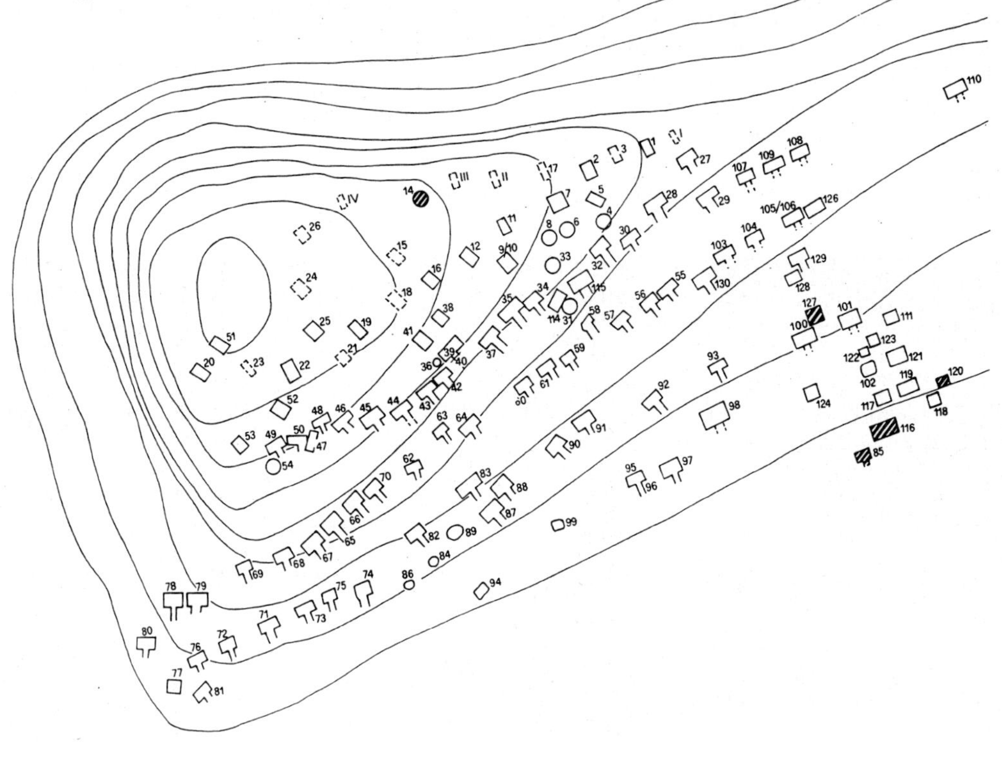

110
1
I
3
2
27
108
109
107
17
III
II
14
IV
7
5
28
29
105/106
126
11
8
6
4
26
30
104
103
15
12
9/10
33
32
129
16
24
34
115
130
55
56
128
18
38
35
114
31
58
57
127
101
111
25
19
41
51
100
123
39
37
36
40
59
93
122
121
20
23
22
21
42
61
60
120
102
119
52
43
92
124
117
118
48
46
45
44
63
64
98
53
49
50
47
91
116
54
90
85
62
95
97
70
83
96
88
66
65
87
99
89
82
68
67
84
69
86
94
78
79
74
75
71
73
80
72
76
77
81

D. Vitali, *Monte Bibele (Monterenzio) und andere Fundstellen der keltischen Epoche im Gebiet von Bologna* (Marburg, 1985); Vitali, in Vitali (ed.), *Celti ed etruschi nell'Italia centro-settentrionale* 309–80; Vitali, in Moscati *et al. The Celts* 288–9; M. Scheeres and K.W. Alt, in Schönfelder *Kelten? Kelten!* 42–5.

THE IMAGE OF THE GAUL

232. Civitalba frieze and Etruscan funerary urn. The terracotta temple frieze from Civitalba (**a**), close to the site of the battle of Sentinum (295 BC) in Umbria, is conventionally dated to the early second century BC. The scene shows a group of armed individuals, some naked, being put to flight by two female divinities and perhaps others. In their disorder, they let various vessels and plates fall to the ground, suggesting that they are temple-robbers losing their booty.

Their nudity and extravagant hair-styles, together with their shields and belts, identify these figures as Gauls, these details corresponding to other figurative depictions and literary descriptions. The theme of the composition also serves to establish who they are: Celts were closely associated with temple-robbing in Greek and Roman historical narratives of the assault on the sanctuary at Delphi (279 BC) and the sack of Rome (387 BC).

The frieze incorporates visually many of the assumptions about the Gauls that were common among Greeks and Romans, particularly their wilful belligerence and hubristic violence against gods and men. Its further implication is that the fate of such violence is, eventually, to meet defeat at the hands of those they have violated. The frieze both commemorates and mythologizes the confrontation with the Gauls in Italy in a fashion akin to monumental developments at Pergamum, where scenes of battles against the Celts (celtomachy) became an important artistic theme in the late third and early second centuries BC.

A series of contemporary funerary 'urns' from Etruria, particularly Clusium (modern Chiusi), provide an Italian context for the development of this theme. This example (**b**) depicts a battle between an armoured warrior in the centre and three opponents, one already fallen to the right, and two others to his left. Behind him stands a winged figure, the Etruscan divinity Vanth.

Celtomachy was a theme with both real and symbolic significance. Romans and Italians had fought long wars against the peoples they called the Gauls since the early fourth century BC. But the Gauls' invasion of Italy and, above all, the Gallic sack of Rome made them into enemies unlike any other: war against Gauls was a fight for survival, not glory (cf. Sall. *Jug.* 114.2), while victory over Gauls meant a release from the fear of annihilation. The appearance of celtomachic scenes on Etruscan grave-reliefs suggests that such attitudes, well attested among Romans, were also current among their Italian allies.

(**a** Museo Archeologico Nazionale delle Marche, Ancona; Archivio Fotografico, Soprintendenza Archaeologica per le Marche neg. 185726; height of figures ranges from 0.5 to 1.1 m).

M. Zuffa, *in Studi in Onore di Aristide Calderini e Roberto Paribeni*, vol. III (Milan, 1956) 267–88; M. Verzar and F.-H. Massa Pairault, in Santoro (ed.) *I Galli e l'Italia* 196–203.

(**b** Museo Civico, Chuisi (980) DAI Rome neg. 68.3388. length 0.7 m; width 0.3 m; height 0.81 m)

232a

232b

H. Brunn and G. Körte *I relievi delle urne etrusche*, vol. III (Berlin, 1916) 160, pl. 118.10; P.R. von Bieńkowski, *Die Darstellungen der Gallier in der hellenistischen Kunst* (Vienna, 1908) 132–3 fig. 140; U. Höckmann, *JDAI* 106 (1991) 199–230 cat. no. 22, pl. 52.2.

THE NEW ROMAN LANDSCAPE

233. Ariminum: town wall masonry (**a**) and cast *biuncia* (**b**) from Arimum, early third century BC. The important Latin colony of Ariminum (modern Rimini) was founded in 268 BC on the site of a previous, perhaps Umbrian, settlement (Strabo V.1.11) in the wake of the defeat of the Gallic Senones in the 280s and the conquest of Picenum in the same year. It was the key to the route northwards over the Apennines from Mediterranean Italy into the Po valley (Polybius III.86.2). Ariminum became an important base for military operations in the north during the Gallic Wars of the 220s and 190s and the Hannibalic War, and the northern military *provincia* was named after it. The colony was surrounded with massive walls for protection, traces of which are seen here (**a**) beneath the later Augustan arch. Military requirements also motivated the construction of the Via Flaminia from Rome to Ariminum in

233a

220 BC. After the north was conquered, it served as the starting-point for the Via Aemilia (187 BC) which terminated at Placentia (modern Piacenza), one of two Latin colonies founded on the river Po in 218 BC (cf. **236**).

Ariminum's status as a bulwark against the fear of invasion from the Gallic north is implicit in the early third-century BC cast bronze coins associated with the colony (**b**, **bi**). They feature the head of a moustachioed man wearing a torque, who must be a Gaul (cf. **226** and **232**). Current opinion dates them to the early years of the colony. An example has been found concealed beneath the third-century wall. Like other cast coin series from eastern Italy, the Ariminese pound (*libra*) was heavier than the Roman (370 g compared with 325 g), and the currency unit, the *as*, was divided into ten *unciae* rather than the Roman twelve. The earliest inhabitants of Latin Ariminum seem to have adapted to local monetary and weight systems rather than simply importing Roman standards: Romanization clearly involved variety and accommodation as well as imposition.

(a DAI Rome neg. 40.1131; **b**, **bi** British Museum (*BMC* Italy, Ariminum 2), diameter 4.5 cm; weight 73.95 g)

G.A. Mansuelli, *Ariminum* (Spoleto, 1941) pl. IIIb; J. Ortalli, in Calbi and Susini *Pro Poplo Ariminese* 469–529; M. H. Crawford, *Coinage and Money under the Roman Republic: Italy and the Mediterranean Economy* (London, 1985) 14–5, 43; S. Balbi di Caro in Moscati *et al. The Celts* 290–1.

234. Cesena centuriation. This aerial picture, taken by the Royal Air Force in 1943, shows the town of Caesenna (modern Cesena) situated in the foothills of the Apennines. The Via Aemilia can be seen passing through, deviating from its otherwise straight course to skirt round the mountains at this point. The landscape to the north betrays the enduring pattern left behind by centuriation, the regular division of the land into squares of 20 × 20 *actus* (710 m), making 200 *iugera* (50 ha), ready for settlement and cultivation by new Latin-speaking colonists. The squares are clearly visible, orientated according to the four compass points, in stark contrast to the non-centuriated areas west of the river Savio and in the foothills. The centuriation in this area does not run parallel to the Via Aemilia as it does further to the north-west, leading some to

233b

234

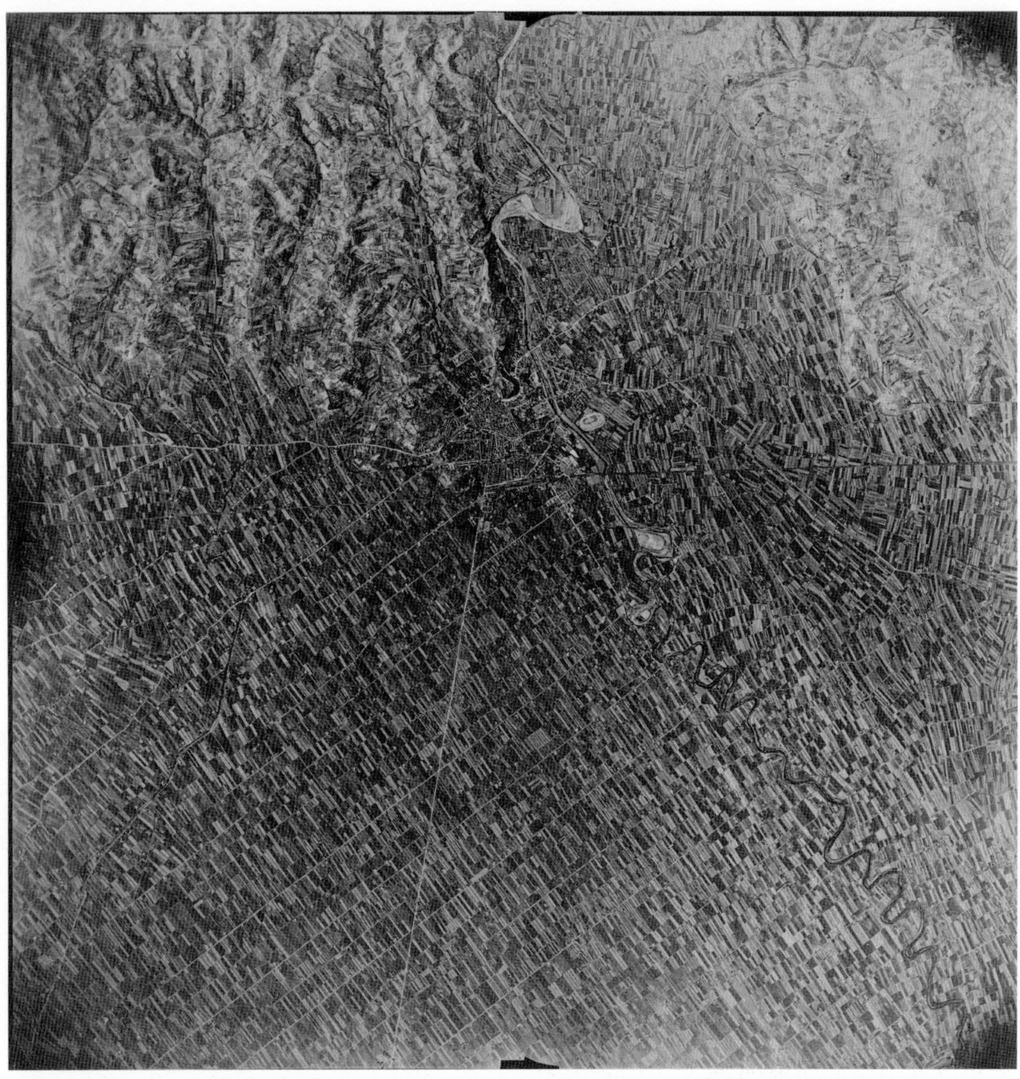

suggest that it predates the great road (187 BC), belonging perhaps to the 232 BC settlements organized by C. Flaminius.

Later Romans noted the absence of the Senones and Boii, the Gallic peoples who had once lived south of the Po, and concluded that they had either been expelled or annihilated. More probably, they had been integrated into the new human landscape represented by the urban foundations and centuriated countryside.

(Air Photo Library, Keele University (10894; 5S/131/3PG; 3.8.43; print 5039))

J. Bradford, *Ancient Landscapes* (London, 1957) 137–9 pl. 38; Peyre *La Cisalpine Gauloise* 34; Chevallier *Romanisation* 44–5 pl. XI; G. Bottazzi, in Calbi and Susini *Pro Poplo Ariminese* 329–54.

235. Statue base from Aquileia (limestone). Transcription:

L.MANLIVS.L.F/ACIDINVS TRIVVIR (*sic*)/AQVILEIAE. COLONIAE/DEDVCVNDAE

(Lucius Manlius, son of Lucius, Acidinus, member of the Board of Three for the founding of the colony of Aquileia)

This second-century BC limestone block from Aquileia once bore a statue of L. Manlius Acidinus, one of three senatorial commissioners appointed in 183 to found the major Latin colony of Aquileia

235

(Livy XXXIX.55.5–6). Situated at the head of the Adriatic, it was initially conceived as a centre from which to counter the threat of invasion from Gauls and other hostile groups to the north-east of Italy. By 181, the Board had gathered 3,000 colonists, each of whom was granted the large area of 50 *iugera* of land (12.5 ha); the officers and equestrians got even more (Livy XL.34.2–3). In 169 a further, 1,500 households were sent by the Senate to reinforce the fledgling colony, which felt itself beleaguered (Livy XLIII.1.5–6, 17.1). New roads lessened its isolation: in 153 BC, probably, the Via Annia connected Aquileia to Bologna on the Via Aemilia, and in 148 Aquileia was chosen as one of the termini of the great Via Postumia which spanned the Po valley and ended at Genoa.

The very location of Aquileia was an expression of Roman triumph over both land and sea, acting as one of the defining vertices of the geographers' triangular Italy and also dominating the Adriatic. The ensuing decades after foundation saw the expansion of Roman interests, military and commercial, into the area. The clearest example of this from our period is the mid-century Alpine gold-rush to the north of Aquileia, which reportedly lowered the gold price in Italy by one-third (Polybius XXXIV.10.10–14).

(Museo Aquileia 2399; DAI Rome neg. 68.3388; 0.72 m × 0.37 m × 0.16 m)

CIL I[2] 621; *ILLRP* 324; *Imagines* 143.

236. Piacenza from the air and plan of Placentine centuriation. After the campaigns of the 220s when the Romans had first ventured over the Apennines into the Po valley and defeated the Gallic tribes, two colonies – Placentia and Cremona – were founded on the banks of the Po in 218 BC. Having suffered at the hands of Hannibal and the Gauls in the ensuing war – Placentia was burned down in 200 (Livy XXXI.10.2–3) – the towns received additional colonists in 190 (Livy XXXVII.46.10–11). This aerial view of Piacenza (**a**), taken during World War II, together with the plan of the traces of centuriation detected within its territory (**b**), indicate the principal features of the new Po valley landscape which developed south of the river through Roman agency during the second century BC – axial roads, urban implantations and rural centuriation.

First, in the case of Placentia and Cremona, came the towns, founded initially in the middle of a potentially hostile zone. They, like the centuriated countryside which which they were later surrounded, were laid out according to an orthogonal plan, still visible in the streets of modern Piacenza. After the long intermission of the Hannibalic War and the subsequent (re-)conquest of the Po valley in the 190s, the Via Aemilia connected Placentia with Ariminum to the south-east (cf. **233**, **234**). The axis of the city plan is taken from the direction of the road – presumably reflecting its post-war reconstruction. It was probably in the second century that the centuriation of the colony's territory was begun in earnest.

In 148 BC the Via Postumia, beginning at Genoa and ending at Aquileia, joined coast to coast, running through both Placentia and Cremona. The two major roads of the north met at Placentia, and each can be seen entering the town. Roads were an important manifestation and symbol of conquest – of both land and people. They also offered new opportunities for further military operations as they brought neighbouring peoples within the reach of Roman arms. However, in the second century BC at least, the Via Postumia was used for this purpose only sporadically and in reaction to occasional threats from the Alps or beyond. The region north of the Po was left mostly uncolonized and uncenturiated during our period, apart from the regions around Cremona and Aquileia. It is, however, probable that there was considerable unofficial immigration over the Po at this time. This would seem to be a necessary precondition for the flourishing Latin literary culture of Transpadane towns such as Milan and Verona

236a

in the first century BC that produced Cornelius Nepos, Catullus and Livy.

(Air Photo Library, Keele University (PR/JB: 60PR/510; 21.6.44; print 4070))

Bradford *Ancient Landscapes* 261–2 pl. 63; P. Tozzi, *Athenaeum* 61 (1983) 494–513; Tozzi, in AA. VV., *Storia di Piacenza*, vol. 1 (Piacenza, 1990) 329–92 esp. 330–44; Chevallier *Romanisation* pl. V, XIV.

IMPERIAL ACTIONS, LOCAL REACTIONS

237. Boundary stone.

sex . atilivs . m . f . saranvs . pro . cos / ex . senati consvlto / inter . atestinos . et . veicetinos / fines . terminosque . statvi . iusit

Sextus Atilius, son of Marcus, Saranus, proconsul, by decree of the Senate, ordered a border-line and boundary-stones to be established between the people of Ateste and Vicetia

How far, and when, did the Romans interfere with the internal affairs of allied states within Italy? Polybius says that the Senate had jurisdiction over serious crimes committed within Italy, such as treason or assassination, and that states and individuals could approach the Senate to arbitrate in disputes (Polybius VI.13.4–5). Short of a real crisis, such as a major war when action was inevitable, direct, and armed, interference to restore order in individual cases was possible, though instances are rare. In 175 BC the Senate was invited to put down a case of civil unrest in Patavium (Padua), and a consul was dispatched (Livy XLI.27.3–4).

Boundary disputes were one common cause of Roman intervention, particularly in Venetia, where a number of inscriptions attest to the phenomenon in the second century BC (cf. also *CIL* I^2 633, 634; *ILS* 2501). This stone records the resolution of such a dispute between Ateste (Este) and Vicetia (Vicenza) by the proconsul Sex. Atilius Saranus in 135 BC. It acts both as a boundary marker and a striking memorial of high-level Roman involvement in

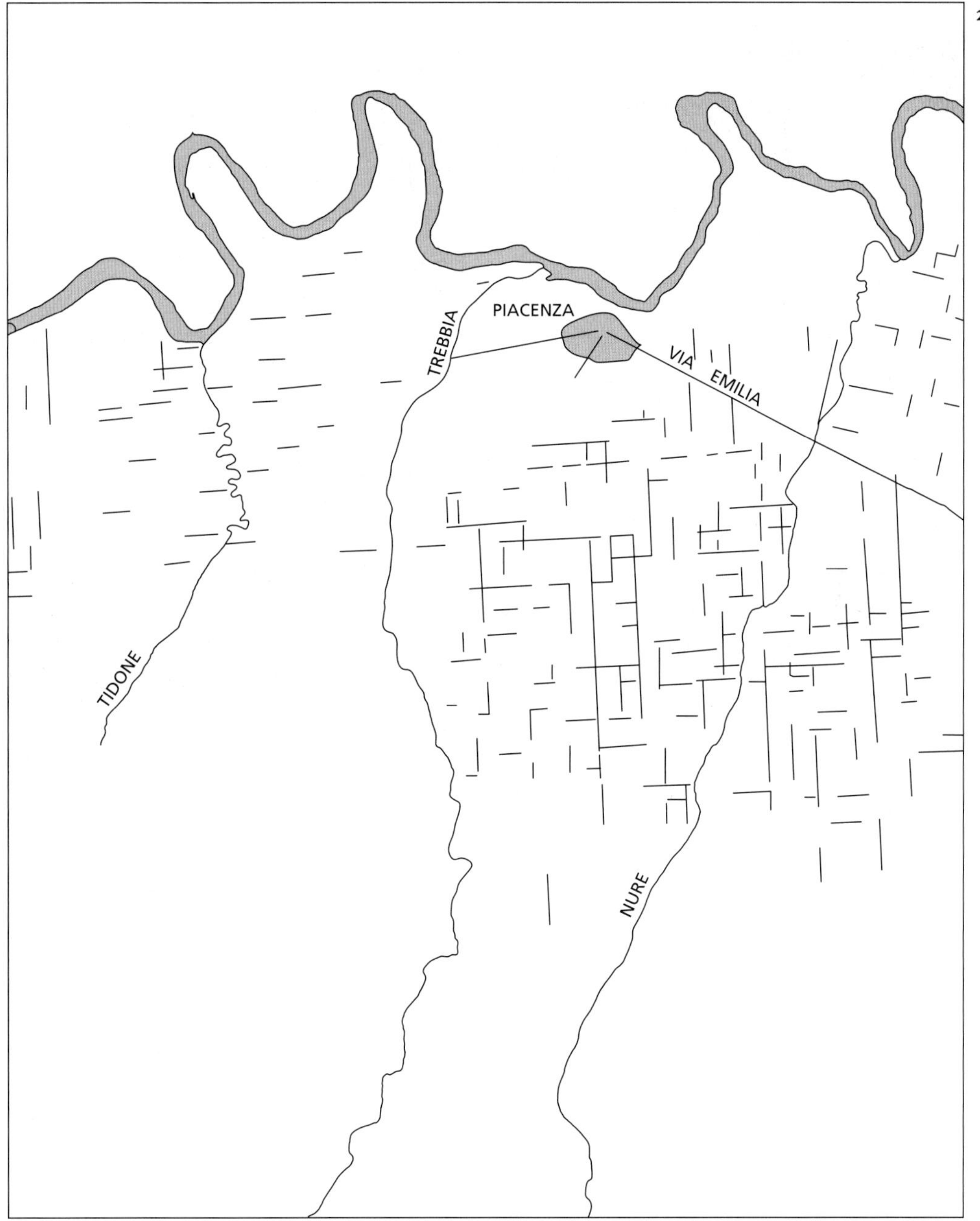

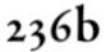

the affairs of two autonomous communities. The Senate had probably been invited to arbitrate in this case, as in many others. In this way, Roman influence could spread in response to local invitation rather than by imperial initiative. Nevertheless, as the inscription makes clear, the Roman proconsul, once asked, issued an order. The ultimate consequences of disobedience are left implicit.

(Museo Maffeiano, Verona; Direzione Civici Musei e Gallerie d' Arte, Sezione Archeologica, Commune di Verona. Height 0.72 m; diameter 1.03 m)

CIL I[2] 636; *ILLRP* 477; *Imagines* 203.

237

238. Northern Italian silver coins. From perhaps as early as the fourth century down to the early first century BC (the chronology is disputed), locally made silver coins circulated in northern Italy, mostly north of the Po. Their designs were modelled on those of the silver drachms of the Greek city of Massalia in southern Gaul which bore a profile head of Artemis on the obverse and a lion on the reverse. In the hands of the peoples of Cisalpine Gaul, the lion design became ever more stylized, finally becoming almost abstract. The Greek inscription on the original (ΜΑΣΣΑ; cf. **221**) developed into a series of abstract patterns and in some varieties was replaced by new inscriptions written in the local script (cf. **224**). The second example shown here (*BM* 25), dating probably to the late second–early first century BC, reads RIKOI (D = r: read from right to left). It is probably an abbreviated form of the name of a king or magistrate in whose name the coins were made.

The persistence of local coinages after Roman conquest is a common phenomenon in the Republican period, also seen in Spain and southern Gaul. The eventual decline of these silver issues in northern Italy and the proliferation of Roman coinage probably had more to do with changes in the supply of precious metal and demand for Roman coin than with official suppression upon the granting of the Latin Right to the communities of Transpadane Italy in 89 BC, as is often argued.

(**a** British Museum BM3; **b** BM25. Diameter 15 mm; weight 3.19 g, 2.03 g respectively)

A. Pautasso, *Sibrium* 7 (1962–3); Crawford *Coinage and Money* 75–83; E. A. Arslan, *Sibrium* 22 (1992–3) 179–215.

238a

238ai

238b